THE TRAVELS OF
IBN BATTUTAH

'Ibn Battutah, whose name translates variously as Son of a Duck, Egg-shaped Bottle and Bad Woman with Ellipsoidal Body, was the greatest flower of a long tradition of Arab travellers . . . An earlier writer had urged Moroccans who wanted to make a name for themselves to "head for the land of the east". Ibn Battutah took him at his word and zigzagged his way across Africa to Egypt, where an ascetic directed him on, towards India and China. In a medieval take on working one's way around the world, Ibn Battutah didn't just pass through these countries, but was employed as a judge and ambassador by several of the rulers he visited. Many showed their gratitude by lavishing on him gifts of gold and possessions that helped him on his way . . . All this is rich material, generally unfingered by British writers and unknown to most British readers'

Anthony Sattin, *Sunday Times*

'A picture of medieval civilisation without equal in detail and brilliance . . . as good an introduction to the great masterpiece of Muslim geography as anyone could want . . . What Mackintosh-Smith conveys in his abridgement is the sheer scope, both geographical and mental, of Islamic civilisation in its climactic phase'

James Buchan, *Guardian*

'An eccentric combination of fable, fantasy, history and theology that whisks the reader off along camel roads and into courts and palaces from China to Tanzania . . . An insight into the medieval world view and a timely reminder of Islamic civilization and learning'

Big Issue

'There's little doubt that Ibn Battutah was, and remains, the greatest traveller of all time . . . He had "a soft heart, a big head, a huge libido" and was "enthralled by saints", according to Mackintosh-Smith, who is himself almost as interesting as I.B.'

Geoffrey Moorhouse, *New York Times*

'Ibn Battutah dined with sultans, khans and emperors; escaped from pirates; sired children on several continents; crossed deserts; dodged the Black Death; found employment as a *qadi* (judge) and courtier *par excellence*. No form of transport then available was unknown to him. He had hopped onto camels, mules and horses, boarded junks, dhows and rafts, clambered onto oxwagons and trudged wearily on foot. The literary fruit of his odyssey, which spanned countries from the Volga to Tanzania, China to Morocco, was *The Precious Gift of Lookers into the Marvels of Cities and Wonders of Travel*, the ultimate travel narrative, at once scholarly and picaresque'

Justin Marozzi, *Spectator*

'Ibn Battutah is long overdue a wider Western audience and he couldn't enjoy a better champion than Mackintosh-Smith'

The Times

Tim Mackintosh-Smith was just twenty-one when he set out for Arabia. For the past eighteen years, when not travelling, he has lived in the Yemeni capital, San'a. His first book, *Yemen: Travels in Dictionary Land*, won the 1998 Thomas Cook/*Daily Telegraph* Travel Book Award. His second, *Travels with a Tangerine: A Journey in the Footnotes of Ibn Battutah*, was published in 2001 to critical acclaim.

THE TRAVELS OF
IBN BATTUTAH

Abridged, introduced and annotated by

TIM MACKINTOSH-SMITH

PICADOR

First published 2002 by Picador

This paperback edition published 2003 by Picador
an imprint of Pan Macmillan, a division of Macmillan Publishers Limited
Pan Macmillan, 20 New Wharf Road, London N1 9RR
Basingstoke and Oxford
Associated companies throughout the world
www.panmacmillan.com

ISBN 978-0-330-41879-9

Abridged from the translation by Professors Sir Hamilton Gibb
and C. F. Beckingham originally published by the Hakluyt Society
in four volumes, 1958–1994.

17 19 18

A CIP catalogue record for this book is available from
the British Library.

Typeset in Sabon by SX Composing DTP, Rayleigh, Essex
Printed and bound by CPI Group
(UK) Ltd, Croydon, CR0 4YY

Visit www.picador.com to read more about all our books and to buy
them. You will also find features, author interviews and news of any author
events, and you can sign up for e-newsletters so that you're always first to hear
about our new releases.

Contents

Foreword
by Tim Mackintosh-Smith

'I know of no person who has journeyed through so many lands as Ibn
Battutah did; and he was withal generous and well-doing.'

IBN MARZUQ OF TLEMCEN (D. 1379)

A few years ago, benighted between Edfu and the Red Sea at the tomb
of a holy man called Sidi Salim, I opened the *Rihlah* of Ibn Battutah
and read aloud to my fellow-travellers. We were on our way to visit
the mausoleum of Abu 'l-Hasan al-Shadhili, seventy miles to the
south; the passage I read out was the story of the death and burial of
this more famous saint.

The story ended to murmurs of approval. I felt pleased to have passed
on to a group of Upper Egyptian saint-fanciers a piece of forgotten lore,
preserved by a fourteenth-century traveller from distant Morocco. Then
one listener, an old man, spoke out: whoever wrote my book had missed
out the most important bit! He told the rest of the tale – a strange and
passionate postscript, stranger still by lamplight in the Egyptian desert.

It is wonderful to see a 650-year-old book sprouting apocrypha.
The *Rihlah* also continues to grow, less passionately, in libraries and
seminars from Berkeley to Beijing, by discussion, explanation and
annotation. Having agreed to reverse the process and abridge it, I
began to feel queasy. To cut into the heart of a living corpus would
be a messy and distasteful operation. And then there was the size of
it: Ibn Battutah's subject is, in short, the world.

It is a world that stretches from the beginning of Africa to the end
of Asia, and, via the Volga, to beyond Zanzibar. It is packed with
people and events, short on landscape and adverbs; enormous, but
seen with the close clear gaze of a miniaturist; diverse, yet God-

ordered. The order is Islamic, and Ibn Battutah has his coordinates in it: Sunni Muslim, Mecca pilgrim, scholar of jurisprudence, judge belonging to the Maliki legal school. Unless you happen to be at least one of these, you are at first triply abroad – not just geographically and temporally, but also culturally. And then, slowly and sidelong, Ibn Battutah reveals himself: snatches of homesickness, intolerance, exasperation, indignation, bemusement, bafflement, disgust, lust; of a traveller who got the runs and got ripped off. They are passing glimpses, but they disclose a stranger abroad like us – and all strangers, as one of the oldest Arabic poems says, are kin.

There are glimpses, too, of a kind of travel literature one might take to be much later in date. To be fleeced by a guide in Turkey and make a joke of it, as Ibn Battutah did, sounds Learish, or Newbyesque. In contrast, the fascinating yet somehow bloodless adventures of Marco Polo, whose life and route overlapped with those of Ibn Battutah, seem to belong to a past age. The Venetian's death, shortly before Ibn Battutah started travelling, was nicely timed.

Ibn Battutah's work, his world, deserves to be known better. So despite my reservations I went ahead and amputated. The book is still vast. Where do we begin?

One day in the spring of 1350, a gathering took place in a garden near Granada. The owner of the garden, a scholar of Islamic law, had invited several notables from the capital to meet two guests. One was a sort of Andalusian John Clare, a poetical peasant who composed verses in the crispest classical Arabic. The other was a Moroccan, a native of Tangier recently returned from the East. 'I was with them in that garden,' recalled a young writer a few years later. 'Shaikh Abu Abdallah*

*Ibn Battutah's full name is Shams al-Din Abu Abdallah Muhammad ibn Abdallah ibn Muhammad ibn Ibrahim Ibn Battutah al-Lawati al-Tanji. Shams al-Din, 'the Sun of Religion', is a typical handle (others are Jamal al-Din, Muhyi al-Din, etc.) given to the names of scholars, mainly in the Islamic East. Abu Abdallah is 'Father of Abdallah'; theoretically but by no means invariably taken from the name of the eldest son, this is the respectful form of address, perhaps the equivalent of 'Mr . . .'. Muhammad is the traveller's personal name, Abdallah that of his father, Muhammad of his grandfather, and so on. Ibn Battutah ('Battutahson', like Johnson or Jackson) is the family name; Battutah, the name of the putative founder of the line, is possibly a pet version of 'Fatimah'. It may also be transcribed delighted us with the stories of his travels. I took down from him the names of famous people he had met, and we profited greatly from him.'

Ibn Battutah's listeners would have been comforted as well as edified by what he had to tell them. Despite the literary salons and splendid buildings (work was about to begin on the Court of the Lions in the Alhambra), Granada was a Moorish rump, the last great city of the Muslims in al-Andalus. Most of Spain had already been lost to the *reconquista* and, even along the few routes still in Muslim hands, travel could be risky: Ibn Battutah himself had a narrow squeak with Christian raiders on his way up the coast near Fuengirola. Here, then, in this threatened island of Islamic civilization in the far west of the known world, it must have been heartening to hear of thriving Muslim states on the Volga, in India and Sumatra, and way down the east coast of Africa.

Ibn Battutah told of a world far-flung yet close-knit. In China he had heard a verse of Sa'di, the poet of Shiraz at the other end of Asia, sung on the river at Hangzhou. Not far away in Fuzhou he bumped into a man from Ceuta, a day's journey from his own home town of Tangier; after leaving Spain, he would stay with the man's brother south of the Atlas Mountains. Even in embattled Granada he met natives of Anatolia, Central Asia and India. As a traveller, Ibn Battutah was by no means unique.

The difference was that he wrote his travels down, or to be exact dictated them. A few years after that meeting in the garden, the Sultan of Morocco commissioned Ibn Juzayy – the young writer who had enjoyed hearing Ibn Battutah's tales – to take down the traveller's memoirs. The result was *Tuhfat al-nuzzar fi ghara'ib al-amsar wa aja'ib al-asfar*, or *A Gift to Those Who Contemplate the Wonders of Cities and the Marvels of Travelling* – the *Rihlah*, or *Travels*, for short. In terms of ground covered, some 75,000 miles, it was, and still probably is, the biggest travel book ever written.

In this aetiological era, the first question most travel writers feel

---

'Battuta'. Al-Lawati is 'of the tribe of Lawatah' (see below), al-Tanji 'of Tanjah', i.e. Tangier. One could also add al-Maliki, 'of the Maliki rite' – one of the four main schools of Sunni Islam; and al-Maghribi, 'the Westerner', i.e. from North Africa west of Egypt or (at this period) al-Andalus, the Iberian Peninsula.

they ought to deal with is 'why?' (Often the real reason is: to write a travel book. This is rarely admitted.) Ibn Battutah gives his answer in a sentence: to make the pilgrimage to Mecca and to visit the Prophet's tomb at al-Madinah. Since the Qur'an says that all Muslims who are able to do so should go on the pilgrimage, his departure from Tangier was a matter not of choice but of duty. But there were other reasons, which his background may help to explain.

Ibn Battutah was born in 1304 into a family of native North African origin. He would have recoiled from the description 'Berber', even though his Lawatah forbears, who had migrated to Morocco from Libya centuries earlier, tend to come under that woolly blanket term. While not ethnically Arabian, he was culturally as Arab-Muslim as could be: the occupation of qadi, judge, he says, 'is my occupation, and that of my fathers before me', and jurisprudence and the allied study of Arabic linguistics were the meat and bones of Islamic science. The Ibn Battutahs were a respected family, but not a distinguished one. The traveller mentions a cousin who was qadi of the town of Ronda in Spain; in Portugal there exists a manuscript of a work entitled *The Qadis of Cordova*, with the ownership inscription of another Ibn Battutah. Our Ibn Battutah could have continued the tradition of worthy provincial obscurity, memorizing *The Beaten Track*, the legal handbook of the Maliki school, and spending the rest of his life writing marriage contracts and dividing inheritances. But, aged twenty-one, he hoped for more, and there was only one way of getting it.

'Travelling in search of knowledge,' wrote Ibn Battutah's younger North African contemporary, Ibn Khaldun, 'is absolutely essential for the acquisition of useful learning and of perfection through meeting authoritative teachers and having contact with scholarly personalities.' The Prophet Muhammad had put it more snappily, 'Travel in search of knowledge, even though the journey take you to China.' Despite the rhetorical injunction, the East for most Maghribis meant Cairo, Damascus and Mecca. The question to ask, then, is not why Ibn Battutah set out, but why he went so far.

Part of the answer is in the timing of the travels, from 1325 to 1354.* The Crusades were a memory and the Tatars, having all but

* On the historical setting of the *Travels*, Ross E. Dunn's *The Adventures of Ibn Battuta*, London and Sydney, 1986, is excellent.

destroyed the eastern Muslim world, had settled down and become generally good Muslims over a huge swathe of Eurasia between the Altai and the Carpathians. Trade routes were open, and Ibn Battutah had a portable and immensely valuable commodity: *fiqh*, Islamic jurisprudence. Its attraction may be harder to understand now; but for rulers who had started out as rude Tatar or Turkic warlords, the cachet of having at court a legal expert from the old Islamic world was irresistible. Ibn Battutah knew this. He bumped up his academic credentials with a crash course in Damascus and with more desultory studies in Mecca, then began a pinball progress through the eastern Islamic lands. He was aiming – if that is the right word for a route that included a 3,000-mile jaunt to Constantinople and numerous other sidetracks – for the big score: Delhi. When at last he arrived there he was not disappointed: the Sultan appointed him Maliki qadi of the city, and assigned him the income of a minor potentate. It was then, perversely, that the rising graph line of Ibn Battutah's fortunes began to plunge, then peak, then plunge again in a series of Candide-like adventures.

But to return to the question of Ibn Battutah's motives. If he himself could be asked why he went so far, I suspect he would have retold the story of his meeting in Alexandria with the saint Burhan al-Din the Lame. Gifted like many of his holy peers with knowledge of future events, he asked Ibn Battutah to pass on his greetings to his spiritual brothers in Sind, India and China. 'I was amazed at his prediction,' Ibn Battutah recalled, 'and the idea of going to these countries having been cast into my mind, my wanderings never ceased until I had met these three.' Shortly afterwards, a more detailed itinerary was revealed by a dream, interpreted by another saint. (Ibn Battutah and his contemporaries lived in a Schopenhauerian world in which our waking and sleeping existences are leaves of the same book: to live is to read them in order, to dream to skim through.) Predestination as an incentive to action may seem paradoxical; but for Ibn Battutah there was no paradox. The quest was part of the destiny.

Nor was there any paradox in Ibn Battutah's simultaneous travel in two worlds, the one furnished with ermine, aloes wood, dinars and robes, the other peopled by saints and seers, *marabouts* and mendicants. He collected horses and slave girls, and he collected holy men – yogis and monks as well as dervishes. His belief in the extraordinary powers of the latter group was unshakeable. One modern Moroccan commentator has said, 'It is strange that Ibn Battutah's critical faculty was absent with regard to the supernatural.' And it is stranger still that a scholar and a compatriot of the traveller could so misunderstand the man and his age: to read the *Travels* you must have faith in the world beyond the senses, or at least suspend your disbelief. A forty-day fast broken by a single bean, the telephonic harvesting of coconuts, pomegranates in mid-winter – these are not curiosities, but the essence of the book.

If the *Travels* is steeped in spirit, it is also rich in solid observation. On the pre-Ottoman Turkoman states of Anatolia, the Khanate of the Golden Horde, the Sultanate of Delhi, the Maldives and the Empire of Mali, Ibn Battutah is the major source of his time. Gibb, his English translator, called him 'the supreme example of *le géographe malgré lui*'. He might have added hagiographer, ethnographer, biographer, anecdotal historian and occasional botanist and gastronome. Quite apart from the geographical scope, it is these polyhedral interests that make the *Travels* such a huge book.

For the same reasons, it was never a bestseller. It went too far beyond the purview of the Maghribi armchair traveller. Courtly suicide in Sumatra? Battles of fruit in China? Judicial gang rape in the Land of the *Barahnakar*? (We still don't know where that is.) And then, for all Ibn Juzayy's best efforts at editing, the literary polish wears thin the further one goes. Fourteenth-century readers were more at home with the well-turned tropes of Ibn Jubair, the earlier travel writer of Valencia, and with the portly tomes of Ibn Rushaid – a superb compilation of the Prophet's sayings masquerading as the most tedious travel book ever written. (Even now the odd pedant fulminates at Ibn Battutah's Arabic prose. Dr Muhammad Mustafa Ziyadah, for instance, lists his 'unacceptable dialecticisms' and grammatical mistakes. The late Abdallah Gannun, a loyal defender of the traveller, produced a counter-list of Dr Muhammad's own syntactic infelicities.)

Even so, judging by the surviving manuscripts, Ibn Battutah's book had a steady readership over the centuries, at least in the western Muslim world. One copy, made in 1484, appears from marginal jottings to have been used as a guidebook by a Maghribi pilgrim to Mecca; another was made in 1634 in Timbuktu; some 250 years later, the *Travels* was wartime reading for a Moroccan prince fighting

the Spaniards.* Ibn Battutah's compatriot and editor, Dr Abdelhadi
Tazi, suggests that the book may have inspired a Moroccan phrase
proverbial for great distances: 'From Tangier to the Land of the Dog.'
(Ibn Battutah described, but did not witness, the use of dog sleds in
the Siberian 'Land of Darkness'.)

European orientalists had heard of the *Travels* by about 1800. A
few years later the explorer Burckhardt got hold of an abridged
version, intending to use it as a guide in West Africa. The first full
printed edition came out in Paris between 1853 and 1858, edited in
part from an incomplete manuscript that may be in the hand of Ibn
Juzayy himself. The complete English translation has been longer
in coming. H. A. R. (later Sir Hamilton) Gibb first proposed the idea
to the Hakluyt Society in 1922. Gibb died in 1971, and the fourth
and final volume of text, prepared by the late Professor Charles
Beckingham, did not appear until 1994. A fifth volume, of indexes,
came out in 2000. The Gibb–Beckingham translation is the basis of
this volume.

A distinguished Arab historian of geography has branded as criminal
all abridgements of Ibn Battutah; but, as the mention of Burckhardt's
copy shows, I am not the first vandal. Another shortened version,
done in seventeenth-century Aleppo, was translated into English by
the Reverend Samuel Lee and published in 1829. (Lee was a Shropshire
carpenter's apprentice who picked up Latin, Greek, Arabic, Hebrew,
Aramaic, Syriac, Persian and Hindustani in his idle moments, and
died in the Regius chair of Hebrew at Cambridge.) Exactly a century
later, Gibb – perhaps sensing the enormity of translation and, especially,
annotation before him – produced a volume of selections. It is
elegantly done, but over-harsh on the first part of the *Travels*. (Here,
admittedly, Ibn Battutah follows the standard Islamic Grand Tour
and is less original than he is later. Not that the concept of originality
meant anything in his time; indeed, unoriginality was *de rigueur*.)
In this new version I have kept more of these earlier sections: it is

*Next to Ibn Battutah's comments on the Mahratta ladies of India – 'they have
in intercourse a deliciousness and a knowledge of erotic movements beyond that
of other women' – the prince scribbled a prayer: 'O God, give me a taste of this
delight!'

important to show where Ibn Battutah came from, as well as where he went.

An abridgement of a translation could be to the original what processed cheese is to a ripe, unpasteurized Stilton. So I have also tried to preserve more of the rich and complex flavour of the full text: for instance, some of the poetical asides of Ibn Juzayy, who is not only Ibn Battutah's editor but also his literary Sancho Panza; some, at least, of the detailed descriptions of court etiquette, with which Ibn Battutah was obsessed; the pious prayers which he (God have mercy on him) appended, as Muslims still do, to the names of spiritual and other VIPs; the beautiful *Litany of the Sea* of the miraculously interred saint al-Shadhili (whom, eventually, I did visit), still recited by pious skippers. (Sir Richard Burton said of his version of it, 'As this prayer is supposed to make all safe upon the ocean wave, I will not selfishly withhold it from the British reader.' Neither will I.) I have also boiled down Gibb and Beckingham's footnotes, amassed over seventy years' work on the text, served them as endnotes and seasoned them with some additions and revisions of my own.*

Much, however, has gone – about three fifths of the full text. I have cut most of the painstaking accounts of the Umayyad Mosque in Damascus and of the holy sites and rites of Mecca – partly because it was the earlier traveller Ibn Jubair who took the pains and Ibn Juzayy who pinched the results, incorporating them into Ibn Battutah's book. Other major excisions include the logorrhoeal panegyric of Ibn Battutah's patron, Sultan Abu Inan (not that he didn't deserve it), and some of the long sections of pure history such as that on the earlier Delhi Sultanate. Most of the actual travelling remains, although I have pruned a few of the stragglier and less eventful offshoots from Ibn Battutah's route (northern Mesopotamia, eastern Anatolia, part of Khurasan). I have also further accelerated his lightning return from China to Morocco which, even in the original, often reads like a package-tour timetable. The occasional collapsing of itinerary that results is, in a way, faithful to the full text: Ibn Juzayy himself seems to have wielded an editorial red pen, for he says at the end of the book, tantalizingly, that he made an epitome of Ibn Battutah's

---

*Many more insights into the first part of Ibn Battutah's text are to be found in my *Travels with a Tangerine: A Journey in the Footnotes of Ibn Battutah*, John Murray, 2001. Other volumes, dealing with the rest of the *Rihlah*, are planned.

composition. Perhaps this explains how in the original the traveller could, for example, have crossed eight hundred miles of Anatolia in an afternoon.

The most painful kind of excision is that of persons. Places mattered less to Ibn Battutah than people, and he mentions more than 1,500 by name – a veritable Court and Social of the fourteenth century. How he remembered them – and, where they can be checked, with generally impressive accuracy – is one of the mysteries of the *Travels*. In at least some places he took notes: 'The tombs of the learned men of Bukhara are inscribed with their names,' he recalled, 'and the titles of their writings. I had copied a great many of these, but they were lost along with all that I lost when the Indian infidels robbed me at sea.' Nowadays, most travel writers would go to pieces if they mislaid their notebooks. Ibn Battutah's education, however, had prepared him for such an event: more stress was placed on rote learning and memorizing in the Maghrib than in any other part of the Islamic world. Add to this his constant name-dropping along the way and the result is that he must have had a well-developed mnemonic muscle, like the poet who boasted,

> My knowledge follows me wherever I'm cast up –
> Its vessel is my breast, and not my travelling-trunk.

To return to that garden near Granada. One of the other guests listening to Ibn Battutah's tales was the octogenarian qadi Ibn al-Balfiqi. Unlike the traveller's future editor, he was not impressed. Ibn Battutah, he said afterwards, claimed to have seen in the church in Constantinople 12,000 bishops. This and other such statements showed that the Moroccan was a liar.

It is possible that Ibn Battutah, inspired by the Andalusian spring and the *al fresco* setting, got carried away. But the *Travels* itself – which mentions the innumerable priests, monks and devotees of the Byzantine capital but is silent on its episcopal population – is a sober document. Despite the wonders and marvels of its full title, it is free from what one might call the Sindbad Syndrome: even Ibn Battutah's 'roc', as the crew of his ship called it, is never described as anything other than a natural phenomenon – perhaps one of those fearsome arch-squalls that haunt the China Sea. (Supernatural feats performed by saints do not come under the heading of earthly *mirabilia*.) Unlike his contemporary Sir John Mandeville who, at least in the later parts of his book, got away with the travel-literary equivalent of murder, Ibn Battutah's veracity was in the dock wherever he went. He travelled not in some imaginary Orient, but in a world full of mobile and well-connected Muslim scholars: any embroidery of his adventures would, sooner or later, have been ripped apart. He knew this, and his audience knew he knew it.

Why then was Ibn al-Balfiqi, the grand old man of Andalusian scholarship, so dismissive of Ibn Battutah's stories? Perhaps it was simple academic snobbery. The first phrase of the main biographical note on the traveller (written, incidentally, by a student of Ibn al-Balfiqi) says that, 'He had a modest share of the sciences . . .'* Next door in Christendom, Mandeville was swallowed whole. In the scholastic, hypercritical Maghrib, the more curiously shaped crudités of travel – when served up by a scholar who was not first-class – stuck in the throat.

The debate over Ibn Battutah's credibility became a minor cause célèbre that found its way into another great Arabic work of the fourteenth century. Intended as the first volume of a world history, Ibn Khaldun's *Prolegomena* jumped the tracks and went off in a runaway train of ideas. At one point, it discusses the importance of keeping an open mind about information which, though beyond one's experience, is not impossible. The passage is worth quoting in full, as it is the longest contemporary reference to the traveller.

> Consider the following fine anecdote. In the time of the Marinid Sultan Abu Inan there arrived in the Maghrib a man from a learned family of Tangier, known as Ibn Battutah. Twenty years earlier, he had set out for the East and knocked about the lands of Iraq, Yemen and India. He entered the city of Delhi, the seat of the ruler of India, Sultan Muhammad Shah. He found favour with the Sultan, who employed him as qadi of the Maliki rite. Then he returned to the Maghrib and met Sultan Abu Inan. He used to tell stories about his travels, and especially about the rule of the Sultan of India. This Sultan, for instance, upon departing on a journey, would have a census made of the people of Delhi – men, women and children – and allot them six months' victuals, which were distributed to them from his own largesse. When the Sultan returned from his journey, the day was one of celebration and the entire population would go

---

*This is probably spot on. The only formal higher education Ibn Battutah seems to have had, in Damascus, lasted no more than a few weeks.

to the outskirts of the city and mill around him; whereupon he would have catapults set up on the backs of the beasts in his procession, from which bags of dinars and dirhams were scattered into the crowd. This would go on all along the route to his palace.

On hearing this and other such tales, people began to whisper that Ibn Battutah was a liar. Eventually it reached the stage where the majority of people disbelieved Ibn Battutah's stories. At this time I met Sultan Abu Inan's vizier, the renowned Faris Ibn Wadrar, and asked his opinion on the matter. The vizier said to me, 'You should never dismiss accounts of other lands merely on the grounds of not having seen them. If you did so, you would be like the vizier's son who grew up in prison. His story is as follows: a certain sultan imprisoned his vizier. The vizier remained in custody for many years, during which his infant son was confined with him. When the boy reached the age of reason, he asked about the meat which was sent in for their meals. His father replied, "This is mutton," at which the boy asked, "What is mutton?" So his father gave him a full and precise description of a sheep. The boy then said, "Father, is a sheep like a rat?" "No," said the vizier. "There is a huge difference between the two!" Similar exchanges took place concerning camel meat and beef. This was all because the only creature the boy had ever seen was the rat: therefore, he considered all creatures to be sub-species of rat.'*

With the vizier Ibn Wadrar and other notable figures – including Ibn Marzuq of Tlemcen, the future Grand Qadi of Cairo – as counsel for the defence, Ibn Battutah was acquitted of lying. But doubts still linger about one or two sections of the *Travels*, like the journey to inland China. Apologists for Ibn Battutah blame such passages on Ibn Juzayy, arguing plausibly that he couldn't resist the occasional urge to stuff the journey with material from guidebooks – a practice not unknown among travel writers today. (There is also an intriguing possibility that both Ibn Juzayy and Marco Polo's own amanuensis, Rustichello of Pisa, might have got some of their Chinese padding from the same source.)

*The eighteenth-century traveller James Bruce used a similar defence. When his account of breakfasting in Abyssinia on steaks cut from live oxen became the tall story of the season, his rebuff was: 'People who have never been out of their own country and others well acquainted with the manners of the world, for they had travelled as far as France, had agreed the thing was impossible, and therefore it was so.'

The dubious passages occupy no more than a few pages. Concerning the rest there are no doubts. Unlike Ibn al-Balfiqi and Ibn Battutah's other contemporary detractors, we now have access to local records of, for example, the Delhi Sultanate, which corroborate the traveller's accounts. Following Ibn Battutah on the ground, I have discovered sometimes startling evidence of his accuracy: to find, for instance, a certain piece of furniture seen by him in an obscure Anatolian mosque, still in the same spot 670 years on, is a spine-tingling experience.

> How many fellow-travellers have I known? I cannot count.
> How many corners of the Earth? I cannot tell.
> Now that my wanderings east and west are done,
> There is but one last corner left: my grave.

So said a travelling poet of the eleventh century. In Ibn Battutah's case, however, life did not imitate art. Back home, he did not die while the laurels were still fresh; he simply faded away into the provincial obscurity from which he had come. There is a glimpse of him by a contemporary, sitting in Sultan Abu Inan's academy in Fez soon after his return; and then an obituary by Ibn Marzuq: 'He lived to the year seventy [1368–9] and died while holding the office of qadi in some town or other.'

Ibn Battutah led a mobile life; it may be appropriate that, even in death, he cannot be precisely pinned down. A tomb in Tangier is attributed to him, but without a wisp of evidence. The *Travels*, however, is a sufficient monument, and not short on epitaphs. Here is one from a holy man in Assam:

'He said to me,' Ibn Battutah remembered, '"You are the traveller of the Arabs." One of his companions who was present said, "And of the non-Arabs, my master." He said, "And of the non-Arabs. Treat him with respect."'

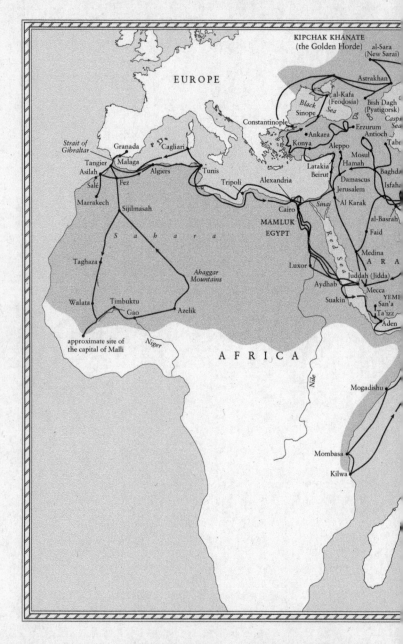

The travels of Ibn Battutah 1325–1354

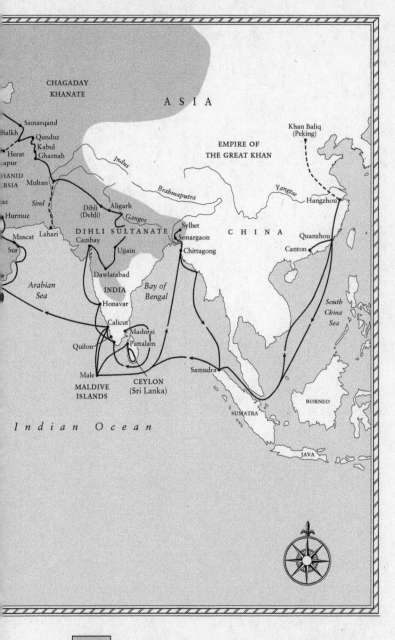

CHAGADAY
KHANATE

ASIA

EMPIRE OF
THE GREAT KHAN

Khan Baliq
(Peking)

Samarqand
Balkh
Qunduz
Kabul
Herat
apur
Ghaznah
HANID
RSIA
az
Hurmuz
Muscat
Sur
Sur

Multan

Indus

Brahmaputra

Yangtse

Hangzhou

CHINA

Quanzhou

Canton

Dihli
(Dehli)
Aligarh
Ganges
DIHLI SULTANATE
Cambay
Ujjain

Sylhet
Sonargaon
Chittagong

Sind
Lahari

*Arabian
Sea*

Dawlatabad

INDIA

Honavar

Calicut

Quilon

Male

MALDIVE
ISLANDS

*Bay of
Bengal*

Madurai
Pattalam

CEYLON
(Sri Lanka)

Samudra

South
China
Sea

BORNEO

SUMATRA

Indian   Ocean

JAVA

Islamic lands ▬▬▬ Ibn Battutah's routes

Introduction by Ibn Juzayy

In the name of God   The Merciful One   The Compassionate

Among those who resorted to the illustrious court of our master Abu Inan Faris,[1] there came the Shaikh learned in the Law, the most trustworthy and veracious traveller, the ranger of the earth and traverser of its climes in length and breadth, Abu Abdallah Muhammad ibn Abdallah ibn Muhammad ibn Ibrahim al-Lawati al-Tanji, known as Ibn Battutah, and in the Eastern lands as Shams al-Din. He, who had encompassed the earth with attentive mind and travelled through its cities with observant eye, and who had investigated the diversities of nations and probed the ways of life of Arabs and non-Arabs, thereafter laid down the staff of the much-travelled in this Sublime Residence.

A gracious direction was transmitted that he should dictate an account of the cities which he had seen in his travels, and of the interesting events which had clung to his memory, and that he should speak of those whom he had met of the rulers of countries, of their distinguished men of learning, and of their pious saints. Accordingly, he dictated upon these subjects a narrative which gave entertainment to the mind and delight to the ears and eyes, with a variety of curious particulars by the exposition of which he gave edification and of marvellous things by adverting to which he aroused interest. The exalted command issued to the slave of their illustrious Highness, who has attached himself with singleness of mind to their gate, and is honoured with employment in the service of their Majesty, Muhammad ibn Muhammad Ibn Juzayy al-Kalbi[2] (may God aid him to serve them and inspire him to gratitude for their bounty), that he should assemble that which the Shaikh Abu Abdallah Ibn Battutah had dictated on these subjects into a compilation which should comprehend what was of profit in them and ensure the full attainment of their objects, giving care to the pruning and polishing of its language and applying himself to its clarification and adaptation to the taste of readers, that they might find enjoyment in these curiosities and that the profit to be derived from their pearls should be increased in stripping them from their shell. He therefore set himself straightway to execute the command laid upon him, and went down to draw from Ibn Battutah's spring, that he might by the aid of God faithfully accomplish this design.

1 North-West Africa and Egypt

The Shaikh Abu Abdallah Ibn Battutah related as follows:

My departure from Tangier, my birthplace, took place on Thursday the second of the month of God, Rajab the Unique, in the year seven hundred and twenty-five,[1] with the object of making the Pilgrimage to the Holy House at Mecca and of visiting the tomb of the Prophet, God's richest blessing and peace be on him, at al-Madinah. I set out alone, having neither fellow-traveller in whose companionship I might find cheer, nor caravan whose party I might join, but swayed by an overmastering impulse within me and a desire long-cherished in my bosom to visit these illustrious sanctuaries. So I braced my resolution to quit all my dear ones, female and male, and forsook my home as birds forsake their nests. My parents being yet in the bonds of life, it weighed sorely upon me to part from them, and both they and I were afflicted with sorrow at this separation. My age at that time was twenty-two lunar years. (Note by Ibn Juzayy: Abu Abdallah told me in the city of Granada that he was born at Tangier on Tuesday 17th Rajab al-Fard of the year seven hundred and three [25 February 1304].)

I came to the city of Tilimsan [Tlemcen], the sultan of which at that time was Abu Tashifin, and my arrival chanced to coincide with the visit of two envoys of the king of Africa.[2] These envoys left the town, and one of the brethren advised me to travel in their company. I consulted the will of Almighty God[3] in regard to this and after a stay of three nights in Tilimsan to procure what I needed, I left, riding after them with all speed, and on reaching the town of Milyanah overtook them there.[4] This was in the time of the summer heats, and both of the doctors of the law fell sick, on account of which we stopped for a space of ten nights. We then set out again, but the illness

3

of one of the envoys, a qadi,[5] had taken a serious turn, so we stopped for three nights by a stream at a distance of four miles from Milyanah. The qadi breathed his last in the forenoon of the fourth day, and his companions returned to Milyanah and buried him there. I left them at this point and pursued my journey with a company of merchants from Tunis.

When we reached Bijaya [Bougie] I was attacked by fever, and one of my fellow travellers advised me to stay there until I was fully recovered. But I refused saying, 'If God decrees my death, then my death shall be on the road, with my face set towards the land of the Hijaz.'[6] 'Well then,' he replied, 'if you are resolved, sell your ass and your heavy baggage, and I shall lend you ass and tent. In this way you may travel with us light, for we must move with all speed for fear of molestation by roving Arabs on the road.' I did as he suggested, and he lent me what he had promised – may God reward him with good! This was the first of the divine mercies which were manifested to me in the course of that journey to the Hijaz.

Continuing our journey, we reached the town of Qusantinah [Constantine] and halted outside it. We were caught by heavy rain, which forced us to leave our tents during the night for the shelter of some buildings there. Next morning the governor of the town came to meet us, and seeing my clothes, for they were all soiled by the rain, he gave orders that they should be washed at his house. The mantle which was amongst them was in rags, so he sent me in its place a mantle of fine Ba'albek cloth, in one of whose corners he had tied two gold dinars. This was the first alms which was bestowed upon me on my journey.

We set out again and came next to the town of Bunah [Bône]. We lodged inside the city, and after we had stopped in it for some days we left there the merchants who had been in our company, on account of the dangers of the road, and travelled light with the utmost speed, pushing on night and day without stopping. I was again attacked by the fever, and I actually tied myself on the saddle with a turban-cloth in case I should fall off by reason of my weakness. It was impossible for me to dismount, on account of the danger. So at last we reached the town of Tunis, and the townsfolk came out to welcome the travellers. On all sides they came forward with greetings and questions to one another, but not a soul said a word of greeting to me, since there was none of them that I knew. I felt so sad at heart on account of my loneliness that I could not restrain the tears that started to my eyes, and wept bitterly. But one of the pilgrims, realizing the cause of my distress, came up to me with a greeting and friendly welcome, and continued to comfort me with friendly talk until I entered the city, where I lodged in the College of the Booksellers.[7]

While still at Tunis I was overtaken by the feast of the Fast-breaking and I joined the company at the *Musalla*.[8] The inhabitants had already assembled in large numbers to celebrate their festival and had come out in brave show and in their richest apparel. The sultan arrived on horseback, accompanied by all his relatives and courtiers and guards of his kingdom walking on foot in a magnificent procession. The prayers were recited, the allocution was discharged, and the people returned to their homes.[9]

Some time later the caravan of pilgrims for the noble Hijaz was organized and they put me forward as qadi of their company. We left Tunis in the last days of the month of Dhu'l-Qa'dah [beginning of November 1325], following the coast road, and came to the township of Susah, which is small but pretty and built on the seashore, forty miles distant from Tunis. We came next to the town of Safaqus [Sfax].

Ibn Juzayy adds: It is of the town of Safaqus that the poet Ali b. Habib al-Tanukhi says:

> God send refreshing rain to the land of Safaqus, city of cisterns
>   and place of prayer!
> His protection be on the bay and extend to the channel, and on
>   its lofty castle of highest fortune!
> A town which seems to say when thou comest to it 'Welcome to
>   home and ease.'
> Methinks the sea, as it now slips away from it, now fills up,
> Is like a lover, seeking to pay a visit, but when it sees the
>   guardians draws back.

Precisely the opposite of these sentiments is expressed in the verses of Abu Abdallah Muhammad b. Abi Tamim, a finished man of letters, and a copious poet:

> Safaqus! may life not be sweet (*safa*) to the dweller therein, and
>   no rain outpouring refresh her soil![10]
> Out on a town where he who alights in her court is assailed by
>   both foes, the Christian and the Arab!
> How many there are who wander distraught on the land,
>   despoiled of their goods! How many who spend their nights on
>   the sea bewailing captivity and perdition!

The sea itself hath beheld such villainy in her dwellers that as oft
as it makes to approach her it turns back in flight.

(Resumes.) We came next to the town of Qabis [Gabes], and put up
inside it. We stopped there over ten nights, on account of incessant
rains. We then left Qabis, making for Atrabulus [Tripoli], and were
escorted for some stages of our journey thither by about a hundred or
more horsemen. There was also in the caravan a troop of archers, with
the result that the roving Arabs, in fear of them, avoided their vicinity, and God preserved us from them. We celebrated the Feast of
Sacrifice[11] on one of the stages of this journey, and on the fourth day
following came to the city of Atrabulus, where we stayed for some
time. I had made a contract of marriage at Safaqus with the daughter
of one of the syndics at Tunis, and she was conducted to me at
Atrabulus.[12] Later, however, I became involved in a dispute with my
father-in-law which made it necessary for me to separate from his
daughter. I then married the daughter of a *talib*[13] of Fez, and when
she was conducted to me at Qasr al-Za'afiyah I gave a wedding feast,
at which I detained the caravan for a whole day, and entertained
them all.

After that, on the 1st of First Jumada [5 April 1326], we arrived at
the city of al-Iskandariyah [Alexandria], may God protect her! She is
a well-guarded frontier citadel and a friendly and hospitable region,
remarkable in appearance and solid of construction, furnished with
all that one could wish for in the way of embellishment and embattle-
ment, and of memorable edifices both secular and religious. Noble
are her dwellings, graceful her qualities and to imposing size her
buildings unite architectural perfection. She is a unique pearl of
glowing opalescence, and a secluded maiden arrayed in her bridal
adornments, glorious in her surpassing beauty, uniting in herself the
excellences that are shared out by other cities between themselves
through her mediating situation between the East and the West. Every
fresh marvel has there its unveiling, every novelty finds its way
thither.[14] Among all the ports in the world I have seen none to equal
it, except the ports of Kawlam [Quilon] and Qaliqut [Calicut] in
India, the port of the infidels [Genoese] at Sudaq in the lands of the
Turks, and the port of Zaitun in China, all of which will be mentioned
later.[15]

The lighthouse.[16] I went to see the lighthouse on this journey and found one of its faces in ruins. One would describe it as a square building soaring into the air. Its door is high above the level of the ground, and opposite its door and at the same height is another building; wooden planks are laid from one to the other, and on these one crosses to the doorway. When they are removed there is no means of approach to it. Inside the door there is a place for the guardian of the lighthouse to sit in, and within the lighthouse itself there are many chambers. The breadth of the passage in its interior is nine spans; and the breadth of the wall ten spans; the breadth of the lighthouse on each of its four faces is 140 spans. It is situated on a high mound and lies at a distance of one farsakh [three miles] from the city on a long tongue of land, encompassed on three sides by the sea up to the point where the sea is immediately adjacent to the city wall, so that the lighthouse cannot be reached by land except from the city. On this peninsula connected with the lighthouse is the cemetery of Alexandria. I visited the lighthouse again on my return to the Maghrib[17] in the year 750 [1349], and found that it had fallen into so ruinous a condition that it was impossible to enter it or to climb up to the doorway. Al-Malik al-Nasir (God's mercy on him) had started to build a similar lighthouse alongside it, which he was prevented by death from completing.[18]

The Pillar of Columns.[19] Another of the marvels of this city is the awe-inspiring marble column outside it, called by them the Pillar of Columns. It is in the midst of a grove of date-palms, but it stands out from amongst the trees, over-topping them in height. It is a single block, skilfully hewn, erected on a plinth of square stones like enormous platforms, and no one knows how it was erected there nor for certain who erected it.

Ibn Juzayy remarks: I have been told by one of my teachers, a much-travelled man, that a man of the corps of archers at Alexandria climbed to the top of this column, taking his bow and quiver with him, and sat himself down there. When the news of this spread, a huge crowd assembled to gaze at him. Everyone was greatly astonished at his feat and puzzled to know how he had contrived to do it. I think that he was either in fear of something or wanting to get something, and his action enabled him to attain his object, on account of the strangeness of his performance. This was the way in which he contrived to ascend the column. He shot an arrow, to the end of which he had tied a long thread, and to the end of the thread a stout rope, so that the arrow passed over the top of the column and exactly transverse to it, and fell on the side opposite to the archer. Thus the thread lay transversely across the top of the column, and he pulled on it until the middle of the rope came to the top of the column in place of the thread. He then secured the rope firmly in the ground at one end and climbed up from the other end, and having taken up his position on top pulled away the rope. He had someone with him who carried it away, so that people had nothing to guide them to his trick and were astonished by his feat.

Some of the learned men of Alexandria. One of these was the qadi of the city, Imad al-Din al-Kindi, a master of the arts of speech, who used to wear a turban of extraordinary size. Never either in the eastern nor in the western lands have I seen a more voluminous headgear than this. I saw him one day sitting in the forepart of a prayer-niche, and his turban was not far short of filling it up completely.

Another of them was the learned, self-denying, pious and humble imam Burhan al-Din the Lame, one of the greatest of ascetics and a devotee of outstanding personality. I met him during my stay in Alexandria and I spent three days as his guest.[20]

A miracle of his

One day, when I had entered his room, he said to me: 'I see that you are fond of travelling and wandering from land to land.' 'Yes,' I replied, 'I am fond of it,' although there had not as yet entered my mind any thought of penetrating to such distant lands as India and China. Then he said: 'You must certainly, if God will, visit my brother Farid al-Din in India, and my brother Rukn al-Din Zakariya in Sind, and my brother Burhan al-Din in China, and when you reach them convey to them a greeting from me.' I was amazed at his prediction, and the idea of going to these countries having been cast into my mind, my wanderings never ceased until I had met these three that he named and conveyed his greeting to them. When I bade him farewell, he gave me some coins as a travelling provision. I kept them as a treasured possession, and never afterwards had need to spend them, until the infidel Indians took them from me at sea with all the other things of which they stripped me.

Another of the religious at Alexandria was the Shaikh Yaqut al-Habashi ('the Ethiopian'), a man of outstanding gifts, who had been the pupil of Abu'l-Abbas of Murcia, who in his turn was the pupil of the famous saint Abu'l-Hasan al-Shadhili, noted for his great miracles and his high degrees of mystical attainment.[21]

A miracle of Abu'l-Hasan al-Shadhili

The Shaikh Yaqut informed me on the authority of his shaikh, Abu'l-Abbas al-Mursi, that Abu'l-Hasan used to go on pilgrimage every year. His custom was to make his way through Upper Egypt, stay at Mecca, fasting and engaging in pious exercises during the month of Rajab and the following months until the close of the Pilgrimage, visit the Holy Tomb of Muhammad at al-Madinah, and return by the main pilgrim road to the town where he resided. One year, however (it was the last year in which he set out), he said to his attendant, 'Take with you a pickaxe, a basket, aromatics for embalming, and all that is necessary for burying the dead.' The servant said to him, 'Why so, O my master?' and he replied, 'In Humaithira you shall see.' Now Humaithira is in the region of Upper Egypt, in the desert of Aidhab, and there is a well of brackish water there and a great many hyenas. When they reached Humaithira, the Shaikh Abu'l-Hasan made a complete ablution, and said a prayer of two prostrations. At the final prostration in his prayers God (Great and Mighty is He) took him and he was buried there. I have visited his tomb; there is a tombstone over it, upon which is inscribed his name and his lineage back to al-Hasan the son of Ali (on him be peace).[22]

The Litany of the Sea attributed to al-Shadhili

He made a journey every year, as we have just said, through Upper Egypt and across the sea of Juddah [the Red Sea],[23] and when he was on board ship he used to recite this litany every day. His disciples still recite it every day, and it runs as follows:

O God, O Exalted, O Mighty, O Forbearing, O All-knowing, Thou
art my Lord and Thy knowledge is my Sufficiency. How excellent
a lord is my Lord, how excellent a sufficiency my sufficiency. Thou
aidest whom Thou wilt, for Thou art the Powerful, the Compassionate.
We pray Thee to guard us from sin in our movements and stillnesses,
our words and designs, and in the stirring of doubts, of unworthy
suggestions and of vain imaginings, that veil from our hearts the
perception of things unseen. Verily *the Believers have been tried
and grievously shaken, and when the time-servers and the sick-
hearted say 'The promises of God and His Apostle to us are naught
but delusion'*,[24] do Thou establish us and succour us, and subject to
us this sea as Thou didst subject the sea unto Moses, and as Thou
didst subject the fire to Abraham, and as Thou didst subject the
mountains and the iron to David, and as Thou didst subject the wind
and the demons and the jinn to Solomon.[25] Subject to us every sea
that is Thine on earth and in heaven, in the world of sense and in
the invisible world, the sea of this life and the sea of the life to come.
Subject to us everything, O Thou in Whose Hand is the rule over
all. *Kaf-Ha-Ya-Ain-Sad.*[26] Succour us, for Thou art *the best of
those that succour*; hear our prayers, for *Thou art the best of those
that open the way*; forgive us our sins, for *Thou art the best of
pardoners*; show mercy upon us, for *Thou art the best of those that
show mercy*; give us our daily bread, for *Thou art the best of
sustainers. Guide us*, and *deliver us from the hand of the evildoers*,
and grant us *a fair wind* according to Thy knowledge; waft it upon
us from *the treasures of Thy mercy*, and carry us thereon with
conveyance of Thy favour, granting us therewith preservation from
sin and wellbeing in our spiritual and our material life and in the
life to come; *verily Thou art disposer of all things*. O God, *smooth
for us* our affairs; give peace to our hearts and our bodies, and grant
us health and wellbeing in our spiritual and our material life. Be
Thou our Companion in our journey, and Guardian of our
households in our absence. Blot out the faces of our enemies, and
transform them into vile creatures in the place where they be; then
shall they not be able to go nor to come against us. *If We will, We
shall blot out their sight, and they shall hasten one with another to
the Bridge;*[27] *how then shall they perceive? If We will, We shall
transform them in their place and they shall not be able to go forth
nor shall they return. Ya-Sin. Faces shall be deformed. Ain-Mim.
Faces shall be humbled before the Living, the Self-Subsistent, and
frustrated is he who bears a burden of wrong-doing. Ta-Sin. Ha-
Mim. Ain-Sin-Qaf. He hath let loose the two seas that meet*

together, between them is a barrier, they cannot pass. Ha-Mim (seven times). The matter is decreed, *Divine aid is at hand,* against us *they shall not be victorious. Ha-Mim. The revelation of the Book is from God, the Mighty, the All-knowing, Who pardoneth sin and accepteth repentance, Whose chastisement is heavy, the Long-suffering; there is no god but He, to Him is the way* of all flesh. *In the name of God* is our door, *Blessed is He* is our walls, *Ya-Sin* is our roof, *Kaf-Ha-Ya-Ain-Sad* is our sufficiency, *Ha-Mim Ain-Sin-Qaf* is our defence. And *God will suffice thee against them, for He is the Hearing, the Knowing.* The curtain of the Throne is extended over us, the Eye of God is watching us, in the Might of God none can harm us. *God is behind them, encompassing! Nay, it is a glorious Qur'an in a Preserved Tablet.* God is the best in keeping, and *He is the most Merciful of them that show mercy. Verily my patron is God, who hath sent down the Book, and He upholdeth the cause of the righteous. My sufficiency is God, other than He there is no god; upon Him have I put my trust and He is the Lord of the Glorious Throne. In the Name of God,* with Whose Name nothing that is on earth or in heaven shall suffer harm, *and He is the Hearing, the Knowing. Each one has attendant angels before him, watching over him at the command of God.* 'There is no Power nor Might save in God, the High, the Great.'

During my stay at Alexandria I heard tell of the pious Shaikh Abu Abdallah al-Murshidi, who lived a life of devotion in retirement from the world, and bestowed gifts from the divine store, for he was indeed one of the great saints who enjoy the vision of the unseen.[28] I was told that he was living in solitary retreat at the village of Munyat Bani Murshid. He had a hermitage there in which he lived alone, with neither servant nor companion. He was sought by the amirs and ministers of state, and parties of men in all ranks of life used to visit him every day, and he would serve them all with food. Every man of them would express his desire to eat some flesh or fruit or sweetmeat at his cell, and to everyone he would bring what he had desired, though that was often out of season. Doctors of the Law used to come to him to ask for appointment to office, and he gave appointments or dismissed from office. All these stories were carried from mouth to mouth far and wide, and al-Malik al-Nasir too had visited him several times in his retreat.

I set out then from the city of Alexandria to seek this shaikh (God profit us by him), and travelled to the town of Fawwa. This town has an attractive appearance, and is as fair as it looks; it has a great many orchards and a remarkable supply of valuable products. In it is the grave of the saintly Shaikh Abu'l-Najah, of celebrated name, the seer of that country.

The retreat of the Shaikh Abu Abdallah al-Murshidi, whom I had come to visit, lies close by the town and separated from it by a canal. On reaching the town I passed through it, and arriving at the cell of this shaikh before the hour of afternoon prayer, I saluted him. When I entered the shaikh's presence (God's mercy upon him) he rose to meet me, embraced me, and calling for food invited me to eat. He was dressed in a black woollen tunic. When the hour of the afternoon prayer arrived, he set me in front as prayer leader (imam), and did the same on every occasion when I was at his cell at the times of prayer during my stay with him. When I prepared to sleep, he said to me, 'Go up to the roof of the cell and sleep there,' for this was during the summer heats.' So I ascended to the roof and found there a straw mattress and a leather mat, vessels for ritual ablutions, a jar of water and a drinking-cup, and I lay down there to sleep.

A miracle of this shaikh

That night, as I was sleeping on the roof of the cell, I dreamed that I was on the wing of a huge bird which flew with me in the direction of the *qiblah*,[29] then made towards the Yaman, then eastwards, then went towards the south, and finally made a long flight towards the east, alighted in some dark and greenish country, and left me there. I was astonished at this dream and said to myself, 'If the shaikh shows me that he knows of my dream, he is all that they say that he is.' Later on, when I had prayed the forenoon prayer, he called me and revealed to me his knowledge of my dream. So I related it to him and he said: 'You shall make the Pilgrimage to Mecca and visit the tomb of the Prophet at al-Madinah, and you shall travel through the lands of al-Yaman and al-Iraq, the land of the Turks, and the land of India. You will stay there for a long time and you will meet there my brother Dilshad the Indian, who will rescue you from a danger into which you will fall.' He then gave me a travelling provision of some small cakes and silver coins, and I bade him farewell and departed. Never since parting from him have I met on my journeys aught but good fortune, and his blessed powers have stood me in good stead.

I travelled next through the Delta to the city of Dimyat [Damietta]. It is a city of spacious quarters and with a diversity of fruits, admirably laid out, and enjoying a share of every good thing. It lies on the bank of the Nile, and the people in the houses next to the river draw water from it in buckets. Many of the houses have steps leading down to the Nile. Banana trees are especially abundant there, and their fruit is carried to Cairo in boats. Its sheep and goats are allowed to pasture at liberty day and night, and for this reason the saying goes of Dimyat, 'Its wall is a sweetmeat and its dogs are sheep.' No one who enters the city may afterwards leave it except by the governor's seal. Persons of repute have a seal stamped on a piece of paper, which they show to the gatekeepers; other persons have the seal stamped on their forearms and must show that.

Sea-fowl are sold in this city in large quantities and are exceedingly fat; in it there are to be had also various preparations of buffalo milk, which are unequalled for sweetness and delicious taste, and the fish called *al-buri*, which is exported from there to Syria, Anatolia, and Cairo.[30] Outside the town there is an island lying between the sea and the river, called al-Barzakh. On this island there is a mosque and a hermitage, in which I met its shaikh, and I spent the night preceding a Friday in his company. With him were a number of pious poor brethren (faqirs),[31] devoted to the religious life and of excellent character, who passed the night in prayers, recitation of the Qur'an, and liturgical exercises.

The present town of Dimyat is of recent construction; the old city was that destroyed by the Franks in the time of al-Malik al-Salih.[32] In it is the hermitage of Shaikh Jamal al-Din al-Sawi, who set the example which is followed by the group known as the Qarandariyah;[33] these are the persons who shave off their beards and eyebrows.

Anecdote

It is said that the reason which led Shaikh Jamal al-Din al-Sawi to shave off his beard and eyebrows was this. He was a man of fine figure and handsome face, and a woman belonging to Sawah conceived a passion for him, and made a habit of sending him letters, of intercepting him in the streets, and inviting him to fulfil her desires.

He for his part rejected all her advances with scorn. When she was baffled by his refusals, she tricked him by sending an old woman who posted herself with a sealed letter in her hand outside a certain house on his way to the mosque. As he passed by her, she said to him, 'Sir, can you read?' He said, 'Yes.' 'This letter,' she told him, 'has reached me from my son; I wish you would read it to me.' He consented, but when he opened the letter she said to him, 'Sir, my son has a wife, and she is in the vestibule of the house. Would you be so kind as to read it between the outer and inner doors of the house, so that she may hear it?' He agreed to do as she asked, and when he was between the two doors the old woman locked the outer door, and the woman herself came out with her attendants. They seized him and carried him into the inner apartments, where the woman tried to seduce him. When he saw that there was no way out for him, he said, 'I shall do as you wish, so show me the closet,' and she showed it to him. He took water in with him, and as he had in his possession a sharp razor, he shaved off his beard and eyebrows and came out before her. She, horrified at his appearance and indignant at what he had done, ordered him to be put out. Since God preserved him from temptation by this means, he retained the same appearance ever after, and all those who follow his way shave the head, beard and eyebrows.[34]

A miracle of this shaikh

The story goes that when he came to the city of Dimyat he never quitted its cemetery. There was in the town a qadi known as Ibn al-Amid, who went out one day to the funeral of one of the notables, and seeing the Shaikh Jamal al-Din in the cemetery said to him, 'You are the innovating shaikh.'[35] He replied, 'And you are the ignorant qadi, riding on your mule among the tombs, although you know that a man should be shown the same respect in death as in life.' The qadi said to him, 'But worse than that is your shaving off your beard.' 'Is it to me that you refer?' said the shaikh; then bowing his head to his knees he raised it again, and lo! he had a magnificent black beard. The qadi was astonished, as were all those who were in his company; and dismounted from his mule as a mark of respect to him. The shaikh then bowed his head a second time and lo! he had a fine white beard. Then he bowed his head a third time, and when he raised it again, he had no beard, just as he appeared to begin with.[36] The qadi kissed his hand, and becoming his pupil, built him a fine hermitage and spent the rest of his life in his company. When at length the shaikh died he was buried in his hermitage, and the qadi, when his own death was at hand, gave instructions that he should be buried at the door of the hermitage, so that every visitor to the tomb of the shaikh should tread upon his grave.

From Dimyat I travelled up the Nile until at length I arrived at the city of Misr [Cairo], mother of cities and seat of pharaoh the tyrant, mistress of broad provinces and fruitful lands, boundless in multitude of buildings, peerless in beauty and splendour, the meeting-place of comer and goer, the stopping-place of feeble and strong. Therein is what you will of learned and simple, grave and gay, prudent and foolish, base and noble, of high estate and low estate, unknown and famous; she surges as the waves of the sea with her throngs of folk and can scarce contain them for all the capacity of her situation and sustaining power. Her youth is ever new in spite of length of days, and the star of her horoscope does not move from the mansion of fortune; her conquering capital (*al-Qahirah*)[37] has subdued the nations, and her kings have grasped the forelocks of both Arab and non-Arab. She has as her peculiar possession the majestic Nile, which dispenses her district from the need of entreating the distillation of the rain; her territory is a month's journey for a hastening traveller, of generous soil, and extending a friendly welcome to strangers.

It is said that in Cairo there are twelve thousand water-carriers who transport water on camels, and thirty thousand hirers of mules and donkeys, and that on its Nile there are thirty-six thousand vessels belonging to the sultan and his subjects, which sail upstream to Upper Egypt and downstream to Alexandria and Damietta, laden with goods and commodities of all kinds. On the bank of the Nile opposite Cairo is the place known as al-Rawdah ['the Garden'], which is a pleasure park and promenade, containing many beautiful gardens. The people of Cairo are fond of pleasure and amusement. I once witnessed a fête there, which was held for al-Malik al-Nasir's recovery from a fracture which he had suffered in his hand. All the merchants decorated their bazaars and had rich stuffs, ornaments, and silken fabrics hung up in their shops for several days.

The mosque of Amr b. al-As, and the colleges, hospital, and convents

The mosque of Amr b. al-As is a noble mosque, highly venerated and widely celebrated.[38] The Friday service is held in it, and the road runs right through it from east to west. To the west of it is the cell where the Imam Abu Abdallah al-Shafi'i used to teach.[39] As for the *madrasahs* in Cairo, they are too many for anyone to count; and as for the *Maristan*, which is 'between the two castles' near the mausoleum of al-Malik al-Mansur Qala'un, no description is adequate to its beauties.[40] It is equipped with innumerable conveniences and medicaments, and its revenue is reported to be a thousand dinars a day. The convents too are numerous, and the amirs in Cairo vie with one another in building them.

Each convent in Cairo is affected to the use of a separate congregation of poor brethren, most of whom are Persians, men of good education and adepts in the 'way' of Sufism. Each has a shaikh as superior and a warden, and the organization of their affairs is admirable. It is one of their customs in the matter of their food that the steward of the house comes in the morning to the faqirs, each of whom then specifies what food he desires. When they assemble for meals, each person is given his bread and soup in a separate dish, none sharing with another. They eat twice a day. They receive winter clothing and summer clothing and a monthly allowance varying from twenty to thirty dirhams each. Every Thursday night they are given sugar cakes, soap to wash their clothes, the price of admission to the bath-house, and oil to feed their lamps. These men are celibate; the married men have separate convents.

The Qarafah of Cairo and its sanctuaries

At Old Cairo too is the cemetery called al-Qarafah, a place of vast repute for blessed power, for it is a part of the mount of al-Muqattam, of which God has promised that it shall be one of the gardens of Paradise. These people build in the Qarafah beautiful domed chapels and surround them by walls, so that they look like houses, and they construct chambers in them and hire the services of Qur'an readers, who recite night and day in beautiful voices. There are some of them who build a religious house or a *madrasah* by the side of the mausoleum. They go out every Thursday evening to spend the night there with their children and womenfolk and make a circuit of the famous sanctuaries.

They go out also to spend the night there on the night of mid-Sha'ban, and the market people take out all kinds of eatables.[41]

Among the celebrated sanctuaries in the city of Cairo is the imposing holy shrine where rests the head of al-Husain b. Ali (on both be peace).[42] Beside it is a vast convent, of wonderful workmanship, on the doors of which there are silver rings, and plates also on them of the same metal. This shrine is paid its full meed of respect and veneration.

The Egyptian Nile[43]

The Egyptian Nile surpasses all rivers of the earth in sweetness of taste, breadth of channel and magnitude of utility. Cities and villages succeed one another along its banks without interruption and have no equal in the inhabited world, nor is any river known whose basin is so intensively cultivated as that of the Nile. The course of the Nile is from south to north, contrary to all the great rivers. One extraordinary thing about it is that it begins to rise in the extreme hot weather, at the time when rivers generally diminish and dry up, and begins to subside at the time when rivers increase in volume and overflow.

The Nile is one of the five great rivers of the world, which are the Nile, Euphrates, Tigris, Saihun [Syr Darya] and Jaihun [Amu Darya]; five other rivers rival these, the river of Sind, which is called Panj Ab [i.e. Five Rivers], the river of Hindustan which is called the Gang [Ganges] – to it the Hindus go on pilgrimage, and when they burn their dead they throw the ashes of them into it, and they say that it comes from Paradise – the river Jun [Yamuna], also in Hindustan, the river Itil [Volga] in the Qifjaq [Kipchak] steppe, on the shore of which is the city of al-Sara, and the river Saru in the land of al-Khita [Cathay], on the banks of which is the city of Khan-Baliq [Peking], whence it descends to the city of al-Khansa [Hangzhou] and from there to the city of Zaitun in the land of China. We shall speak of all these in their proper places, if God will.

The pyramids and berbas[44]

These are among the marvels which have been celebrated through the course of ages, and there is much talk and theorizing amongst men about them, their significance and the origin of their construction. They aver that all branches of knowledge which came into existence before the Deluge were derived from Hermes the Ancient, who lived in the remotest part of the Sa'id [Upper Egypt]; he is also called by the name of Khanukh [Enoch] that is Idris (on him be peace). It is said that he was the first to speculate on the movements of the spheres and the celestial bodies, and the first to construct temples and glorify God in them; and that he warned men of the coming of the Deluge, and fearing for the disappearance of knowledge and destruction of the practical arts built the pyramids and the berbas, in which he depicted all the practical arts and their tools, and made diagrams of the sciences, in order that they might remain immortalized.

The pyramids is an edifice of solid hewn stone, of immense height and circular plan, broad at the base and narrow at the top, like the figure of a cone.[45] They have no doorways and the manner of their erection is unknown. Now when the caliphate devolved upon the Commander of the Faithful al-Mamun,[46] he proposed to pull them down, and although one of the Egyptian shaikhs advised him not to do so he persisted in his design and ordered that they should be breached from the north side. So they set about lighting fires up against them and then sprinkling them with vinegar and battering them with a mangonel, until the breach which is still to be seen in them was opened up. There they found, facing the hole, a sum of money which the Commander of the Faithful ordered to be weighed. He then calculated what had been spent on making the breach, and finding the two sums equal, was greatly astonished.

The Sultan of Egypt

The sultan of Egypt at the time of my entry was al-Malik al-Nasir Abu'l-Fath Muhammad, son of al-Malik al-Mansur Saif al-Din Qala'un al-Salihi. Qala'un was known as al-Alfi ['the Thousandman'] because al-Malik al-Salih bought him for a thousand dinars of gold.[47] He came originally from Qifjaq [Kipchak]. Al-Malik al-Nasir (God's mercy upon him) was a man of generous character and great virtues, and sufficient proof of his nobility is furnished by his devotion to the service of the two holy sanctuaries of Mecca and al-Madinah and the works of beneficence which he does every year to assist the pilgrims, in furnishing camels loaded with provisions and water for those without means and the helpless, and for carrying those who cannot keep up with the caravan or are too weak to walk on foot, both on the Egyptian pilgrim road and on that from Damascus.

Some of the amirs of Cairo

Among them was the cup-bearer of al-Malik al-Nasir, the amir Buktumur;[48] it was he whom al-Malik al-Nasir put to death by poison. Another was al-Malik al-Nasir's deputy, Arghun the Dawadar, and it is he who comes next to Buktumur in rank. Another was Tushtu, who was known as 'Green Chickpeas'; he was one of the best of the amirs and had to his credit many charities to orphans for clothing and upkeep, and payment of a salary to a teacher to instruct them in the Qur'an. He also made large benefactions to the vagabonds known as *harafish*, who are a large organized body, hard-faced folk and lewd. Al-Malik al-Nasir once imprisoned Tushtu, and the *harafish* assembled in thousands, took up their stand below the citadel and shouted as with a single tongue: 'Ho, thou ill-starred limper (meaning al-Malik al-Nasir), fetch him out!'[49] So he released him from his place of confinement. He imprisoned him a second time, but the orphans made a like scene, and he set him free again.

Next came my journey from Cairo by the route of the Sa'id,[50] with the object of crossing to the noble Hijaz. I stayed on the night following my departure at the convent which the Sahib Taj al-Din ibn Hanna built at Dair al-Tin. It is an enormous convent built by him for the sake of certain possessions of great pride and illustrious relics that he deposited in it, namely, a fragment of the wooden basin of the Prophet (God's blessing and peace upon him), the pencil with which he used to apply kohl to his eyes, the *dirafsh*, that is to say, the awl, which he used for sewing his sandals, and the Qur'an of the Commander of the Faithful Ali b. Abi Talib, written in his own hand (God be pleased with him). The sahib, it is said, bought the illustrious relics of the Prophet which we have mentioned for a thousand dirhams, and built the convent, and endowed it with funds to supply food to all comers and goers and to maintain the guardians of these sacred relics – God Most High profit him by his blessed purpose.[51]

From this convent I travelled upriver to the town of Munyat Ibn Khasib, a widely spaced town covering an extensive area, and built on the bank of the Nile.[52] And in truth, in truth, it excels all the other towns of the Sa'id, having colleges and sanctuaries, religious houses and mosques. In ancient times it was a village belonging to Khasib, the governor of Egypt.

The story of Khasib

It is told that one of the caliphs of the house of al-Abbas (God be pleased with them), angered with the people of Egypt, swore to appoint as governor over them the most contemptible and abject of his slaves, with the object of humiliating them and inflicting upon them a signal punishment. Now Khasib was the lowest of the slaves, since he was charged with the duty of heating the bath. The caliph conferred upon him a robe of honour and made him amir over Egypt, thinking that he would conduct himself towards them in an evil manner and seek occasions to injure them, as usually happens in the case of those who are given authority with no previous experience of high office. When, however, Khasib found himself settled in Egypt, he conducted himself towards its inhabitants with the utmost magnanimity, and acquired a name for liberality and open-handedness. The relatives of the caliphs, amongst others, used to visit him, when he would make them munificent gifts, and they returned to Baghdad full of gratitude for his generosity towards them. The story goes on that the caliph remarked the absence of a certain member of the Abbasid family, and that he was away from him for some time and then came back. So the caliph asked him the reason of his absence, and he told him that he had gone to visit Khasib, and stated what Khasib had given him, which was a considerable gift. The caliph was enraged, and commanded that Khasib should have his eyes put out, be fetched up from Egypt to Baghdad, and thrown into the bazaars there.

When the order to arrest him arrived, he was denied entrance into his house, but he had on his hand a jewel of great value, which he hid on his person and sewed up by night into one of his garments. After he had suffered the loss of his eyes and was thrown into the bazaars of Baghdad, he was accosted by a certain poet who said to him. 'O Khasib, I went from Baghdad to seek you in Egypt, in order to sing your praises in an ode, but my arrival there happened to coincide with your departure; still I should like you to hear it.' 'What use is there in my hearing it,' exclaimed Khasib, 'when I am as you see me?' 'All that I want,' said the poet, 'is that you should hear it; as for the gift, you have given to others, and that lavishly – God reward you with good.' 'Go on then,' said he, and the poet recited:

> Khasib, the fruitful to bestow, by Egypt's Nile alights;
> Let high the golden tide o'erflow, since sea with sea unites.

When he came to the end of the ode, Khasib said to him, 'Unpick this piece of sewing,' and when he had done so bade him take the jewel. He refused, but Khasib adjured him to take it, so he took it and went off with it to the jewellers' bazaar. When he displayed it to them they said, 'Such a jewel is fitting for none but the caliph.' They brought it therefore to the notice of the caliph, who commanded that the poet should be sent for, and questioned him on the subject of the jewel. The poet told him the story of it, whereupon the caliph repented of what he had done to Khasib, and commanding him to be brought into his presence, gave him a large sum of money and bade him choose what he would like. He requested the caliph to give him this village, the request was granted, and Khasib lived in it until his death, bequeathing it to his descendants until they became extinct.

The qadi of this Munya at the time of my arrival there was Fakhr al-Din al-Nuwairi al-Maliki and its governor was Shams al-Din, an excellent and generous amir. One day I entered the bath-house in this township, and found the men in it wearing no covering. This appeared a shocking thing to me, and I went to the governor and informed him of it. He told me not to leave and ordered the lessees of all the bath-houses to be brought before him. Articles were formally drawn up there and then making them subject to penalties if any person should enter a bath without a waist-wrapper, and the governor behaved to them with the greatest severity, after which I took leave of him.

From Munyat ibn Khasib I travelled to the town of Manfalut, a town of pleasant appearance and elegant construction, on the bank of the Nile, and of celebrated sanctity.

Anecdote

The people of this town told me that al-Malik al-Nasir (God's mercy upon him) gave orders for the construction of a large mimbar[53] of solid workmanship and admirable style, which was intended for the Sacred Mosque of Mecca (God increase it in nobility and veneration). When it was completed, he gave orders that it should be taken up the Nile, in order to be transported to the sea of Juddah, and then on to Mecca (God ennoble her). But when the vessel which carried it reached Manfalut and drew level with its congregational mosque, it stopped and refused to proceed, in spite of the assistance of the wind. Those on board were intensely amazed at its behaviour, and as they stayed there for several days while the boat refused to move with them, they wrote an account of the incident to al-Malik al-Nasir (God's mercy upon him). He ordered that mimbar to be placed in the congregational mosque of the town of Manfalut, which was done, and I saw it there with my own eyes.

I travelled from this town to the town of Asyut, a handsome town with choice bazaars. Its qadi was known far and wide by the nickname of 'Revenue Nil', which originated in this way. The qadis in Egypt and Syria administer the *waqfs*[54] and alms for the benefit of travellers. When a poor man comes to any of the towns, he goes to the qadi of the place, who gives him whatever amount is assigned to him. Now this qadi, when any poor person applied to him, used to say to him, 'revenue nil', that is, there is nothing left of the money produced by the endowments. So he came to be called by this nickname and it stuck to him.

Thence I journeyed to the town of Ikhmim, which is a place solidly built and of imposing appearance. Here is the *berba* which is known by the name of the town. It is built of stones, and in the interior there are sculptures and writing of the ancients, which is not understood in these days, and images of the spheres and stars. They assert that it was built when the Flying Eagle was in the sign of the Scorpion. It contains also images of animals and other things, and the people tell a number of fanciful stories, over which it is not necessary to linger, on the subject of these images.

I continued on my way from Ikhmim to the town of Hu, a large town on the bank of the Nile. In this town lives the Sayyid Sharif Abu Muhammad Abdallah al-Hasani, one of the saintliest of men.[55]

A miracle of his

I went to visit this sharif, for the sake of the blessing conferred by seeing and greeting him. When he asked me what I proposed to do, and I told him that I intended to make the Pilgrimage to the Holy House by way of Juddah, he replied, 'You will not succeed in doing that on this occasion. Go back, for you will make your first Pilgrimage by the Syrian Road and no other.' So I took leave of him; but instead of acting upon his advice I continued on my way until I got to Aidhab, and then, as I could not manage to complete the journey, I turned back and retraced my steps to Cairo, and from there on to Syria, and my route on the first of my Pilgrimages was indeed along the Syrian Road, just as the sharif had told me (God profit us by him).

Leaving Hu, I continued upriver through the towns of Qina, Qus, al-Aqsur [Luxor] and Asna, until I came to the town of Adfu [Edfu], between which and Asna is a day and a night's journey through desert country. Then, crossing the Nile, we hired camels and set out with a party of Arabs through a desert totally devoid of settlements but quite safe for travelling. At one of our halts on the way we encamped at Humaithira, the site of the tomb of the saint Abu'l-Hasan al-Shadhili, whose miraculous foretelling that he would die there we have related above.[56] The place is infested with hyenas, and during the night of our stay there we were continually occupied in driving them off. Indeed one of the animals got at my baggage, ripped up a camel-sack which was amongst it, dragged out a small skin of dates and made off with it. We found the skin when we rose next morning, torn to pieces and with most of the contents eaten.

At length, after travelling for fifteen days through the desert, we reached the town of Aidhab, a large town, well supplied with fish and milk;[57] dates and grain are imported from Upper Egypt. Its inhabitants are the Bujah, black-skinned people, who wrap themselves in yellow blankets and tie headbands, each about a fingerbreadth wide, round their heads. They give daughters no share in their inheritance. Their food is camel's milk and they ride on *mahri* dromedaries. One-third of the city belongs to the sultan of Egypt al-Malik al-Nasir, and two-thirds to the king of the Bujah, who is called al-Hadrabi.[58]

On reaching Aidhab we found that al-Hadrabi had fallen out with the officers of al-Nasir, that he had sunk the ships, and the Turks had fled before him. It was impossible for us to make the sea-crossing, so we sold the provisions that we had made ready, and returning to Upper Egypt with the Arabs from whom we had hired the camels, arrived back at the town of Qus. We sailed thence down the Nile (it was the flood season), and after a passage of eight nights arrived at Cairo.

2 Syria

I stayed only one night in Cairo before setting out for Syria. This was in the middle of Sha'ban of the year 26.[1] I then travelled to the town of Balbais; it is a large town with many fruit gardens, but I did not see there anyone whom I should wish to mention. I came next to al-Salihiyah, after which we entered the sands and halted at the post-stations on the way through. At each of these stations there is a hostelry which they call a *khan*, where travellers alight with their beasts, and outside each *khan* is a public watering-place and a shop at which the traveller may buy what he requires for himself and his beast. Amongst these stations is the well-known place called Qatya, where *zakat* is collected from the merchants, their goods are examined, and their baggage most rigorously searched.[2] There are government offices here, with officers, clerks and notaries, and its daily revenue is a thousand gold dinars. No one may pass this place in the direction of Syria without a passport from Egypt, nor into Egypt without a passport from Syria, as a measure of protection for a person's property and of precaution against spies from Iraq.[3] This road is under guarantee of the bedouins (that is to say, they have been made responsible for guarding it). At nightfall they smooth down the sand so that no mark is left on it, then the governor comes in the morning and examines the sand. If he finds any track on it he requires the Arabs to fetch the person who made it, and they set out in pursuit of him and never fail to catch him. They then bring him to the governor, who punishes him as he sees fit.

The governor at Qatya showed me hospitality, treated me honourably, and gave free passage to those who were with me. On his staff was the inspector Abd al-Jalil al-Maghribi, who was familiar with the Maghribis and their lands, and whose duty it was to ask of each of them who arrived from what country he came, so that there might be no doubt as to their identity; for the Maghribis are allowed to pass through Qatya without hindrance.

From there we went on to the town of Ghazzah [Gaza], which is the first of the towns of Syria on the borders of Egypt,[4] a place of spacious dimensions and large population, with fine bazaars. It contains numerous mosques, and there is no wall round it.

Next I travelled from Ghazzah to the town of al-Khalil [Hebron] – God bless and give peace to our Prophet and to him.[5] It is a town of small extent but high distinction and shining splendours, pleasant in outward appearance and admirable in inner quality, lying in the hollow of a valley. Its mosque is an elegant edifice, substantially built, of striking beauty and imposing height, and constructed of squared stones. In one angle of it there is a stone, one of whose faces measures thirty-seven spans. It is said that Solomon (peace be on him) commanded the jinn to build it. In the interior of the mosque is the honourable and sanctified cave containing the tomb of Abraham, Isaac, and Jacob – God's blessings upon our Prophet and on them – and facing them are three other tombs, which are those of their wives. To the right of the *mimbar* and adjoining the wall containing the *qiblah*[6] is a place from which one descends by marble steps of solid construction into a narrow passage which leads to a marble-paved hall, containing cenotaphs of the three tombs, and one is told that these are above the real tombs. There used formerly to be in the same place a passageway into the blessed cave, but it is now blocked up. I have gone down into this place several times.

I continued my journey thereafter from this town to al-Quds [Jerusalem]. On my way there I visited Bait Lahm [Bethlehem], the birthplace of Jesus – on him be peace – where the trace of the palm trunk is still to be seen surmounted by a vast edifice.[7] The Christians regard it with intense veneration and hospitably entertain all who alight at it.

We then arrived at Bait al-Muqaddas [Jerusalem][8] – God ennoble it – third in excellence after the two sacred mosques of Mecca and al-Madinah, and the place of ascension of the Apostle of God – God bless him and give him peace – whence he was caught up into heaven.[9] The town is large and imposing, and built of squared stones.

The Sacred Mosque

This is one of those surpassingly beautiful mosques which excite
wonder and admiration. It is said that there is not upon the face of
the earth a mosque larger than it. Its length from east to west is seven
hundred and fifty-two cubits, measuring in royal cubits, and its
breadth from south to north four hundred and thirty-five cubits. The
entire mosque is an open court, unroofed except for the mosque of al-
Aqsa; this has a roof of the utmost perfection of architecture and skill
in execution, and is embellished with gold and brilliant colours.

The Dome of the Rock

This is one of the most marvellous of buildings, of the most perfect in
architecture and strangest in shape; it has been endowed with a
plentiful share of loveliness, and has received a choice portion of
every rare beauty. It stands on an elevation in the centre of the
mosque and is reached by ascending a flight of marble steps. It has
four doors. The court around it is also paved with marble, of
excellent workmanship, and its interior likewise. Both on its exterior
and inside it is adorned with such a variety of decorations and such
brilliance of execution as to defy description. The greater part of this
decoration is surfaced with gold, so that it glows like a mass of light
and flashes with the gleam of lightning; the eyes of him who would
gaze on its splendours are dazzled and the tongue of the beholder
finds no words to represent them. In the centre of the Dome is the
blessed Rock of which mention is made in the Traditions, for the
Prophet (God bless him and give him peace) ascended from it to
heaven. It is a solid piece of rock, projecting about a man's height,
and underneath it there is a cave the size of a small room and of about
a man's height also, with steps leading down to it.

Some of the gracious sanctuaries in the Holy City of Jerusalem

Among these there is, on the farther side of the valley called the Valley
of Jahannam, to the east of the town, and on a lofty hill there, a
building which is said to mark the place whence Jesus (on him be

peace) ascended to heaven. In the hollow of the valley already mentioned is a church venerated by the Christians, who say that it contains the grave of Mary (peace be upon her). At Jerusalem also there is another venerated church to which the Christians come on pilgrimage. This is the church about which they lie and are persuaded that it contains the grave of Jesus (on him be peace).[10] All who come on pilgrimage to it are liable to a stipulated tax to the Muslims and various humiliations, which they suffer very unwillingly.

I then set out from Jerusalem the Holy to visit the frontier fortress of Asqalan [Ascalon]. It is lying in ruins, and has become no more than shapeless remains and mouldering walls. Yet seldom has one town united so many advantages as were united in Asqalan – solidity, fine situation, natural strength of position, and combination of the resources of both land and sea. From there I went on next to the town of Sur [Tyre], which is in ruins, but outside it there is an inhabited village, most of whose population are Rafidis.[11] I stopped there at a place with some water, to make the ritual ablutions, and one of the men of this village also came up to make his ablutions. Well, he began by washing his feet, then he washed his face, without rinsing out his mouth or snuffing water up his nostrils, and ended by wiping his hand over a part of his head. I reproved him for doing this, but he said to me, 'In building, the place to begin is at the foundation.' It is this city of Sur which has become proverbial for strength of fortification and inaccessibility, because the sea surrounds it on three of its sides, and it has two gates, one on the landward side and one on the sea. That gate which gives access to the land has four covered passages, each with parapets, protecting it, and that which opens to the sea stands between two great towers. For sheer masonry there is no more marvellous or more remarkable construction in any town in the world; for the sea surrounds it on three sides and on the fourth side is a wall underneath which ships may enter and come to anchor. In former times there was an iron chain between the two towers as a barrier, so that there was no way in at that point, nor way out, until it had been lowered. It was under the charge of guards and inspectors, and none might enter or leave but with their knowledge. Akkah[12] also had a harbour like this, but it could hold only small vessels.

Then I went on from there to the town of Saida [Sidon], which is on the coast, a pleasant place and rich in fruits; figs, raisins and olive oil are exported from it to the cities of Egypt. We travelled next to the town of Bairut. It is a small place, but with fine bazaars, and its congregational mosque is of striking beauty. Fruit and iron are exported from there to Egypt. We made an excursion from Bairut to visit the tomb of Abu Ya'qub Yusuf, who, they say, was one of the kings of the Maghrib. The tomb is at a place called Karak Nuh in the Biqa al-Aziz, and by it is a religious house at which food is provided for all who come and go.[13] It is said that the Sultan Salah al-Din [Saladin] assigned the religious endowments for its upkeep, but some say it was the Sultan Nur al-Din, who was a man of saintly life and of whom it is told that he used to weave mats and live on the proceeds of their sale.[14]

The story of the above-mentioned
Abu Ya'qub Yusuf

It is related that after coming to the city of Damascus he fell ill there of a grievous malady and remained for some time lying on the ground in the bazaars. When he recovered from his illness, he went out to the outskirts of Damascus to seek some orchard for which he might serve as keeper. He was engaged to keep an orchard belonging to the king Nur al-Din and continued to tend it for six months. When the fruit was due to ripen the sultan came to that garden, and the super-intendent of the garden bade Abu Ya'qub fetch some pomegranates for the sultan to partake of. He brought him some pomegranates accordingly, but the superintendent, finding them sour, bade him fetch some others. He did so, and the superintendent, finding them sour also, said to him, 'Have you been looking after this orchard for six months and cannot tell the sweet from the sour?' He replied, 'It was for keeping that you hired me, not for eating,' whereupon the superintendent came to the king and told him the whole story. The king sent for him, for he had seen in a dream that he should meet with Abu Ya'qub and that some advantage would accrue to himself from him, and he had an intuition that this was he. So he said to him, 'You are Abu Ya'qub?' and on receiving his answer, 'Yes,' he rose to welcome him, embraced him, and bade him sit beside him. After that he took him in his cortège to his own residence, where he entertained him. Abu Ya'qub stayed with him for some time, but subsequently left Damascus in solitary flight during the season of severe cold, and came to one of the villages in the district. There was in this place a man of humble station, who invited him to stay in his house and, on his consenting, prepared soup for him and killed a chicken and brought it to him with barley bread. Having partaken of this, Abu Ya'qub prayed for a blessing upon his host. Now the man had several children, one of them being a girl who was shortly to be conducted to her husband. It is one of their customs in that country that the girl receives an 'outfit' from her father, the greater part of which consists of copper utensils. These are regarded by them with much pride and are made the subject of special stipulations in the marriage contract. So Abu Ya'qub said to the man, 'Have you any copper in your house?' 'Yes,' he replied, 'I have just bought some in order to give this girl her outfit.' 'Fetch it to me,' he said, and when the man had brought it added, 'Now borrow all the copper that you can from your neighbours.' So he did so and laid all the vessels out before him. Then Abu Ya'qub lit fires around them, and taking out a purse which he had containing the elixir, he threw some of it upon the copper and the whole collection turned into gold. After putting these into a locked chamber, Abu Ya'qub wrote a letter to Nur al-Din, the king of Damascus, telling him about them and exhorting him to build a hospital for sick strangers and to constitute endowments for it. He bade him also build religious houses on the highways, satisfy the owners of the copper vessels and provide for the maintenance of the owner of the house, and concluded his letter with these words: 'If Ibrahim b. Ad'ham[15] renounced the kingdom of Khurasan as he did, I too have renounced the kingdom of the Maghrib, and now renounce also this art. Farewell.' He at once took to flight, and the owner of the house brought the letter to the King Nur al-Din, who came to that village and carried off the gold, after satisfying the owners of the copper vessels and the man himself. He made search for Abu Ya'qub, but failing to find any trace or light upon any news of him, returned to Damascus, where he built the hospital which is known by his name and which has not its equal in the inhabited world.

I came next to the town of Atrabulus [Tripoli], one of the capitals of Syria and of its great cities, traversed by flowing streams, and surrounded by gardens and trees, flanked by the sea with its copious resources and by the land with its sustaining bounties, and possessed of admirable bazaars and fertile lands. The sea is at a distance of two miles from it, and the town itself is of recent construction. There are in this city some fine bath-houses, among them being the bath-house of Sandamur, who was a former governor of the city, and of whose severity to evildoers many stories are told. For example, a woman complained to him that one of his private mamluks had seized from her some milk that she was selling and had drunk it. She had no evidence to support her tale, but Sandamur gave orders that he should be cut in two, and the milk came out of his entrails. From Tripoli I went inland, via Hisn al-Akrad and Hims,[16] to the town of Hamah. This is one of the dignified metropolitan centres and elegant cities of Syria, of exceeding comeliness and surpassing beauty, and surrounded by orchards and gardens, supplied by waterwheels [*norias*] like revolving spheres. It is traversed by the great river called al-Asi ['the Rebel'].[17] Hamah produces great quantities of fruit, amongst them being the almond apricot; when you break open its kernel you find a sweet almond inside it.

Ibn Juzayy adds: it is this city and her river, waterwheels and orchards that form the subject of the following verses by the man of letters and traveller, Ibn Sa'id of Gharnatah.

May God guard those scenes in Hamah that border both banks of
   her river
By which I have lingered with hearing and musing and sight!
The doves in her gardens are singing, the boughs in the breeze are
   aquiver,
Her buildings so brave that they baffle the tongue to indite.
Men chide me because I rebel at restraint and at reason's
   repression,
And homage I pay to the cup and to revel and cheer.
If the river itself be a rebel in Hamah why hold it transgression
That I follow its lead and I drink of the wine strong and clear?
My voice in its ringing descant keeps time with her *norias'*
   screeching,
My hand with their ladling, but swifter the dance of my feet.
Lamenting, they scatter incessant their tears, like to lovers
   beseeching
With passion to see their beloved and her favours entreat.

We travelled from there to the town of Sarmin, a pretty place with a great quantity of orchards, their principal tree being the olive. Brick soap is manufactured there and exported to Cairo and Damascus; they manufacture also perfumed soap, for washing the hands, and this they dye with red and yellow. At Sarmin too are manufactured fine cotton fabrics, which are known by its name. Its population are revilers, who hate 'the Ten', and – an extraordinary thing – never mention the word 'ten'.[18] When their brokers are selling goods by auction in their bazaars and come to ten, they say 'nine and one'. One day a Turk happened to be there, and hearing a broker cry 'nine and one', he laid his club about his head saying, 'say ten', whereupon quoth he, 'Ten for the sake of the club.' There is a congregational mosque there with nine domes, and they avoided making them ten, in accordance with their detestable doctrine.

We journeyed thereafter to the city of Halab [Aleppo], that city of the first magnitude and vast metropolis. Abu'l-Husain Ibn Jubair[19] has expressed himself thus describing it: 'Honourable is her rank, and far-flung in every age her name, many the kings who have sought her hand, and privileged her position in all hearts. How many a hand-to-hand combat has she excited, how many gleaming blades have been unscabbarded for her! She has a citadel famed for natural strength, conspicuous in height, and exempted by inaccessibility from being sought or won, whose flanks are of squared stones, and which is erected in the proportion of symmetry and stability of elevation.' The citadel of Halab is called al-Shahba;[20] within it are two wells fed with water from springs, whence it has no fear of thirst. It is encompassed by two walls and around it between the two walls is a great trench, also fed with water from springs. Its inner wall is close set with towers, in which there have been contrived marvellous upper rooms, pierced with windows, and every tower amongst them is inhabited. Foodstuffs do not corrupt in this castle in spite of long-keeping. In it there is a sanctuary which is visited by some persons, and of which it is told that al-Khalil [Abraham] – upon him be peace – was wont to make his devotions there.

Halab is one of the most illustrious of cities, and one which has no rival in beauty of plan and perfection of arrangement, and in the spaciousness and symmetrical disposition of the bazaars. Its *qaisariyah*[21] cannot be paralleled for beauty and size; it encircles the chief mosque of the city, and each of its arcades faces one of the doors of the mosque. The congregational mosque itself is one of the most splendid buildings of its kind. In the court there is a pool of water, which is surrounded by a pavement of vast extent, and its pulpit is of exquisite workmanship, inlaid with ivory and ebony.[22] The spirit feels in the environs of the city of Aleppo an exhilaration, gladness and spright-liness which are not experienced elsewhere, and it is one of the cities which is worthy to be the seat of the Caliphate.

From Aleppo I journeyed north, visiting Antioch, then turned south once more and entered the mountains. Here I passed by the castle of al-Qadmus, the castle of al-Mainaqah, the castle of al-Ullaiqah, the castle of Masyaf, and the castle of al-Kahf. These castles belong to a sect called the Isma'iliyah, known also as the Fidawis, and none may visit them there save members of their sect.[23] They are the arrows of al-Malik al-Nasir, by means of whom he strikes down those of his enemies who take refuge from him in al-Iraq and other lands, and they receive fixed emoluments. When the sultan desires to send one of them to assassinate some foe of his, he pays him his blood money. If he escapes after carrying out what is desired of him, the money is his, but if he is caught it goes to his children. They have poisoned knives, with which they strike the victim of their mission, but some-times their devices do not succeed and they themselves are killed.

I then journeyed from the castles of the Fidawis to the town of Jabalah, a place of perennial streams and trees, and about a mile distant from the sea.[24] It contains the tomb of the pious and cele-brated saint Ibrahim ibn Ad'ham (God be pleased with him), he who renounced the kingly state and consecrated himself to God Most High, as all the world knows. But Ibrahim was not of royal lineage, as most people imagine; he inherited the kingdom from his maternal, not his paternal, grandfather. His father Ad'ham was one of the pious wan-dering mendicants, who give themselves up to devotions, and live in abstinence, cut off from the world.[25]

The story of Ad'ham

It is related that he passed one day through the gardens of the city of Bukhara and had made his ablutions in one of the canals which traverse them, when he saw an apple being carried along by the current of the stream. Saying to himself, 'This is absolutely valueless,' he ate it. But later on there arose in his mind some scruple at what he had done, and he determined to ask pardon of the owner of the orchard, and knocked at its gate. A slave girl came out to him, and he bade her call the owner of the dwelling. When she informed him that it belonged to a woman, he said, 'Ask permission for me to come to her.' She did so, and Ad'ham told the woman the story of the apple. She said to him, 'This orchard belongs half to me and half to the sultan' (the sultan being then at Balkh, which is ten nights' journey from Bukhara), and absolved him as far as her half was concerned. He went on to Balkh, and there the sultan with all his suite happened to cross his path. He told him the story and begged for his pardon, and was bidden to return to him on the morrow.

Now the sultan had a daughter of surpassing beauty, who had been sought in marriage by the sons of kings, but she obstinately remained virgin, taking pleasure only in religious exercises and an inclination towards pious devotees, for it was her desire to marry some ascetic who scorned the things of this world. When the sultan returned to his abode, he told his daughter the story of Ad'ham, and added, 'I have never seen a more God-fearing man than this – he comes from Bukhara to Balkh for the sake of half an apple.' She at once expressed a desire to marry him, so when Ad'ham came to him the following day, the sultan said to him, 'I shall not absolve you unless you marry my daughter.' He submitted to this condition after some opposition and resistance, and was married to her. When he entered her chamber, he found her decked in bridal finery, and the room also adorned with carpets and other furnishings, and retiring to a corner of the room he set to his prayers and kept on praying until morning. He continued to do this during all the nights of the bridal week. Meanwhile the sultan had withheld his absolution, and when Ad'ham sent to him to grant it, he replied, 'I shall not absolve you until your cohabitation with your wife takes place.' That night therefore he lay with her, and then, after making a complete ablution, he prepared to begin his prayers, when he gave a cry, prostrated himself on his prayer-mat, and was found dead – God have mercy on him. The princess, however, conceived by him and bore Ibrahim, and as his grandfather had no son, he assigned the kingdom to him. After that came the incident of his divesting himself of the kingship, according to the well-known story.

The majority of the people of these coasts compose the sect of the Nusairiyah, who hold the belief that Ali b. Abi Talib is a god.[26] They do not pray the ritual prayers, nor do they purify themselves, nor fast. Al-Malik al-Zahir Baibars compelled them to build mosques in their villages, so in every village they put up a mosque far away from their houses, and they neither enter it nor keep it in repair. It often serves as a refuge for their cattle and their asses. Frequently too a stranger on coming to a village of theirs will stop at the mosque and recite the call to prayer, and then they call out to him, 'Stop braying; your fodder is coming to you.' The number of these people is considerable.

I travelled next to the city of al-Ladhiqiyah [Latakiya], which is an ancient town on the sea coast. Near this town is the monastery known as Dair al-Farus, which is the largest monastery in Syria and Egypt. It is inhabited by monks, and Christians visit it from all quarters. Every Muslim who stops there is entertained by the Christians; their food is bread, cheese, olives, vinegar and capers.

I went on from there to Jabal Lubnan.[27] This is among the most fertile mountain ranges in the world; in it are to be found all manner of fruits, and water fountains and thick coverts. It is never without a number of recluses who have renounced the world for the service of God Most High, and of ascetics and devotees, for the place is noted for this, and I myself saw there several saintly men of obscure name who had become recluses in the service of God Most High.

After Jabal Lubnan we came to the city of Ba'labakk, a beautiful and ancient place and one of the most agreeable cities in Syria, surrounded by glorious orchards and superb gardens, with flowing streams traversing its land, and rivalling Damascus in its boundless amenities. It has such an abundance of cherries as is not to be found elsewhere, and in it is manufactured the *dibs* which is called by its name. It is a kind of thick fruit juice which they make from grapes; they have a kind of clay which they add to this, with the result that it solidifies. The jar into which the paste is put can then be broken and the contents will remain in one piece. From this *dibs* is manufactured a sweetmeat, into which pistachios and almonds are put, and which they call *al-mulabban*. Another name which they give to it is 'horse skin'.[28] Another industry at Ba'labakk is the making of wooden vessels and spoons that have no equal in the world. Frequently they make a large dish, then make a second which fits into the hollow of the first, and another in the hollow of that, and so on to as many as ten, which anyone seeing them would imagine to be a single dish. In the same way with spoons, they make a series of ten, one within the hollow of the other, and make a leather covering for them. A man will carry this in his belt and, on joining in a meal with his friends, will take it out; those who see it think it to be a single spoon, whereupon he produces nine others from within it.

When I entered Ba'labakk night was already falling, but I left early the following day, because of my eager desire to reach Damascus; and on Thursday, the ninth of the month of Ramadan the Exalted in the year seven hundred and twenty-six, I arrived at this city, Dimashq al-Sham.[29] I lodged there at the college of the Malikis, which is called al-Sharabishiyah.[30] Damascus is the city which surpasses all other cities in beauty and takes precedence of them in loveliness.

Ibn Juzayy adds: what the poets have said in description of the beauties of Damascus is beyond all computation. My father (God's mercy on him) used frequently to recite in description of her these verses, which belong to Sharaf al-Din Abu'l-Mahasin (God Most High have mercy on him):

> Damascus! my longing for her is a lover's torment,
>   let false friends importune, let critics condemn as they please!
> A land where the pebbles are pearls and the soil is amber,
>   and fragrant and heady as wine is the northerly breeze.
> Her waters glide softly with rippling chains, yet unfettered,
>   and healthy yet languid the zephyr that plays o'er her leas.

This is poetry of a high order. Arqalah the Damascene said of her:

> Who would anticipate celestial joys,
> Here is Damascus, here those maids and boys![31]
> Here never moonfaced youth sang to his lute,
> But piping merle and ouzel followed suit.
> O lovely when the wind's soft fingers weave
> Ringed mail upon its streams – but make-believe!

But let us return to the narrative of the Shaikh Abu Abdallah.

The congregational mosque of Damascus, known as the Mosque of the Umayyads

This is the greatest mosque on earth in point of magnificence, the most perfect in architecture, and the most exquisite in beauty, grace, and consummate achievement; no rival to it is known, no equal to it is in existence. The man who was responsible for its construction and architectural perfection was the Commander of the Faithful, al-Walid b. Abd al-Malik b. Marwan.[32] He applied to the king of the Greeks at Constantinople, bidding him send craftsmen to him, and the king sent him twelve thousand of them. The site of the mosque was a church, and when the Muslims conquered Damascus Khalid b. al-Walid (God be pleased with him) entered from one side by the sword and penetrated as far as the middle of the church, while Abu Ubaidah b. al-Jarrah (God be pleased with him) entered by capitulation from the western side and also advanced as far as the middle of the church. Consequently the Muslims made of that half of the church which they had entered by force a mosque, and the half which they occupied under the terms of the capitulation remained a church. When al-Walid determined to enlarge the mosque by incorporating the church, he asked the Greeks to sell him that church of theirs for whatsoever equivalent they desired, but they would not yield to him, so he seized it from their hands. The Christians used to assert that the destroyer of the church would be stricken with madness, and they told that to al-Walid. But he replied, 'I shall be the first to be stricken with madness in the service of God,' and, taking an axe, he set to work to knock it down with his own hands. When the Muslims saw this, they joined one after another in the work of destruction, and God gave the lie to the assertion of the Greeks.

The inner faces of all the walls of this mosque are decorated with cut stones of gold known as *fusaifisa*, intermingled with various colours of extraordinary beauty.[33] The size of the mosque in length from east to west is two hundred paces, that is three hundred cubits, and its breadth from south to north a hundred and thirty-five paces, that is two hundred cubits.

The courtyard of the mosque is encircled by three arcades, one on each of its eastern, western and northern sides, the breadth of each arcade being ten paces. They contain thirty-three columns and fourteen plaster piers. The breadth of the court is a hundred cubits. It is one of the most graceful and most perfectly beautiful of sights. The people of the city gather there in the evenings, some reading, some conversing, and some walking up and down, and they disperse after the last prayer of the night. When any of their principal men, among the jurists or others, meets a friend of his, each of them hastens towards the other and bows his head.

This mosque is renowned for its special virtue. I have read in regard to the peculiar merits of Damascus the following tradition: 'Verily, the prayer in the mosque of Damascus is equivalent to thirty thousand prayers.' Moreover in the Tradition handed down from the Prophet (God bless and save him), it is related that he said: 'God shall be worshipped in it for forty years after the destruction of the world.'

The professors and teachers at the mosque

There are in this mosque several 'circles' of instruction in the various branches of sacred knowledge, while the traditionists read the books of Tradition, sitting in high chairs, and the Qur'an readers recite in pleasing voices morning and evening. It contains also a number of teachers of the Book of God, each of whom leans his back upon one of the pillars of the mosque, dictating to the children and making them recite, for they abstain from writing down the Qur'an on their tablets out of reverence for the Book of God lest it suffer pollution, and so recite it from dictation only. The teacher of writing is a different person from the teacher of the Qur'an, and he uses books of poetry and the like for teaching them. The pupil moves from the class for religious instruction to the writing class, and then becomes expert in calligraphy, because the teacher of writing teaches nothing else.

Among the sanctuaries of Damascus which are celebrated for their blessed power is the Mosque of the Footprints, which lies two miles to the south of Damascus, alongside the main highway which leads to the illustrious Hijaz, Jerusalem and Egypt. It is a large mosque, abundant in blessing, and possessing many endowments, and the people of Damascus hold it in great veneration. The footprints from which it derives its name are certain marks impressed upon a rock there, which are said to be the print of the foot of Moses (on him be peace).[34] Within this mosque there is a small chamber containing a stone with the following inscription upon it: 'A certain saintly man used to see the Chosen One [i.e. Muhammad] (God bless and give him peace) in his sleep, and he would say to him, "Here is the grave of my brother Moses (on him be peace)".'

Anecdote

I witnessed at the time of the Great Plague[35] at Damascus in the latter part of the month of Second Rabi of the year 49 [July 1348], a remarkable instance of the veneration of the people of Damascus for this mosque. Arghun-Shah, king of the amirs and the sultan's viceroy, ordered a crier to proclaim through Damascus that the people should fast for three days and that no one should cook in the bazaar during the daytime anything to be eaten (for most of the people there eat no food but what has been prepared in the bazaar). So the people fasted for three successive days, the last of which was a Thursday. At the end of this period the amirs, sharifs, qadis, doctors of the Law, and all other classes of the people in their several degrees, assembled in the Great Mosque, until it was filled to overflowing with them, and spent the Thursday night there in prayers and liturgies and supplications. Then, after performing the dawn prayer on the Friday morning, they all went out together, walking barefoot and carrying Qur'ans in their hands. The entire population of the city joined in the exodus, male and female, small and large; the Jews went out with their book of the Law and the Christians with their Gospel, their women and children with them; the whole concourse of them in tears and humble supplications, imploring the favour of God through His Books and His Prophets. They made their way to the Mosque of the Footprints and remained there in supplication and invocation until near midday, then returned to the city and held the Friday service. God Most High lightened their affliction; the number of deaths in a single day reached a maximum of two thousand, whereas the number rose in Cairo and Old Cairo to twenty-four thousand in a day.

The pious endowments at Damascus, and some of the merits and customs of its inhabitants

The varieties of the endowments at Damascus and their expenditure are beyond computation, so numerous are they. There are endowments in aid of persons who cannot undertake the Pilgrimage, out of which are paid to those who go in their stead sums sufficient for their needs. There are endowments for supplying wedding outfits to girls, to those namely whose families are unable to provide them with the customary paraphernalia. There are endowments for the freeing of prisoners, and endowments for travellers, out of which they are given food, clothing, and the expenses of conveyance to their countries. There are endowments for the improvement and paving of the streets, because the lanes in Damascus all have a pavement on either side on which the foot passengers walk, while riders use the roadway in between. Besides these there are endowments for other charitable purposes.

Anecdote

As I went one day along a lane in Damascus, I saw in it a young slave boy out of whose hand there had just fallen a Chinese porcelain dish. It had broken to bits. A crowd gathered round him and one of them said to him, 'Pick up the pieces, and take them with you to the custodian of the endowments for utensils.' So he picked them up, and the man went with him to the custodian, to whom the slave showed the broken pieces and thereupon received from him enough to buy a similar platter. This endowment is one of the best of good works, for the boy's master would undoubtedly have beaten him for breaking the dish, or at least have scolded him, while he too would have been heartbroken and upset because of that. The benefaction is thus indeed a mender of hearts – may God well reward him whose charitable zeal rose to the height of such an action.

The people of Damascus vie with one another in the building and endowment of mosques, religious houses, colleges, and sanctuaries. They have a high opinion of the Moors and freely entrust them with the care of their moneys, wives and children. Every man of them who comes to the end of his resources in any district of Damascus finds without exception some means of livelihood opened to him, either as imam in a mosque, or as a reciter in a college, or by occupation of a cell in a mosque, where his daily requirements are supplied to him, or by recitation of the Qur'an, or employment as a keeper at one of the blessed sanctuaries, or else he may be included in the company of Sufis who live in the convents, in receipt of a regular allowance of upkeep-money and clothing. Anyone who is a stranger there living on charity is always protected from having to earn it at the expense of his self-respect, and carefully sheltered from anything that might injure his dignity. Those who are manual workers or in domestic service find other means of livelihood, for example as guardian of an orchard or intendant of a mill, or in charge of children, going with them in the morning to their lessons and coming back with them in the evening, and anyone who wishes to pursue a course of studies or to devote himself to the religious life receives every aid to the execution of his purpose.

It is one of the laudable customs of the people of Damascus that not a man of them breaks his fast during the nights of Ramadan entirely alone. Those of the standing of amirs, qadis and notables invite their friends and a number of faqirs to breakfast at their houses. Merchants and substantial traders follow the same practice; the poor and the country folk for their part assemble each night in the house of one of their own number or in a mosque, each brings what he has, and they all breakfast together.

When I first came to Damascus, a friendship grew up between the Maliki Professor Nur al-Din as-Sakhawi and me, and he urged me to breakfast at his house during the nights of Ramadan. After I had visited him for four nights I had a stroke of fever and absented myself. He sent out in search of me, and although I excused myself on the ground of illness he would accept no excuse from me, so I went back to his house and spent the night there. When I wished to take leave the next morning, he would not hear of it but said to me, 'Consider my house as your own, or as the house of your father or brother,' and gave orders to send for a doctor and to have prepared for my use in his own house everything that the doctor should prescribe in the way of medicine or diet. I remained in his house in this condition until the day of the Feast of the Fast-breaking, when I joined in the festival prayers at the *musalla* and God Most High healed me of what had befallen me. Meanwhile all the money I had for my expenses was exhausted. Nur al-Din, learning this, hired camels for me and gave me travelling provisions, etc., and money in addition, saying to me, 'It will come in useful for anything of importance that you may be in need of' – may God reward him well!

In the Umayyad mosque (God keep it ever filled with His praise) I heard the whole of the *Sahih* of the Imam al-Bukhari[36] (God be pleased with him) explained by the aged shaikh, the goal of travel from all quarters, the conjoiner of the younger with the elder generations, Shihab al-Din Ahmad Ibn al-Shihnah al-Hajjar; it was completed in fourteen sittings, the first of them on Tuesday the 15th of Ramadan the Exalted, in the year seven hundred and twenty-six, and the last on Monday the 28th of the same, the text being read by the imam and *hafiz*, the historian of Damascus, Alam al-Din al-Birzali, of Seville by origin and of Damascus by residence, in the presence of a large audience.

3 The Pilgrimage to Mecca

When the new moon of Shawwal appeared in the above-mentioned year [1 September 1326], the Hijaz caravan went out to the outskirts of Damascus and encamped at the village called al-Kiswah, and I set out on the move with them. We marched to the town of Bosra, and thence to the castle of al-Karak.

Al-Karak is one of the most marvellous, inaccessible, and celebrated of fortresses, and it is called 'the Castle of the Raven'.[1] The riverbed encircles it on all sides, and it has but one gate, the entrance to which is hewn in the living rock, as also is the entrance to its vestibule. The caravan stopped outside al-Karak for four days, at a place called al-Thaniyah, and made preparations for entering the wilderness. Thence we travelled to Ma'an, which is the last town in Syria, and descended through the Pass of al-Sawan into the desert, of which the saying goes: 'He who enters it is lost, and he who leaves it is born.' After a march of two days we halted at Dhat Hajj, a place of subterranean waterbeds with no habitations, then on to Wadi Baldah (but there is no water in it), and then to Tabuk. This is the place which was raided by the Apostle of God (God bless and give him peace). It has a spring which used to yield a scanty supply of water, but when the Apostle of God (God bless and give him peace) went down to it and used it for his ablutions it gave an abundant flow of running water and continues to do so to this day, through the blessed power of the Apostle of God (God bless and give him peace). It is the custom of the Syrian pilgrims, on reaching the camping ground of Tabuk, to take their weapons and unsheath their swords, charge upon the camp and strike the palms with their swords, saying, 'Thus did the Apostle of God (God bless and give him peace) enter it.'

The huge caravan encamps near the spring referred to, and every

43

one of them slakes his thirst from it. They remain here for four days to rest themselves and to water the camels and lay in supplies of water for the fearsome wilderness between Tabuk and al-Ula. It is the practice of the water-carriers to take up their positions at the sides of this spring, and they have tanks made of buffalo hides, like great reservoirs, from which they water the camels and fill the large waterbags and ordinary waterskins. Each amir or person of rank has a private tank from which his camels and those of his retinue are watered, and their waterbags filled; the rest of the people arrange with the water-carriers to water the camel and fill the waterskin of each person for a fixed sum of money.

The caravan then sets out from Tabuk and pushes on speedily night and day, for fear of this wilderness. Halfway through is the valley of al-Ukhaidir, which might well be the valley of Hell (God preserve us from it). One year the pilgrims suffered severe distress in this place, by reason of the *samum*-wind which blows there, their water supplies dried up, and the price of a drink of water rose to a thousand dinars, but both seller and buyer perished.[2] The story of this is inscribed on one of the rocks in the valley. Going on from there, the caravan halts at the Pool of al-Mu'azzam, a vast basin, called after al-Malik al-Mu'azzam of the house of Ayyub, in which the rainwater collects in certain years, but which is generally dry in others.

On the fifth day after leaving Tabuk, they reach the well of al-Hijr – the Hijr of Thamud – which has an abundance of water, but not one of the pilgrims draws of it, however violent their thirst, following the example set by the Apostle of God (God bless and give him peace), when he passed it by on the expedition to Tabuk. For he drove on his riding camel, giving orders that none should water from it, and those who had used it to make dough fed their camels with it. At this place are the dwellings of Thamud, in some hills of red rock.[3] They are hewn out and have carved thresholds, such that anyone seeing them would take them to be of recent construction. Their bones lie crumbling inside these houses – 'verily, in that is a warning example'. The place of kneeling of the she-camel of Salih (on him be peace) is between two hills there, and in the space between them are the traces of a mosque, in which the pilgrims perform a prayer.

From al-Hijr to al-Ula is half a day's journey or less. Al-Ula is a large and pleasant village with palm gardens and watersprings at which the pilgrims halt for the space of four nights. They provision themselves and wash their clothes, and also deposit here any surplus of provisions they may have, taking on with them only the amount of their strict necessities. The inhabitants of this village are trustworthy persons. This is the limit to which the Christian merchants of Syria may come, and beyond which they may not pass, and they trade in provisions and other goods with the pilgrims here.

The caravan then sets out from al-Ula and encamps on the day following the resumption of the journey in the valley known as al-Itas. It is a place of violent heat, in which the fatal samoom-wind blows. It blew up one year on the caravan, and none but a few of the pilgrims escaped with their lives; that year is known as the year of the Amir al-Jaliqi. After this they encamp at Hadiyah, which is a place of subterranean waterbeds in a valley; they dig pits in it and the water comes up, but brackish. On the third day they alight outside the sanctified city of al-Madinah, the holy and illustrious.

Taibah, the city of the Apostle of God (God bless and give him peace, exalt and ennoble him!)[4]

On the evening of the same day, after sunset, we entered the holy sanctuary and reached at length the illustrious mosque. We halted at the Gate of Peace to pay our respects, and prayed at the noble Garden between the tomb of the Apostle and the noble pulpit.[5] We kissed the fragment that remains of the palm trunk that whimpered for the Apostle of God (God bless and give him peace), which is now attached to a pillar standing between the tomb and the mimbar, on the right as one faces the *qiblah*. We paid the meed of salutation to the lord of men, first and last, the intercessor for sinners and transgressors, the apostle-prophet of the tribe of Hashim from the Vale of Mecca, Muhammad (God bless and give him peace, exalt and ennoble him), and the meed of salutation to his two companions who share his tomb, Abu Bakr al-Siddiq and Abu Hafs Umar al-Faruq (God be pleased with them).[6] We then retired to our camp, rejoicing at this most signal favour, with hearts cheered at obtaining this most great bounty, praising God Most High for our safe arrival at the sacred abodes of His Apostle and his glorious and sublime sanctuaries, and praying Him to grant that this be not our last association with them and that we might be of those whose visitation is accepted and whose journey upon the path of God has been ordained.

Our stay at al-Madinah the Illustrious on this journey lasted four days. We spent each night in the holy mosque, where everyone engaged in pious exercises; some, having formed circles in the court and lit a quantity of candles, and with book-rests in their midst on which were placed volumes of the Holy Qur'an, were reciting from it; some were intoning hymns of praise to God; others were occupied in contemplation of the Immaculate Tomb (God increase it in sweetness); while on every side were singers chanting in eulogy of the Apostle of God (God bless and give him peace). This is the custom observed by all visitors to al-Madinah during those blessed nights, and they also bestow large sums in alms upon the 'sojourners' and the needy.

Then came our departure from al-Madinah to go to Mecca (God Most High ennoble her). We halted near the mosque of Dhu'l-Hulaifah, where the Apostle of God (God bless and give him peace) assumed the pilgrim garb. It is at a distance of five miles from al-Madinah, of whose sacred territory it forms the limit, and not far from it is the *wadi* of al-Aqiq. Here I divested myself of my tailored clothes, bathed, put on the garment of my consecration, and made a prayer of two bowings. I entered the pilgrim state and in my enthusiasm I did not cease crying *Labbaika Allahumma*[7] through every valley and hill and rise and descent.

Thus prepared for the Pilgrimage, we marched for a further eight days until at last we encamped in the Bottom of Marr, a fertile valley with numerous date-palms and a gushing spring of flowing water which serves for the irrigation of that district. From this valley fruit and vegetables are brought to Mecca (God Most High ennoble her). We set out again at night from this blessed valley, with hearts full of gladness at reaching the goal of their hopes, rejoicing in their present condition and future state, and arrived in the morning at the City of Surety, Mecca (God Most High ennoble her).

Of the wondrous doings of God Most High is this, that He has created the hearts of men with an instinctive desire to seek these sublime sanctuaries, and yearning to present themselves at their illustrious sites, and has given the love of them such power over men's hearts that none alights in them but they seize his whole heart, nor quits them but with grief at separation from them, sorrowing at his far journey away from them, filled with longing for them, and purposing to repeat his visitation to them. For their blessed soil is the focus of all eyes, and love of it the marrow of all hearts, in virtue of a wise disposition of God which achieves its sublime purpose, and in fulfilment of the prayer of His Friend [Abraham] (upon him be peace). Intensity of yearning brings them near while yet far off, presents them to the eye while yet unseen, and makes of little account to him who seeks them the fatigues which he meets and the distress which he endures. How many a weakling sees death before reaching them, and beholds destruction on their road, yet when God brings him safely to them he welcomes them with joy and gladness, as though he had not tasted bitterness, nor suffered torment and affliction for their sakes! Truly this is a divine thing and a God-given benefit, a proof uncontaminated by ambiguity, unobscured by dubiety, and inaccessible to deception, which is of compelling cogency in the perception of men of understanding, and shatters the rationalism of the intellectuals. He whose soul God Most High hath sustained by granting him to alight in those regions and to present himself in that court, upon him hath God bestowed the greatest of all favours and possession of the best of both abodes, that of his present world and the other of the world to come. It is meet for him, therefore, that he should abundantly give thanks for what He has bestowed upon him. May God Most High number us amongst those whose visitation is accepted, whose merchandise[8] in seeking to perform it brings him gain in the world to come, whose actions in the cause of God are written in the Book of Life, and whose burdens of sin are effaced by the acceptance of the merit earned by Pilgrimage, through His loving kindness and graciousness.

The venerable city of Mecca

Mecca is a large town, compactly built and oblong in shape, situated in the hollow of a valley which is so shut in by hills that the visitor to her sees nothing of her until he actually reaches her. These hills that overlook her are of no exceeding elevation. She lies, as God has related in His glorious Book, 'in a valley bare of corn', but the blessed prayer of Abraham has anticipated her needs, so that every delicacy is brought to her, and fruits of every kind are gathered for her. I myself have eaten there fruits, such as grapes, figs, peaches, and fresh dates, that have not their equal in the world; likewise the melons which are transported to her have none to compare with them for flavour and sweetness. The flesh-meats in Mecca are fat and exceedingly delicious in taste. All the commodities that are dispersed in different countries find assembly in her.

The Meccans: their good qualities

The citizens of Mecca are given to well-doing, of consummate generosity and good disposition, liberal to the poor and to those who have renounced the world, and kindly towards strangers. One of their generous customs is that when any of them makes a feast, he begins by giving food to the poor brethren who have devoted themselves to the religious life and are sojourning at the Sanctuary, first inviting them with courtesy, kindness and delicacy, and then giving them to eat. The majority of these destitute devotees are to be found by the public ovens, where the people bake their bread. When anyone has his bread baked and takes it away to his house, the destitute follow him up and he gives each one of them whatever he assigns to him, sending none away disappointed. Even if he has but a single loaf, he gives away a third or a half of it, conceding it cheerfully and without grudgingness.

Another good habit of theirs is that orphan children make a practice of sitting in the bazaar, each with two baskets, one large and one small. A man of the townsfolk of Mecca comes to the bazaar, where he buys grain, meat and vegetables, and passes these to a boy, who puts the grain in one of his baskets and the meat and vegetables in the other, and takes them to the man's house, so that his meal may be prepared from them. Meanwhile the man goes about his devotions and his business. There is no instance related of any of the boys having ever abused their trust in this matter – on the contrary he delivers what he has been given to carry, with the most scrupulous honesty. They receive for this a fixed fee of a few coppers.

The Meccans are elegant and clean in their dress, and as they mostly wear white their garments always appear spotless and snowy. They use perfume freely, paint their eyes with kohl, and are constantly polishing their teeth with twigs of green arak-wood.[9] The

Meccan women are of rare and surpassing beauty, pious and chaste. They too make much use of perfumes, to such a degree that a woman will spend the night hungry and buy perfume with the price of her food. They make a practice of performing the circuit of the House on the eve of each Friday, and come in their finest apparel, and the Sanctuary is saturated with the smell of their perfume. When one of these women goes away, the odour of the perfume clings as an effluvium to the place after she has gone.

Anecdote of blessed import

I had a dream in the days of my residence in Mecca (God ennoble her), while I was living in the Muzaffariyah college there, that the Apostle of God (God bless and give him peace) was sitting in the classroom of this college, beside the window from which one looks out upon the illustrious Ka'bah, and the people were taking his hand and swearing allegiance to him. I saw in my dream that the Shaikh Abu Abdallah called Khalil came in, squatted before the Apostle of God (God bless and give him peace), and placing his hand in the hand of the Apostle of God (God bless and give him peace) he said, 'I give thee my allegiance to do thus and thus', and enumerated a number of things including 'never to turn away a destitute man from my house disappointed'. This was the last phrase of his oath, and I was surprised to hear him saying it, and thought to myself: 'How can he say this and carry out his word, seeing the multitude of the poor of Mecca itself and those who come hither from the Yaman, Zaila, al-Iraq, Persia, Egypt and Syria?' As I saw him in my dream, he was wearing a short white tunic of the cotton fabric called *fushtan*,[10] which he used sometimes to put on. Next morning, after performing the dawn prayer, I went to him and told him of my dream. It gave him great pleasure and he wept and said to me: 'This tunic was given by one of the saints to my grandfather and for that reason I put it on sometimes for the sake of the blessing.' I never saw him after that turn away a suppliant disappointed. He used to bid his servants bake bread and cook food and bring it to me after the afternoon prayer every day. The people of Mecca eat only once in the day, after the afternoon prayer, and content themselves with that until the same time on the following day. If anyone wishes to eat at any other time of day, he eats dried dates, and it is for that reason that their bodies are healthy and that diseases and infirmities are rarely found amongst them.

There lived in Mecca in the days of my sojourn there Hasan the Maghribi, the demoniac, a man of strange life and remarkable character. He had formerly been sound in mind and a servitor of the saint Najm al-Din al-Isbahani during the lifetime of the latter.

His story

Hasan the demoniac was assiduous in making circuits of the Ka'bah by night, and he used to see during his nightly circuits a faqir busily circuiting whom he never saw by day. This faqir came up to him one night, asked him how he was, and said to him, 'O Hasan, your mother is weeping for you and longing to see you.' (She was one of the handmaidens of God.) 'Would you like to see her?' 'Yes,' he replied, 'but I have no means of doing that.' The faqir said to him, 'We shall meet here tomorrow night, if God Most High will.' The following night, which was the eve of Friday, Hasan found him at the spot which he had appointed for their meeting, and they made the circuit of the House together many times. The faqir then went out of the Sanctuary, Hasan following close behind him, to the Ma'la Gate; when they arrived there he bade him shut his eyes and hold fast to his garment. Hasan did so. After a time the faqir asked: 'Would you recognize your own town?' 'Yes,' said Hasan. 'Well, here it is,' he said. Hasan opened his eyes and lo! he was at the gate of his mother's house. So he went in to her, without telling her anything of what had happened, and stayed with her for a fortnight – I think his town was the city of Asafi. He then went out to the cemetery where he found his friend the faqir, who said to him, 'How are you?' He replied: 'O sir, I have been longing to see Shaikh Najm al-Din, for I went out of his house in my usual way and have been away from him all these days, and I should like you to take me back to him.' The faqir, saying, 'Yes certainly,' made an appointment to meet him at the cemetery by night. When Hasan came to him there, he bade him do as he had done at Mecca (God ennoble her), that is, close his eyes and grip his skirt. He did so, and lo! he was in Mecca (God ennoble her)! The faqir charged him to speak no word to Najm al-Din of what had happened, nor to speak of it to any other person, but when he came into Najm al-Din the saint said to him, 'Where have you been, Hasan, during your absence?' Hasan at first would not tell him, but when Najm al-Din pressed him, he told him the story. The shaikh then said, 'Show me the man,' and came with him by night. The man came according to his usual custom, and when he passed them Hasan said to his master, 'Sir, this is he.' The man heard him and struck him on the mouth with his hand saying, 'Be silent, God make thee silent.' Immediately his tongue became tied, and his reason went. So he remained in the Sanctuary, a demented man, making circuits night and day without either ablutions or prayers, while the people looked upon him as a means of blessing and clothed him. When he felt hungry he went out to the market which is between al-Safa and Marwa, where he would make for one of the booths and eat what he liked from it; nobody would drive him off or hinder him – on the contrary, everyone from whose stock he ate anything was rejoiced, and it procured for that person blessing and increase in his sales and profits. Whenever he came into the market, the stallkeepers would crane their necks towards him, on account of the experience they had gained of the blessing which he conferred. He did exactly the same with the water-carriers when he wished to drink. This continued to be his way of living until the year seven hundred and twenty-eight, when the Amir Saif al-Din Yalmalak came on pilgrimage and took him back with him to Egypt. From that time no further news of him was heard – God Most High profit us by him!

The departure from Mecca
(God Most High ennoble her)

Having performed the rites of Pilgrimage, on the twentieth day precisely of Dhu 'l-Hijjah[11] I went out of Mecca in company with the commander of the caravan of al-Iraq. He hired for me the half of a double litter as far as Baghdad, paying its cost from his own purse, and took me under his protection. We went out to the Bottom of Marr, after performing the Farewell Circuit with a host of men of al-Iraq, Khurasan, Fars and other eastern lands, of uncountable multitude, so many that the earth surged with them as the sea surges with dashing waves and their advance was like the march of high-piled clouds. Anyone who left the caravan for a natural want and had no mark by which to guide himself to his place could not find it again for the vast number of people. Included in this caravan were many water-carrying camels for the poorer pilgrims, who could obtain drinking water from them, and other camels to carry provisions for issue as alms and to carry medicines, potions and sugar for those who should be attacked by illness. Whenever the caravan halted food was cooked in great brass cauldrons, and supplied from them to the poorer pilgrims and those who had no provisions. With the caravan also was a number of spare camels for the carriage of those who were unable to walk. All of this was due to the benefactions and generosity of the Sultan Abu Sa'id.[12]

This caravan contained also animated bazaars and great supplies of luxuries and all kinds of food and fruit. They used to march during the night and light torches in front of the file of camels and litters, so that you saw the countryside gleaming with light and the darkness turned into radiant day.

We at length reached Taibah, the City of the Apostle of God (God bless and give him peace), and were privileged to visit once again the tomb of the Apostle of God (God bless and give him peace).

We stayed at al-Madinah (God Most High glorify her) for six days, and taking with us from there water for a three nights' journey, we set out from her. On the third night we encamped at Wadi 'l-Arus, where we provided ourselves with water from underground water-beds. They dig holes above them in the ground, and procure sweet flowing water. We then left Wadi 'l-Arus and entered the land of the Najd, which is a level stretch of country extending as far as eye can see, and inhaled its sweet-scented air. We halted after covering four stages at a water-point known as al-Usailah, and going on from there halted at a water-point known as al-Naqirah, where there are the remains of cisterns like vast reservoirs. Thence we marched to a water-point known as al-Qarurah, being certain tanks filled with rainwater, of those which were constructed by order of Zubaidah, daughter of Ja'far (God's mercy and favour upon her).[13] This place is the centre of the land of Najd, spacious, with sweet air and healthy climate, clean-soiled, and temperate in every season of the year. Then, leaving al-Qarurah, we stopped at al-Hajir, where there are tanks for water, but as they often dry up water has to be procured by digging temporary wells, and going on from there stopped next at Samirah, which is a patch of low-lying ground situated in a plain where there is a kind of fortified and inhabited enceinte. The water at Samirah is plentiful and drawn from cased wells, but it is brackish. The bedouins of that district bring sheep, melted butter and curdled milk, and sell these to the pilgrims for pieces of coarse cotton cloth, and they will not exchange them for anything but this. We resumed our journey and halted at the 'Hill with the Hole', which lies in a tract of desert land and has at its summit a perforation from side to side through which the wind blows. We proceeded from there to Wadi 'l-Kurush, which is waterless in spite of its name, and after marching on through the night came in the morning to the fort of Faid.

Faid is a large fortified enceinte on a level plain and surrounded by a wall, with a suburb outside it. Its inhabitants are Arabs, who make a living off the pilgrims by selling and trading. At that point the pilgrims leave some part of their provisions at the time of their arrival from al-Iraq on the way to Mecca (God Most High ennoble her), and on the return journey they pick them up again. It lies halfway between Mecca and Baghdad, and from it to Kufah is a twelve days' journey by an easy road furnished with supplies of water in tanks. It is the practice of the caravan to enter this place in military formation and warlike array, in order to overawe the Arabs who are assembled there in considerable numbers and to cut short their hopes of despoiling the caravan. We met there in two amirs of the Arabs, Fayyad and Hiyar, sons of the Amir Muhanna b. Isa, accompanied by a body of Arab horsemen and foot soldiers not to be reckoned for multitude; both of them displayed zeal for the safety and protection of the pilgrims and their possessions. The Arabs brought camels and sheep for sale and the pilgrims bought from them what they could afford.

We set out again and halted at the place known as al-Ajfur and made famous through the romantic lovers Jamil and Buthainah.[14] Then travelling on we halted in the open desert, and again marching through the night halted at Zarud, a level plain, in which there are extensive sands. The place itself has some small dwellings, which they have surrounded by a sort of fortified enceinte, and there are wells of water there but they are unpalatable. Proceeding, we halted at al-Tha'labiyah, where there is a ruined fort, opposite which is an enormous reservoir reached by a stairway and containing a quantity of rainwater enough to meet the needs of the whole caravan. A great host of bedouin Arabs assemble at this place and they sell camels, sheep, melted butter and milk. From there to al-Kufah are three marches. We continued our journey and halted at Birkat al-Marjum ('The Pool of the Stoned'), the latter being a tomb in the roadway with a great heap of stones upon it, and everyone who passes by throws a stone at it. It is related that the person who is thus stoned was a Rafidi; he set out with the caravan to make the Pilgrimage, but a dispute broke out between him and some Turks, followers of the Sunnah, in the course of which he reviled one of the Companions of the Prophet, so they killed him by throwing stones. At this place there are many tents of the bedouins, who come to the caravan bringing melted butter, curdled milk and so on, and there is also a large reservoir enough to supply the needs of the entire caravan. This too is one of those constructed by Zubaidah (God's mercy upon her); indeed, every reservoir, pool or well on this road which goes from Mecca to Baghdad is due to her munificent bounty – God give her goodly reward and recompense her for them in full; for, had it not been for her concern on behalf of this road, it would not be usable by anyone.

Continuing our journey, we halted at a place known as al-Mashquq ['the Cleft'], where there are two reservoirs containing fresh sweet water. Everyone emptied out what water was still in his possession and took a fresh supply from them. Then we went on and after halting at a place called al-Tananir ['the Ovens'], where there is a reservoir filled with water, we made a night march from there and sometime after sunrise arrived before Zumalah, an inhabited village with a fortified grange belonging to some Arabs, two reservoirs of water and many wells. This place is one of the natural watering-places on this road. We set out again and halted at al-Haithaman, where there are two reservoirs of water; then continuing on our way halted below the defile known as Aqabat al-Shaitan ['Devil's Pass']. We climbed the defile on the following day. There is no steep place on that road except this, and even it is neither difficult nor considerable. We halted next at a place called Waqisah, where there is a large fortified grange and reservoirs of water. It is inhabited by bedouin Arabs, and is the last of the natural watering-places on this road, for thereafter until al-Kufah there is no conspicuous watering-place except the watercourses derived from the Euphrates. At this point many of the people of al-Kufah come out to meet the pilgrim caravan, bringing flour, bread, dried dates and fruit, and the travellers congratulate one another on their safe journey. We then halted at a place known as

Lawrah, where there is a large reservoir for water; then at a place known as al-Masajid ['the Mosques'], where there are three reservoirs; then at a place known as Manarat al-Qurun ['the Tower of Horns'], this being a tower in a desert locality, conspicuous in height and decorated on top with horns of gazelles, with no habitation around it. We halted next at a place known as al-Udhaib, which is a fruitful valley covered with dwellings and cultivation and surrounded by a plain abounding in pasture and affording a pleasant prospect to the eyes. Thereafter we halted at al-Qadisiyah, where the famous battle was fought against the Persians, in which God manifested the triumph of the Faith of Islam, and subdued the Magians, the fire-worshippers, so that after it no foot was left for them to stand on and God extirpated their root.[15] The commander of the Muslims at that time was Sa'd b. Abi Waqqas (God be pleased with him), and al-Qadisiyah was a great city which Sa'd took by force, but it fell into ruins so that nothing now remains of it except as much as constitutes a large village. The place contains some palm groves and at it there are water courses of Euphrates water.

We went on from there and halted at the town of Mashhad Ali b. Abi Talib (God be pleased with him) at al-Najaf.[16] It is a fine city, situated in a wide rocky plain – one of the finest, most populous, and most substantially built cities of al-Iraq, and it has beautiful clean bazaars. We entered it by the outer Bab al-Hadrah and made our way through the bazaar of the greengrocers, cooks, and butchers, then through the fruit-market, then the bazaar of the tailors and the *qaisariyah*, then the perfumers' bazaar, and so came to the inner Bab al-Hadrah, where is the tomb which they claim to be the tomb of Ali (peace be upon him). Fronting it are a number of colleges, religious houses and convents, most beautifully adorned, their walls being faced with *qashani*, tiles, which resemble the *zalij*[17] in our country but are more lustrous in colour and more finely decorated.

The mausoleum and tombs contained in it

One enters through the Bab al-Hadrah into a vast college, inhabited by students and sufis belonging to the Shi'ah. Everyone who visits it receives hospitality for three days – namely, bread, meat, and dried dates twice daily. From this college one gains access to the gateway of the domed shrine, which is guarded by a number of doorkeepers, chamberlains and eunuchs. As the visitor to the tomb approaches, one of them rises to meet him or all of them do, this being regulated by the visitor's rank. They stand beside him on the threshold and ask permission for him to enter, saying: 'By your leave, O Commander of the Faithful, this feeble creature asks permission for his entry to the sublime mausoleum. If ye grant it to him so be it, but if not, he will turn back; and though he be not worthy of this favour, ye are the possessor of generous qualities and of dignity.' They then bid him kiss the threshold, which is of silver, as also are the doorposts. Having done so, he enters the shrine, which is carpeted with various sorts of carpets of silk and other materials, and contains candelabra of gold and silver, large and small. In the centre of the space beneath the dome is a square platform, faced with wood, upon which are carved golden plaques of excellent workmanship, hammered on with silver nails, which have so completely masked the wood that none of it is visible. The height of the platform is less than the stature of a man, and on top of it are three tombs, of which they assert that one is the tomb of Adam (upon him be blessing and peace), the second the tomb of Noah (upon him be blessing and peace), and the third the tomb of Ali (God be pleased with him). Between the tombs are dishes of gold and silver, containing rose-water, musk and various kinds of perfumes. The visitor dips his hand in this and anoints his face with it for a blessing. The shrine has another door the threshold of which is likewise of silver, and with hangings of coloured silk over it. This leads to a mosque laid with beautiful carpets, its walls and ceiling concealed by silken hangings, and having four doorways with thresholds of silver and covered by silken hangings.

The inhabitants of this city are all of them Rafidis, and at this mausoleum certain miracles are operated, whereby it is established, so they claim, that the mausoleum does indeed contain the grave of Ali (God be pleased with him). One of these miracles is that on the eve of the twenty-seventh of Rajab, which is called by them 'the night of life', all the crippled are brought to this mausoleum from the two Iraqs, Khurasan, and the countries of Fars and Rum,[18] so that there are assembled some thirty or forty of them. After the last ritual prayer of the night, they are placed upon the sanctified tomb, while the people wait in expectation of their rising and pass the time, some in praying, others in reciting liturgies, or reading the Qur'an, or in contemplation of the mausoleum. When the night is half over, or two-thirds or so, the whole company arise sound in body, with no trace of disease, and saying: 'There is no God but God; Muhammad is the Apostle of God; Ali is the Friend of God.' This is a thing much spoken of among them; I heard of it from trustworthy persons, but I was not actually present on any such night. I saw, however, in the Guests' College three men, one from the land of Rum, the second from Isfahan and the third from Khurasan, who were cripples, and when I asked them about themselves they told me that they had missed the 'Night of Life' and were waiting for its time to come round next year. This night serves as occasion for a gathering of the people from the district, and they hold a great fair lasting for ten days.

In this town there is no tax, no farmer of market or *octroi* dues, and no royal governor, but the government over them is exercised solely by the marshal of the Sharifs.[19] Its inhabitants are merchants, who travel far and wide; they are courageous and open-handed, and their protégé suffers no wrong on his journeyings with them, so that their company is highly commended. But they are fanatical about Ali (God be pleased with him). There are some people in the land of al-Iraq and other lands who, if attacked by illness, vow to make a votive offering to the mausoleum when they recover. In other cases a man suffering from illness in the head will make a head of gold or silver and bring it to the mausoleum, and the marshal puts it into the treasury; likewise with hand or foot, or any other member. The treasury of the mausoleum is enormous, and contains such a quantity of riches as defies exact computation.

4 Southern Persia and Iraq

After we had enjoyed the privilege of visiting the tomb of the Commander of the Faithful Ali (peace be on him), the caravan went on to Baghdad. But I set out for al-Basrah, in company with a large troop of the Khafajah Arabs, who are the occupants of that country. They are very powerful and violent, and there is no way to travel in those regions save in their company, so I hired a camel through the commander of that troop. Our way lay alongside the Euphrates by the place known as al-Idhar, which is a water-logged jungle of reeds, inhabited by nomad Arabs called al-Ma'adi.[1] They are brigands, of the Rafidi sect. They came out upon a party of poor brethren who had fallen behind our troop, and stripped them of everything down to their shoes and wooden bowls. They fortify themselves as it were with this jungle and are able to defend themselves in it against all attacks. Savage beasts also inhabit this jungle, in large numbers. Our journey through this Idhar took three days' march, and thereafter we arrived at the city of Wasit.[2]

The city of Wasit

It has fine quarters and an abundance of orchards and fruit trees, and is famed for its notable men, the living teachers among whom furnish lessons for meditation. Its inhabitants are among the best people in al-Iraq – indeed, the very best of them without qualification. Most of them can recite the Holy Qur'an from memory and are expert in the art of its melodious recitation with the correct reading.

When we halted at the city of Wasit the caravan stopped outside it for three nights in order to trade. This gave me the opportunity of visiting the grave of the saint Abu'l-Abbas Ahmad al-Rifa'i, which is one day's journey from Wasit.³ It is a vast convent in which there are thousands of poor brethren.

When the afternoon prayers had been said in this convent, drums and kettle-drums were beaten and the poor brethren began to dance. After this they prayed the sunset prayer and brought in the repast, consisting of rice-bread, fish, milk and dates. When all had eaten and prayed the first night prayer, they began to recite their *dhikr*,⁴ then they began the musical recital. They had prepared loads of firewood which they kindled into a flame, and went into the midst of it dancing; some of them rolled in the fire, and others ate it in their mouths, until finally they extinguished it entirely. This is their regular custom and it is the peculiar characteristic of this corporation of Ahmadi brethren. Some of them will take a large snake and bite its head with their teeth until they bite clean through.

After making the visitation of the Shaikh Abu'l-Abbas al-Rifa'i (God give us good of him) I returned to the city of Wasit. From there we went on and camped in the vicinity of al-Basrah, and on resuming our march we entered the city on the forenoon of the following day.

The city of al-Basrah is one of the metropolitan cities of al-Iraq, renowned throughout the whole world, spacious in area and elegant in its courts, remarkable for its numerous fruit-gardens and its choice fruits; blessed with an abounding portion of plenty and of fruit-fulness, since it is the meeting place of the two seas, the salt and the fresh. No place on earth exceeds it in quantity of palm-groves. The qadi there, Hujjat al-Din, sent me a hamper of dates that a man could scarcely carry; I sent them to be sold and they fetched nine dirhams, three of which were taken by the porter as the charge for carrying them from the house to the market.

The people of al-Basrah are of generous nature, hospitable to the stranger and readily doing their duty by him, so that no stranger feels lonely amongst them. They hold the Friday prayers in the mosque of the Commander of the Faithful Ali (God be pleased with him). This is one of the finest of mosques.

An anecdote, for reflection

I was present one day at the Friday service in this mosque and when the preacher rose and recited his discourse he committed in it many gross errors of grammar. I was astonished at his conduct and spoke of it to the Qadi Hujjat al-Din, who said to me, 'In this town there is not a man left who knows anything of the science of grammar.' Here is a lesson for men to reflect on – magnified be He who changes all things and inverts all conditions. This Basrah, to whose inhabitants fell the mastery in the science of grammar, from whose soil sprang its trunk and its branches, and from whose people arose its leader whose primacy is undisputed – the preacher in this town cannot deliver a Friday discourse according to its rules for all his efforts![5]

This mosque has seven minarets, one of them the minaret which shakes, or so they say, when the name of Ali ibn Abi Talib (God be pleased with him) is mentioned. I climbed up to this minaret from the top of the roof of the mosque, accompanied by one of the inhabitants of al-Basrah, and I found in one angle of it a wooden handgrip nailed into it, resembling the handle of a builder's trowel. The man who was with me placed his hand on that handgrip and said, 'By right of the head of the Commander of the Faithful Ali (God be pleased with him), shake,' and he shook the handgrip, whereupon the whole minaret quivered. I in my turn placed my hand on the handgrip and said to him, 'And I say, by right of the head of Abu Bakr, the successor of the Apostle of God (God give him blessing and peace), shake,' and I shook the handgrip and the whole minaret quivered. They were astonished at this. The people of al-Basrah are followers of the Sunnah and the Community, and no one who does as I did has anything to fear from them, but if anything like this were to happen at Mashhad Ali [Najaf] or Mashhad al-Husain [Karbala] or at al-Hillah or al-Bahrain or Qumm or Qashan or Sawah or Awah or Tus, whoever did it would perish, because they are fanatical Shi'ites.[6]

Al-Basrah is on the banks of the Euphrates and Tigris, and there is high tide and low tide there. The channel of salt water which comes up from the Sea of Fars[7] is at a distance of ten miles from the town, and at high tide the salt water overpowers the sweet but at low tide the sweet water overpowers the salt. The inhabitants of al-Basrah draw this water for use in their houses and for this reason the saying goes that their water is brackish.

Ibn Juzayy remarks: it is for the same reason that the air of al-Basrah is unhealthy and that the complexions of its inhabitants are yellowish and sallow, to such an extent that they have become pro-verbial. A certain poet said of a citron:

61

A citron here amongst us shows
the image of the lachrymose.
So God hath clothed in sickly hue
the slaves of love – the Basrans too!

(To return.) Thereafter, from the strand of al-Basrah, I embarked in a *sumbuq*, that is a small boat, for al-Ubullah. The distance between them is ten miles, through an uninterrupted succession of fruit gardens and overshadowing palmgroves both to right and left, with traders sitting in the shade of the trees, selling bread, fish, dates, milk and fruit. The sailors in this country row standing up.

Al-Ubullah was in former times a great city, frequented by merchants from India and Fars, but it fell into decay and is now a village, though it preserves traces of palaces and other buildings which indicate its former greatness. Here we embarked on the channel which comes up from the Sea of Fars in a small ship belonging to a man from al-Ubullah named Mughamis. It was after sunset when we sailed and in the early morning we reached Abbadan, a large village on a salt marsh, with no cultivation but containing many mosques and cells and hermitages for devotees.[8] It is three miles from the strand.

On the shore of Abbadan there is a hermitage which is called after the name of al-Khidr and Ilyas (peace be upon them), and alongside it a convent inhabited by four poor brethren with their children. Everyone who passes by them gives them alms. The men of this convent told me that there was at Abbadan a devotee of great merit, living entirely alone. He used to come down to this sea once a month and catch there enough fish for a month's provision, and would not be seen again until the end of the next month. This had been his custom for many years. When we reached Abbadan I had no other care than to seek him out, so while those who were with me were occupied in prayers in the mosque and cells, I went off in search of him. I came to a mosque in a ruinous condition and found him praying in it, so I sat down beside him. He shortened his prayer, and after pronouncing the benedictions took my hand and said to me, 'May God grant you your desire in this world and the next.' I have indeed – praise be to God – attained my desire in this world, which was to travel through the earth, and I have attained in this respect what no other person has attained to my knowledge. The world to come remains, but my hope is strong in the mercy and clemency of

God, and the attainment of my desire to enter the Garden.

When I came back to my companions and told them what had happened to me with this man and indicated his place to them, they went to see him, but they could not find him nor come to any information about him and they were filled with amazement at this incident. We returned in the evening to the convent and put up in it for the night. After the last night prayer one of the four poor brethren came into our room. It was the custom of this brother to go into Abbadan every night and light the lamps in the mosques, after which he returned to his convent. When he reached Abbadan that evening, he found the devotee, who gave him a fresh fish, saying to him, 'Take this to the guest who came today.' So the poor brother said to us as he came in, 'Which of you saw the shaikh today?' I replied, 'It is I who saw him,' and he said, 'He says to you "This is your hospitality gift".' I thanked God for that and the poor brother cooked that fish for us and we all ate of it. I have never tasted better fish. For a moment I entertained the idea of spending the rest of my life in the service of this shaikh, but I was dissuaded from it by the pertinacity of my spirit.[9]

On the next morning we resumed our sea-voyage, making for the town of Machul. It was a habit of mine on my travels never, so far as possible, to retrace any road that I had once travelled over. I was desirous of making for Baghdad in al-Iraq, and a man at al-Basrah advised me to travel to the country of the Lurs, and from there to Iraq al-Ajam and then on to Iraq al-Arab, and I followed his advice. Four days later we reached the town of Machul, a small place on the coast of this channel which we have described as coming out of the Sea of Fars. Its ground is saline, without trees or vegetation, and it has an immense bazaar, one of the largest of its kind. I stayed there only one day and after that I hired from some merchants who bring grain from Ramiz to Machul a mount for my conveyance. We travelled for three nights across open country inhabited by Kurds in hair-tents, who are said to be Arabs by origin, and then reached the town of Ramiz, a fine city with fruit trees and rivers. I stayed only one night in the town of Ramiz, after which we continued our journey for three nights more across a plain where there are villages inhabited by Kurds. At the end of each stage of this journey there was a hospice at which every traveller was supplied with bread, meat and sweetmeats. Their sweetmeats are made with grape-syrup mixed with flour and ghee.

I came next to the city of Tustar,[10] which is situated at the edge of the plain in the dominion of the Atabek and the beginning of the mountains – a large city, splendid and flourishing, with noble orchards and superb gardens, and possessed of rare attractions and well-stocked markets. It is encircled by the river called al-Azraq, which is a marvel, unsurpassed in its clearness and exceedingly cold during the hot season. I have never seen any river as blue except the river of Balakhshan. On both banks of the river, there are orchards and water-wheels; the river itself is deep and over it, leading to the travellers' gate, there is a bridge upon boats.

When I entered this city I was attacked by a fever, for visitors to these countries in the hot season generally suffer from fever, as happens also in Damascus and other cities which have abundant waters and fruits. The fever attacked my companions also and one of them died. During my illness I had no appetite for the dishes which were prepared for me.

When I had recovered, we set out from the city of Tustar, travelling for the space of three nights through towering mountains, at each stage there being a hospice, and came to the city of Idhaj, also called Mal al-Amir, the capital of the Sultan Atabek.[11] On my arrival there I met with its shaikh of shaikhs, the learned and pious Nur al-Din al-Kirmani, who has the supervision of all the hospices (which these people call by the term *madrasah*). The sultan venerates him and comes to visit him, and so also the officers of state and the chief men of the capital visit him morning and evening. He received me honourably and hospitably and lodged me in a hospice where I stayed for some days. My arrival was at the period of the summer heats; we used to pray the night prayers and then lie down to sleep on the top of the roof of the hospice and descend to the hospice itself in the early morning. I had in my company twelve poor brethren including an imam, two skilled reciters of the Qur'an and a servitor so that we made a well-organized party.

Account of the king of Idhaj and Tustar

The king of Idhaj at the time of my entry into it was the Sultan Atabek Afrasiyab, son of the Sultan Atabek Ahmad, *atabek* being with them a title common to every king who rules that country, and the country itself is called the country of the Lurs.[12] I wished to see this Sultan Afrasiyab, but that was not easily come by as he goes out only on Fridays, owing to his addiction to wine. He had one son and one only, who was designated heir, and who fell ill at this time. On a certain night one of his servants came to me and made enquiries of me about myself; when I told him he went away and came back later after the sunset prayer, bringing with him two great platters, one with food and the other with fruit, and a pouch containing money. Accompanying him were musicians with their instruments and he said to them, 'Make music, so that these poor brethren will dance and pray for the sultan's son.' I said to him, 'My associates have no knowledge of either music or dancing,' but we prayed for the sultan and his son, and I divided the money among the poor brethren. In the middle of the night we heard cries and lamentations, for the sick boy had died.

On the following morning the shaikh of the hospice and some of the townsfolk came into my room and said, 'All the principal men of the city, qadis, faqihs,[13] sharifs and amirs, have gone to the sultan's palace for the ceremony of condolence, and it is your duty to go along in company with them.' I refused to go, but when they insisted with me and I had no alternative but to go, I set out with them. I found the audience hall in the sultan's palace filled with men and youths – slaves, sons of princes, viziers and soldiers – all wearing sacks of coarse cloth and horses' saddle-cloths; they had put dust and straw on their heads and some of them had cut off their forelocks. They were divided into two groups, one group at the top end of the hall and another at its lower end, and each group would advance towards the other, all beating their breasts with their hands and crying *khundikarima*, which means 'our master'. The spectacle that I witnessed there was an appalling thing and a disgraceful sight, the like of which I have never encountered.

Anecdote

A strange thing that happened to me that day was that, when I entered, I saw that the qadis, the khatibs and the sharifs had taken up positions with their backs to the walls of the hall. The place was crammed with them on all sides, some of them weeping, some pretending to, some with eyes fixed on the ground, and all of them wearing on top of their robes unbleached lengths of rough cotton stuff, not properly tailored and inside out, with the face of the cloth next their bodies. Each one of them also had on his head a bit of rag or a black veil. They continue to do the same until forty days have passed, this being for them the end of the period of mourning, and thereafter the sultan sends a complete set of clothing to every one who has done so.

When I saw all parts of the audience hall crowded with people I looked right and left, searching for a place to seat myself. Then I saw there a dais, raised above the ground about a span; at one corner of it there was a man, apart from the crowd, sitting there, and wearing a woollen robe like the felt coat which the poor people in that country wear on days of rain or snow and on journeys. So I went up to where this man was; my companions fell back behind me when they saw me going towards him and were amazed at my action, whereas I had no knowledge at all of what he was. I mounted the dais and gave the word of greeting to the man; he returned my greeting and raised himself from the ground as if he intended to rise, a gesture which they call 'half-rising', and I sat down in the corner opposite him. Then I observed that the people present had fixed their eyes on me, everyone of them; I was surprised at them, and I looked at the faqihs and shaikhs and sharifs, all with their backs to the wall behind the dais. One of the qadis made a sign to me that I should come beside him, but I did not do so, and then I began to suspect that the man was the sultan. At the end of an hour or so, the Chief Shaikh Nur al-Din al-Kirmani, whose name we have mentioned above, came forward, mounted the dais and saluted the man; he rose up to him, and the shaikh then sat down between me and him; thereupon I knew for certain that the man was the sultan. Next, the bier was brought in, surrounded by citron lemon and orange trees, the branches of which they had loaded with their fruits, the trees themselves being carried by men, so that the bier seemed to be a moving orchard, with torches on tall lances carried before it, and candles likewise. Prayers were recited over it, and those present went out with it to the burial ground of the kings.

Some days later the sultan sent to me the messenger who had brought the hospitality gift previously, to invite me to visit him. So I went with the messenger to a gate called the Cypress Gate and we mounted a long flight of steps, finally reaching a room which was uncarpeted, on account of the mourning that they were observing at the time. The sultan was sitting on a cushion, with two goblets in front of him which had been covered up, one of gold and the other of silver. There was in the chamber a green prayer-rug; this was laid out for me near him, and I sat down on it. No one else was in the room but his chamberlain, the faqih Mahmud, and a boon companion of his, whose name I do not know. He put questions to me about myself and my country, and asked me about al-Malik al-Nasir and the land of al-Hijaz, and I answered him on these points. At this juncture there came in a great faqih, who was chief of the doctors of the law in that country, and the sultan said to me, 'This is Mawlana Fadil,' for in all the lands of the Persians a faqih is never called by any title other than *mawlana*, and is so addressed by the sultan and everyone else. The sultan then began to recite the praises of the faqih just mentioned, and it became clear to me that he was under the influence of intoxication, for I had already learned of his addiction to wine. Afterwards he said to me in Arabic (which he spoke well), 'Speak.' I said to him, 'If you will listen to me, I say to you, "You are the son of the Sultan Atabek Ahmad, who was noted for piety and self-restraint, and there is nothing to be laid against you as a ruler but this",' and I pointed to the two goblets. He was overcome with confusion at what I said and sat silent. I wished to go but he bade me sit down and said to me, 'To meet with men like you is a mercy.' But then I saw him reeling and on the point of falling asleep, so I withdrew. I had left my sandals at the door but I could not find them, so the faqih Mahmud went down in search of them, while the faqih Fadil went to look for them inside the chamber, found them in a window embrasure there, and brought them to me. His kindness shamed me, and I began to apologize to him, but at that he kissed my sandals, placed them on his head, and said, 'God bless you. What you said to our sultan no one could say but you. I sincerely hope, by God, that this will make an impression on him.'

A few days later came my departure from the city of Idhaj. For ten days we continued to travel through the territories of Sultan Afrasiyab amidst lofty mountains, and on each night we would halt at a *madrasah* where food was served. Some of these *madrasahs* are in cultivated country, and some have no cultivation in the vicinity at all, but everything that they require is transported to them. On the tenth day we halted at a *madrasah* by the name of Madrasah Kiriwa 'l-rukh, which marks the end of the territories of this king.

We travelled on from there across a well-watered plain belonging to the province of the city of Isfahan, and thereafter reached the town of Ushturkan, a pleasant township, with numbers of running streams and orchards, and possessed of a very fine mosque intersected by the river. From this place we went on to the city of Firuzan, which is a small town with streams, trees and orchards. We arrived there after the hour of afternoon prayer, and found that its population had gone out to escort a funeral. Behind and before the bier they had lit torches, and they followed it up with fifes and singers, singing all sorts of merry songs. We were astonished at this behaviour of theirs. After spending one night there, we passed on the following morning through a village called Nablan; this is a big village on a broad river, beside which there is a mosque of the utmost beauty. One goes up to it by a flight of steps, and it is surrounded by orchards.

We travelled on for the whole of this day between orchards and streams and fine villages with many pigeon-towers, and after the time of the afternoon prayer we reached the city of Isfahan, also called Ispahan, in Persian Iraq. The city of Isfahan is one of the largest and fairest of cities, but it is now in ruins for the greater part, as the result of the feud there between the Sunnis and the Rafidis, which continues to rage between them still to the present day, so that they never cease to fight. It is rich in fruits, especially the wonderful watermelons whose like is not to be found in the world, except for the watermelons of Bukhara and Khwarizm. Their rind is green, and the inside is red; they are preserved as dried figs are preserved in the Maghrib, and are exceedingly sweet. When anyone is not used to eating them, they relax him on his first experience of them – and so indeed it happened to me when I ate them at Isfahan.

The people of Isfahan have fine figures and clear white skins tinged with red; their dominant qualities are bravery and pugnacity, together with generosity[14] and a strong spirit of rivalry between them in procuring luxurious viands. Some curious stories are told of this last trait in them. Sometimes one of them will invite his friend and will say to him, 'Come along with me for a meal of *nan* and *mas*' – that is bread and curdled milk in their language; then, when his friend goes along with him, he sets before him all sorts of wonderful dishes, with the aim of outdoing him by this display. The members of each craft appoint one of their own number as headman over them, whom they call the *kilu*, and so do the leading citizens from outside the ranks of the craftsmen. One company, for example, will be composed of young bachelors. These companies try to outdo one another and invite one another to banquets, displaying all the resources at their disposal and making a great show in regard to the dishes and everything else. I was told that one company of them invited another, and cooked their viands with lighted candles, then the second company returned the invitations and cooked their viands with silk.

My lodging at Isfahan was in a convent which is attributed to the Shaikh Ali b. Sahl, the disciple of al-Junaid.[15] It is held in great veneration and is visited by the people of those regions, who seek to obtain blessing by visiting it. Food is served in it to all wayfarers, and it has a magnificent bath, paved with marble, and with *qashani* tiles on its walls. It is endowed for the service of God, so that nothing is required of any person in order to enter it. The shaikh of this convent was a pious and scrupulous devotee named Qutb al-Din Husain. He went to great lengths in honouring me, showed me generous hospitality, and presented me with a fine set of garments. At the very hour of my arrival at the convent he sent me food and three of those watermelons which we have mentioned already, and which I had not seen nor eaten previously.

A grace of this shaikh's

One day he came to visit me in the part of the hospice where I was staying. This place looked out over a garden belonging to the shaikh, and on that day his garments had been washed and spread out in the garden to dry. Among them I saw a white tunic with a lining, of the kind called by them *hazarmikhi*.[16] I admired it and said to myself, 'This is the kind of thing that I was wanting.' When the shaikh came into my room, he looked out towards the garden and said to one of his servants, 'Fetch me that *hazarmikhi* robe,' then when they brought it, he put it upon me. I threw myself at his feet, kissing them, and begged him to clothe me also with a skull-cap from his head, and to give me the same authorization in transmitting this that he had received from his father on the authority of the latter's shaikhs. He invested me with it accordingly on the fourteenth of Latter Jumada in the year 727[17] in his convent aforementioned, as he had been invested with it by his father Shams al-Din and his father had been invested with it by his father Taj al-Din Mahmud, and Mahmud by his father Shihab al-Din Ali al-Raja, and Ali by the Imam Shihab al-Din Abu Hafs Omar b. Muhammad b. Abdallah al-Suhrawardi.

From Isfahan we travelled to the town of Shiraz. In the whole East there is no city except Shiraz which approaches Damascus in the beauty of its bazaars, fruit gardens and rivers, and in the handsome figures of its inhabitants. It is situated in a plain, surrounded by orchards on all sides and intersected by five streams; one of these is the stream known as Rukn Abad, the water of which is sweet, very cold in summer and warm in winter, and gushes out of a fountain on the lower slope of a hill.[18]

The people of Shiraz are distinguished by piety, sound religion, and purity of manners, especially the women. These wear boots, and when out of doors are swathed in mantles and head-veils, so that no part of them is to be seen, and they are noted for their charitable alms and their liberality. One of their strange customs is that they meet in the principal mosque every Monday, Thursday and Friday, to listen to the preacher, sometimes one or two thousand of them, carrying fans in their hands with which they fan themselves on account of the great heat. I have never seen in any land an assembly of women in such numbers.

On my entry into the city of Shiraz I had no desire but to seek out the shaikh, the qadi, the imam, the pole of the saints and solitaire of the age, noted for his evident 'graces', Majd al-Din Isma'il b. Muhammad b. Khudhadad (*Khudhadad* meaning 'gift of God').[19] I arrived at the *madrasah*, called after him the Majdiyah, in which is his residence, it being in fact his own foundation, and went in to visit him with three of my companions. When I saluted him, he embraced me and took me by the hand until he came to his prayer-mat, then let go my hand and signed to me to pray alongside him, and I did so. After he had prayed the afternoon prayer, the notables of the city came forward to salute him, as was their custom with him morning and evening, and then he asked me about myself and how I had come, and questioned me about the Maghrib, Egypt, Syria and al-Hijaz, to all of which I answered. He gave orders for my lodging to his servants, who lodged me accordingly in a very small chamber in the *madrasah*.

**Narrative of the reason of their esteem for this shaikh,
which is an example of manifest grace**

The late king of al-Iraq, the Sultan Muhammad Khudabandah, had
as an associate, while yet in his state of infidelity, a doctor of law of
the Imami sect of the Rafidis.[20] When this sultan embraced Islam and
the Tatars were converted by his conversion, he showed even greater
esteem for this *faqih*; the latter consequently gave him a beguiling
view of the Rafidis and its superiority over the other Islamic schools.
The sultan, accordingly, gave orders that the people should be forced
to subscribe to the Rafidi doctrines. The people of Shiraz, Isfahan and
Baghdad, however, refused to do so. Whereupon he ordered the qadis
of the three cities to be fetched, and the first of them who was brought
was the Qadi Majd al-Din, the qadi of Shiraz, the sultan being at that
time at a place called Qarabagh, which is his summer residence.[21]
When the qadi arrived, the sultan gave orders that he should be
thrown to the dogs which he had there – these are enormous dogs,
with chains on their necks, and trained to eat human beings. When
anyone is brought to be delivered to the dogs, he is set at liberty and
without chains in a wide plain; those dogs are then loosed on him, so
they overtake him, tear him to pieces, and eat his flesh. But when the
dogs were loosed on the Qadi Majd al-Din and reached him, they
fawned on him and wagged their tails before him without attacking
him in any way.

On being informed of this, the sultan went out from his residence,
bare-footed, prostrated himself at the qadi's feet, kissing them, took
him by the hand and placed upon him all the garments that he was
wearing. This is the highest mark of distinction which a sultan can
confer in their usage. Among the gifts which he made to him were one
hundred of the villages of Jamakan, which is a valley like a trench
between two mountains, twenty-four *farsakhs* in length and traversed
by a great river, with the villages ranged on both sides of it.

I had a second opportunity to meet the Qadi Majd al-Din at the
time when I left India. I went to visit him from Hurmuz, to gain the
blessing of a meeting with him, in the year 48.[22] It is thirty-five days'
journey from Hurmuz to Shiraz. When I entered his chamber (though
he had then become too weak to walk) and saluted him, he recognized
me, rose up to welcome me, and embraced me. My hand happened to
touch his elbow, and I felt his skin clinging to the bone without any

flesh between them. He lodged me in the same *madrasah* where he had lodged me the first time. I visited him one day and found the king of Shiraz sitting in front of him, holding his own ear in his hand. This is the height of good manners amongst them, and all the people do so when they are seated in presence of the king.

Among the great sanctuaries of Shiraz is the mausoleum of the imam and pole, the saint Abu Abdallah b. Khafif, who is known by them simply as 'the Shaikh'.[23] He is the paragon of the whole land of Fars, and his mausoleum is highly venerated by them; they come to it morning and evening, and rub their hands on it for a blessing. I myself saw the Qadi Majd al-Din come to it on visitation and kiss it. The Shaikh Abu Abdallah b. Khafif occupies a high rank among the saints and is widely celebrated. It was he who revealed the track of the mountain of Sarandib in the island of Ceylon in the land of India.

A miracle of this shaikh

It is related that on one occasion he set out for the mountain of Sarandib, accompanied by about thirty poor brethren. They were assailed by hunger on the way to the mountain, in an uninhabited locality, and lost their bearings. They asked the shaikh to allow them to catch one of the small elephants, which are exceedingly numerous in that place and are transported thence to the capital of the king of India. The shaikh forbade them, but their hunger got the better of them; they disobeyed his instruction and, seizing a small elephant, they slaughtered it and ate its flesh. The shaikh, however, refused to eat it. That night, as they slept, the elephants gathered from every direction and came upon them, and they went smelling each man and killing him until they had made an end of them all. They smelled the shaikh too, but offered no violence to him; one of them took hold of him, wrapped its trunk round him, set him on its back, and brought him to the place where there was some habitation. When the people of the place saw him thus, they were astonished at it, and went out to meet him and find out all about him. Then the elephant, as it came near them, seized him with its trunk, and lifted him off its back down to the ground in full view of them. These people then came up to him, touched the fringes of his robe for a blessing and took him to their king. There they made known the story of his adventure – all of them being infidels – and he stayed with them for some days. That place lies on a *khawr* called 'Bamboo Khawr', *khawr* meaning river. In the same place there is a pearl fishery, and it is recounted that the shaikh, one day during his stay there, dived in the presence of their king and came out with both hands closed. He said to the king, 'Choose what is in one of them.' The king chose what was in his right hand, where-upon he passed over to him what it contained. They were three stones of ruby, unequalled in quality, and they are still in the possession of their kings, set in their crown and inherited by them in succession.

I visited this island of Ceylon. Its people still remain in a state of infidelity, yet they hold the poor brethren of the Muslims in great respect, lodge them in their houses and give them food, and these Muslims will be in their rooms amidst their wives and children.

All of the sanctuaries of Shiraz are inside the city, and so also are most of the graves of its inhabitants. For if the son or the wife of one of them dies, he prepares a tomb for him or her in one of the chambers of his house and buries him there. The members of the household look after the tomb, cover it with carpets, and light lamps over it, so that the deceased person is, as it were, still present with them; and it was told me that they prepare every day the deceased person's portion of food and give it away in alms on his behalf.

Anecdote

I was passing one day through one of the bazaars in the city of Shiraz when I saw there a mosque, substantially built and handsomely carpeted. Inside it there were copies of the Qur'an, placed in silken bags laid upon a rostrum. On the northern side of the mosque was a cell with a grille opening in the direction of the bazaar, and there sat an old man, of handsome appearance and garments, with a Qur'an before him, in which he was reading. I saluted him and sat down facing him, and, after he had asked me where I came from and I had replied to him, I questioned him on the subject of his mosque. He told me that it was he who had built it and endowed it with the revenues from a number of properties, for the maintenance of Qur'an readers and others, and that this cell in which I had sat down with him was the site of his grave, if God should decree his death in that city. He then lifted a carpet which was underneath him, and there was the grave, covered over with planks of wood. He showed me also a chest, which was at the other side of him, and said, 'In this chest is my shroud and the spices for my burial, and some money that I earned by hiring myself to dig a well for a saintly man, and when he paid me this money I put it aside to meet the expenses of my interment, and any of it left over is to be distributed in alms.' I was astonished at what he told me and made ready to withdraw, but he adjured me to stay and served me with food in that place.

Among the sanctuaries outside Shiraz is the grave of the pious shaikh known as al-Sa'di,[24] who was the greatest poet of his time in the Persian language and sometimes introduced Arabic verses into his compositions. It has attached to it a hospice which he had built in that place, a fine building with a beautiful garden inside it, close by the source of the great river known as Rukn Abad. The shaikh had constructed there some small cisterns in marble to wash clothes in. People go out from the city to visit his tomb, and they eat from his table, wash their clothes in that river and return home. I did the same thing at his tomb – may God have mercy upon him.

Then followed my departure from Shiraz with the object of visiting the grave of the pious Shaikh Abu Ishaq al-Kazaruni, at Kazarun, which is at a distance of two days' journey from Shiraz.[25] We arrived there in the evening of the second day and went to the hospice of the Shaikh Abu Ishaq (God benefit us by him), where we passed that night.

This Shaikh Abu Ishaq is highly venerated by the people of India and China. Travellers on the Sea of China make a practice when the wind turns against them and they fear pirates, of making vows to Abu Ishaq, and each one of them sets down in writing the obligation he has undertaken in his vow. Then, when they come safely on land, the servitors of the hospice go on board the ship, take the inventory, and exact the amount of his vow from each person who has pledged himself. There is not a ship that comes from China or from India but has thousands of dinars in it vowed to the saint, and the agents on behalf of the intendant of the hospice come to take delivery of that sum.

From Kazarun we returned to al-Iraq, visiting the city of al-Kufah and the sanctuary of al-Husain b. Ali (peace be upon them both) at al-Karbala. We travelled on from there to Baghdad.

The city of Baghdad

She is the Abode of Peace and capital of al-Islam, of illustrious rank and supreme preeminence, abode of caliphs and residence of scholars. Abu'l-Hasan Ibn Jubair (God be pleased with him) has said: 'And this illustrious city, although she still remains the capital of the Abbasid Caliphate, and centre of allegiance to the Imams of Quraish, yet her outward lineaments have departed and nothing remains of her but the name. By comparison with her former state, before the assault of misfortunes upon her and the fixing of the eyes of calamities in her direction, she is as the vanishing trace of an encampment or the image of the departing dream-visitant. There is no beauty in her that arrests the eye, or summons the busy passer-by to forget his business and to gaze – except the Tigris, which lies between her eastern and western quarters like a mirror set off between two panels, or a necklace ranged between two breasts; she goes down to drink of it and never suffers thirst, and views herself by it in a polished mirror that never suffers rust; and between her air and her water feminine beauty is brought to its flowering.'

Ibn Juzayy remarks: one would imagine that Abu Tammam[26] had witnessed with his own eyes what befell her in the end, when he said of her:

> Over Baghdad is stationed death's loud herald—
> Weep for her, then, weep for time's rapine there!
> Erstwhile, upon her stream by war imperilled,
> When in her streets its flames were briefly bated,
> Men hoped her happy fortunes reinstated.
> Now all their hopes have turned to dull despair!
> Since she, from youth to eldritch age declined,
> Has lost the beauty that once charmed mankind.

(Resumes.) There are two bridges in Baghdad, and the population are continually crossing them, night and day, men and women; indeed they find in this unending pleasure. Of mosques in Baghdad in which the Friday services are held there are eleven, eight of them on the west bank and three on the east bank. As for the other mosques, they are very numerous, and so too are the colleges, although these have fallen into ruin. The bath-houses in Baghdad also are numerous; they are among the most sumptuous of baths, and the majority of them are painted and plastered with pitch, so that it appears to the spectator to be black marble. This pitch is brought from a spring between al-Kufah and al-Basrah, from which it flows continuously and gathers at its sides like black clay; it is shovelled up from there and transported to Baghdad. In each of these bath-houses there are a large number of cubicles, each one of them floored with pitch and having the lower half of its wall also coated with it, and the upper half coated with a gleaming white gypsum plaster; the two opposites are thus brought together in contrasting beauty. Inside each cubicle is a marble basin fitted with two pipes, one flowing with hot water and the other with cold water. A person goes into one of the cubicles by himself, nobody else sharing it with him unless he so desires. In the corner of each cubicle is another basin for washing in, and this also has two pipes with hot and cold water. Every one on entering is given three towels; one of them he ties round his waist on coming out, and with the third he dries the water from his body. I have never seen such an elaboration as all this in any city other than Baghdad.

The western side of the city was the one first built, but is now for the most part in ruins. In contrast, the eastern part of Baghdad has magnificent bazaars and is splendidly laid out. The largest of its bazaars is one called the Tuesday bazaar, in which each craft occupies a section by itself. In the centre of this bazaar is the wonderful Nizamiyah College, the splendour of which is commemorated in a number of proverbial phrases, and at the end of it is the Mustansiriyah College, named after the Commander of the Faithful al-Mustansir.[27] All four schools are included in it, each school having a separate wing, with its own mosque and lecture room. The teacher takes his place under a small wooden canopy, on a chair covered with rugs; he sits on this in a grave and quiet attitude, wearing robes of black and his black turban, and with two assistants on his right and left, who repeat everything that he dictates. This same system is followed in every formal lecture of all four sections. Inside this college there is a bath-house for the students and a chamber of ablutions.

On this eastern side there are three mosques in which the Friday prayers are held. One is the caliphs' mosque, which is adjacent to the palaces and residences of the caliphs. It is a large cathedral mosque, containing fountains and many lavatories for ablutions and baths. The second cathedral mosque is the sultan's mosque, which is situated outside the town, and in proximity to it are palaces designated as the sultan's. The third cathedral mosque is that of al-Rusafah, which is about a mile from the sultan's mosque.

My arrival at Baghdad coincided with the presence in it of the king of al-Iraq, so let us speak of him here.

Account of the sultan of the two Iraqs and of Khurasan

Namely the illustrious Sultan Abu Sa'id Bahadur Khan (*Khan* in their language meaning 'king'), son of the illustrious Sultan Muhammad Khudabandah – he was the one of the line of kings of the Tatars who was converted to Islam.[28] His name is differently pronounced; some say Khudhabandah, with *dh*, but as to *bandah* there is no dispute. The interpretation of the name according to the latter pronunciation is Abdallah [i.e. slave of God], because *Khudha* in Persian is the name of God (High and Mighty is He) and *bandah* is 'servant' or 'slave' or words to that effect. It is said also that it is really Kharbandah, *khar* in Persian meaning 'ass'. What a world of difference there is between these two statements! But yet it is this latter name that is the best known, and the former was the name to which he changed it out of religious zeal. It is said that the reason why he was called by this latter name is that the Tatars name a new-born child after the first person to enter the house after its birth; when this sultan was born the first person to enter was a mule-driver, whom they call *kharbandah*, so he was given this name. Kharbandah's brother in turn was called Qazghan, which the people pronounce Qazan. *Qazghan* means a cooking pot, and the story goes that he was given this name because, when he was born, a slave girl entered carrying a cooking pot.

It was this Khudhabandah who embraced Islam – we have previously related the story of his relations with the Qadi Majd al-Din. When he died, there succeeded to the kingdom his son Abu Sa'id Bahadur Khan. He was an excellent and a generous king. He became king while of tender age, and when I saw him in Baghdad he was still a youth, the most beautiful of God's creatures in features, and without any growth on his cheeks. I saw both the sultan and his vizier one day on the Tigris in a launch; in front of him was Dimashq Khwajah, son of the Amir al-Juban who held the mastery over Abu Sa'id, and to right and left of him were two launches, carrying musicians and dancers. I was witness to one of his acts of generosity

77

on the same day; he was accosted by a company of blind men, who complained to him of their miserable state, and he ordered each one of them to be given a garment, a slave to lead him, and a regular allowance for his maintenance.

When the Sultan Abu Sa'id succeeded, being a young boy, as we have mentioned, the chief of the amirs, al-Juban, gained control over him and deprived him of all powers of administration, so that nothing of sovereignty remained in his hands but the name. Later, however, he asserted his authority. Al-Juban fled, but was captured and killed; his head was sent to Baghdad. Having now become sole master in the kingdom, Abu Sa'id decided to marry al-Juban's daughter; she was named Baghdad Khatun[29] and was one of the most beautiful of women. This khatun gained an ascendancy over Abu Sa'id, and he preferred her to all the other wives. She continued to enjoy this position for almost the whole period of his life; but he subsequently married a woman called Dilshad, whom he loved with a violent passion, and neglected Baghdad Khatun. She became jealous in consequence, and administered poison to him in a kerchief, with which she wiped him after conjugal relations. So he died, and his line became extinct, and his amirs seized the provinces for themselves. When the amirs learned that it was Baghdad Khatun who had poisoned him they resolved to kill her. The Greek slave Khwajah Lu'lu, who was one of the principal and senior amirs, took the initiative in this; he came to her while she was in the bath-house and beat her to death with his club. Her body lay there for some days, with only her pudenda covered with a piece of sacking.

Let us return now to the matter that we were dealing with. I left Baghdad after this in the *mahallah*[30] of the Sultan Abu Sa'id, on purpose to see the ceremonial observed by the king of al-Iraq in his journeying and encamping, and the manner of his transportation and travel. It is their custom to set out with the rising of the dawn and to encamp in the late forenoon. Their ceremonial on setting out is as follows: each of the amirs comes up with his troops, his drums and his standards, and halts in a position that has been assigned to him, not a step further, either on the right wing or the left wing. When they have all taken up their positions and their ranks are set in perfect order, the king mounts, and the drums, trumpets and fifes are sounded for the departure. Each of the amirs advances, salutes the king, and returns to his place; then the chamberlains and the marshals move forward ahead of the king, and are followed by the musicians. These number about a hundred men, wearing handsome robes, and behind them comes the sultan's cavalcade. Ahead of the musicians there are ten horsemen, with ten drums carried on slings round their necks, and five other horsemen carrying five reed-pipes, which are called in our country *ghaitahs*. They make music with these drums and pipes and then stop, and ten of the musicians sing their piece; when they finish it those drums and pipes play again, and when they stop, ten others sing their piece, and so on until ten pieces are completed, whereupon the encampment takes place. On the sultan's right and left during his march are the great amirs, who number about fifty, and behind him are the standard-bearers, drums, fifes and trumpets, then the sultan's mamluks, and after them the amirs according to their ranks. Each amir has his own standards, drums and trumpets. The organization of all this is supervised by the amir jandar, who has a large corps under his command.[31] The punishment of anyone who lags behind his unit and his corps is that his boots are taken off, filled with sand, and hung around his neck. He walks on his bare feet until finally, on reaching the encampment, he is brought before the amir jandar, thrown face downwards on the ground, and beaten with twenty-five lashes on his back; whether he be of high degree or low degree, they except no one from this punishment.

I travelled in this *mahallah* for ten days, and thereafter accompanied the amir Ala al-Din Muhammad, one of the great and distinguished amirs, to the city of Tabriz. We arrived at Tabriz after ten days' journey, and encamped outside it in a place called al-Sham. At that place is the grave of Qazan, king of al-Iraq, and alongside it a fine *madrasah* and a hospice in which food is supplied to all wayfarers, consisting of bread, meat, rice cooked in ghee, and sweetmeats. The amir arranged for my lodging in this hospice, which is situated among rushing streams and leafy trees. On the following morning I entered the city by a gate called the Baghdad Gate, and we came to an immense bazaar called the Qazan bazaar, one of the finest bazaars I have seen the world over. Each trade has its own location in it, separate from every other. I passed through the jewellers' bazaar, and my eyes were dazzled by the varieties of precious stones that I saw; they were displayed in the hands of beautiful slave boys, wearing rich robes and their waists girt with sashes of silk, who stood in front of the merchants exhibiting the jewels to the wives of the Turks, while the women were buying them in large quantities and trying to outdo one another. What I saw of all this was a scandal – may God preserve us from such! We went into the ambergris and musk bazaar also and saw the like of this again, or worse.

We spent one night in Tabriz. On the following morning the amir Ala al-Din received the order of the Sultan Abu Sa'id to rejoin him, so I returned along with him, without having met any of the scholars of Tabriz. We continued our journey until we reached the sultan's *mahallah*, where this amir told the sultan about me and introduced me into his presence. He asked me about my country, and gave me a robe and a horse. The amir told him that I was intending to travel to the noble Hijaz, whereupon he gave orders for me to be supplied with provisions and mounts in the pilgrim caravan accompanying the *Mahmil*,[32] and wrote instructions to that effect on my behalf to the governor of Baghdad, Khwajah Ma'ruf. I returned therefore to the city of Baghdad, and received in full what the sultan had ordered for me.

The governor assigned me the half of a camel litter and provisions and water for four men, writing out an order to that effect for me, then sent for the commander of the pilgrim caravan, who was the Bahlawan Muhammad al-Hawih, and commended me to him. I already had an acquaintance with the latter which went back to my journey from Mecca, but our friendship was strengthened by this and I remained under his protection and favoured by his bounty, for he gave me even more than had been ordered for me. As we left al-Kufah I fell ill of a diarrhoea and they had to dismount me from the litter many times during the day; during all this time the commander of the caravan kept enquiring for me and giving instructions that I should be looked after. My illness continued until after I reached Mecca, the sanctuary of God Most High (may He exalt her in honour and veneration). I made the prescribed circuits of the Holy House (God Most High ennoble it) on arrival, but I was so weak that I had to carry out the ordinances seated, so I made the circuits riding on the horse of the amir al-Hawih mentioned above.

We made the 'Standing'[33] at Arafat that year on a Monday, and when we camped at Mina I began to feel relief and to recover from my malady. At the end of the Pilgrimage I remained as a 'sojourner' at Mecca for the following three years. I led a most agreeable existence, giving myself up to circuits, pious exercises and frequent performances of the Lesser Pilgrimage.

5 Southern Arabia, East Africa and the Arabian Gulf

Following the Pilgrimage of the year 730, I set out from Mecca (God Most High ennoble her) intending to travel to the land of al-Yaman, and came to Juddah, an old town on the sea coast, which is said to have been founded by the Persians. This year was one of little rain, so water was brought to Juddah from the distance of a day's journey, and the pilgrims used to beg for water from the owners of the houses.

Anecdote

A strange thing happened to me in Juddah. There stopped at my door a blind beggar led by a boy, to ask for water. He saluted me, called me by my name and took me by the hand, although I had no acquaintance with him, nor did he know me. I was astonished at his doing so; but next he grasped my finger with his hand and said, 'Where is the *fatkhah*?' (meaning the ring). Now, as I was going out from Mecca, I had been accosted by a certain poor brother, who asked me for alms, and as I had nothing with me at that time I handed him my ring. So when this blind man asked about it, I told him that I had given it to a poor brother, and he said, 'Go back and look for it, for there are names written on it which contain a great secret.' Great was my astonishment at him and at his knowledge of all this – God knows best who and what he was.

We then embarked from Juddah on a vessel that they call a *jalbah*,[1] which belonged to Rashid al-Din al-Alfi of al-Yaman, and of Abyssinia by origin. The Sharif Mansur b. Abu Numayy embarked on another *jalbah* and desired me to accompany him, but I did not do so on account of there being a number of camels with him in his

81

jalbah, and I was frightened of this, never having travelled by sea before. There were there a number of men of al-Yaman, who had placed their provisions and goods in *jalbahs*, in preparation for the voyage.

Anecdote

When we got on board, the Sharif Mansur ordered one of his slaves to fetch him an *adilah* (that is half a camel load) of flour and a cruse of ghee, taking them from the *jalbahs* of the men of al-Yaman. When the man brought them to him, the merchants came to me weeping, stated to me that inside that *adilah* there were ten thousand dirhams of silver, and begged me to speak to him, to send it back and take another instead. So I went to him and spoke to him on the matter, saying, 'The merchants have something inside this *adilah*.' He replied, 'If it is an intoxicant, I shall not return it to them, but if it is anything else they shall have it.' They opened the sack then and found the dirhams, so he gave it back to them, saying to me, 'If it had been Ajlan, he would not have given it back,' Ajlan being the son of his brother Rumaithah; he had about that time entered the house of a Damascus merchant who was intending to go to al-Yaman, and had made off with most of what was in it. Ajlan is the amir of Mecca at the present time, and he has reformed his conduct and shown himself just and upright.

We then travelled on this sea with a favouring wind for two days, but thereafter the wind changed and drove us off the course which we had intended. The waves of the sea entered in amongst us in the vessel, and the passengers fell grievously sick. We continued in stormy weather until we emerged at a roadstead called Ra's Dawa'ir, between Aidhab and Sawakin.[2] We landed there and found on the shore a hut of reeds, shaped like a mosque, and inside a large number of ostrich eggshells filled with water, so we drank from these and cooked some food.

I saw in that roadstead a marvellous thing. This is a channel something like a riverbed which fills with water flowing out from the sea. The people there would take a length of cloth, holding it by its ends, and bring it out filled with fish, each about a cubit long, which they call by the name of *buri*. These people then cooked and broiled a large quantity of them. A party of the Bujah came to meet us; we hired camels from them and travelled with them through a desert country with many gazelles. The Bujah do not eat them, so they are sociable with human beings and do not flee from them.

After two days' travelling we came to the island of Sawakin. It is about six miles off the coast, and has neither water, nor cereal crops, nor trees. Water is brought to it in boats, and on it there are cisterns in which rainwater is collected. It is a large island, and in it is to be had the flesh of ostriches, gazelles and wild asses; its inhabitants have goats also in large numbers, together with milk products and ghee, which is exported from it to Mecca.

We took ship from the island of Sawakin, making for the land of al-Yaman. No sailing is done on this sea at night because of the large number of rocks in it. They travel on it only from sunrise to sunset, then anchor and disembark, and at dawn they mount into the ship again. The captain of the ship remains constantly in the bow of the vessel to warn the steersman of rocks. Six days after leaving the island of Sawakin we reached the city of Hali,[3] where the ruler assigned me a lodging as his guest for some days. I embarked on a ship of his and reached the township of al-Sarjah, a small town inhabited by a body of merchants of al-Yaman, most of whom are inhabitants of Sa'da.[4] They are men of generosity and open-handedness, and make a practice of supplying food to wayfarers, and assist pilgrims, transporting them in their vessels and giving them provisions from their own funds. They are indeed noted and famed for this, and God has multiplied their wealth and given them increase of His bounty and aided them to their work of charity.

We stayed at al-Sarjah only one night, enjoying the hospitality of these merchants, then continued our journey to the roadstead of al-Ahwab, and then rode to the city of Zabid, a great city in al-Yaman.[5] Between it and San'a is a distance of forty farsakhs, and after San'a there is no place in al-Yaman that is larger than it nor whose population is wealthier. It lies amid luxuriant gardens with many streams and fruits, such as bananas and others, and is in the interior, not on the coast, and one of the capital cities of al-Yaman. It is a great and populous city, and contains groves of palms, orchards and running streams – in fact the pleasantest and most beautiful town in al-Yaman. Its inhabitants are courteous in manners, upright in conduct, and handsome in figure, and its women are of exceeding and preeminent beauty. This is the 'vale of al-Husaib' of which it is related in certain Traditions that the Apostle of God (God bless and give him peace) said to Mu'adh in his admonition to him: 'O Mu'adh, when you come to the vale of al-Husaib, quicken your pace.'[6]

The people of this city hold the famous junketings called *subut al-nakhl* in this wise. They go out, during the season of the colouring and ripening of the dates, to the palm-groves on every Saturday. Not a soul remains in the town, whether of the townsfolk or of the strangers. The musicians go out to entertain them and the bazaar folk sell fruit and sweetmeats. The women go out riding on camels in litters. Together with the exceeding beauty that we have already mentioned, they are virtuous and generous in character, and they have a predilection for the stranger and do not refuse to marry him, as the women of our country do. When he wishes to travel, his wife goes out with him and bids him farewell; and if there should be a child between them, it is she who takes care of it and supplies what is needed for it until its father returns. During his absence she makes no demands on him for maintenance or clothes or anything else, and when he is resident she is content with little from him for upkeep and clothes; but the women never leave their own town and would not consent to do so even if one of them were offered any sum that might be offered to her on condition that she should leave her town.

The scholars and doctors of the law in this country are upright, pious, trustworthy, generous, and of fine character. During my conversations with them, mention happened to be made of the ascetic and humble devotee Ahmad b. al-Ujail al-Yamani, who was one of the greatest of men and of those favoured with miraculous powers.[7]

A miraculous grace

They relate that the jurists and leading men of the Zaidiyah came once on visitation to the Shaikh Ahmad b. al-Ujail. He sat awaiting them outside the hospice, and his associates went to meet them but the shaikh himself did not budge from his place. After they had saluted him and he had shaken hands with them and bidden them welcome, a discussion arose between them on the question of predestination. They maintained that there is no predestined decree and that the creature who is made responsible for carrying out the ordinances of God creates his own actions, whereupon the shaikh said to them: 'Well, if the matter is as you say, rise up from this place where you are.' They tried to rise up but could not, and the shaikh left them as they were and went into the hospice. They remained thus until, when the heat afflicted them sorely and the blaze of the sun smote them, they complained loudly of what had befallen them, then the shaikh's associates went in to him and said to him, 'These men have repented to God and recanted their false doctrine.' The shaikh then went out to them and, taking them by their hand, he exacted a pledge from them to return to the truth and abandon their evil doctrine. He brought them into his hospice, where they remained as his guests for three nights, and then returned to their own towns.

I went out to visit the grave of this saintly man, which is in a village called Ghassanah, outside Zabid, and met his pious son Abu'l-Walid Isma'il. He received me hospitably and I spent the night with him. After visiting the shaikh's tomb, I stayed three nights more with him and set out in company with him to visit the jurist Abu'l-Hasan al-Zaila'i. He is one of the great saints and leads the pilgrims from al-Yaman when they go on the Pilgrimage. The inhabitants of that country, and its bedouins as well, hold him in great esteem and veneration. We came to Jublah,[8] a small and pretty town with palms, fruit trees and streams, and when the jurist Abu'l-Hasan al-Zaila'i heard of the arrival of the Shaikh Abu'l-Walid he came out to meet him and lodged him in his hospice. I saluted him together with the shaikh, and we enjoyed a most agreeable residence with him for three days. When we left he sent one of the poor brethren with us and we proceeded to the city of Ta'izz, the capital of the king of al-Yaman. It is one of the finest and largest of the cities of al-Yaman. Its people are overbearing, insolent and rude, as is generally the case in towns where kings have their seats.[9] It is composed of three quarters; one of them is the residence of the sultan, his mamluks and courtiers, and the officers of his government, and is called by a name that I do not remember; the second is inhabited by the amirs and troops and is called Udainah; the third is inhabited by the common people and contains the principal bazaar, and it is called al-Mahalib.

Account of the sultan of al-Yaman

He is the Sultan al-Mujahid Nur al-Din Ali of the Rasulid dynasty.[10] His ancestor became widely known by the appellation of *Rasul* ['Envoy'] because one of the Abbasid caliphs sent him to al-Yaman to be a governor there, and later on his sons gained the royal power for themselves. On the fourth day of my stay in Ta'izz, I was introduced to him and I saluted him. The method of saluting him is that one touches the ground with his index finger, then raises it to the head and says, 'May God prolong thy majesty.' He then questioned me about my country, about our Master, the Commander of Faithful, the prince of liberality, Abu Sa'id[11] (God be pleased with him), and about the king of Egypt, the king of al-Iraq, and the king of the Lurs, and I answered all the questions that he asked concerning them. His vizier was in his presence, and the king commanded him to treat me honourably and arrange for my lodging.

The ceremonial at the public session of this king is as follows. He takes his seat on a platform carpeted and decorated with silken fabric; to right and left of him are the men-at-arms, those nearest him holding swords and shields, and next to them the bowmen; in front of them to the right and left are the chamberlain and the officers of government and the private secretary. The amir jandar is in attendance on him, and the men-at-arms, who form part of the corps of jandars, are stationed at a distance. When the sultan takes his seat they cry with one voice *'Bismillah'*,[12] and when he rises they do the same, so that all those in the audience hall know the moment of his rising and the moment of his sitting. When he has settled in his seat, each one of those persons whose custom it is to salute him enters, makes his salutation, and stands in the place appointed for him on the right and on the left. No person goes beyond his place or sits down, except those who are bidden to sit. The sultan says to the amir jandar 'Command so-and-so to sit down,' whereupon the person so commanded to sit advances a little way from his place and sits down on a carpet there in front of those standing on the right and the left. The food is then brought, and it is of two sorts, the food of the commons and the food of the high officers. The superior food is partaken of by the sultan, the grand qadi, the principal sharifs and jurists and the guests; the common food eaten by the rest of the sharifs, jurists and qadis, the shaikhs, the amirs and the officers of the troops. The seat of each person at the meal is fixed; he does not move from it, nor does anyone of them jostle another. On exactly this same pattern is the ceremonial of the king of India at his meal, but I do not know whether the sultans of India took it over from the sultans of al-Yaman or the sultans of al-Yaman took it over from the sultans of India.

After I had remained for some days as the guest of the sultan of al-Yaman, during which he treated me generously and provided me with a horse, I took leave to continue my journey to the city of San'a.[13] It is the former capital of the country of al-Yaman, a large and well-constructed city, built with bricks and plaster, with many trees and fruits, and with a temperate climate and good water. It is a curious thing that the rain in the lands of India, al-Yaman and Abyssinia falls during the period of summer heat, and mostly during the afternoon of every day in that season, so that travellers make haste when the sun begins to decline, to avoid being caught by rain, and the womenfolk retire to their dwellings, because these rains are heavy downpours. The whole city of San'a is paved and when the rain falls it washes and cleans all its streets. The cathedral mosque of San'a is one of the finest of mosques, and contains the grave of one of the prophets (peace be upon them).

I travelled from there next to the city of Adan, the port of the land of al-Yaman, on the coast of the great sea. It is surrounded by mountains and there is no way into it except from one side only. It is a large city, but has no crops, trees, or water, and has reservoirs in which water is collected during the rainy season.[14] This water is at some distance from it and the bedouins often cut off the approach to it and prevent the townsfolk from obtaining it until the latter buy their consent with money and pieces of cloth. It is an exceedingly hot place, and is the port of the merchants of India, to which come great vessels from Kinbayah [Cambay], Tanah, Kawlam [Quilon], Qaliqut, Fandaraina, al-Shaliyat, Manjarur [Mangalore], Fakanur, Hinawr [Honavar], Sandabur [Goa], and other places.[15] The merchants of India live there, and the merchants of Egypt also. The inhabitants of Adan are either merchants or porters or fishermen. The merchants among them have enormous wealth; sometimes a single man may possess a great ship with all it contains, no one sharing in it with him, because of the vast capital at his disposal, and there is ostentation and rivalry between them in this respect.

Anecdote

It was told me that one of them sent a slave boy of his to buy for him a ram, and another of them sent a slave boy for the same purpose. It happened that there was only a single ram in the bazaar on that day, so there ensued a contest for it between the two slaves, bidding against one another, until its price rose to four hundred dinars. Then one of them got possession of it and said, 'The sum of my wealth is four hundred dinars, and if my master gives me its price, good and well, but if not, I shall pay out of my own capital for it, and I shall have vindicated myself and defeated my rival.' He went off with the ram to his master, and when the latter learned what had happened he freed him and gave him a thousand dinars. The other returned to his master empty-handed, and he beat him, took his money and drove him out of his service.

I lodged in Adan with a merchant called Nasir al-Din al-Fa'ri. There used to come to his table every night about twenty of the merchants, and he had slaves and servants in still larger numbers. Yet with all this, they are men of piety, humility, uprightness and generous qualities, doing good to the stranger, giving liberally to the poor brother, and paying God's due in tithes as the Law commands.

I travelled from the city of Adan by sea for four days, and arrived at the city of Zaila, the city of the Barbarah, who are a people of the negroes.[16] Their country is a desert extending for two months' journey, beginning at Zaila and ending at Maqdashaw. Their cattle are camels, and they also have sheep which are famed for their fat. Zaila is a large city with a great bazaar, but it is in the dirtiest, most disagreeable, and most stinking town in the world. The reason for its stench is the quantity of its fish and the blood of the camels that they slaughter in the streets. When we arrived there we chose to spend the night at sea in spite of its extreme roughness, rather than pass a night in the town, because of its filth.

We sailed on from there for fifteen nights and came to Maqdashaw, which is a town of enormous size. Its inhabitants are merchants possessed of vast resources; they own large numbers of camels, of which they slaughter hundreds every day for food, and also have quantities of sheep.[17] It is the custom of the people of this town that, when a vessel reaches the anchorage, the *sumbuqs*, which are small boats, come out to it. In each *sumbuq* there are a number of young men of the town, each one of whom brings a covered platter containing food and presents it to one of the merchants on the ship saying, 'This is my guest,' and each of the others does the same.

When the young men came on board the vessel in which I was, one of them came up to me. My companions said to him, 'This man is not a merchant, but a doctor of the law,' whereupon he called out to his friends and said to them 'This is the guest of the qadi.' There was among them one of the qadi's men, who informed him of this, and he came down to the beach with a number of students and sent one of them to me. I then disembarked with my companions and saluted him and his party. He said to me, 'In the name of God, let us go to salute the shaikh.' 'And who is the shaikh?' I said, and he answered, 'The sultan,' for it is their custom to call the sultan 'the shaikh'. Then I said to him, 'When I am lodged, I shall go to him,' but he said to me, 'It is the custom that whenever there comes a jurist or a sharif or a man of religion, he must first see the sultan before taking a lodging.' So I went with him to the sultan, as they asked.

Account of the sultan of Maqdashaw

The sultan of Maqdashaw is Abu Bakr, son of the Shaikh Omar; he is by origin of the Barbarah and he speaks in Maqdishi, but knows the Arabic language.

When I arrived with the qadi I have mentioned, who was called Ibn al-Burhan, an Egyptian by origin, at the sultan's residence, one of the serving boys came out bringing a plate on which were some leaves of betel and areca nuts. He gave me ten leaves along with a few of the nuts, the same to the qadi, and what was left on the plate to my companions and the qadi's students. He brought also a jug of rose-water of Damascus, which he poured over me and over the qadi [i.e. over our hands], and said, 'Our master commands that he be lodged in the students' house,' this being a building equipped for the entertainment of students of religion. The qadi took me by the hand and we went to this house, which is in the vicinity of the shaikh's residence, and furnished with carpets and all necessary appointments. Later on the serving boy brought food from the shaikh's residence. With him came one of his viziers, who was responsible for the care of the guests, and who said, 'Our master greets you and says to you that you are heartily welcome.' He then set down the food and we ate. Their food is rice cooked with ghee, which they put into a large wooden platter, and on top of this they set platters of *kushan*. This is the seasoning, made of chickens, flesh-meat, fish and vegetables. They cook unripe bananas in fresh milk and put this in one dish, and in another dish they put curdled milk, on which they place pieces of pickled lemon, bunches of pickled pepper steeped in vinegar and salted, green ginger, and mangoes. These resemble apples, but have a stone; when ripe they are exceedingly sweet and are eaten like other fruit, but before ripening they are acid like lemons, and they pickle them in vinegar. When they take a mouthful of rice, they eat some of these salted and pickled conserves after it. A single person of the people of Maqdashaw eats as much as a whole company of us would eat, as a matter of habit, and they are corpulent and fat in the extreme.

I then sailed from the city of Maqdashaw, making for the country of the Sawahil [Coastlands], with the object of visiting the city of Kulwa in the land of the Zinj people. We came to the island of Mambasa, a large island two days' journey by sea from the Sawahil country.[18] It has no mainland territory, and its trees are the banana, the lemon, and the citron. Its people have a fruit which they call *jammun*, resembling an olive and with a stone like its stone.[19] The inhabitants of this island sow no grain, and it has to be transported to them from the Sawahil. Their food consists mostly of bananas and fish. They are Shafi'ites in rite, pious, honourable, and upright, and their mosques are of wood, admirably constructed. At each of the gates of the mosques there are one or two wells (their wells have a depth of one or two cubits), and they draw up water from them in a wooden vessel, into which has been fixed a thin stick of the length of one cubit. The ground round the well and the mosque is paved; anyone who intends to go into the mosque washes his feet before entering, and at its gate there is a piece of thick matting on which he rubs his feet. If one intends to make an ablution, he holds the vessel between his thighs, pours water on his hands and performs the ritual washings. All the people walk with bare feet.

We stayed one night in this island and sailed on to the city of Kulwa, a large city on the seacoast, most of whose inhabitants are Zinj, jet-black in colour. They have tattoo marks on their faces. We then sailed from Kulwa to the city of Zafar, which is at the extremity of the land of al-Yaman, on the coast of the Indian Sea.[20] From it thoroughbred horses are exported to India, and the sea between it and the land of India can be crossed with the aid of the wind in a full month. I myself crossed it once from Qaliqut in the land of India to Zafar in twenty-eight days with a favouring wind, sailing continuously by night and by day. The city of Zafar lies in an isolated desert region, in which there is not a village, and it has no dependencies. The bazaar is outside the city in a suburb called al-Harja, and it is one of the dirtiest, most stinking and fly-ridden of bazaars, because of the quantity of fruit and fish sold in it. Most of the fish in it are the species called *sardin*, which are extremely fat there. It is a strange fact that their beasts have as their sole fodder these sardines, and likewise their flocks, and I have never seen this in any other place. Most of the sellers in the bazaar are female slaves, who are dressed in black.

The people of this city are men of humility, good dispositions, virtue, and affection for strangers. Their clothes are made of cotton, which is brought to them from India, and they wear wrappers fastened round their waists in place of drawers. Most of them wear only one wrapper tied round the waist and put another over their backs, because of the violent heat, and they bathe several times a day. There is prevalent among the inhabitants, both men and women, the disease called elephantiasis, which is a swelling of both feet, and most of the men suffer from hernia – God preserve us!

A strange thing is that the people of this city of all men most closely resemble the people of the Maghrib in their ways. I lodged in the house of the khatib in its principal mosque, who was Isa b. Ali, a man of great distinction and a generous soul. He had a number of slave girls, who were called by the same names as the female slaves in the Maghrib; one was named Bukhait and another Zad al-Mal, and I have never heard these names in any other country. Most of its inhabitants leave their heads uncovered, and do not wear a turban. In every one of their houses there is a prayer-mat of palm leaves hung up inside the house, on which the master of the house performs his prayers, exactly as the people of the Maghrib do, and their food also is millet. All of this similarity between them is of a nature to strengthen the opinion that the Sanhajah and other tribes of the Maghrib originate from Himyar.[21]

In the vicinity of this city and among its groves is the hospice of the pious shaikh and devotee Abu Muhammad b. Abu Bakr b. Isa, of the people of Zafar.[22] I went out to this hospice and spent a night in it, enjoying the hospitality of the two sons of the Shaikh Abu Bakr, and I found them to be men of great benevolence. When we washed our hands after the meal, one of them, Abu'l-Abbas, took that water in which we had washed, drank some of it, and sent the servant with the rest of it to his wives and children, and they too drank it. This is what they do with all visitors to them in whom they perceive indications of goodness.

This city of Zafar has groves in which grow large numbers of bananas of great size; one of them was weighed in my presence and its weight was twelve ounces. They are pleasant to the taste and very sweet. There too are betel and coconut (known as 'Indian nut'), which are to be found only in the land of India and in this city of Zafar, because of its similarity and proximity to India – except, however, that in the city of Zabid, in the sultan's garden, there are some few coconut trees. Since the mention of betel and coconuts has come up, I shall now proceed to describe them and give an account of their properties.

Account of the betel tree

The betel is a tree which is cultivated in the same manner as the grapevine; trellises of cane are made for it, just as for gravevines, or else the betel trees are planted close to coconut trees, so that they may climb upon them in the same way that vines climb, and as the pepper climbs. The betel has no fruit, and is grown only for the sake of its leaves, which resemble the leaves of the bramble, and the best ones are the yellow. Its leaves are picked every day. The Indians attach immense importance to betel, and when a man comes to the house of his friend and the latter gives him five leaves of it, it is as though he had given him the world, especially if he is an amir or some great man. The gift of betel is for them a far greater matter and more indicative of esteem than the gift of silver and gold. The manner of its use is that before eating it one takes areca nut; this is like a nutmeg but is broken up until it is reduced to small pellets, and one places these in his mouth and chews them. Then he takes the leaves of betel, puts a little chalk on them, and masticates them along with the betel. Their specific property is that they sweeten the breath, remove foul odours of the mouth, aid digestion of food, and stop the injurious effect of drinking water on an empty stomach; the eating of them gives a sense of exhilaration and promotes cohabitation, and a man will put some by his head at nights so that, if he wakes up or is awakened by his wife or slave girl, he may take a few of them and they will remove any foul odour there may be in his mouth. I have been told, indeed, that the slave girls of the sultan and of the amirs in India eat nothing else. I shall speak of this again in describing the land of India.

Account of the coconut

This is the 'Indian nut'. These trees are among the most peculiar trees in kind and most astonishing in habit. They look exactly like date-palms, without any difference between them except that the one produces nuts as its fruits and the other produces dates. The nut of a coconut tree resembles a man's head, for in it are what look like two eyes and a mouth, and the inside of it when it is green looks like the brain, and attached to it is a fibre which looks like hair. They make from this cords with which they sew up ships instead of using iron nails, and they also make from it cables for vessels. The coconut, especially that in the islands of Dhibat al-Mahal [Maldives], is the size of a human head, and they tell this story: a certain philosopher in India in past ages was in the service of one of the kings and was held by him in high esteem. The king had a vizier, between whom and this philosopher there was enmity. The philosopher said to the king, 'If this vizier's head is cut off and buried, there will bring advantage to the people of India and other peoples in the world.' The king said to him, 'And what if this that you have stated does not come from the head of the vizier?' He replied, 'If it does not, do with my head as you have done with his.' So the king gave orders to cut off the vizier's head, and the philosopher took it, planted a date-stone in his brain, and tended it until it grew into a tree and produced this nut as its fruit. This story is a fiction, but we have related it because of its wide circulation among them.

Among the properties of this nut are that it strengthens the body, fattens quickly, and adds to the redness of the face. As for its aphrodisiac quality, its action in this respect is wonderful. One of the marvellous things about it is that at the beginning of its growth it is green, and if one cuts out a piece of its rind with a knife and makes a hole in the head of the nut, he drinks out of it a liquid of extreme sweetness and coolness, but whose temperament is hot and aphrodisiac. After drinking this liquid, he takes a piece of the rind and fashions it like a spoon, and with this he scoops out the pulp which is inside the nut. The taste of this is like that of an egg which has been broiled but not fully cooked, and one uses it for food. This was what I lived on during my stay in the islands of Dhibat al-Mahal for a period of a year and a half.

From Zafar we sailed towards Oman in a small vessel belonging to an inhabitant of the island of Masirah. On the day following our embarkation we alighted at the roadstead of Hasik, in which there are a number of Arabs, who are fishermen and live there. They possess incense trees; these have thin leaves, and when a leaf is slashed there drips from it a sap like milk, which then turns into a gum. This gum is the incense, and it is very plentiful there. The only means of livelihood for the inhabitants of this port is from fishing, and the fish that they catch is called *lukham*, which is like a dogfish. It is cut open, dried in the sun, and used for food; their huts also are built with fish bones, and roofed with camel hides.[23] We continued our journey from the roadstead of Hasik for four days, and came to the Hill of Lum'an, in the midst of the sea.[24] On top of it is a hermitage built of stone, with a roofing of fish bones, and with a pool of collected rainwater outside it.

Account of a saint whom we met on this hill

When we cast anchor under this hill, we climbed up to this hermitage, and found there an old man lying asleep. We saluted him, and he woke up and returned our greeting by signs; then we spoke to him, but he did not speak to us and kept shaking his head. The ship's company offered him food, but he refused to accept it. We then begged of him a prayer on our behalf, and he kept moving his lips, though we did not know what he was saying. He was wearing a patched robe and a felt bonnet, but had no skin bag nor jug nor staff nor sandals. The ship's company declared that they had never before seen him on this hill. We spent that night on the beach of the hill and prayed the afternoon and sunset prayers with him. We offered him food, but he refused it and continued to pray until the hour of the last night-prayer, when he pronounced the call to prayer and we prayed along with him. He had a beautiful voice in his reciting of the Qur'an and in his modulation of it. When he ended the last night prayer, he signed to us to withdraw, so, bidding him farewell, we did so, with astonishment at what we had seen of him. Afterwards, when we had left, I wished to return to him, but on approaching him I felt in awe of him; fear got the better of me, and when my companions returned for me, I went off with them.

We resumed our voyage and after two days reached the Island of Birds, which is uninhabited.[25] We cast anchor and went ashore on it, and found it full of birds like blackbirds, except that these were bigger. The sailors brought some eggs of those birds, cooked and ate them, and also caught and cooked some of the birds themselves without slitting their throats, and ate them. There was sitting along-side me a merchant, of the people of the island of Masirah, but living in Zafari, named Muslim; I saw him eating these birds along with them, and reproved him for it. He was greatly abashed and said to me, 'I thought that they had slaughtered them,' but he kept aloof from me thereafter out of shame and would not come near me until I called him. My food during those days on that ship was dried dates and fish. We celebrated the Feast of Sacrifice at sea;[26] on that very day there blew up against us a violent wind after daybreak and it lasted until sunrise and almost sunk us.

A miraculous grace

There was accompanying us in the vessel a pilgrim, a man from India named Khidr, but he was called *Mawlana* because he knew the Qur'an by heart and could write excellently. When he saw the storminess of the sea, he wrapped his head in a mantle that he had and pretended to sleep. When God gave us relief from what had befallen us, I said to him, 'O Mawlana Khidr, what kind of thing did you see?' He replied, 'When the storm came, I kept my eyes open, watching to see whether the angels who receive men's souls had come. As I could not see them I said "Praise be to God. If any of us were to be drowned, they would come to take the souls." Then I would close my eyes and after a while open them again, to watch in the same manner, until God relieved us.' A ship belonging to one of the merchants had gone ahead of us, and it sank, and only one man escaped from it – he got out by swimming after suffering severely.

We came next to the island of Masirah, to which the master of the ship that we were sailing on belonged.[27] It is a large island, whose inhabitants have nothing to eat but fish. We did not land on it, because of the distance of the anchorage from the shore; besides I had taken a dislike to these people when I saw them eating the birds without proper slaughtering. We stayed there one day, while the master of the ship went ashore to his home and came back to join us.

We continued our voyage for a day and a night and came to the roadstead of a large village on the seashore called Sur, from which we saw the city of Qalhat on the slope of a hill, and seeming to us to be close by.[28] We had arrived at the anchorage just after noon or before it, and when the city appeared to us I felt a desire to walk to it and spend the night there, since I had taken a dislike to the company of the ship's folk. I made enquiries about the way to it and was told that I should reach it by mid-afternoon, so I hired one of the sailors to guide me on the road. I was accompanied by Khidr the Indian, who has been already mentioned, and I left my associates with my possessions on the ship to rejoin me on the following day. I took some pieces of clothing of mine and gave them to the man I had hired as a guide, to spare me the fatigue of carrying them, and myself carried a spear in my hand. Now that guide wanted to make off with my garments, so he led us to a channel, an inlet from the sea in which there was a tidal flow and ebb, and was about to cross it with my garments, but I said to him, 'You cross over by yourself and leave the clothes with us; if we can cross, we shall, but if not we shall go up higher to look for a ford.' He drew back and afterwards we saw some men who crossed it by swimming, so we were convinced that he had meant to drown us and make away with the garments. Thereupon I made a show of vigour and took a firm attitude; I girt up my waist and kept brandishing the spear, so that the guide went in awe of me. We went up higher until we found a ford, and then came out into a waterless desert, where we suffered from thirst and were in a desperate plight. But God sent us a horseman with a number of his companions, one of whom had in his hand a waterskin and gave me and my companion to drink. We went on, thinking that the city was close at hand, whereas in reality we were separated from it by nullahs through which we walked for many miles.

When the evening came the guide wanted to lead us down towards the shore, where there was no road, for the coast there is nothing but rocks. He wanted us to get stuck amongst them and to make off with the garments, but I said to him, 'We shall just keep walking along this track that we are following,' there being a distance of about a mile between us and the sea. When it became dark he said to us, 'The city is no distance from us, so come, let us walk on so that we can stop overnight in its outskirts.' But I was afraid that we might be molested by someone on our road, and was not sure how far we still had to go, so I said to him, 'The right course is to turn off the track and sleep, and in the morning we shall reach the town, if God will.' I had observed a party of men on a hillside thereabouts, and fearing that they might be robbers said to myself, 'It is preferable to go into hiding.' My companion was overcome by thirst and did not agree to this, but I turned off the road and made for a tree of Umm Ghailan.[29] Although I was worn out and suffering from exhaustion, I made a show of strength and vigour for fear of the guide; as for my companion, he was ill and incapacitated. So I placed the guide between him and me, put the garments between my robe and my skin, and held the spear firmly in my hand. My companion went to sleep and so did the guide, but I stayed on watch, and every time the guide moved I spoke to him and showed him that I was awake. We remained thus till daybreak, when we came out to the road and found people going to the town with various kinds of produce. So I sent the guide to fetch water for us, and my companion took the garments. There were still some steep slopes and nullahs between us and the city, but the guide brought us water and we drank, this being the season of heat.

Finally we reached the city of Qalhat, arriving at it in a state of great exhaustion. My feet had become so swollen in my shoes that the blood was almost starting under the nails. Then, when we reached the city gate, the finishing touch to our distress was that the gatekeeper said to us, 'You must go with me to the governor of the city, that he may be informed of what you are doing and where you have come from.' So I went with him to the governor, and found him to be an excellent man and of good disposition. He asked me about myself and made me his guest, and I stayed with him for six days, during which I was powerless to rise to my feet because of the pains that they had sustained.

The city of Qalhat is on the seacoast; it has fine bazaars and one of the most beautiful mosques. Its walls are tiled with *qashani*, which is like *zalij*, and it occupies a lofty situation from which it commands a view of the sea and the anchorage. It was built by the saintly woman Bibi Maryam, *bibi* meaning in their speech 'noble lady'.[30] I ate in this city fish such as I have never eaten in any other region; I preferred it to all kinds of flesh and used to eat nothing else. They broil it on the leaves of trees, place it on rice, and eat it thus; the rice is brought to them from India. They are traders, and make a livelihood by what comes to them on the Indian Sea. When a vessel arrives at their town, they show the greatest joy. Their speech is incorrect although they are Arabs, and every sentence that they speak they follow up with *la* ['no']. So, for example, they say, 'You eat, no; you walk, no; you do so-and-so, no.'

We set out thereafter for the land of Oman,[31] and after travelling for six days through desert country we reached it on the seventh. It is fertile, with streams, trees, orchards, palm groves and abundant fruit of various kinds. We came to the capital of this land, which is the city of Nazwa – a city at the foot of a mountain, enveloped by orchards and streams, and with fine bazaars and splendid clean mosques. Their womenfolk, however, are much given to corruption, and the men show no jealousy nor disapproval of such conduct.

Anecdote

One day I was in the presence of the sultan of Oman, Abu Muhammad Ibn Nabhan, when a women came to him, young, pretty and with unveiled face. She stood before him and said to him, 'O Abu Muhammad, the devil is in revolt in my head.' He said to her, 'Go and drive out the devil.' She said, 'I cannot, and I am under your protection, O Abu Muhammad.' Then he said to her, 'Go and do what you want.' I was told that this girl and anyone who does as she did are under the sultan's protection and engage in debauchery. Neither her father nor any of her relatives can punish her, and if they kill her they are put to death in retaliation for her, because she is under the sultan's protection.

I travelled next from the land of Oman to the land of Hurmuz. Hurmuz is a city on the sea-coast, and is also called Mughistan.

Opposite it in the sea is New Hurmuz, and between them is a sea passage of three *farsakhs*. We came to New Hurmuz, which is an island whose city is called Jarawn.[32] It is a fine large city, with magnificent bazaars, as it is the port of India and Sind, from which the wares of India are exported to the two Iraqs, Fars and Khurasan. I saw a remarkable thing there – near the gate of the cathedral mosque, between it and the bazaar, the head of a fish as large as a hillock and with eyes like doors, and you would see persons going in by one eye and coming out by the other.

We left the city of Jarawn and, after crossing the strait, hired mounts from the Turkmens;[33] they are the inhabitants of that country, and no travelling can be done through it except in their company, because of their bravery and knowledge of the roads. In these parts there is a desert extending over four nights' journey, which is the haunt of Arab brigands and in which the *samum* wind blows up in the two months of June and July. All those whom it overtakes there it kills; indeed, I was told that when a man is killed by that wind and his friends attempt to wash him for burial all his limbs fall apart. There are many graves in it of those who have succumbed there in this wind. We used to travel by night, and when the sun rose we would halt in the shade of the Umm Ghailan trees, resuming our journey in the late afternoon and going on until sunrise.

Eventually we arrived in the city of Qais, also called Siraf.[34] It is on the coast of the Indian Sea, and its people draw their water from springs that gush out from its hills; they are Persians of noble stock, and among them is a body of Arabs. It is these latter who dive for pearls.

Account of the pearl fishery

The pearl fishery is situated between Siraf and al-Bahrain, in a calm channel like a great river. When the month of April and the month of May come round, large numbers of boats come to this place with divers and merchants of Fars, al-Bahrain and al-Qutaif. The diver, when he makes ready to dive, puts over his face a covering made of the shell of the tortoise, and makes of this same shell a sort of thing like scissors which he fastens on his nose, then ties a rope round his waist and submerges. They differ in their endurance under water, some of them being able to stay under water for an hour or two hours or less.[35] When the diver reaches the bottom of the sea he finds the shells there, stuck in the sand among small stones, and pulls them out by hand or cuts them loose with a knife that he has for that purpose, and puts them in a leather bag slung round his neck. When his breath becomes restricted he pulls on the rope, and the man who is holding the rope on the surface feels the movement and pulls him up to the boat. The bag is then taken from him and the shells are opened. Inside them are found pieces of flesh which are cut out with a knife, and when they come into contact with the air they solidify and turn into pearls. All of these are collected, whether small or large; the sultan takes his fifth and the remainder are bought by the merchants who are there in the boats. Most of them are creditors of the divers, and they take the pearls in quittance of their debts, or so much of them as is their due.

We then travelled from Siraf to the city of al-Bahrain, a fine large city with gardens, trees and streams. Water is easy to get at there – one digs with one's hands in the sand and there it is. The city has groves of date-palms, pomegranates, and citrons, and cotton is grown there. It is exceedingly hot there and very sandy, and the sand often encroaches on some of its dwellings. From al-Bahrain I made my way to Mecca, and performed the Pilgrimage for the year 732.

6 Asia Minor, the Steppe and Constantinople

When the Pilgrimage ended, I went to Juddah, with the intention of sailing to al-Yaman and India. But that was not decreed for me; I was unable to find a companion and I stayed in Juddah about forty days. There was a ship there belonging to a man called Abdallah al-Tunisi, who was intending to go to al-Qusair,[1] so I boarded it to see what state it was in, but it did not please me and I disliked the idea of travelling by it. This was an act of providence of God Most High, for the ship sailed and when it was in the open sea it foundered. Its master and some merchants escaped in a ship's boat after severe distress and were on the point of death; even some of these perished, and all the rest were drowned, including about seventy of the pilgrims who were on it.

Some time later I sailed in a *sumbuq* for Aidhab but the wind drove us back to a roadstead called Ra's Dawa'ir, and from there we travelled by land with the Bujah. We made our way through a desert full of ostriches and gazelles. Since our provisions were exhausted we purchased sheep from some of the Bujah whom we found in the wilderness, and prepared a store of their flesh. I saw in this wilderness an Arab boy who spoke to me in Arabic and told me that the Bujah had captured him; he declared that for a whole year he had eaten no meat and had no other food than camel's milk. Later on that meat that we had bought ran out on us and we had no provisions left. But I had with me about a load of dried dates, intended as presents to my friends, so I distributed them to the company and we lived on them for three nights' journey.

After a passage of nine days from Ra's Dawa'ir we reached Aidhab. From here I followed my earlier route via Cairo into Syria, arriving at length in al-Ladhiqiyah. From al-Ladhiqiyah we embarked on a large vessel belonging to the Genoese, the master of which was called Martalamin, and made for the country of the Turks, known as Bilad al-Rum.[2] We travelled on the sea for ten nights with a favouring wind, and the Christians treated us honourably and took no passage money from us. On the tenth day we arrived at the city of al-Alaya, which is the beginning of the land of al-Rum.[3] This country called Bilad al-Rum is one of the finest regions in the world; in it God has brought together the good things dispersed through other lands. Its inhabitants are the comeliest of men in form, the cleanest in dress, the most delicious in food, and the kindliest of God's creatures. This is why the saying goes, 'Blessing in Syria and kindliness in al-Rum', since what is meant by the phrase is the people of this land. Wherever we stopped in this land, whether at hospice or private house, our neighbours both men and women (who do not veil themselves) came to ask after our needs. When we left them to continue our journey, they bade us farewell as though they were our relatives and our own kin, and you would see the women weeping out of grief at our departure. One of their customs in that country is that they bake bread on only one day each week, making provision on that day for enough to keep them for the rest of the week. Their men used to bring us warm bread on the day it was baked, together with delicious viands to go with it, as a special treat for us, and would say to us, 'The women have sent this to you and beg of you a prayer.'

All of the people of this land belong to the school of the Imam Abu Hanifah (God be pleased with him) and are firmly attached to the Sunnah – there is not a Qadari, nor a Rafidi, nor a Mu'tazili, nor a Khariji, nor any innovator amongst them.[4] This is a virtue by which God Most High has distinguished them, but they consume hashish and think nothing wrong in that.

The city of al-Alaya that we have mentioned is a large place on the sea coast. It is inhabited by Turkmens, and is visited by the merchants of Cairo, Alexandria, and Syria. It has quantities of wood, which is exported from there to Alexandria and Dimyat, and thence carried to the other parts of Egypt. There is at the top of the town a magnificent and formidable citadel, built by the illustrious Sultan Ala al-Din al-Rumi.

From there I went on to the city of Antaliyah.[5] It is one of the finest of cities, enormous in extent and bulk, among the most handsome of cities to be seen anywhere, as well as the most populous and best organized. Each section of its inhabitants live by themselves, separated from each other section. Thus the Christian merchants reside in a part of it called al-Mina and are encircled by a wall, the gates of which are shut upon them from without at night and during the Friday prayer service; the Rum [Greek Christians], who were its inhabitants in former times, live by themselves in another part, also encircled by a wall; the Jews in another part, with a wall round them; while the king and his officers and mamluks live in a separate township, which also is surrounded by a wall that encircles it and separates it from the sections that we have mentioned. The rest of the population, the Muslims, live in the main city. We stayed in the college in this city, the shaikh of which was Shihab al-Din al-Hamawi.

Account of the Young Akhis[6]

They exist in all the lands of the Turkmens of al-Rum, in every district, city, and village. Nowhere in the world are there to be found any to compare with them in solicitude for strangers, and in ardour to serve food and satisfy wants, to restrain the hands of the tyrannous, and to kill the agents of police and those ruffians who join with them. An Akhi, in their idiom, is a man whom the assembled members of his trade, together with others of the young unmarried men and those who have adopted the celibate life, choose to be their leader. The Akhi builds a hospice and furnishes it with rugs, lamps, and what other equipment it requires. His associates work during the day to gain their livelihood, and after the afternoon prayer they bring him their collective earnings; with this they buy fruit, food, and the other things needed for consumption in the hospice. If, during that day, a traveller alights at the town, they give him lodging with them; what they have purchased serves for their hospitality to him and he remains with them until his departure. If no newcomer arrives, they assemble themselves to partake of the food, and after eating they sing and dance. On the morrow they disperse to their occupations, and after the afternoon prayer they bring their collective earnings to their leader. The members are called *fityan*, and their leader, as we have said, is the Akhi. Nowhere in the world have I seen men more chivalrous in conduct than they are.

On the day after that of our arrival in this city one of these *fityan* came to the Shaikh Shihab al-Din al-Hamawi and spoke with him in Turkish, which I did not understand at that time. He was wearing shabby clothes and had a felt bonnet on his head. The shaikh said to me, 'Do you know what this man is saying?' 'No,' said I, 'I do not know what he said.' Then he said to me, 'He is inviting you to a meal with him, you and your companions.' I was surprised at this, but I said to him, 'Very well,' and when the man had gone I said to the shaikh, 'This is a poor man, and he has not the means to entertain us and we do not like to impose a burden on him.' Whereupon the shaikh burst out laughing and said to me, 'He is one of the shaikhs of the Young Akhis. He is a cobbler, and a man of generous disposition. His associates number about two hundred men of different trades, who have elected him as their leader and have built a hospice to entertain guests in, and all that they earn by day they spend at night.'

So, after I had prayed the sunset prayer, the same man came back for us and we went with him to the hospice. We found it to be a fine building, carpeted with beautiful Rumi rugs, and with a large number of lustres of Iraqi glass. Standing in rows in the chamber were a number of young men wearing long cloaks, and with boots on their feet. Each one of them had a knife about two cubits long attached to a girdle round his waist, and on their heads were white bonnets of wool with a piece of stuff about a cubit long and two fingers broad attached to the peak of each bonnet. When they take their places in the chamber, each one of them removes his bonnet and puts it down in front him, but retains on his head another bonnet, an ornamental one, of silk taffeta or some other fabric. In the centre of their hall was a sort of platform placed there for visitors. When we had taken our places among them, they brought in a great banquet, with fruits and sweetmeats, after which they began their singing and dancing. Everything about them filled us with admiration and we were greatly astonished at their generosity and innate nobility. We took leave of them at the end of the night and left them in their hospice.

From Antaliyah we travelled to the city of Akridur, a great and populous city with fine bazaars and running streams, fruit trees and orchards.[7] It has a lake of sweet water, on which a vessel plies in two days to Aqshahr and Baqshahr and other towns and villages. We lodged there in a college opposite the main congregational mosque, and occupied by the learned Professor Muslih al-Din. He had studied in Egypt and Syria, and lived for a time in al-Iraq; he was elegant in speech and eloquent in expression, a prodigy among the rare spirits of the age, and he received us with the utmost generosity and lavishly supplied our needs.

Account of the sultan of Akridur

Its sultan is Abu Ishaq Bak, son of al-Dundar Bak, one of the great sultans of that land. He lived in Egypt during his father's lifetime and made the Pilgrimage. He is a man of upright conduct, and makes a practice of attending the afternoon prayers in the congregational mosque every day. When these prayers are concluded, he sits with his back to the wall of the *qiblah*; the Qur'an readers take their seats in front of him on a high wooden platform and recite with beautiful voices, that work upon men's souls and at which hearts are humbled, skins creep, and eyes fill with tears. After this he returns to his residence.

We left there for the city of Qul Hisar, a small town surrounded on every side by water in which there is a thick growth of rushes.[8] There is no way to reach it except by a path like a bridge constructed between the rushes and the water, and broad enough only for one horseman. The city is on a hill in the midst of the waters and is formidably protected and impregnable. We lodged there in the hospice of one of the Young Akhis.

The sultan of Qul Hisar sent a number of horsemen with us to escort us to the city of Ladhiq, which is also called Dun Ghuzluh, which means 'town of the swine'.[9]

This is one of the most attractive and immense cities. In it there are seven mosques for the observance of Friday prayers, and it has splendid gardens, perennial streams, and gushing springs. Its bazaars are very fine, and in them are manufactured cotton fabrics edged with gold embroidery, unequalled in their kind, and long lived on account of the excellence of their cotton and strength of their spun thread. Most of the artisans there are Greek women, for in it there are many Greeks who are subject to the Muslims and who pay dues to the sultan, including the *jizyah*,[10] and other taxes. The distinctive mark of the Greeks there is their wearing of tall pointed hats, some red and some white, and the Greek women for their part wear capacious turbans.

The inhabitants of this city make no effort to stamp out immorality

– indeed, the same applies to the whole population of these regions. They buy beautiful Greek slave girls and put them out to prostitution, and each girl has to pay a regular due to her master. I heard it said there that the girls go into the bath-houses along with the men, and anyone who wishes to indulge in depravity does so in the bath-house and nobody tries to stop him. I was told that the qadi in this city himself owns slave girls employed in this way.

On our entry into this city, as we passed through one of the bazaars, some men came down from their booths and seized the bridles of our horses. Then certain other men quarrelled with them for doing so, and the altercation between them grew so hot that some of them drew knives. All this time we had no idea what they were saying, and we began to be afraid of them, thinking that they were brigands, who infest the roads in the environs of this city, and reckoning that they were out to rob us. At length God sent us a man, a pilgrim, who knew Arabic, and I asked what they wanted of us. He replied that they belonged to the *fityan*, that those who had been the first to reach us were the associates of the Young Akhi Sinan, while the others were the associates of the Young Akhi Tuman, and that each party wanted us to lodge with them. We were amazed at their native generosity. Finally they came to an agreement to cast lots, and that we should lodge first with the one whose lot was drawn. The lot of Akhi Sinan won, and on learning of this he came to meet us with a body of his associates. They greeted us and we were lodged in a hospice of his, where we were served with a variety of dishes. The Akhi then conducted us to the bath and came in with us; he himself took over the office of serving me, while his associates undertook the service of my companions, three or four of them waiting on each one of the latter. Then, when we came out of the bath, they served us a great banquet with sweetmeats and quantities of fruit, and after we finished eating and the Qur'an readers had recited verses from the Exalted Book they began their singing and dancing. They sent word about us to the sultan, and on the following day he sent for us in the evening, and we went to visit him and his son.

From Ladhiq we visited the towns of Mughlah and Milas, before making for the city of Quniyah,[11] a great city with fine buildings and abundant watercourses, streams, gardens and fruits. It is said that this city was founded by Alexander. In it is the mausoleum of the shaikh and pious imam, the Pole Jalal al-Din, known as *Mawlana*.

Anecdote

It is related that in early life Jalal al-Din was a legist and professor, to whom students used to flock at his college in Quniyah. One day there came into the college a man selling sweetmeats, who carried on his head a trayful of them, cut up into pieces which he would sell for a copper apiece. When he came into the lecture hall the shaikh said to him, 'Bring your tray here.' The sweet-seller took a piece of his wares and gave it to the shaikh, the latter took it with his hand and ate it, whereupon the sweet-seller went out without offering anything to anyone other than the shaikh. The shaikh, abandoning his lecture, went out to follow him up; and the students, when he delayed to return and they had waited a long time, went out to seek for him, but they could not discover where he was living. Subsequently he came back to them, after many years, but he had become demented and would speak only in Persian rhymed couplets which no one could understand. His disciples used to follow him and write down that poetry as it issued from him, and they collected it into a book called the *Mathnawi*. The inhabitants of that country greatly revere that book, meditate on its contents, teach it and recite it in their hospices on Thursday nights.

Leaving Quniyah, we toured the eastern part of Bilad al-Rum, reaching the city of Arz al-Rum.[12] From here we journeyed westward once more, arriving in the city of Birgi.[13] We met one of its inhabitants and enquired of him for the hospice of the Akhi there. He replied, 'I will guide you to it,' so we followed him and he conducted us to his own residence, in a garden that he had, and put us up on the roof of his house, overshadowed by trees, for this was the season of extreme heat. He brought us all kinds of fruit, and gave us excellent hospitality and fodder for our beasts, and we spent that night with him.

We had already learned that there was in this city an eminent professor named Muhyi al-Din. Our host for the night, who was a student of religion, took us to the college, and there was the professor just arriving, mounted on a lively mule and wearing magnificent robes, open in front and embroidered with gold, with his slaves and servants to right and left of him and preceded by the students. When we saluted him he bade us welcome, greeted us and spoke to us most graciously, and, taking me by the hand, made me sit beside him. Later on, he began to lecture on the sciences, both fundamental and accessory.

When he had finished his lecture, he went to a small chamber in the college, ordered it to be furnished, put me up in it, and sent a superb meal.

Later on, after the sunset prayer, he sent an invitation to me, and I went to him. I found him in a reception chamber in a garden of his, where there was an ornamental pool into which the water was flowing down from a white marble basin edged with enamelled tiles. In front of him were a number of the students, and his slaves and servants were standing on either side of him, while he himself was sitting on a dais covered with beautiful embroidered rugs. When I saw him in so stately a setting I took him for a prince. He rose up and came forward to welcome me, took me by the hand, and made me sit beside him on the dais. Food was then brought, and after we had eaten we returned to the college. One of the students told me that all of the students who were present at the professor's that night were regular attendants at his meal every night. This professor wrote to the sultan a letter, composed in laudatory terms, to inform him about us. The sultan was at the time living on a mountain thereabouts, passing the summer there on account of the severe heat; this mountain was cool, and it was his practice to pass the summer there.[14]

Account of the sultan of Birgi

He is the Sultan Muhammad, son of Aydın, one of the best, most generous, and worthiest of sultans.[15] When the professor sent to inform him about me, he despatched his deputy to me with an invitation to visit him, but the professor advised me to wait until the sultan sent for me again. He himself was at the time suffering from a boil that had broken out on his foot, on account of which he was unable to ride and had ceased to go to college. Later on the sultan sent for me again. This gave great distress to the professor and he said, 'It is impossible for me to ride on horseback, although it was my intention to go with you in order to reaffirm to the sultan what is due to you.' He braced himself, however, wrapped his foot in bandages, and mounted, without putting his foot in the stirrup. I and my companions mounted also and we climbed up to the mountain by a road that had been hewn in its side and evened out. We arrived at the sultan's place just after noon and alighted by a stream of water under the shade of walnut trees. On hearing of our arrival the sultan sent me a tent of the kind which is called by them *kharqah*, and consists of wooden laths put together in the shape of a cupola and covered with pieces of felt.[16] The upper part of it can be opened to admit light and air, like a ventilation pipe, and can be closed when required. They also brought rugs and furnished it. I sat down with my companions, outside the tent under the shade of walnut trees. It was very cold in that place, and on that night a horse of mine died from the sharpness of the cold.

On the following morning the professor rode to visit the sultan and spoke about me in terms dictated by his own generous qualities. He then returned to me and told me about this, and after a while the sultan sent to summon both of us. On reaching his place of residence we found him standing up; we saluted him and sat down, the doctor on his right and I next to the doctor. He enquired of me about myself and my coming, and then questioned me about al-Hijaz, Egypt, Syria, al-Yaman, the two Iraqs, and the lands of the Persians. Food was then served, and we ate and withdrew. He sent presents of rice, flour, and butter in sheep's stomachs, this being a practice of the Turks. We continued in this way for several days, being sent for every day to join in his meal. One day he came to visit us after the noon prayer and asked me to write down for him a number of *hadiths*, of the sayings of the Apostle of God (God bless and give him peace), and when I had written them for him and the doctor presented them to him in the same hour, he commanded the latter to write an exposition of them for him in the Turkish language.[17] He then rose and went out, and observing that our servants were cooking food for us under the shade of the walnut trees without any spices or greens, commanded that his storekeeper should be punished, and sent spices and butter.

Our stay on this mountain lasted so long that I began to weary and wished to take my leave. But at length he went down to the city, and we with him. He called to us and bade us come into his palace with him. On our arrival at the vestibule of the palace, we found about twenty of his servants, of surpassingly beautiful appearance, wearing robes of silk, with their hair parted and hanging loose, and in colour of a resplendent whiteness tinged with red. I said to the doctor, 'What are these beautiful figures?' and he replied, 'These are Greek pages.' We climbed a long flight of stairs with the sultan and came eventually into a fine audience hall, with an ornamental pool of water in the centre and the figure of a lion in bronze at each corner of it, spouting water from its mouth. Round this hall there was a succession of benches covered with rugs, on one of which was the sultan's cushion. When we came up to this bench, the sultan pushed away his cushion with his hand and sat down alongside us on the rugs. The doctor sat on his right, the qadi next to him, and I next to the qadi. The Qur'an readers sat down below the bench, for there are always Qur'an readers in attendance on him in his audiences, wherever he may be. The servants then brought in gold and silver bowls filled with sherbet of raisins steeped in water, into which citron juice had been squeezed, with small pieces of biscuits in it, along with gold and silver spoons. At the same time they brought some porcelain bowls containing the same beverage and with wooden spoons, and any who felt scruples about using the gold and silver vessels used the porcelain bowls and wooden spoons. I made a speech of thanks to the sultan and eulogized the doctor, sparing no efforts in doing so, and this gave much pleasure and satisfaction to the sultan.

Anecdote

While we were still sitting with the sultan there came in an elderly man, wearing on his head a turban with a tassel, who saluted him. The qadi and the doctor stood up as he came in, and he sat down in front of the sultan, on the bench, with the Qur'an readers beneath him. I said to the doctor, 'Who is this shaikh?' He just laughed and said nothing, but when I repeated the question he said to me, 'This man is a Jew, a physician. All of us need his services, and it was for this reason that we acted as you saw in standing up at his entry.' At this my indignation flared up and I said to the Jew, 'You God-damned son of a God-damned father, how dare you sit up there above the readers of the Qur'an, and you a Jew?' and went on berating him in loud tones. The sultan was surprised and asked what I was saying. The doctor told him, while the Jew grew angry and left the chamber in the most crestfallen state. When we took our leave, the doctor said to me, 'Well done, may God bless you. Nobody but you would dare to speak to him in that way, and you have let him know just what he is.'[18]

Another anecdote

In the course of this audience the sultan asked me this question: 'Have you ever seen a stone that fell from the sky?' I replied, 'I have never seen one, nor ever heard tell of one.' 'Well,' he said, 'a stone did fall from the sky outside this town of ours,' and then called some men and told them to bring the stone. They brought in a great black stone, very hard and with a glitter in it – I reckoned its weight to amount to a hundredweight. The sultan ordered the stone-breakers to be summoned, and four of them came and on his command to strike it they beat upon it as one man four times with iron hammers, but made no impression on it. I was astonished at this phenomenon, and he ordered it to be taken back to its place.

Every night of our stay the sultan used to send food, fruit, sweet-meats and candles, and finally he sent to me a hundred mithqals of gold,[19] a thousand dirhams, a complete set of garments, a horse, and a Greek slave called Mikha'il, and to each of my companions a robe and some dirhams – all this owing to the friendly offices of the Professor Muhyi al-Din, God Most High reward him with good. He bade us farewell and we left, having spent fourteen days with him on the mountain and in the city.

We went on to the city of Aya Suluq, a large and ancient city venerated by the Greeks, in which there is a great church built with huge stones, each measuring ten or less cubits in length and most skilfully hewn.[20] The congregational mosque in this city is one of the most magnificent mosques in the world and unequalled in beauty. It was formerly a church of the Greeks, greatly venerated among them, which they used to visit from all parts, and when the Muslims captured the city they made it a congregational mosque. Its walls are of marble of different colours, and it is paved with white marble and roofed with lead. It contains eleven domes, differing in size, with a water pool in the centre of the area under each dome. The city is traversed by the river, which has on either side of it trees of different species, grapevines, and trellises of jasmine, and it has fifteen gates. I bought in this city a Greek slave girl, a virgin, for forty gold dinars.

We went on next to the city of Yazmir, a large city on the sea coast, mostly in ruins, with a citadel adjoining its upper end.[21] The amir of this city is Omar Bak, son of the Sultan Muhammad b. Aydin mentioned above. This amir was a generous and pious prince, and continually engaged in jihad against the Christians. He had war galleys with which he used to make raids on the environs of Constantinople the Great and to seize prisoners and booty, then after spending it all in gifts and largesse he would go out again to the jihad. Eventually his pressure became so galling to the Greeks that they appealed to the Pope, who ordered the Christians of Genoa and France to attack him, and attack him they did. The Pope sent an army from Rome, and the combined forces made an assault on the city by night with a large number of galleys, capturing the harbour and the town. The Amir Omar came down from the citadel to engage them, but died a martyr's death together with a great number of his men. The Christians established themselves in the town, but could not capture the citadel because of its impregnability.

We continued our journey from this city to the city of Maghnisiyah,[22] a large and fine city on a mountain slope. Its sultan is called Saru-khan, and when we arrived in this town we found him at the mausoleum of his son, who had died some months before. He and the boy's mother spent the eve of the festival and the following morning at the tomb. The boy had been embalmed and placed in a coffin of wood with a lid of tinned iron; the coffin was raised on high trestles in a domed chamber without a roof, so that its odour should escape, and after this the dome would be roofed in and the boy's coffin placed where it could be seen on ground level, and his garments laid upon it.[23]

We continued our journey from Maghnisiyah and came to the city of Barghamah, a city in ruins, with a great and formidable fortress on top of a hill.[24] It is related that the philosopher Aflatun [Plato] was an inhabitant of this city, and his house is known by his name to the present day. We now hired a man to guide us on the road, and travelled over steep and rugged mountains until we came to the city of Bali Kasri.[25] Its sultan is named Dumur Khan, and is a worthless person. It was his father who built this city, and during the reign of this son of his it acquired a large population of good for nothings, for, 'Like king like people'. I visited him and he sent me a silk robe. I bought in this city a Greek slave girl named Marghalitah.

We went on next day to the city of Bursa, a great and important city with fine bazaars and wide streets, surrounded on all sides by gardens and running springs. In its outskirts there is a river of exceedingly hot water which flows into a large pond; beside this have been built two bath-houses, one for men and the other for women.

Sick persons seek a cure in this hot pool and come to it from the most distant parts of the country.[26] I met in this city the pious Shaikh Abdallah al-Misri, the traveller, and a man of saintly life. He journeyed through the earth, but he never went into China nor the island of Ceylon, nor the Maghrib, nor al-Andalus, nor the Negro-lands, so that I have outdone him by visiting these regions.

Account of the sultan of Bursa

Its sultan is Urkhan Bak, son of the Sultan Othman Chuq.[27] This sultan is the greatest of the kings of the Turkmens and the richest in wealth, lands and military forces. Of fortresses he possesses nearly a hundred, and for most of his time he is continually engaged in making the round of them, staying in each fortress for some days to put it into good order and examine its condition. It is said that he has never stayed for a whole month in any one town. He also fights with the infidels continually and keeps them under siege. It was his father who captured the city of Bursa from the hands of the Greeks, and his tomb is in its mosque, which was formerly a church of the Christians.

We continued our journey to the city of Yaznik.[28] It is now in a mouldering condition and uninhabited except for a few men in Sultan Urkhan's service. In it lives also his wife Bayalun Khatun, who is in command of them, a pious and excellent woman. I visited her and she treated me honourably, gave me hospitality, and sent gifts. Some days after our arrival the sultan came to this city. I stayed in it about forty days, on account of the illness of a horse of mine, but when I became impatient at the delay I left it behind and set out with three of my companions, and a slave girl and two slave boys. We had no one with us who could speak Turkish and translate for us. We had a translator previously but he left us in this city.

After our departure from it we spent the night at a village called Makaja with a legist there who treated us well and gave us hospitality.[29] On continuing our journey from this village we were preceded by a Turkish woman on a horse, and accompanied by a servant, who was making for the city of Yanija, while we followed her up. She came to a great river which is called Saqari, as though it took its name from *Saqar* (God preserve us from it). She went right on to ford the river, but when she was in the middle of it the horse nearly sank with her and threw her off its back. The servant who was with her tried to rescue her, but the river carried them both away. There were some men on the opposite bank who threw themselves in and swam after them; they brought out the woman with a spark of life still in her, but the man had perished – God's mercy on him. These men told us that the ford was below that place, so we went down to it. It consists of four balks of wood, tied together with ropes, on which they place the horses' saddles and the baggage; it is pulled over by men from the opposite bank, with the passengers riding on it, while the horses are led across swimming, and that was how we crossed.

We came the same night to Kawiyah,[30] where we lodged in the hospice of one of the Akhis. We spoke to him in Arabic, and he did not understand us; he spoke to us in Turkish, and we did not understand him. Then he said, 'Call the doctor of the law, for he knows Arabic,' so the legist came and spoke to us in Persian. We addressed him in Arabic, but he did not understand us, and said to the Young Brother in Persian, '*Ishan arabi kuhna miquwan waman arabi naw midanam.*' *Ishan* means 'these men', *kuhna* means 'old', *miquwan* 'they say', *naw* 'new', and *midanam* 'I know'. What the legist intended by this statement was to shield himself from disgrace, when they thought that he knew the Arabic language, although he did not know it. So he said to them, 'These men speak the ancient Arabic speech and I know only the new Arabic.' However, the Young Brother thought that matters really were as the man of law said, and this did us good service with him. He showed us the utmost respect, saying, 'These men must be honourably treated because they speak the ancient Arabic language, which was the language of the Prophet (God bless and give him peace) and of his Companions.' I did not understand what the legist said at that time, but I retained the sound of his words in my memory, and when I learned the Persian language I understood its meaning.

We spent the night in the hospice, and the Young Brother sent a guide with us to Yanija, a large and fine township. We searched there for the Akhi's hospice, and found one of the demented poor brothers. When I said to him, 'Is this the Akhi's hospice?' he replied, '*na'am*' [yes] and I was filled with joy at this, thinking that I had found someone who understood Arabic. But when I tested him further the secret came to light, that he knew nothing at all of Arabic except the word *na'am*. We lodged in the hospice, and one of the students brought us food, since the Akhi was away. We became on friendly terms with this student, and although he knew no Arabic he offered his services and spoke to the deputy governor of the town, who supplied us with one of his mounted men.

This man went with us to Kainuk, which is a small town inhabited by infidel Greeks under the government of the Muslims.[31] We lodged in the house of an old woman, an infidel; this was the season of snow and rain, so we gave her some money and spent that night in her house. This town has no trees or grapevines nor is anything cultivated there but saffron, and this old woman brought us a great quantity of saffron, thinking we were merchants and would buy it from her.

In the morning when we mounted our horses, the horseman whom the Young Brother had sent with us from Kainuk came to us and sent with us another horseman to conduct us to the city of Muturni. There had been a heavy fall of snow during the night, which obliterated the road, so that the horseman went ahead of us and we followed in his tracks. Later, however, he decamped, leaving us with no idea which way to go, and with no road visible to us. We made an effort to find traces of the road under the snow and to follow it, until about sunset we came to a hill where the track was shown by a great quantity of stones. I was afraid that both I and my companions would perish, as I expected more snow to fall in the night, and the place was uninhabited; if we dismounted we were doomed, and if we continued on through the night we should not know which way to go. I had a good horse, however, a thoroughbred, so I planned a way of escape, saying to myself, 'If I reach safety, perhaps I may contrive some means to save my companions,' and it happened so. I commended them to God Most High and set out. Now the people of that country build over their graves wooden chambers, which anyone who sees them would take to be habitations, but finds to be graves. I saw a large number of these, but after the hour of the night prayer I came to some houses and said, 'O God, grant that they be inhabited.' I found that they were inhabited, and God Most High guided me to the gate of a certain building. I saw by it an old man and spoke to him in Arabic; he replied to me in Turkish and signed to me to enter. I told him about my companions, but he did not understand me. It happened by the providential goodness of God that that building was a hospice of some poor brethren, and that the man standing by the gate was its shaikh. When the brethren inside the hospice heard me speaking with the shaikh, one of them came out; he was a man with whom I had an acquaintance, and when he greeted me I told him the tale of my companions, and advised him to go with the brethren to rescue them. They did so and went with me to rejoin my companions, and we came back together to the hospice, praising God Most High for our safety.

We rode on at dawn and reached the city of Muturni at the hour of the congregational prayer. There was a strange thing happened to us there. I sent one of the servants to buy chopped straw for the beasts, and one of them to buy ghee. Number one came back with the straw, but number two came back empty-handed and laughing. We asked him what he was laughing at, and he replied, 'We stopped at a stall in the bazaar and asked him for *samn* [ghee]. He signed to us to wait, and spoke to a boy with him, to whom we then gave the money. He was away for a long time, and came back with some straw. We took it from him and said, "We want *samn*," whereupon he said, "This is *samn*."' It came to light that they say *samn* for chopped straw in Turkish, and ghee is called by them *rughan*.

In Muturni we met in with a pilgrim who knew Arabic, whom we besought to travel with us to Qastamuniyah, which is ten days' journey from this town.[32] I presented him with an Egyptian robe, one of my own, gave him also ready money, which he left to meet the expenses of his family, assigned him an animal to ride, and promised him a good reward. When he set out with us it became evident from his conduct that he was a man of substantial wealth, who had made loans to a number of persons, but of mean ambitions, base character, and evil actions. We used to give him money for our expenses and he would take what bread was left over and trade it for spices, vegetables and salt, and appropriate the money that he got by selling these. I was told too that he used to steal some of the money for our expenses as well. We had to put up with him because of our difficulties through not knowing Turkish, but the thing went so far that we openly accused him and would say to him at the end of the day, 'Well, Hajji, how much of the expense money have you stolen today?' He would reply, 'So much,' and we would laugh at him and make the best of it.

One of his base actions was that, when a horse of ours died at one of the halts of our journey, he did the job of skinning it with his own hands and sold the hide. Another occurred when we lodged for the night with a sister of his in a village. She brought us food and fruit, namely pears, apples, apricots and peaches, all of them dried and then cooked in water until they soften, when they are eaten and their juice drunk. We wanted to pay her, but when he learned of this he said, 'Don't give her anything, but give that amount to me.' So we gave the money to him to satisfy him, but we also gave her something secretly, in such a way that he did not know of it.

We came next to the city of Buli.[33] When we were nearly there, we came upon a river which seemed, to all appearances, a small one, but when some of my companions got into the stream, they found it exceedingly fast and impetuous. They all crossed it, however, except for a young slave girl whom they were afraid to take across. Since my horse was a better one than theirs, I mounted her behind me and started to cross the river. But when I was in the middle of it, my horse stumbled with me and the girl fell off. My companions got her out with a spark of life still in her, and I for my part came out safely.

On entering the city, we sought out the hospice of one of the Young Akhis. When we entered it we found the fire alight, so I took off my clothes, put on others, and warmed myself at the fire; and the Akhi not only brought food and fruit but lavished them. What an excellent body of men these are, how noble-minded, how unselfish and full of compassion for the stranger, how kindly affectionate to the visitor, how magnanimous in their solicitude for him! The coming of a stranger to them is exactly as if he were coming to the dearest of his own kin.

We continued our journey via Garadai Buli and Burlu,[34] and at length arrived in the city of Qastamuniyah, one of the largest and finest of cities, where commodities are abundant and prices low. We lodged there in the hospice of a shaikh called al-Utrush ['the deaf'], because of his hardness of hearing, and I witnessed an astonishing thing in connection with him, namely that one of the students would write for him with his finger in the air, or sometimes on the ground, and he would understand what he meant and reply. Long stories were told to him in this way, and he would grasp them.

We stayed in this city about forty days. We used to buy a quarter of fat mutton for two dirhams and bread for two dirhams – this would satisfy our needs for a day, and there were ten of us. We would buy sweetmeats made of honey for two dirhams, and they would be enough for us all, and walnuts for a dirham or chestnuts at the same price, and after all of us had eaten of them there would be some left over. We used to buy a load of firewood for a single dirham, and this in the season of extreme cold. I have never in any country seen a city where prices were lower than there.

I met there the aged and pious Shaikh Dada Amir Ali. I visited this man in his hospice, in the vicinity of the horse market, and found him lying on his back. One of his servants assisted him to sit up and one of them raised his eyelids from his eyes; on opening them he addressed me in pure Arabic, saying, 'You are heartily welcome.' I asked him his age and he said, 'I was an associate of the Caliph al-Mustansir, and at his death I was thirty years old, and my age now is one hundred and sixty-three years.'³⁵ I asked him to invoke a blessing on me; he did so, and I withdrew.

We continued our journey across lofty mountains to the city of Sanub, a superb city which combines fortification with beautification.³⁶ It is encompassed by sea on all sides except one, namely the east, and it has on that side a single gateway through which no one may enter except by permission of its governor. When permission for us had been obtained from him, we entered the town and lodged in the hospice of Akhi Chalabi, which is outside the Sea Gate. From there one can climb up to a mountain projecting into the sea on which there are orchards, cultivated fields and streams, most of its fruits being figs and grapes. It is an inaccessible mountain that cannot be taken by escalade. On it there are eleven villages inhabited by Greek infidels under the government of the Muslims, and on top of it is a hermitage called after al-Khidr and Ilyas (on both of them be peace), which is never without a resident devotee. Beside it is a spring of water, and prayer made in it is answered.

In Sanub I heard tell of its former ruler, Ghazi Chalabi, a brave and audacious man, endowed by God with a special gift of endurance under water and power of swimming.³⁷ He used to make expeditions in war galleys to fight the Greeks, and when the fleets met and everybody was occupied with the fighting he would dive under the water, carrying in his hand an iron tool with which to hole the enemy's galleys, and they would know nothing of what had befallen them until the foundering of their ships took them unawares. On one occasion a fleet of galleys belonging to the enemy made a surprise attack on the harbour of Sanub, and he holed them and captured all the men who were on board. He possessed indeed a talent that was unmatched, but they relate that he used to consume an excessive quantity of hashish, and it was because of this that he died. He went out one day hunting (to which he was passionately addicted) and pursued a gazelle, which led him on among some trees; he spurred his horse on too hard and was intercepted by a tree, which struck and crushed in his head. So he died. It is said that the present ruler too consumes as much as his predecessor did, but the people of all the districts of al-Rum show no disapproval of consuming it. Indeed, I passed one day by the gate of the congregational mosque in Sanub, outside of which there are benches where the inhabitants sit, and I saw several of the superior officers of the army with an orderly of theirs in front of them holding in his hand a bag filled with something resembling henna. One of them took a spoonful of it and ate it, as I was looking at him; I had no idea what there was in the bag, but I enquired of the person who was with me, and he told me that it was hashish.

Our stay in this city lasted for about forty days, while we were awaiting an occasion to travel by sea to the city of al-Qiram.[38] We then hired a vessel belonging to the Greeks and remained eleven days more waiting for a favourable wind. At length we began the voyage, but when we were out in the open sea, after three nights, a storm blew up against us and we were in sore straits, with destruction visibly before our eyes. I was in the cabin, along with a man from the Maghrib named Abu Bakr, and I bade him go up on deck to observe the state of the sea. He did so and came back to me in the cabin saying to me, 'I commend you to God.' The storm raged against us with unparalleled fury, then the wind changed and drove us back nearly to the very city of Sanub from which we had started. One of its merchants wanted to go down to its harbour, but I prevented the master of the ship from disembarking him. Afterwards the wind fell, and we resumed our journey, but when we were in the open sea a storm blew up again and the same thing happened to us as before; then eventually the wind became favourable and we saw the mountains on the mainland.

We made for a harbour called Karsh,[39] intending to put in there, but some persons who were on the mountain made signs to us not to enter, so, fearing that we might run into danger and thinking that there were galleys of the enemy in the port, we turned back along the coast. As we approached the land, I said to the master of the ship, 'I wish to descend here,' so he put me ashore. I saw a church so we made towards it. In it I found a monk, and on one of the walls of the church

I saw the figure of an Arab man wearing a turban, girt with a sword, and carrying a spear in his hand, and in front of him a lamp, which was alight. I said to the monk, 'What is this figure?' and when he replied, 'This is the figure of the prophet Ali,' I was filled with astonishment. We spent the night in that church, and cooked some fowls, but we could not eat them because they were among the provisions that we had taken with us on the ship, and everything that had been on board was impregnated with the smell of the sea.

This place where we landed was in the wilderness known as Dasht-i Qifjaq (*dasht* in the language of the Turks means 'wilderness').[40] This wilderness is green and grassy, with neither trees nor hills, high or low, nor narrow pass nor firewood. What they use for burning is animal dung (which they call *tazak*), and you can see even their men of rank gathering it up and putting it in the skirts of their robes. There is no means of travelling in this desert except in waggons, and it extends for six months' journey, three of them in the territories of the Sultan Muhammad Uzbak, and three in those of other princes.[41] On the day after our arrival at this roadstead, one of the merchants in our company went to some of the tribesmen known as Qifjaq who inhabit this desert and profess the Christian religion, and hired from them a waggon drawn by horses. We rode in this, and came to the city of al-Kafa, which is a great city along the sea coast inhabited by Christians, most of them Genoese, who have a governor called al-Damdir.[42] We lodged there in the mosque of the Muslims.

Anecdote

When we alighted at this mosque and stayed in it for an hour or so, we heard the sounds of clappers on every side, and never having heard them before I was alarmed at this and bade my companions ascend the minaret and chant the Qur'an and praises to God, and recite the call to prayer. They did so, when suddenly a man came in wearing breastplate and weapons and saluted us. We asked him what was his business, and he told us that he was the qadi of the Muslims there, and said, 'When I heard the chanting and the call to prayer, I feared for your safety and came as you see.' Then he went away, but no evil befell us.

On the following day the governor came to visit us and prepared a banquet, which we ate in his residence. We made a circuit of the city and found it provided with fine bazaars, but all the inhabitants are infidels. We went down to its port, where we saw a wonderful harbour with about two hundred vessels in it, both ships of war and trading vessels, small and large, for it is one of the world's celebrated ports.

We then hired a waggon and travelled to the city of al-Qiram,[43] a large and fine city in the territories of the illustrious Sultan Muhammad Uzbak Khan. There is an amir who governs it on his behalf, named Tuluktumur. We lodged in a hospice, whose shaikh, Zadah al-Khurasani, welcomed us and treated us honourably and generously. This Shaikh Zadah told me that outside this city there was a Christian monk living in a monastery, who devoted himself to ascetic exercises and used frequently to fast, and that he eventually reached the point of being able to fast for forty days at a stretch, after which he would break his fast with a single bean; also that he had the faculty of revealing secret things. He desired me to go with him to visit the man, but I refused, although afterwards I regretted not having seen him and found out the truth of what was said about him.

The Amir Tuluktumur was ill, but we visited him and he received us honourably and made gifts to us. He was on the point of setting out for the city of al-Sara,[44] the capital of the Sultan Muhammad Uzbak, so I planned to travel in his company and bought some waggons for that purpose.

Account of the waggons in which one journeys in this country

They are waggons with four large wheels, some of them drawn by two horses, and some drawn by more than two, and they are drawn also by oxen and camels, according to the weight or lightness of the waggon. The man who services the waggon rides on one of the horses that draw it, which has a saddle on it, and carries in his hand a whip with which he urges them to go and a large stick by which he brings them back to the right direction when they turn aside from it. There is placed upon the waggon a kind of cupola made of wooden laths tied together with thin strips of hide; this is light to carry, and covered with felt or blanket-cloth, and in it there are grilled windows. The person who is inside the tent can see other persons without their seeing him, and he can employ himself in it as he likes, sleeping or eating or reading or writing, while he is still journeying. Those of the waggons that carry the baggage, the provisions and the chests of eatables are covered with a sort of tent much as we have described, with a lock on it. When I decided to make the journey, I prepared for my own conveyance a waggon covered with felt, taking with me in it a slave girl of mine, another small waggon for my associate Afif al-Din al-Tuzari, and for the rest of my companions a large waggon drawn by three camels, one of which was ridden by the conductor of the waggon.

We set out in company with the Amir Tuluktumur, his brother Isa, and his two sons Qutludumur and Sarubak. The habit of the Turks is to organize the journey through this desert in the same way as that of the pilgrims to Mecca. They set out after the dawn prayer and halt in the mid-forenoon, then set out again after noon and halt in the evening. When they halt they loose the horses, camels and oxen from the waggons and drive them out to pasture at liberty, night and day. Their animals pasture without keepers or guards; this is due to the severity of their laws against theft. Their law in this matter is that any person found in possession of a stolen horse is obliged to restore it to its owner and to give him along with it nine like it; if he cannot do that, his sons are taken instead, and if he has no sons he is slaughtered just as a sheep is slaughtered.

These Turks do not eat bread nor any solid food, but they prepare a dish made from a thing in their country like millet, which they call *dugi*. They put water over a fire; when it boils they pour into it some of this *dugi*, and if they have any meat they cut it in small pieces and cook it along with the *dugi*. Then every man is given his portion in a dish, and they pour over it curdled milk and sup it. Sometimes they sup with it mares' milk, which they call *qumizz*.[45] They are powerful and hardy men, with good constitutions. They have also a fermented drink which they make from the grain of the *dugi* mentioned above. They regard the eating of sweetmeats as a disgrace. To give an instance of this I went one day to the audience of the Sultan Uzbak during the month of Ramadan. There was served horseflesh (this is the meat that they most often eat) and sheep's flesh, and *rishta*, which is a kind of macaroni cooked and supped with milk. I brought for him that night a plate of sweetmeats made by one of my companions, and when I presented them before him he touched them with his finger and put it to his mouth, and that was all he did. The Amir Tuluktumur told me of one of the high-ranking mamluks of this sultan, who had between sons and sons' sons about forty descendants, that the sultan said to him one day, 'Eat sweetmeats, and I free you all,' but he refused, saying, 'If you were to kill me I would not eat them.'

From al-Qiram we travelled for twenty-one days to Azaq, then continued on our way to the city of al-Machar, a large town, one of the finest of the cities of the Turks, on a great river, and possessed of gardens and fruits in abundance.[46] In the *qaisariyah* of this city I saw a Jew who saluted me and spoke to me in Arabic. I asked him what country he came from and he told me that he was from the land of al-Andalus and had come from it over land, without travelling by sea, but by way of Constantinople the Great, the land of al-Rum and the land of the Jarkas, and stated that it was four months since he had left al-Andalus.[47] The travelling merchants who have experience of this matter assured me of the truth of his statement.

I witnessed in this country a remarkable thing, namely the respect in which women are held by them, indeed they are higher in dignity than the men. As for the wives of the amirs, the first occasion on which I saw them was when, on my departure from al-Qiram, I saw the khatun, the wife of the Amir Saltiyah, in a waggon of hers. The entire waggon was covered with rich blue woollen cloth, the windows and doors of the tent were open, and there were in attendance on her four girls of excelling beauty and exquisitely dressed. Behind her were a number of waggons in which were girls belonging to her suite. When she came near the encampment of the amir, she descended from the waggon to the ground and with her alighted about thirty of the girls to carry her train. Her robes were furnished with loops of which each girl would take one, and altogether they would lift the skirts clear of the ground on every side. She walked thus in a stately manner until she reached the amir, when he rose before her, saluted her, and sat her beside him, while her maidens stood around her. Skins of *qumizz* were brought and she, having poured some of it into a bowl, went down on her knees before the amir and handed the bowl to him. After he had drunk, she poured out for his brother, and the amir poured out for her. The food was then served and she ate with him, he gave her a robe and she withdrew. Such is the style of the wives of the amirs, and we shall mention that of the wives of the king later on. As for the wives of the traders and the commonalty, I have seen them, when one of them would be in a waggon, being drawn by horses, and in attendance on her three or four girls to carry her train, wearing on her head a *bughtaq*, which is a conical headdress decorated with precious stones and surmounted by peacock feathers. The windows of the tent would be open and her face would be visible, for the womenfolk of the Turks do not veil themselves. One such woman will come to the bazaar in this style, accompanied by her male slaves with sheep and milk, and will sell them for spice-wares. Sometimes one of the women will be in the company of her husband and anyone seeing him would take him to be one of her servants; he wears no garments other than a sheepskin cloak and on his head a high cap to match it, which they call a *kulah*.

We made preparations to travel from the city of al-Machar to the sultan's camp, which was four days' march from al-Machar at a place called Bish Dagh.[48] *Bish* in their language means 'five' and *dagh* means 'mountain'. In these Five Mountains there is a hot spring in which the Turks bathe, and they claim that anyone who bathes in it will not be attacked by disease. We set out for the site of the *mahallah* and reached it on the first day of Ramadan,[49] but found that the *mahallah* had left, so we returned to the place from which we started, because the *mahallah* was encamping in its vicinity. I set up my tent on a low hill thereabouts, fixed my flag in front of the tent, and drew up my horses and waggons behind. Then the *mahallah* came up – they call it the *urdu*[50] – and we saw a vast city on the move with its inhabitants, with mosques and bazaars in it, the smoke of the kitchens rising in the air (for they cook while on the march), and horse-drawn waggons transporting the people. On reaching the camping place they took down the tents from the waggons and set them on the ground, for they are light to carry, and so likewise they did with the mosques and shops.

Account of the exalted Sultan Muhammad Uzbak Khan

His name is Muhammad Uzbak, and khan in their language means 'sultan'. This sultan is mighty in sovereignty, exceedingly powerful, great in dignity, lofty in station, victor over the enemies of God, the people of Constantinople the Great, and diligent in the jihad against them. His territories are vast and his cities great; they include al-Kafa, al-Qiram, al-Machar, Azaq, Surdaq and Khwarizm,[51] and his capital is al-Sara. He is one of the seven kings who are the great and mighty kings of the world.

He observes, in his public sittings, his journeys, and his affairs in general, a marvellous and magnificent ceremonial. It is his custom to sit every Friday, after the prayers, in a pavilion, magnificently decorated, called the Gold Pavilion. It is constructed of wooden rods covered with plaques of gold, and in the centre of it is a wooden couch covered with plaques of silver gilt, its legs being of pure silver and their bases encrusted with precious stones. The sultan sits on the throne, having on his right hand the Khatun Taitughli and next to her the Khatun Kabak, and on his left the Khatun Bayalun and next to her the Khatun Urduja. As for Taitughli, who is the queen and the one of them most favoured by him, he advances to the entrance of the pavilion to meet her, salutes her, takes her by the hand, and only after she has mounted to the couch and taken her seat does the sultan himself sit down. All this is done in full view of those present, without any use of veils. The people hold Taitughli in great honour because of his honouring her; otherwise, she is the most close-fisted of the khatuns. I was told for a fact by one in whom I have confidence, a person well acquainted with matters relating to this queen, that the sultan is enamoured of her because of a peculiar property in her, namely that he finds her every night just like a virgin. Another person related to me that she is of the lineage of that queen on whose account, it is said, the kingdom was withdrawn from Solomon (on whom be peace), and whom, when his kingdom was restored to him, he commanded to be placed in an uninhabited desert, so she was deposited in the desert of Qifjaq.[52] He related also that the vagina of this khatun has a conformation like a ring, and likewise all of those who are descendants of the woman mentioned. I never met, whether in the desert of Qifjaq or elsewhere, any person who said that he had seen a woman formed in this way, or heard tell of one other than this khatun – except, however, that one of the inhabitants of China told me that in China there is a class of women with this conformation. But nothing like that ever came into my hands nor have I learned what truth there is in it.

On the day after my meeting with the sultan, I visited this khatun. She was sitting in the midst of ten elderly women, who seemed to be attendants waiting on her, and in front of her were about fifty young slave girls, whom the Turks call 'girls' and before whom there were gold and silver salvers filled with cherries which they were cleaning. In front of the khatun also there was a golden tray filled with cherries, and she was cleaning them. We saluted her, and among my companions there was a Qur'an reader who recited the Qur'an according to the method of the Egyptians, in a pleasing manner and agreeable voice, and he gave a recitation. She then ordered *qumizz* to be served, and it was brought in light and elegant wooden bowls, whereupon she took a bowl in her hand and offered it to me. This is the highest of honours in their estimation. I had never drunk *qumizz* before, but there was nothing for me to do but to accept it. I tasted it and finding it disagreeable passed it on to one of my companions. She asked me many questions concerning our journey, and after answering her we withdrew. We went to visit her first because of the great position she has with the king.

I paid my respects to the other three khatuns, among them Bayalun, the daughter of the king of Constantinople the Great, the Sultan Takfur.[53] When we visited this khatun, she was sitting on an inlaid couch with silver legs; before her were about a hundred slave girls, Greek, Turkish and Nubian, some standing and some sitting, and pages were standing behind her and chamberlains in front of her, men of the Greeks. She asked about us and our journey hither and the distance of our native lands, and she wept in pity and compassion and wiped her face with a handkerchief that lay before her. She then called for food, which was brought, and we ate before her, while she looked on at us. When we made to withdraw, she said, 'Do not stay away from us, but come to us and inform us of your needs.' She showed herself to be of a generous nature, and sent after us food, a great quantity of bread, ghee, sheep, money, a fine robe, three horses of good breed and ten of ordinary stock. It was with this khatun that my journey to Constantinople the Great was made, as we shall relate below.

Account of my journey to the city of Bulghar[54]

I had heard of the city of Bulghar and desired to go to it, to see for myself what they tell of the extreme shortness of the night there, and the shortness of the day, too, in the opposite season. Between it and the sultan's camp was a ten nights' journey, so I requested him to furnish me with a guide to it, and he sent with me a man who escorted me there and brought me back again. I reached it during the month of Ramadan, and when we had prayed the sunset prayer we broke our fast; the call to the night prayer was made during our eating of this meal, and by the time that we had prayed the dawn broke. So too the daytime becomes as short there in the season of its brevity. I stayed there three days.

Account of the Land of Darkness

I had intended to enter the Land of Darkness, which is reached from Bulghar after a journey of forty days. But I renounced this project in view of the immense effort and expense that it required and the small profit to be got from it. The journey to it can be made only in small waggons drawn by large dogs, for in that desert there is ice, so that neither the foot of man nor the hoof of beast has a firm hold on it, whereas the dogs have claws and so their feet remain firm on the ice. No one can go into this desert except merchants with great resources, each of whom will have a hundred waggons or thereabouts loaded with his food, drink and firewood, for there are no trees in it, nor stones, nor habitations. The guide in that land is the dog that had already made the journey in it many times, and its price is as high as a thousand dinars or so. The waggon is fastened to its neck, and three other dogs are yoked with it; it is the leader and all the other dogs follow it with the waggons and stop when it stops. This dog is never beaten nor berated by its owner, who, when food is prepared, feeds the dogs first before the humans, otherwise the dog is angered and escapes, leaving its owner to perish. When the travellers have completed forty stages in this desert they alight at the Darkness. Each one of them leaves thereabouts the goods that he has brought and they return to their usual camping-ground. Next day they go back to seek their goods, and they find alongside them skins of sable, miniver, and ermine. If the owner of the goods is satisfied with what he has found alongside his goods he takes it, but if it does not satisfy him he leaves it, and then they add more skins, and sometimes they (I mean the people of the Darkness) take away their goods and leave those of the merchant. This is their method of selling and buying, and those who go to those parts do not know who it is who do this trading with them, whether they are of the jinn or of men, for they never see anyone.

I returned from the city of Bulghar with the amir whom the sultan had sent to accompany me, and found the sultan's *mahallah* by the place known as Bish Dagh on the twenty-eighth of Ramadan. I attended in his company the festival prayers, and the day of the festival happened to be a Friday.[55] The sultan was late in coming, and some said that he would not come because drunkenness had got the better of him, and others said that he would not fail to attend the Friday service. When it was well past the time he arrived, swaying, and greeted the sayyid sharif, smiled at him, and kept addressing him as Ata, which means 'father' in the Turkish language. We then prayed the Friday prayers and the people withdrew to their residences.

After this, when the festival had ended, we set out in company with the sultan and the *mahallah* and came to the city of al-Hajj Tarkhan, one of the finest of cities, with great bazaars, built on the river Itil, which is one of the great rivers of the world.[56] It is there that the sultan resides until the cold grows severe and this river freezes over, as well as the waters connected with it. The sultan gives orders to the people of that land, and they bring thousands of loads of straw, which they spread over the ice congealed upon the river. The inhabitants travel in waggons over this river and the adjacent waters for a space of three days' journey, and sometimes caravans cross over it at the end of the winter season and perish by drowning.

When we reached the city of al-Hajj Tarkhan, the Khatun Bayalun, the daughter of the king of the Greeks, begged of the sultan to permit her to visit her father, that she might give birth to her child at the latter's residence, and then return to him. When he gave her permission I too begged of him to allow me to go in her company to see Constantinople the Great for myself. He forbade me, out of fear for my safety, but I solicited him tactfully and said to him, 'It is under your protection and patronage that I shall visit it, so I shall have nothing to fear from anyone.' He then gave me permission, and when we took leave of him he presented me with 1500 dinars, a robe, and a large number of horses, and each of the khatuns gave me ingots of silver. The sultan's daughter gave me more than they did, along with a robe and a horse, and altogether I had a large collection of horses, robes, and furs of miniver and sable.

Account of my journey to Constantinople

We set out on the tenth of Shawwal[57] in the company of the Khatun Bayalun and under her protection. The sultan came out to escort her for one stage, then returned, he and the queen and his heir designate; the other khatuns travelled in her company for a second stage and then they returned. The Amir Baidarah, with five thousand of his troops, travelled along with her, and the khatun's own troops numbered about five hundred, some two hundred of whom were slaves and Greeks in attendance on her, and the remainder Turks. She had with her about two hundred slave girls, most of them Greeks, and about four hundred waggons with about two thousand horses to draw them and for riding, as well as some three hundred oxen and two hundred camels to draw them. She also had ten Greek pages with her, and the same number of Indian pages, whose leader in chief was named Sumbul the Indian; the leader of the Greeks was named Mikha'il (the Turks used to call him Lu'lu), and was a man of great bravery. She left most of her slave girls and of her baggage in the sultan's *mahallah*, since she had set out with the intention only of paying a visit and of giving birth to her child.

We made for the city of Ukak,[58] a city of middling size, with fine buildings and abundant commodities, and extremely cold. Between it and al-Sara, the sultan's capital, it is ten nights' march, and one day's march from this city are the mountains of the Rus, who are Christians; they have red hair, blue eyes, and ugly faces, and are treacherous folk.

After travelling for fifty-two days, first to the town of Baba Saltuq and then across an uninhabited waste, we came to the fortress of Mahtuli, at the beginning of the territory of the Greeks.[59] The Greeks had been informed of the journey of this khatun to their land, and there came to join her at this castle the Greek Kifali Niqulah, with a great body of troops and a large hospitality gift, as well as the khatuns and nurses from the palace of her father, the king of Constantinople. Here the Amir Baidarah turned back with his troops, and none but her own people travelled on with the khatun. She left her mosque behind at this castle and the prescription of the call to prayer was discontinued. Wines were brought to her as part of her hospitality gift, and she would drink them, and not only so but even swine, and one of her personal attendants told me that she ate them. No one was left with her who observed the Muslim prayers except a certain Turk, who used to pray with us. Inner sentiments concealed hitherto suffered a change through our entry into the land of infidelity, but the khatun charged the Amir Kifali to treat me honourably, and on one occasion he beat one of his mamluks when he laughed at our prayer.

For three weeks we travelled through the territory of the Greeks. Finally we camped at a distance of ten miles from Constantinople, and on the following day its population, men, women and children, came out riding or on foot in their finest array and richest apparel. At dawn the drums, trumpets and fifes were sounded, the troops mounted, and the sultan and his wife, the mother of this khatun, came out with the officers of state and the courtiers. Over the king's head there was a canopy, carried by a number of horsemen and men on foot, who held in their hands long staves, each surmounted by something like a ball of leather with which they hoisted the canopy. In the middle of the canopy was a sort of pavilion supported by horsemen with staves. When the sultan drew near, the troops became entangled with one another and there was much dust. I was unable to make my way in among them, so I kept with the khatun's baggage and party, fearing for my life. I was told, however, that when the khatun approached her parents, she dismounted and kissed the ground before them, and then kissed the two hoofs of their horses, and the principal men of her suite did the same.

Our entry into Constantinople the Great was made about noon or a little later, and they beat their church gongs until the very skies shook with the mingling of their sounds. When we reached the first of the gates of the king's palace we found it guarded by about a hundred men, who had an officer of theirs with them on top of a platform, and I heard them saying *Sarakinu, Sarakinu*, which means 'Muslims'.[60] They would not let us enter, and when the members of the khatun's party told them that we had come in her suite they answered, 'They cannot enter except by permission,' so we stayed by the gate. One of the khatun's party sent a messenger to tell her of this while she was still with her father. She told him about us, whereupon he gave orders to admit us and assigned us a house near the residence of the khatun. He wrote also on our behalf an order that we should not be molested wheresoever we might go in the city, and this order was proclaimed in the bazaars. We remained indoors for three nights, during which hospitality gifts were sent to us of flour, bread, sheep, fowls, ghee, fruit, fish, money and rugs, and on the fourth day we had audience of the sultan.

Account of the sultan of Constantinople

His name is Takfur, son of the Sultan Jirjis.[61] His father the Sultan Jirjis was still in the bond of life, but had renounced the world and had become a monk, devoting himself to religious exercises in the churches, and had resigned the kingship to his son. We shall speak of him later. On the fourth day from our arrival at Constantinople, the khatun sent her page Sumbul the Indian to me, and he took my hand and led me into the palace. We passed through four gateways, each of which had porticoes in which were footsoldiers with their weapons, their officer being on a carpeted platform. When we reached the fifth gateway the page Sumbul left me, and going inside returned with four Greek pages, who searched me to see that I had no knife on my person. The officer said to me, 'This is a custom of theirs; every person who enters the king's presence, be he noble or commoner, foreigner or native, must be searched.' The same practice is observed in the land of India.

Then, after they had searched me, the man in charge of the gate rose, took me by the hand, and opened the door. Four of the men surrounded me, two holding my sleeves and two behind me, and brought me into a large audience hall, whose walls were of mosaic work, in which were pictured figures of creatures, both animate and inanimate. In the centre of it was a water channel with trees on either side of it, and men were standing to right and left, silent, not one of them speaking. In the midst of the hall there were three men standing, to whom those four men delivered me. These took hold of my garments as the others had done and so on a signal from another man led me forward. One of them was a Jew and he said to me in Arabic, 'Don't be afraid, for this is their custom that they use with every visitor. I am the interpreter and I am originally from Syria.' So I asked him how I should salute, and he told me to say *al-salamu alaikum*.

I came then to a great pavilion; the sultan was there on his throne, with his wife, the mother of this khatun, before him, and at the foot of the throne were the khatun and her brothers. To the right of him were six men, to his left four, and behind him four, every one of them armed. He signed to me, before I had saluted and reached him, to sit down for a moment, so that my apprehension might be calmed, and I did so. Then I approached him and saluted him, and he signed to me to sit down, but I did not do so. He questioned me about Jerusalem, the Sacred Rock, the Church called al-Qumamah,[62] the cradle of Jesus, and Bethlehem, and about the city of al-Khalil (peace be upon him) [Hebron], then about Damascus, Cairo, al-Iraq and the land of al-Rum, and I answered him on all of his questions, the Jew interpreting between us. He was pleased with my replies and said to his sons, 'Honour this man and ensure his safety.' He then bestowed on me a robe of honour and ordered for me a horse with saddle and bridle, and a parasol of the kind that the king has carried above his head, that being a sign of protection. I asked him to designate someone to ride about the city with me every day, that I might see its wonders and curious sights and tell of them in my own country, and he designated such a guide for me.

Account of the city

It is enormous in magnitude and divided into two parts, between which there is a great river, in which there is a flow and ebb of tide. The name of this river is Absumi.[63] One of the two parts of the city is called Astanbul; it is on the eastern bank of the river, and includes the places of residence of the sultan, his officers of state, and the rest of the population. As for the other section of it, it is called al-Ghalatah, and lies on the western bank of the river, somewhat like Ribat al-Fath in its proximity to the river. This section is reserved for the Christians of the Franks dwelling there. They are of different kinds including Genoese, Venetians, men of Rome and people of France. They are required to pay a tax every year to the king of Constantinople, but they often rebel against his authority and then he makes war on them until the Pope restores peace between them. They are all men of commerce, and their port is one of the greatest of ports; I saw in it about a hundred galleys, such as merchant vessels and other large ships, and as for the small ships they were too numerous to be counted. The bazaars in this section are good, but overlaid with all kinds of filth, and traversed by a small, dirty and filth-laden stream. Their churches too are dirty and mean.

Account of the great church

I can describe only its exterior; as for its interior I did not see it. It is called in their language *Aya Sufiya*, and is one of the greatest churches of the Greeks; around it is a wall which encircles it so that it looks like a city in itself. Its gates are thirteen in number, and it has a sacred enclosure, which is about a mile long and closed by a great gate. No one is prevented from entering the enclosure, and in fact I went into it with the king's father, who will be mentioned later; it is like an audience hall, paved with marble and traversed by a water channel which issues from the church. At the door of the church there are porticoes where the attendants sit who sweep its paths, light its lamps and close its doors. They allow no person to enter it until he prostrates himself to the huge cross at their place, which they claim to be a relic of the wood on which the double of Jesus (on whom be peace) was crucified.[64] This is over the door of the church, set in a golden frame about ten cubits in height, across which they have placed a similar golden frame so that it forms a cross. This door is covered with plaques of silver and gold, and its two rings are of pure gold. I was told that the number of monks and priests in this church runs into thousands, and that some of them are descendants of the Apostles, also that inside it is another church exclusively for women, containing more than a thousand virgins consecrated to religious devotions, and a still greater number of aged and widowed women.

Account of the monasteries in Constantinople

A *manistar* is among them what a *zawiyah* is among Muslims. There are a great many of such monasteries in the city; they display great magnificence in building them, constructing them of marble and mosaic work. I went into a monastery with the Greek whom the king had designated to accompany me on my rides. It was traversed by a stream, and in it was a church containing about five hundred virgins wearing cilices, and with their heads shaved and covered with felt bonnets. They were of exceeding beauty and showed the traces of their austerities. A boy was sitting on a pulpit reading the gospel to them in the most beautiful voice that I have ever heard; round him were eight other boys on pulpits accompanied by their priest, and when this boy finished another boy began. The Greek said to me, 'These girls are kings' daughters who have given themselves to the service of this church, and the boys who are reading also are kings' sons.' In his company I entered churches in which were virgin daughters of the principal men of the city, and churches in which were aged and elderly women, and churches where there were monks, numbering a hundred men or more or less in each church. Most of the inhabitants of this city are monks, devotees, and priests, and its churches are numerous beyond computation. The men of the city, both soldiers and others, small and great, carry over their heads huge parasols, both in winter and summer, and the women wear voluminous turbans.

Account of the King Jirjis, who became a monk[65]

This king invested his son with the kingdom, consecrated himself to the service of God, and built a monastery (as we have related) outside the city, on the bank of its river. I was out one day with the Greek appointed to ride with me when we chanced to meet this king, walking on foot, wearing hair-cloth garments, and with a felt bonnet on his head. He had a long white beard and a fine face, which bore traces of his austerities; before and behind him was a body of monks, and he had a pastoral staff in his hand and a rosary on his neck. When the Greek saw him he dismounted and said to me, 'Dismount, for this is the king's father.' When the Greek saluted him the king asked about me, then stopped and said to the Greek (who knew the Arabic tongue), 'Say to this Saracen (meaning Muslim), "I clasp the hand that has entered Jerusalem and the foot that has walked within the Dome of the Rock and the great church called Qumamah, and Bethlehem",' and so saying he put his hand upon my feet and passed it over his face. I was amazed at their belief in the merits of one who, though not of their religion, had entered these places. He then took me by the hand and as I walked with him asked me about Jerusalem and the Christians living there, and questioned me at length. I entered with him into the enclosure of the church which we have described. When he approached the great door, there came out a number of priests and monks to salute him, for he is one of their great men in the monastic life, and when he saw them he let go my hand. I said to him,

'I should like to go into the church with you,' but he said to the inter-preter, 'Tell him that every one who enters it must needs prostrate himself before the great cross, for this is a rule laid down by the ancients and it cannot be contravened.' So I left him and he entered alone and I did not see him again.

Account of my departure from Constantinople

When it became clear to the Turks who were in the khatun's company that she professed her father's religion and wished to remain with him, they asked her permission to return to their own country. She gave them permission and made them rich presents, and sent with them to escort them to their country an amir with five hundred horsemen. She sent for me and gave me three hundred dinars in their gold coinage (they call this *al-barbarah*, and it is not good money),[66] two thousand Venetian dirhams, a length of woollen cloth of the work of the girls (this is the best kind of such cloth), ten robes of silk, linen, and wool, and two horses, this being the gift of her father. I bade her farewell and left, having spent one month and six days in their city.[67]

We arrived at length at the frontier of their territory, where we had left our associates and our waggons. We then rode in the waggons and entered the desert. This was in the depth of winter, and I used to put on three fur coats and two pairs of trousers, one of them quilted, and on my feet I had woollen boots, with a pair of boots quilted with linen cloth on top of them, and on top of these again a pair of boots of horseskin lined with bearskin. I used to perform my ablutions with hot water close to the fire, but not a drop of water fell without being frozen on the instant. When I washed my face, the water would run down my beard and freeze, then I would shake it and there would fall from it a kind of snow. The moisture that dripped from the nose would freeze on the moustache. I was unable to mount a horse because of the quantity of clothes I had on, so that my associates had to help me into the saddle.

After this I arrived at the city of al-Hajj Tarkhan, where we had parted from the Sultan Uzbak. We found that he had moved and had settled at the capital of his kingdom, so we travelled to it for three nights on the river Itil [Volga] and its joining waters, which were frozen over. Whenever we needed water we used to cut out pieces of ice, put the ice in a cauldron until it turned into water, and then use this for drinking and cooking. On the fourth day we reached the city of al-Sara, which is the capital of the Sultan Uzbak. We had an audience of the sultan; he asked us how our journey had gone and about the king of the Greeks and his city, and after we had answered him he gave orders for our lodging and for the issue to us of what was needed for our maintenance.

The city of al-Sara is one of the finest of cities, of boundless size, situated in a plain, choked with the throng of its inhabitants, and possessing good bazaars and broad streets. We rode out one day with one of its principal men, intending to make a circuit of the city and find out its extent. Our lodging place was at one end of it and we set out from it in the early morning, and it was after midday when we reached the other end. There are various groups of people among its inhabitants; these include the Mughals, who are the dwellers in this country and its sultans, and some of whom are Muslims, then the As,[68] who are Muslims, the Qifjaq, the Jarkas, the Rus, and the Rum – all of these are Christians. Each group lives in a separate quarter with its own bazaars. Merchants and strangers from the two Iraqs, Egypt, Syria and elsewhere, live in a quarter which is surrounded by a wall for the protection of the properties of the merchants. The sultan's palace in it is called Altun Tash, *altun* meaning 'gold', and *tash* 'head'.[69]

After making the acquaintance of some of the pious and learned Muslims in this place, I set out for Khwarizm.[70] Between Khwarizm and the capital city of al-Sara is a desert of forty days' march, in the latter stages of which horses cannot travel owing to lack of fodder, and only camels are employed to draw the waggons.

7 Turkestan and Afghanistan

After ten days' journey from al-Sara we reached the city of Sarachuq (*chuq* meaning 'little', so that it is as if they said 'little Sara'), which lies on the bank of a great and swollen river called Ulusu, meaning 'the great stream'.[1] At this city we reached the limit of the journey with the horses that draw the waggons. We sold them at the rate of four silver dinars per head, and even less, on account of their exhaustion and the cheapness of horses in this town, and hired camels to draw the waggons.

From this place we went on for thirty days by forced marches, halting only for two hours each day, one in the forenoon and the other at sunset. The length of the halt was just as long as the time needed to cook and sup *dugi*, and this is cooked with a single boiling. They would have with them pieces of dried meat, which they put on top of this and they pour sour milk over the whole. Everybody eats and sleeps in his waggon while it is actually on the move, and I had in my waggon three slave girls. It is the custom of travellers in this wilderness to use the utmost speed, because of the scarcity of herbage. Of the camels that cross it the majority perish and the remainder are of no use except a year later, after they are fattened up. The water in this desert is at certain known waterpoints, separated by two or three days' march, and is rainwater in surface pools and shallow wells under the sand.

After journeying through this desert we arrived at Khwarizm, which is the largest, greatest, most beautiful and most important city of the Turks. It has fine bazaars and broad streets, a great number of buildings and abundance of commodities; it shakes under the weight of its population, by reason of their multitude, and is agitated by them in a manner resembling the waves of the sea. I rode out one day on horseback and went into the bazaar, but when I got halfway through it and reached the densest pressure of the crowd, I could not advance any further because of the multitude of the press, and when I tried to go back I was unable to do that either, because of the crowd of people. So I remained as I was, in perplexity, and only with great exertions did I manage to return.

This city is in the dominions of the Sultan Uzbak, who is represented in it by a great amir called Qutludumur. Never have I seen in all the lands of the world men more excellent in conduct than the Khwarizmians, more generous in soul, or more friendly to strangers. They have a praise-worthy custom in regard to the observance of prayer services which I have not seen elsewhere, namely that each of the muezzins in their mosques goes round the houses of those persons neighbouring his mosque, giving them notice of the approaching hour of prayer. Any person who absents himself from the communal prayers is beaten by the imam who leads the prayers in the presence of the congregation, and in every mosque there is a whip hung up for this purpose. He is also fined five dinars, which go towards the expenses of upkeep of the mosque, or of supplying food to the poor and the destitute.

Outside Khwarizm is the river Jaihun, one of the four rivers which flow from Paradise.[2] It freezes over in the cold season in the same way as the river Itil freezes over, and people walk upon it. It remains frozen for the space of five months, and often they walk over it when it is beginning to melt and perish in consequence.

During my stay in Khwarizm I used to attend the Friday prayers in company with the Qadi Abu Hafs Omar in his own mosque, and on the conclusion of the service I went with him to his house, which is close to the mosque. I would then go with him into his reception hall, a most magnificent chamber, furnished with rich carpets, its walls hung with cloth, and a large number of arcaded niches in it, with vessels of silver gilt and Iraqi glass in every niche. Such is the custom followed by the people of this country in the adornment of their houses. He would then produce a copious meal, being a man amply endowed with great wealth and landed property.

The amir of Khwarizm

He is the great Amir Qutludumur, and the meaning of his name is 'Blessed Iron', because *qutlu* is in Turkish 'blessed' and *dumur* is 'iron'.

This amir is the son of the maternal aunt of the exalted Sultan Muhammad Uzbak and the greatest of his amirs. I rode with the qadi to visit him. On reaching his residence we entered a large audience-hall, most of the partitions of which were of wood, and went into a small hall; this had a wooden cupola with ornamental embellishments, its walls hung with coloured woollen cloths and its ceiling with gold-embroidered silk. The amir was sitting on a silk carpet spread for him, and had a cover over his legs on account of the gout with which they were affected, this being a malady very common among the Turks. I saluted him and he bade me sit beside him. He questioned me about his sultan, the King Muhammad Uzbak, and about the Khatun Bayalun, and her father and the city of Constantinople. After I had replied to him on all these subjects, tables were brought in with food of different kinds, roasted fowls, cranes, young pigeons, bread baked with butter, which they call *kulija*, biscuits and sweetmeats. After these were brought other tables with fruit, seeded pomegranates in gold and silver vessels with gold spoons, and some in vessels of Iraqi glass with wooden spoons, grapes and wonderful melons.

Turabak, the governor's wife, also gave a banquet in my honour, for which she assembled the doctors of the law and the principal citizens. This was held in the hospice built by her, where food is supplied to all wayfarers from her benefaction. She sent a furred robe of sable and an excellent horse. She is one of the most virtuous, pious, and generous of women – God reward her with good.

Anecdote

When I left the banquet which this khatun had given for me, and went out of the hospice, I found myself face to face with a woman in the gateway. She was wearing soiled garments, had a veil over her head, and was accompanied by several women – I do not know how many. She gave me the word of salutation, and I returned it, but did not stop with her nor give her any attention. Then when I had gone out, a certain person overtook me and said to me, 'The woman that saluted you is the khatun.' I was covered with confusion on hearing this, and tried to go back to her, but I found that she had departed. So I sent my salutations to her through one of her attendants, together with my apologies for my action, the result of my having no acquaintance with her.

Account of the melons of Khwarizm

The melons of Khwarizm have no equal in any country of the world, East or West, except it may be the melons of Bukhara, and next to them the melons of Isfahan. Their rind is green, and the flesh is red, of extreme sweetness and firm texture. A remarkable thing is that they are cut into strips, dried in the sun, and packed in reed baskets, as is done in our country with dried figs and Malaga figs. They are exported from Khwarizm to the remotest parts of India and China, and of all the dried fruits there are none which excel them in sweetness. During my stay at Dihli in India, whenever a party of travellers arrived, I used to send someone to buy sliced melon for me from them. The king of India, too, when any of it was brought to him, used to send it to me, knowing as he did my fondness for it. It was his way to give pleasure to the foreigners by sending to them the fruit of their own countries, and he used to give special attention to learning their desires and supplying them accordingly.

When I prepared to leave Khwarizm I hired camels and bought a double litter, the second side of which was occupied by Afif al-Din al-Tuzari.[3] The servants rode some of the horses and we put horse-cloths on the rest because of the cold. In this wise we began our journey through the wilderness which lies between Khwarizm and Bukhara, eighteen days' march in sands with no permanent settlement in them save one small township.

After travelling for four days we came to the city of al-Kat, the only settled place on this road, small and pretty. We encamped outside it, by a lake which was frozen over because of the cold, and the boys were playing on it and sliding over it. We then continued our journey for six nights without water, at the end of which we reached the town of Wabkanah, one day's journey from Bukhara. It is a pretty town, with streams and fruit gardens. Its inhabitants preserve grapes from year to year, and they have there a fruit which they call *allu*.[4] They dry it, and people carry the dried fruit to India and China. One steeps it in water and drinks the liquid. In its green state the fruit is sweet, but when dried it acquires a slight acidity, and it has a great deal of pulp.

I have never seen the like of it in al-Andalus, nor in the Maghrib nor in Syria.

Thereafter we travelled for a whole day through contiguous orchards, with streams, trees and habitations, and arrived at the city of Bukhara. This city was formerly the capital of the lands beyond the river Jaihun, but was laid in ruins by the accursed Tankiz, the Tatar, the ancestor of the kings of al-Iraq.[5] So at the present time its mosques, colleges and bazaars are in ruins, all but a few, and its inhabitants are looked down upon and their evidence in legal cases is not accepted in Khwarizm or elsewhere, because of their reputation for factionalism, and making false claims, and denial of the truth. There is not one person in it today who possesses any religious learning or who shows any concern for acquiring it.

I visited at Bukhara the tomb of the learned Imam Abu Abdallah al-Bukhari, compiler of *al-Jami al-Sahih*, the shaikh of the Muslims (God be pleased with him), and over it is inscribed: 'This is the grave of Muhammad b. Isma'il al-Bukhari, who composed such-and-such books.'[6] In the same manner, the tombs of the learned men of Bukhara are inscribed with their names and the titles of their writings. I had copied a great many of these, but they were lost along with all that I lost when the Indian infidels robbed me at sea.

We resumed our journey from Bukhara, making for the camp of the pious and exalted Sultan Ala al-Din Tarmashirin, of whom we shall speak presently.[7] We went by way of Nakhshab; it is small and surrounded by gardens and streams. We lodged outside it, in a house that belonged to its governor. I had with me a slave girl, who was close to the time of her delivery, and I had intended to transport her to Samarqand, so that she might have the child there. It happened that she was inside a litter; the litter was put on a camel and our associates set off during the night, taking her with them, as well as the provisions and other effects of mine. For myself, I remained behind, in order to travel in the daytime, along with some of those who were with me, but the first party went by one road, while I went by another. So we arrived at this sultan's camp late in the evening, very hungry, and alighted at some distance from the bazaar. One of our party bought enough food to stave off our hunger, and one of the merchants lent us a tent in which we spent that night. Our companions set off next morning to look for the camels and the rest of the party, found them in the evening, and returned with them.

The sultan was absent from the *mahallah* on a hunting party, so I met his deputy, the amir Taqbugha, who assigned me a camping ground close to his mosque, and gave me a *kharqah* – this is a kind of tent, a description of which we have given previously. I put the slave girl into this *kharqah*, and she gave birth to a child that same night. They told me that it was a male child, although it was not so, but after the ceremony of the *aqiqah*[8] one of my companions informed me that the child was a girl. So I summoned the slave girls and questioned them, and they confirmed the statement. This girl was born under a lucky star, and I experienced everything to give me joy and satisfaction from the time of her birth. She died two months after my arrival in India, as will be related in the sequel.

Account of the sultan of Transoxiana

He is the exalted Sultan Ala al-Din Tarmashirin, a man of great distinction, possessed of numerous troops and regiments of cavalry, a vast kingdom and immense power, and just in his government. His territories lie between four of the great kings of the earth, namely the king of China, the king of India, the king of al-Iraq, and the King Uzbak, all of whom send him gifts and hold him in high respect and honour. When I entered the king's presence, inside his tent, I found him seated on a chair, resembling a mosque pulpit and covered with silk embroidered in gold. The interior of the tent was lined with silken cloth of gold, and a crown set with jewels and precious stones was suspended over the sultan's head at the height of a cubit. The principal amirs were ranged on chairs to right and left of him, and in front of him were the sons of the kings holding fly-whisks in their hands.

Anecdote

The following is an instance of the virtues of this king. One day I attended the afternoon prayer in the mosque. The sultan had not yet come, but one of his pages came in with a prayer rug and spread it in front of the *mihrab*, where it was his custom to pray, saying to the imam, 'Our master desires you to hold back the prayer for him a moment while he performs his ablutions.' The imam rose up and said,

'Is prayer for God or for Tarmashirin?' He then ordered the muezzin to recite the second call for the prayer. The sultan arrived when two bowings had already been completed, and he made the two latter bowings where the ranks ended, that is at the place where people's shoes are left near the door of the mosque. He then performed the bowings that he had missed and went up laughing to the imam to shake his hand, and after sitting down opposite to the mihrab with the shaikh (that is, the imam) beside him, and I alongside the imam, he said to me, 'When you return to your country, tell how a Persian mendicant behaved like this towards the sultan of the Turks.'

When I resolved to proceed on my journey after staying at this sultan's camp for fifty-four days,[9] the sultan gave me seven hundred silver dinars and a sable coat worth a hundred dinars. I had asked him for this on account of the cold weather, and when I mentioned it to him he took hold of my sleeves and kissed his hand after touching them, with his natural humility, generosity and goodness of character. He gave me two horses and two camels also. When I wished to take leave of him, I encountered him in the midst of his way to his hunting ground. The day was a bitterly cold one, and I swear that I could not utter a single word owing to the severity of the cold, but he understood this, and laughed and gave me his hand, and so I departed.

When I took leave of the Sultan Tarmashirin I journeyed to the city of Samarqand, which is one of the greatest and finest of cities, and most perfect of them in beauty. It is built on the bank of the river called Wadi 'l-Qassarin, along which there are *norias* to supply water to the orchards.[10] The population of the town gather there after the afternoon prayer to divert themselves and to promenade. Benches and seats are provided for them to sit on alongside the river, and there are booths in which fruit and other edibles are sold. There were formerly great palaces on its bank, and constructions which bear witness to the lofty aspirations of the townsfolk, but most of this is obliterated, and most of the city itself has also fallen into ruin. It has no city wall, and no gates, and there are gardens inside it. The inhabitants of Samarqand possess generous qualities; they are affectionate towards the stranger and are better than the people of Bukhara.

We set out from Samarqand and came to Tirmidh,[11] a large city with fine buildings and bazaars, traversed by canals, and with many gardens. It abounds in grapes and quinces of exquisite flavour, as well as in flesh-meats and milk of all kinds. Its inhabitants wash their heads in the bath-house with milk instead of fuller's earth; the proprietor of every bath-house has large jars filled with milk, and each man as he enters the establishment takes some of it in a small jug, and then washes his head. It makes the hair fresh and glossy. Similarly, the Indians put oil of sesame on their heads and afterwards wash their hair with fuller's earth. This gives a smoothness to the body and makes the hair glossy and long, and that is the reason why the Indians and those who live among them have long beards.

Next we crossed the river Jaihun, and marched for a day and a half after leaving Tirmidh and crossing the river through uninhabited desert and sands to the city of Balkh.[12] It is completely dilapidated and unin-habited, but anyone seeing it would think it to be inhabited because of the solidity of its construction (for it was a vast and important city), and its mosques and colleges preserve their outward appearance even now, with the inscriptions on their buildings incised with lapis-blue paints.

The accursed Tankiz devastated this city and pulled down about a third of its mosque because of a treasure which he was told lay under one of its columns. It is one of the finest and most spacious mosques in the world; the mosque of Ribat al-Fath in the Maghrib resembles it in the size of its columns, but the mosque of Balkh is more beautiful than it in all other respects.[13]

Anecdote

I was told by a certain historian that the mosque at Balkh was built by a woman whose husband was governor of Balkh for the Abbasid Caliphs, and was called Da'ud b. Ali. It happened that the caliph on one occasion, in a fit of anger against the people of Balkh for some rebellious act on their part, sent an agent to them to exact a crushing indemnity from them. On his arrival at Balkh, the women and the children of the city came to this woman who had built the mosque, i.e. the wife of their governor, and complained of their situation and the suffering which they had to endure because of this indemnity. Thereupon she sent to the amir who had come to levy this tax on them a garment of her own, embroidered with jewels and of a value greater than the indemnity that he had been ordered to collect, with a message to him, saying, 'Take this robe to the caliph, for I give it to him as alms on behalf of the people of Balkh, in view of their poverty.' So he went off with it to the caliph, laid the robe before him, and related the story to him. The caliph was covered with shame and exclaiming, 'Shall the woman be more generous than we?' commanded him to annul the indemnity extracted from the inhabitants of Balkh, and to return there to restore the woman's robe to her. He also remitted one year's taxes to the people of Balkh. When the amir returned to Balkh, he went to the woman's dwelling, related to her what the caliph had said, and gave the robe back to her. Then she said to him, 'Did the caliph's eye light upon this robe?' He said, 'Yes.' She said, 'I shall not wear a robe upon which there has lighted the eye of any man other than those within the forbidden degrees of relationship to me.'[14] She ordered the robe to be sold and built with its price the mosque, the hospice, and a convent for sufi devotees opposite it, the latter built of tufa and still in habitable condition today. After the buildings were completed there remained of the price of the robe as much as one-third, and the story goes that she ordered it to be buried under one of the columns of the mosque, that it might be available and come to light if it should be needed. This tradition was related to Tankiz, who gave orders in consequence to pull down the columns in the mosque. After about a third had been pulled down without finding anything, he left the rest as they were.

I continued my journey from this city to Qundus and Baghlan, which are regions of villages where there are to be found shaikhs and pious men, and with fruit gardens and streams.[15] We encamped at Qundus by a flowing river, where there was a hospice belonging to one of the shaikhs of the poor brethren, an Egyptian who was called Shir Siyah, and that means 'The Black Lion'. We were entertained there by the governor of that land, who was a man from al-Mawsil, living in a large garden thereabouts. We remained on the outskirts of this village for about forty days, in order to pasture the camels and horses. At that place there are excellent pastures and quantities of herbage, and security there is universally established by reason of the severity of the code of law current among them. The people there leave their animals to graze at will, without any herdsman, after each one has branded his animals on their thighs, and so also did we do in this country. It happened that we made a check of our horses after we had camped there for ten nights, and found three of them missing, but after half a month the Tatars brought them to us at our camp, for fear of what might befall them from the application of the laws.

Another reason for our halt was fear of the snow. For upon this road there is a mountain called Hindukush, which means 'the slayer of the Indians', because the slave boys and girls who are brought from the land of India die there in large numbers as a result of the extreme cold and the great quantity of snow. The passage of it extends for a whole day's march. We stayed until the warm weather had definitely set in and crossed this mountain, setting out about the end of the night and travelling on it all day long until sunset. We kept spreading felt cloths in front of the camels for them to tread on, so that they should not sink in the snow. We found on this mountain a spring of warm water, but when we washed our faces with it the skin peeled off and we suffered sorely in consequence.

After crossing the mountain we halted at a place called Banj Hir (*banj* means 'five' and *hir* means 'mountain', so that the name means 'five mountains').[16] There was there in former times a fine and populous city on a great river of blue water, resembling a sea, which comes down from the mountains of Badakhshan (it is in these mountains that there are found the rubies that are called by people *balakhsh*). This land was devastated by Tankiz, the king of the Tatars, and has not recovered its prosperity since.

We came to the mountains of Pashay,[17] where there is the hospice of the saintly Shaikh Ata Awliya. *Ata* means, in Turkish, 'father', and *awliya* is Arabic [meaning 'saints'], so his name means 'Father of the Saints'. He is called also by the name Sisad Salah, *sisad* in Persian meaning 'three hundred', and *salah* meaning 'year', since they state that his age is three hundred and fifty years. We encamped by a river near his hospice and went to visit him, and when I saluted him he embraced me. His skin is fresh and smoother than any that I have seen; anyone seeing him would take him to be fifty years old. He informed me that every hundred years there grew on him new hair and teeth. I asked him whether he had any Traditions of the Prophet to transmit, and he told me a lot of tales. I had some doubts about him, and God knows how much truth there was in what he claimed.

We then journeyed to the city of Ghaznah, the town associated with the sultan and warrior for the Faith Mahmud b. Subuktakin, of famous name.[18] He was one of the greatest of rulers and made frequent incursions into the land of India, where he captured cities and fortresses. His tomb is in this city, with a hospice around it. The greater part of the town is in ruins, with nothing but a fraction of it still standing, although it was formerly a great city. It has an exceedingly cold climate, and the inhabitants move out of it in the cold season to the city of al-Qandahar.[19] This is a large and fertile place, but I did not visit it; it is three nights' journey from Ghaznah. We encamped outside Ghaznah, in a village there on a stream that flows below its citadel. We were honourably received by its governor, Mardak Agha (*mardak* meaning in Persian 'little man' and *agha* meaning 'of great family').

We travelled next to Kabul. This was in former times a great city, and on its site there is now a village inhabited by a tribe of Persians called al-Afghan.[20] They hold mountains and defiles and have power-ful forces at their disposal, and the majority of them are brigands. Their principal mountain is called Kuh Sulaiman. It is related that the Prophet of God Sulaiman (peace be upon him) climbed this mountain and looked out over the land of India, which was then covered with darkness, but returned without entering it, so the mountain was named after him. It is in this mountain that the king of al-Afghan resides.

From there we rode to Karmash, which is a fortress between two mountains, where the Afghan intercept travellers. During our passage on the defile we had an engagement with them. They were on the slope of the mountain, but we shot arrows at them and they fled. Our party was travelling light without baggage-train and had with them about four thousand horses. I had some camels, as a result of which I got separated from the caravan, along with a company, some of them being Afghan. We jettisoned some of our provisions, and abandoned the loads of those camels that were jaded on the way, but next day our horsemen returned to the place and picked them up. We rejoined the caravan after the last evening prayer, and spent the night at the station of Shashnagar, which is the last inhabited place on the confines of the land of the Turks. From there we entered the great desert, which extends for a space of fifteen nights' march; it cannot be entered except in one season of the year, namely after the rains have fallen in the land of Sind and India, which is in the first days of the month of July. There blows in this desert the deadly *samum* wind, which causes bodies to crumble through putrefaction, so that when a man dies his limbs fall apart. We have already mentioned that this wind blows also in the desert between Hurmuz and Shiraz. A large party had preceded us, and they lost by death many camels and horses. Our company arrived safely (praise be to God Most High) at Banj Ab, which is the water of Sind.[21] *Banj* means 'five' and *ab* means 'water', so the whole name means 'the five rivers'. These flow into the main river and irrigate those districts, as we shall mention later, if God will. Our arrival at this river was on the last day of Dhu 'l-Hijjah, and there rose upon us that night the new moon of al-Muharram of the year 734.

8 Sind and North-Western India

Banj Ab is one of the greatest rivers on earth. It rises in flood in the hot season, and the inhabitants of that country sow at the time of its flood, just as the people of Egypt do during the Nile flood. This river is the frontier of the territories of the exalted Sultan Muhammad Shah, king of Hind and Sind.[1]

When we reached this river the officials of the intelligence service came to us and wrote a report about us. From the province of Sind to the sultan's capital, the city of Dihli, it is fifty days' journey, but when the intelligence officers write to the sultan from Sind the letter reaches him in five days by the postal service.

Description of the *Barid* [Postal Service]

The service of couriers on foot has within the space of each mile three relays. The manner of its organization is as follows. At every third of a mile there is an inhabited village, outside which there are three pavilions. In these sit men girded up ready to move off, each of whom has a rod two cubits long with copper bells at the top. When a courier leaves the town he takes the letter in the fingers of one hand and the rod with the bells in the other, and runs with all his might. The men in the pavilions, on hearing the sound of the bells, get ready to meet him and when he reaches them one of them takes the letter in his hand and passes on, running with all his might and shaking his rod until he reaches the next relay, and so they continue until the letter reaches its destination. This post is quicker than the mounted post, and they often use it to transport fruits from Khurasan which are regarded as great luxuries in India; the couriers put them on woven baskets like plates and carry them with great speed to the sultan. In the same way they transport the principal criminals; they place each man on a stretcher and run carrying the stretcher on their heads. Likewise they bring the sultan's drinking water when he resides at Dawlat Abad,[2] carrying it from the river Gang [Ganges], to which the Hindus go on pilgrimage and which is at a distance of forty days' journey from there.

When the intelligence officials write to the sultan informing him of those who arrive in his country, the letter is written with the utmost precision and fulness of description. They report to him that a certain man has arrived of such-and-such appearance and dress, and note the number of his party, slaves and servants and beasts, his behaviour both on the move and at rest, and all his doings, omitting no details relating to all of these. When the newcomer reaches the town of Multan, which is the capital of Sind, he stays there until the sultan's order is received regarding his entry and the degree of hospitality to be extended to him. A man is honoured in that country only according to what may be seen of his actions, conduct, and zeal, since no one there knows anything of his family or parentage. The king of India, the Sultan Abu'l-Mujahid Muhammad Shah, makes a practice of honouring strangers and showing affection to them and singling them out for governorships or high dignities of state. The majority of his courtiers, palace officials, ministers of state, judges, and relatives by marriage are foreigners, and he has issued a decree that foreigners are to be called in his country by the title of Aziz [Honourable], so that this has become a proper name for them.

Every person proceeding to the court of this king must needs have a gift ready to present to him in person, in order to gain his favour. The sultan requites him for it by a gift many times its value. We shall have much to tell later on about the presents made to him by foreigners. When people became familiar with this habit of his, the merchants in Sind and India began to furnish each person who came to visit the sultan with thousands of dinars as a loan, and to supply him with whatever he might desire to offer as a gift or for his own use, such as riding animals, camels and goods. They place both their money and their persons at his service, and stand before him like attendants. When he reaches the sultan, he receives a magnificent gift from him and pays off his debts and his dues to them in full. So they ran a flourishing trade and made vast profits, and it became an established usage amongst them. On reaching Sind I followed this practice and bought horses, camels, white slaves and other goods from the merchants. I had already bought in Ghaznah from an Iraqi merchant about thirty horses and a camel with a load of arrows, for this is one of the things presented to the sultan. This merchant went off to Khurasan and on returning later to India received his money from me. He made an enormous profit through me and became one of the principal merchants. I met him many years later, in the city of Aleppo, when the infidels had robbed me of everything I possessed, but I received no kindness from him.

Description of the rhinoceros

After crossing the river of Sind called Banj Ab, we entered a forest of reeds, following the track which led through the midst of it, when we were confronted by a rhinoceros. In appearance it is a black animal with a huge body and a disproportionately large head. For this reason it has become the subject of a proverb, as the saying goes, '*Al-karkaddan ras bila badan*' (rhinoceros, head and no torso). It is smaller than an elephant but its head is many times larger than an elephant's. It has a single horn between its eyes, about three cubits in length and about a span in breadth. When it came out against us one of the horsemen got in its way; it struck the horse which he was riding with its horn, pierced his thigh and knocked him down, then went back into the thicket and we could not get at it. I saw a rhinoceros a second time on this road after the hour of afternoon prayer. It was feeding on plants but when we approached it it ran away. I saw a rhinoceros yet another time when in the company of the king of India we had entered a jungle of reeds. The sultan was mounted on an elephant and we too were mounted on elephants along with him. The foot-soldiers and horsemen went in and beat it up, killed it and conveyed its head to the camp.

After two days' march from the crossing of the river of Sind we reached the town of Janani, a large and fine town on the bank of the river Sind.[3] It has beautiful bazaars and has been inhabited from ancient times by a people called the Samirah, whose ancestors established themselves there on the conquest of Sind in the time of al-Hajjaj [AD 712], as the chroniclers of the conquest of Sind have noted.

These Samirah never eat with anyone nor may anyone observe them while they are eating, nor do they marry anyone outside their clan, nor do they allow anyone to marry into it.

From Janani we travelled to Siwasitan [Sehwan],[4] a large town, outside which is a sandy desert, treeless except for acacias. Nothing is grown on the river here except melons, and the food of the inhabitants consists of sorghum and peas, which they call *mushunk* and of which they make bread. There is a plentiful supply of fish and buffalo milk, and the people there eat skinks. These are little animals resembling the lizard (which the Moroccans call the garden snakelet)[5] except that it has no tail. I have seen them digging the sand and fetching it out of it; they slit open its stomach, throw out the contents and stuff it with turmeric. This takes the place of saffron with them. When I saw this small animal and them eating it, I took a loathing to it and would not eat it. We entered Siwasitan during the hottest period of the summer. The heat was intense, and my companions used to sit naked except that each had a cloth round his waist and another soaked with water on his shoulders; this would dry in a very short time and he had to keep constantly wetting it again.

In this town I met its preacher, whose name was al-Shaibani. He showed me the letter of the Commander of the Faithful, the Caliph Omar ibn Abd al-Aziz (God be pleased with him) to his remote ancestor, appointing him to the office of preacher to this town, which they have inherited generation after generation from that time to the present day.

Not long before my arrival in Siwasitan a rebellion had taken place there. News of the revolt was brought to Imad al-Mulk Sartiz, the sultan's mamluk, who was at that time chief amir in Sind and residing in Multan, whereupon he assembled his troops and equipped an expedition both by land and on the river Sind. It is a ten days' journey from Siwasitan to Multan. The rebels came out to meet him, but they were ignominiously defeated and barricaded themselves in the town. Sartiz besieged them, setting up siege artillery against them, and when the siege had gone on for forty days and they were hard pressed by it, they asked for and were granted terms. When they came out to him, however, he broke his word to them, seized their property and ordered their execution. Every day he would strike off the heads of some of them, cut some of them in half, flay others of them alive and fill their skins with straw and hang them on the city wall. The greater part of the wall was covered with these skins fixed on crosses, striking with terror those who saw them. He also collected their heads in the middle of the town where they formed a mound of some size. It was shortly after these events that I lodged at a large college in this town. I used to sleep on the roof of the college and when I woke up during the night I would see these skins attached to the crosses; they filled me with horror and I could not bear to stay in the college, so I went elsewhere.

Now the worthy and equitable jurist Ala al-Mulk of Khurasan had come to join the service of the king of India, and had been appointed governor of the town and dependencies of Lahari in Sind.[6] I resolved to travel with him to the town of Lahari. He had fifteen ships with which he had come on the river of Sind, carrying his baggage-train, so I set out with him.

The journey on the river of Sind and the order observed during it

The jurist Ala al-Mulk had amongst his vessels one called by the name of *ahawrah*. In the centre of it there was a wooden cabin to which one climbed up by steps, and on the top of this there was a place prepared for the governor to sit in. His suite sat in front of him and the mamluks stood to right and left, while the crew of about forty men rowed. Accompanying the *ahawrah* were four vessels to right and left, two of which carried the governor's 'honours', i.e. standards, kettledrums, trumpets, bugles and reed pipes, and the other two carried singers. First the drums and trumpets would be sounded and then the musicians would sing, and they kept this up alternately from early morning to the hour of the midday meal. When this moment arrived the ships came together and closed up with one another and gangways were placed from one to the other. The musicians then came on board the governor's *ahawrah* and sang until he finished eating, when they had their meal and at the end of it returned to their vessel. They then set off again on their journey in the manner described until nightfall. When it became dark, the camp was set up on the bank of the river, the governor disembarked and went to his tents, the repast was spread and most of the troops joined in the meal. After the last evening prayer, sentries were posted for the night in reliefs. As each relief finished its tour of duty one of them cried in a loud voice, 'O lord king, so many hours of the night are past.'[7] Then the next relief would come on duty, and when it finished its tour, their spokesman also called out to give notice of how many hours had passed. At dawn the trumpets and drums sounded and the dawn prayer was said, then food was brought, and when the meal was finished they resumed their journey.

After I had travelled for five days with Ala al-Mulk, we reached the site of his province. This is the city of Lahari, a fine town on the sea coast where the river of Sind discharges itself into the ocean. It possesses a large harbour, visited by merchants from al-Yaman, Fars, and elsewhere. For this reason its contributions to the treasury and its revenues are considerable.

A curiosity which I visited outside this town

I rode out one day with Ala al-Mulk, and we came to a plain called Tarna, seven miles from Lahari, where I saw an innumerable quantity of stones resembling the shapes of men and animals. Many of them were disfigured and their forms effaced, but there remained among them the figure of a head or a foot or something of the sort. Some of the stones also had the shape of grains of wheat, chickpeas, beans and lentils and there were remains of a city wall and house walls. We saw too the ruins of a house with a chamber of hewn stones, in the midst of which there was a platform of hewn stones resembling a single block, surmounted by a human figure, except that its head was elongated and its mouth on one side of its face and its hands behind its back like a pinioned captive. The place had pools of stinking water and an inscription on one of the walls in Indian characters. Ala al-Mulk told me that the historians assert that in this place there was a great city whose inhabitants were so given to depravity that they turned to stone, and that it is their king who is on the platform in the house we have described, which is still called 'the king's palace'. They add that the inscription on one of the walls there in Indian characters gives the date of the destruction of the people of that city, which occurred about a thousand years ago.

When I had spent five days in this city with Ala al-Mulk, he gave me a generous travelling provision and I left for the city of Bakar, a fine city intersected by a channel from the river of Sind.[8] Thereafter I came to the city of Ujah [Uch], a large and well-built town which lies on the bank of the river of Sind and has fine bazaars and good buildings.[9] In the town of Ujah I met the devout and ascetic shaikh the Sharif Qutb al-Din Haidar al-Alawi, who invested me with the patched robe. He was one of the great saints, and the garment in which he robed me remained in my possession down to the time when the infidel Hindus despoiled me at sea.

From Ujah I travelled to the city of Multan, the capital of the land of Sind and residence of its ruling amir. On the road to Multan and ten miles distant from it is the river called Khusru Abad, a large river that cannot be crossed except by boat.[10] At this point the goods of all who pass are subjected to a rigorous examination and their baggage searched. Their practice at the time of our arrival was to take a quarter of everything brought in by the merchants, and to exact a duty of seven dinars for every horse. When we set about the crossing of this river and the baggage was examined, the idea of having my baggage searched was very disagreeable to me, for though there was nothing much in it, it seemed a great deal in the eyes of the people, and I did not like having it looked into. By the grace of God Most High there arrived on the scene one of the principal officers on behalf of Qutb al-Mulk, the governor of Multan, who gave orders that I should not be subjected to examination or search. And so it happened, and I gave thanks to God for the mercies which He had vouchsafed me. We spent that night on the bank of the river and next morning were visited by the postmaster. I was introduced to him and went in his company to visit the governor of Multan.

The governor of Multan and the ordering of affairs at his court

The Governor of Multan is Qutb al-Mulk, one of the greatest and most excellent of the amirs. When I entered his presence, he rose to greet me, shook my hand, and bade me sit beside him. I presented him with a white slave, a horse, and some raisins and almonds. These are among the greatest gifts that can be made to them, since they do not grow in their land but are imported from Khurasan. This governor in his public audience sat on a large carpeted dais, having the qadi and the preacher beside him. To right and left of him were ranged the commanders of the troops, and armed men stood at his back, while the troops were passed in review before him. They had a number of bows there, and when anyone comes desiring to be enrolled in the army as an archer he is given one of the bows to draw. They differ in stiffness and his pay is graduated according to the strength he shows in drawing them. For anyone desiring to be enrolled as a trooper there is a target set up; he puts his horse into a run and tries to hit it with his lance. There is a ring there too, suspended to a low wall; the candidate puts his horse into a run until he comes level with the ring, and if he lifts it off with his lance he is accounted among them a good horseman. For those wishing to be enrolled as mounted archers, there is a ball placed on the ground; each man gallops towards it and shoots at it, and his pay is proportioned to his accuracy in hitting it.

Two months after we reached Multan two of the sultan's chamberlains arrived in the town. They had instructions to arrange for the journey to Dihli of all those who had come on one mission or another.[11] They came to me together and asked me why I had come to India. I told them that I had come to enter permanently the service of Khund Alam ['Master of the World'], namely the sultan, this being how he is called in his dominions. He had given orders that no one coming from Khurasan should be allowed to enter India unless he came with the intention of staying there. So when I told them that I had come to stay they summoned the qadi and notaries and drew up a contract binding me and those of my company who wished to remain in India, but some of them refused to take this engagement.

We then set out on the journey to the capital, which is forty days' march from Multan through continuously inhabited country. The first town we entered was the city of Abuhar,[12] which is the first of these lands of Hind, a small but pretty place with a large population, and with flowing streams and trees. There are not to be found in India any trees of our country except the lote-tree, but there it is of great girth and its fruit is about as large as a gall nut, and very sweet. They have many trees none of which are to be found either in our country or elsewhere. One of them is the *anbah* [mango]; it is a tree which resembles orange trees but is larger in size and more leafy. The shade which it gives is the densest of any, but it is oppressive and if one sleeps beneath it he becomes enervated. Its fruit is of the size of a large pear. When the fruit is green and not yet fully ripe the people gather those of them that fall, put salt on them and pickle them as limes and lemons are pickled in our country. The Indians pickle also green ginger and clusters of pepper, which they eat with meat dishes, taking after each mouthful a little of these pickled fruits. When the mango ripens in the season of autumn rains its fruit becomes yellow and then they eat it like apples, some people cutting it with a knife while others simply suck it. The fruit is sweet, with a little acidity mingled with its sweetness, and has a large stone which they plant, like orange pips and other fruit stones, and the trees sprout from them.

To return to what we were saying, we continued our journey from the city of Abuhar across open country extending for a day's journey. On its borders are formidable mountains, inhabited by Hindu infidels who frequently hold up parties of travellers. Of the inhabitants of India the majority are infidels. Some of them are subjects under Muslim rule; others of them are rebels and warriors, who maintain themselves in the fastness of the mountains and plunder travellers.

Account of an engagement which we had on this road, being the first engagement which I witnessed in India

When we made ready to set out from Abuhar, the main party left the town in the early morning, but I stayed there with a small party of my companions until midday. We then set out too, numbering in all twenty-two horsemen, partly Arabs and partly non-Arabs [i.e. Persians and Turks], and were attacked in the open country there by eighty infidels on foot with two horsemen. My companions were men of courage and vigour and we fought stoutly with them, killing one of their horsemen and about twelve of the footsoldiers, and capturing the horse of the former. I was hit by an arrow and my horse by another, but God in His grace preserved me from them, for there is no force in their arrows. One of our party had his horse wounded, but we gave him in exchange the horse we had captured from the infidel, and killed the wounded horse, which was eaten by the Turks of our party. We carried the heads of the slain to the castle of Abu Bak'har, which we reached about midnight, and suspended them from the wall.

After two days' journey from this place we reached the town of Ajudahan, a small town belonging to the pious Shaikh Farid al-Din al-Badhawuni, the very person whom the pious Shaikh and Saint

Burhan al-Din the lame had told me, at Alexandria, that I should meet.[13] And meet him I did, God be praised. He was the spiritual preceptor of the king of India, who made him a gift of this town. But he is afflicted by secret imaginings (God preserve us from them); thus he never shakes anyone by the hand, nor comes near him, and if his robe should brush against the garment of any other person he washes it. I went into his hospice and when I met him I gave him the greetings of Shaikh Burhan al-Din. He was astonished and said, 'I am not worthy of that.'

Account of the Indians who burn themselves to death

As I returned from visiting this shaikh, I saw people hurrying out from our camp, and some of our party along with them. I asked them what was happening and they told me that one of the Hindu infidels had died, that a fire had been kindled to burn him, and his wife would burn herself along with him. After the burning my companions came back and told me that she had embraced the dead man until she herself was burned with him. Later on I used often to see in that country an infidel Hindu woman, richly dressed, riding on horseback, followed by both Muslims and infidels and preceded by drums and trumpets; she was accompanied by Brahmans, who are the chiefs of the Hindus. In the sultan's dominions they ask his permission to burn her, which he accords them, and then they burn her.

Sometime later I happened to be in a town inhabited by a majority of infidels, called Amjari.[14] Its governor was a Muslim, one of the Samirah of Sind. In its neighbourhood were some unsubdued infidels, and when one day they made an attack on the road the Muslim amir went out to engage them, together with his subjects both Muslim and infidel. There was severe fighting between them, in the course of which seven of the infidel subjects were killed, three of whom had wives, and the three widows agreed to burn themselves. The burning of the wife after her husband's death is regarded by them as a commendable act, but is not compulsory; but when a widow burns herself her family acquire a certain prestige by it and gain a reputation for fidelity. A widow who does not burn herself dresses in coarse garments and lives with her own people in misery, despised for her lack of fidelity, but she is not forced to burn herself.

When these three women to whom we have referred made a compact to burn themselves, they spent three days preceding the event in concerts of music and singing and festivals of eating and drinking, as though they were bidding farewell to the world, and the women from all around came to take part. On the morning of the fourth day each one of them had a horse brought to her and mounted it, richly dressed and perfumed. In her right hand she held a coconut, with which she played, and in her left a mirror, in which she could see her face. They were surrounded by Brahmans and accompanied by their own relatives, and were preceded by drums, trumpets and bugles. Every one of the infidels would say to one of them, 'Take greetings from me to my father, or brother, or mother, or friend,' and she would say, 'Yes,' and smile at them. I rode out with my companions to see what exactly these women did in this ceremony of burning. After travelling about three miles with them we came to a dark place with much water and trees with heavy shade, amongst which there were four pavilions, each containing a stone idol. Between the pavilions there was a basin of water over which a dense shade was cast by trees so thickly set that the sun could not penetrate them. The place looked like a spot in hell – God preserve us from it! On reaching these pavilions they descended to the pool, plunged into it and divested themselves of their clothes and ornaments, which they distributed as alms. Each one was then given an unsewn garment of coarse cotton and tied part of it round her waist and part over her head and shoulders. Meanwhile, the fires had been lit near this basin in a lowlying spot, and oil of sesame poured over them so that the flames were increased. There were about fifteen men there with faggots of thin wood, and with them about ten others with heavy baulks in their hands, while the drummers and trumpeters were standing by waiting for the women's coming. The fire was screened off by a blanket held by some men in their hands, so that they should not be frightened by the sight of it. I saw one of them, on coming to the blanket, pull it violently out of the men's hands, saying to them with a laugh, 'Is it with the fire that you frighten me? I know that it is a blazing fire.' Thereupon she joined her hands above her head in salutation to the fire and cast herself into it. At the same moment the drums, trumpets and bugles were sounded, and men threw on her the firewood they were carrying and the others put those heavy baulks on top of her to prevent her moving, cries were raised and there was a loud clamour. When I saw this I had all but fallen off my horse, if my companions had not quickly brought water to me and laved my face, after which I withdrew.

The Indians have a similar practice of drowning themselves, and many of them do so in the river Gang, the river to which they go on pilgrimage, and into which the ashes of these burned persons are cast. They say that it is a river of Paradise. When one of them comes to drown himself he says to those present with him, 'Do not think that I drown myself for any worldly reason or through penury; my purpose is solely to seek approach to Kusay,' Kusay being the name of God in their language.[15] He then drowns himself, and when he is dead they take him out and burn him and cast his ashes into this river.

Let us return to our original topic. We set out from the town of Ajudahan, and travelled via the towns of Sarasati, Hansi and Mas'ud Abad.[16] At length we arrived at the royal residence of Dihli, the metropolis of the land of al-Hind, a vast and magnificent city, uniting beauty with strength. It is surrounded by a wall whose equal is not known in any country in the world, and is the largest city in India, nay rather the largest of all the cities of Islam in the East.

9 The City of Dihli and Sultan Muhammad ibn Tughluq

Description of the city

The city of Dihli is of vast extent and population, and made up now of four neighbouring and contiguous towns. One of them is the city called by this name, Dihli; it is the old city built by the infidels and captured in the year 584 [AD 1188].[1] The second is called Siri. The third is called Tughluq Abad, after its founder, the Sultan Tughluq, the father of the sultan of India to whose court we came. The reason why he built it was that one day as he stood before the Sultan Qutb al-Din he said to him, 'O master of the world, it were fitting that a city should be built here.' The sultan replied to him ironically, 'When you are sultan, build it.' It came to pass by the decree of God that he became sultan, so he built it and called it by his own name. The fourth is called Jahan Panah, and is set apart for the residence of the Sultan Muhammad Shah, the reigning king of India, to whose court we had come. He was the founder of it, and it was his intention to unite these four towns within a single wall, but after building part of it he gave up the rest because of the great expense entailed in its construction.

Description of the wall of Dihli

The wall which surrounds the city of Dihli is unparalleled. The breadth of the wall itself is eleven cubits, and inside it there are rooms where nightwatchmen and keepers of the gates are lodged. The wall contains also stores for provisions, which they call granaries, as well as stores for war equipment and for mangonels and stone-throwing machines. Grain keeps in it for a very long time without going bad or becoming damaged. I have seen rice brought out of one of these stores, and although it had gone black in colour it was still good to the taste. I have also seen millet taken out of them. All these stores had been laid up by the Sultan Balaban ninety years before. There is room inside the wall for horsemen and infantry to march from one end of the town to the other, and it has window openings pierced on the town side, through which the light enters. The lower courses of this wall are constructed with stone and the upper courses with baked brick, and its towers are numerous and set at short intervals.

Description of the mosque of Dihli[2]

The Cathedral Mosque occupies a vast area; its walls, roof, and paving are all constructed of white stones, admirably squared and firmly cemented with lead. There is no wood in it at all. It has thirteen domes of stone, its *mimbar* also is of stone, and it has four courts. In the centre of the mosque is the awe-inspiring column of which it is said nobody knows of what metal it is constructed. One of their learned men told me that it is called Haft Jush, which means 'seven metals', and that it is composed of these seven. A part of this column, of a finger's length, has been polished, and this polished part gives out a brilliant gleam. Iron makes no impression on it. It is thirty cubits high, and we rolled a turban round it, and the portion which encircled it measured eight cubits. At the eastern gate of the mosque there are two enormous idols of brass prostrate on the ground and held by stones, and everyone entering or leaving the mosque treads on them. The site was formerly occupied by a *budkhanah*, that is an idol temple, and was converted into a mosque on the conquest of the city. In the northern court of the mosque is the minaret, which has no parallel in the lands of Islam.[3] It is built of red stone, unlike the stone used for the rest of the mosque, for that is white, and the stones of the minaret are decoratively carved. The minaret itself is of great height; the ball on top of it is of glistening white marble and its 'apples' are of pure gold. The passage is so wide that elephants can go up by it. A person in whom I have confidence told me that when it was built he saw an elephant climbing with stones to the top. It was built by the Sultan Mu'izz al-Din. The Sultan Qutb al-Din wished to build in the western court an even larger minaret, but was cut off by death when only a third of it had been completed. The Sultan Muhammad intended to bring it to completion, but afterwards gave up the idea as being unlucky. This unfinished minaret is one of the wonders of the world for size, and the width of its passage is such that three elephants could mount it abreast. The third of it built equals in height the whole of the other minaret we have mentioned in the northern court. I climbed to the top of it on one occasion; I saw most of the houses of the city, and the walls for all their elevation and loftiness looked to me quite low. The people at the foot of the minaret appeared to me like little children, although to one looking at it from below it does not seem so high because of its great bulk and breadth.

Description of the two great tanks outside Dihli

Outside Dihli is the large reservoir named after the Sultan Shams al-Din Lalmish, from which the inhabitants of the city draw their drinking water.[4] It lies close to the *musalla*. Its contents are collected from rain water, and it is about two miles in length by half that breadth. Its western side, in the direction of the *musalla*, is constructed with stones, and disposed like a series of terraces one above the other, and beneath each terrace are steps leading down to the water. Beside each terrace there is a stone pavilion containing seats for those who have come out to visit the place and to enjoy its attractions. In the centre of the tank there is a great pavilion built of dressed stones, two storeys high. When the reservoir is filled with water it can be reached only in boats, but when the water is low the people go into it. Inside it is a mosque, and at most times it is occupied by poor brethren devoted to the service of God and placing their trust in Him [i.e. dependent upon charity]. When the water dries up at the sides of this reservoir, they sow sugar canes, gherkins, cucumbers, and green and yellow melons there; the latter are very sweet but of small size. Between Dihli and the 'Abode of the Caliphate' is the 'private tank', which is larger than that of the Sultan Shams al-Din. Along its sides there are forty pavilions, and round about it live the musicians. Their place is called Tarab Abad ['City of Music'] and they have there a most extensive bazaar, a cathedral mosque, and many other mosques besides.

Account of some of its scholars and pious men

Among them is the pious and learned Shaikh Mahmud al-Kubba;[5] he is one of the great saints and the people assert he is able to draw on the resources of creation, because to all outward seeming he has no property of his own, yet he supplies food to all comers and makes gifts of gold and silver coins and garments. Many miraculous graces have been operated through him and he has acquired a great reputation for them. I saw him many times and profited from his blessed power. Another is the pious and learned Shaikh Ala al-Din called al-Nili as though he were named after the Egyptian Nile, but God knows. He was a disciple of the learned and pious Shaikh Nizam al-Din al-Badhawuni. He preaches to the people every Friday and multitudes of them repent before him and shave their heads and fall into ecstasies of lamentation, and some of them faint.

Anecdote

I was present one day when he was preaching, and the Qur'an reader recited in his presence, 'O ye men, fear your Lord. Verily the quaking of the earth at the Hour is a thing of terror. On the day when ye see it every nursing woman shall be unmindful of what she has suckled, and every carrying female shall bring forth her burden, and thou shalt see men reeling as drunkards, yet are they not drunkards, but the chastisement of God is terrible.' When the reader finished, the doctor Ala al-Din repeated these words, and a certain poor brother somewhere in the mosque uttered a loud cry. The shaikh repeated the verse and the faqir cried out again and fell dead. I was one of those who prayed over him and joined in his funeral cortège.

Another of the pious men of Dihli is the learned and saintly imam, the abstinent and humble-minded devotee, Kamal al-Din Abdallah al-Ghari, the outstanding and unique personality of his age.[6] He is called al-Ghari ['the cave-man'] from a cave which he used to inhabit outside Dihli, near the hospice of Shaikh Nizam al-Din al-Badhawuni. I visited him in this cave three times.

A miraculous grace of his

I had a slave boy who ran away from me, and whom I found in the possession of a certain Turk. I had in mind to reclaim the slave from him, but the shaikh said to me, 'This boy is no good to you. Don't take him.' The Turk wished to come to an arrangement, so I settled with him that he paid me a hundred dinars and I left him the boy. Six months later the boy killed his master and was taken before the sultan, who ordered him to be handed over to his master's sons, and they put him to death. When I experienced this miracle on the part of the shaikh I attached myself entirely to him, withdrawing from the world and giving all that I possessed to the poor and needy. I stayed with him for some time, and I used to see him fast for ten and twenty days on end and remain standing in prayer most of the night. I continued with him until the sultan sent for me and I became entangled in the world once again – may God give me a good ending! Later on, if God will, I shall tell the whole story, and how it was that I returned to the world.

The Sultan Abu 'l-Mujahid Muhammad Shah, son of the Sultan Ghiyath al-Din Tughluq Shah, King of al-Hind and al-Sind, at whose court we presented ourselves

Concerning the manner of his succession, I was told that his father, the late Sultan Tughluq, had been on an expedition to the land of Laknawti.[7] When he approached the capital on returning from this expedition he ordered his son to build him a palace, which they call a *kushk*, by a riverbed in those parts which is called Afghan-bur.[8] Muhammad Shah built it in three days, constructing it mostly of wood, raised upon wooden pillars to some height above the ground. He had it skilfully built on a plan which was supervised by al-Malik Zadah, known later by the title of Khwajah Jahan, the chief of the viziers of Sultan Muhammad, who was at that time the controller of buildings. The scheme which they excogitated for this kiosk was that whenever the elephants should tread on one particular side of it, the whole building would fall in ruins. The sultan alighted at the kiosk and after he had given a meal to his troops and they had dispersed, his son asked his permission to parade the elephants before him in their ceremonial trappings, and he granted it.

My informant, the Shaikh Rukn al-Din, told me that on that day he was with the sultan, and the sultan's favourite son Mahmud was in their company. Muhammad came and said to the shaikh, '*Ya khund* ["master"], it is the hour of the afternoon prayer; go down and pray.' The shaikh continued the story to me as follows: 'So I went down, and the elephants were led up from one direction, as they had planned. When they walked on that side the pavilion fell in upon the sultan and his son Mahmud. On hearing the noise I went back without finishing the prayer and found the pavilion in ruins. Muhammad gave orders to fetch axes and mattocks in order to dig for them, but he made a sign to delay and in consequence they were not brought until after sunset. They then cleared away the ruins and found the sultan with his back bent over his son to protect him from death; some said that he was brought out dead, but others assert that he was brought out alive and despatched. He was carried by night to the mausoleum which he had built for himself outside the town called Tughluq Abad after him, and he was buried there.'[9]

We have already related the reason for his building of this town, which contained the treasuries and palaces of Tughluq. In it was the great palace whose tiles he had gilded, so that when the sun rose they shone with a brilliant light and a blinding glow, that made it impossible to keep one's eyes fixed on it. He deposited in this town vast stores of wealth and it is told that he constructed a tank and poured into it molten gold so that it became a single block. All these treasures were spent by his son Muhammad Shah when he became sultan. It was to the mechanical skill, which we have described, of the Vizier Khwajah Jahan in constructing the pavilion which fell down upon Tughluq that he owed his privileged position with his son Muhammad Shah and the special favour shown to him by the latter, for there was no one, whether of the vizier or of any others, who came near to enjoying the same position with the sultan nor stood to him on the same level.

When the Sultan Tughluq died his son Muhammad took posses-sion of the kingdom without competition or opposition. His name was Jawnah, but when he became king he called himself Muhammad and took the *kunyah* name of Abu 'l-Mujahid.[10] My statements about this king are based for the most part on what I myself witnessed in the days when I was in his land.

Description of him

This king is of all men the most addicted to the making of gifts and the shedding of blood. His gate is never without some poor man enriched or some living man executed, and there are current amongst the people many stories of his generosity and courage and of his cruelty and violence towards criminals. For all that, he is of all men the most humble and the readiest to show equity and to acknowledge the right. The ceremonies of religion are strictly complied with at his court, and he is severe in the matter of attendance at prayer and in punishing those who neglect it. He is one of those kings whose felicity is unimpaired and whose success in his affairs surpasses all ordinary experience, but his dominant quality is generosity. We shall mention some examples of this that are marvellous beyond anything heard tell of anyone before him, and I call God and His Angels and His Prophets to witness that all that I shall relate of his extraordinary generosity is absolute truth, and God is a sufficient witness. I know that some of the stories I shall tell on this subject will be unacceptable to the minds of many persons, and that they will regard them as quite impossible in the normal order of things; but in a matter which I have seen with my own eyes and of which I know the accuracy and have myself had a large share, I cannot do otherwise than speak the truth. In addition, most of these facts are established by numerous independent authorities in the lands of the East.

Description of his gates and audience hall and of the ceremonial observed therein

The sultan's palace at Dihli is called Dar Sara and contains many gates.[11] At the first gate there are posted a number of men in charge of it, and beside it sit buglers, trumpeters and pipe-players. When any amir or person of note arrives, they sound their instruments and say during this fanfare, 'So-and-so has come, so-and-so has come.' The same takes place also at the second and third gates. Outside the first gate are platforms on which sit the executioners, for the custom among them is that when the sultan orders a man to be executed, the sentence is carried out at the gate of the public audience hall, and the body lies there three nights. Between the first and second gates there is a large vestibule with platforms built along both sides, on which sit those troops whose turn of duty it is to guard the gates. At the second gate also there are seated the porters who are in charge of it. Between the second and third gates there is a large platform on which the principal *naqib*[12] sits; in front of him there is a gold mace, which he holds in his hand, and on his head he wears a tall jewelled cap of gold, surmounted by peacock feathers. The other *naqibs* stand before him, each wearing a low gilded cap on his head and a girdle round his waist and holding in his hand a whip with a gold or silver handle. This second gate leads to a large and commodious audience hall in which the people sit.

At the third gate there are platforms occupied by the scribes of the door. One of their customs is that none may pass through this gate except those whom the sultan has expressly designated to enter, and for each person he prescribes a number of his companions and men who may enter along with him. Whenever any person comes to this gate the scribes write down, 'So-and-so came at the first hour' or the second or later hours, until the close of the day, and the sultan studies this report after the last evening prayer. They also take note of everything of any kind that happens at the gate, and certain of the sons of the maliks are appointed to transmit what they write to the sultan. Another of their customs is that anyone who absents himself from the sultan's palace for three days or more, with or without excuse, may not enter this door thereafter except by the sultan's permission. If he has an excuse of illness or otherwise he presents before him a gift such as is suitable for one of his rank or office to offer to the sultan. So also do those who present themselves at the court on return from their journeys; the doctor of the law presents a copy of the Qur'an or a book or the like, the faqir presents a prayer-carpet, rosary, tooth-cleaning stick, etc., and the amirs and such present horses, camels and weapons. This third door opens into the immense and vast hall called Hazar Ustun, which means in Persian 'A thousand pillars'.[13] The pillars are of painted wood and support a wooden roof, most exquisitely carved. The people sit under this, and it is in this hall that the sultan sits for public audience.

The order of his public audience

As a rule his audiences are held after the afternoon prayer, although he often holds them early in the day. He sits on a raised seat standing on a dais carpeted in white, with a large cushion behind him and two others as arm-rests on his right and left. His left foot is tucked under him in the same way that one sits when reciting the creed during prayers; this is the way in which all the people of India sit. When he takes his seat, the vizier stands in front of him, the secretaries behind the vizier, then the chamberlains behind them. The chief of the chamberlains is Firuz Malik, the son of the sultan's uncle and his deputy, and he is that one of the chamberlains who stands closest to the sultan.[14]

As the sultan sits down the chamberlains and *naqibs* say in their loudest voice '*Bismillah*'. Then the 'great king' Qabulah takes his place behind the sultan, standing with a flywhisk in his hand to drive off the flies. A hundred armour-bearers stand on the right of the sultan and a like number on the left, carrying shields, swords, and bows. To right and left all the way down the hall stand the grand qadi, next to him the chief preacher, then the rest of the qadis, then the chief jurists, then the chiefs of the sharifs [descendants of the Prophet], then the shaikhs, then the sultan's brothers and relations by marriage, then the principal amirs, then the chiefs of those called *aziz* (that is to say the foreigners), then the *qa'ids*.[15]

Then they bring in sixty horses saddled and bridled with the royal harness, some of them with the trappings of the caliphate, namely those with bridles and girths of black silk gilded, and some with the same in white silk gilded, which are reserved for the sultan's exclusive use. Half of these horses are ranged on the right and half on the left, where the sultan can see them. Next fifty elephants are brought in; these are adorned with silken and gold cloths, and have their tusks shod with iron for service in killing criminals. On the necks of each elephant is its mahout, who carries a sort of iron battle-axe with which he punishes it and directs it to do what is required of it. Each elephant has on its back a sort of large box capable of holding twenty warriors or more or less, according to its bulk and the size of its body. At the corners of each such box there are fixed four banners. These elephants are trained to make obeisance to the sultan and to incline their heads, and when they do so the chamberlains cry in a loud voice, '*Bismillah*'. They also are arranged half on the right and half on the left, behind the persons already standing there. As each person enters who has an appointed place of standing on the right or left, he makes obeisance on reaching the station of the chamberlains, and the chamberlains say, '*Bismillah*', regulating the loudness of their utterance by the height of reputation of the person who is making his obeisance, and who then retires to his appointed place on the right or left, beyond which he never passes. If it is one of the infidel Hindus who makes obeisance, the chamberlains and the *naqibs* say to him, 'God guide thee'. The sultan's slaves stand behind all those in attendance, having in their hands shields and swords, and no one can come in to the hall between their ranks, but only by passing before the chamberlains who stand in front of the sultan.

How he goes out for the two festivals

On the morning of the feast day all the elephants are adorned with silk, gold, and precious stones. There are sixteen of these elephants which no one rides, but they are reserved to be ridden by the sultan himself, and over them are carried sixteen parasols of silk embroidered with jewels, each one with a shaft of pure gold. On each elephant is a silk cushion adorned with precious stones. The sultan himself rides on one of these elephants, and in front of him there is carried aloft the *ghashiyah*, that is his saddle-cover, which is adorned with the most precious jewels. In front of him walk his slaves and his *mamluks*, each one of them wearing on his head a cap of gold and round his waist a girdle of gold, which some of them adorn with jewels. In front of him also walk the *naqibs*, about three hundred in number, each one of them wearing on his head a golden *aqruf* [high conical hat] and round his waist a golden girdle, and carrying in his hand a whip with a handle of gold. Those who ride are the qadis, and the principal foreigners among the Khurasanians, Iraqis, Syrians, Egyptians, and Moors, each one of them mounted on an elephant. All foreigners are called by them Khurasanians. The muezzins also ride on elephants and they keep on calling out, '*Allahu akbar.*'

When the sultan reaches the gate of the *musalla* he halts by the gate and orders the judges, the principal amirs, and the chiefs of the foreigners to enter. Then he himself alights, and the imam leads the prayers and delivers the address. If it should be the Feast of the Sacrifice, the sultan brings a camel and stabs it in the throat with a javelin, first putting on over his clothes a silk wrapper to protect himself from the blood; then he mounts the elephant and returns to his palace.

One of their customs on the feast day is that there is set up the great cassolette, which is a sort of tower of pure gold composed of separate pieces; when they wish to put it together they join them up, and each section of it is carried by a number of men. Inside it are three chambers which are entered by incense-burners, who set fire to *qamari* and *qaquli* aloes-wood, ambergris and benzoin, so that the smoke from them fills the whole hall.[16] There are also gold and silver barrels carried by pages and filled with rose-water, with which they sprinkle those present broadcast.

His ceremonial on his return from a journey

When the sultan comes back from his journeys, the elephants are decorated, and over sixteen of them are raised sixteen parasols, some brocaded and some set with jewels. In front of him is carried the *ghashiyah*, that is the saddle-cover, set with precious stones. Wooden pavilions are built, several storeys high, and covered with silk cloths, and in each storey there are singing girls wearing the most beautiful dresses and ornaments, with dancing girls amongst them. In the centre of each pavilion there is fashioned a large tank made of skins and filled with rose-syrup dissolved in water, from which all the people, that is to say all comers, natives or strangers, may drink, and everyone who drinks receives at the same time betel leaves and areca nuts. The space between the pavilions is carpeted with silk cloths, on which the sultan's horse treads. The walls of the street along which he passes from the gate of the city to the gate of the palace are hung with silk cloths. In front of him march footmen from his own slaves, several thousands in number, and behind come the squadrons and mounted troops. On one of his entries into the capital I saw three or four small catapults set up on elephants throwing dinars and dirhams amongst the people, and they would be scrambling to pick them up, from the moment when he entered the city until he reached the palace.[17]

The ceremonial at the public meals

At the sultan's public meals, the food is brought from the kitchen preceded by the *naqibs* crying out, '*Bismillah*'; the head of the *naqibs* walks in front of them carrying a golden mace, and with him is his deputy carrying a silver mace. The food consists of thin rounds of bread, roast meat, round cakes filled with sweet confections, rice, chickens, and *samusak*.[18] It is their custom that the principal place at the banquet should be taken by the qadis, the preachers, doctors of law, sharifs and shaikhs; after them come the sultan's relatives, then the principal amirs and then the rest of the people. No one sits down except in a place assigned to him, so that there is no pushing and elbowing between them at all. When they sit down, the *shurbadars*, that is to say cup-bearers, come bearing vessels of gold, silver, brass and glass, filled with candy-water. The guests drink this before beginning to eat, and when they have drunk the chamberlains say, '*Bismillah*'. They then start eating and there is set before each person a portion of every dish of which the meal is composed; he eats of it by himself and no person eats with another out of the same dish. When they finish eating barley-water is brought to them in tin mugs, and when they have taken this the chamberlains say, '*Bismillah*'. Then trays are brought in with betel and areca-nut and each person is given a spoonful of crushed areca with fifteen leaves of betel tied in a bunch with red silk thread. When those present take the betel the chamberlains say, '*Bismillah*' and thereupon they all stand up. The amir who is appointed to preside at the banquet does homage and they all do homage with him and then withdraw. They have meals twice a day, once before noon, and again after the afternoon prayer.

The sultan's generosity and open-handedness

Especially well known is his generosity to foreigners, for he prefers them to the people of India, singles them out for favour, showers his benefits upon them and clothes them in an ample garment of bounty, appoints them to high offices of state, and confers upon them magnificent gifts. One indication of his generous treatment of them is that he has called them by the designation of *aziz*[19] and has prohibited their being called strangers, for, he said, when a person is called 'stranger' he feels dispirited and downcast.

Account of the gift which he made to the preacher from Tirmidh, Nasir al-Din

This doctor of the law and homiletic preacher had come to the sultan's court, and after staying for a year as a pensioner on his bounty, he wished to return to his own country. The sultan gave him permission to do so, although he had not yet heard him in discourse or homily. When however, the sultan prepared to set out on an expedition to the land of al-Ma'bar he desired to hear him before his departure, and gave orders that there should be prepared for him a pulpit of white sandalwood, called *maqasiri*, and its nails and plaques were made of gold and at the top of it there was inserted an immense ruby.[20] Nasir al-Din was invested with an Abbasid robe, black, embroidered with gold and encrusted with precious stones, and his turban was to match. The pulpit was set up for him inside the sultan's tent. The sultan took his seat on his throne with the principal officers on his right and left, and the judges, doctors of law and amirs took their places; then he delivered an eloquent address followed by a homily and exhortation. There was nothing remarkable in what he did, but his good fortune befriended him, and when he came down from the pulpit the sultan rose up and came to him, embraced him, mounted him on an elephant and ordered all those present, of whom I was one, to walk before him to a tent which had been pitched for him in face of the sultan's tent. This enclosure was made entirely of coloured silk and its marquee and private tent were both made of silk also. He sat there for a reception in which we joined, each sitting in his place. At one side of the tent there were some golden vessels which the sultan had given him, namely a large vase for holding lamps, which was big enough to accommodate a man sitting inside it, two cooking pots, plates, I cannot say how many, a number of jugs, a waterskin, a table with four legs and a book stand, all of these in pure gold. Imad al-Din al-Simnani held up two of the tent pegs, one of them brass, the other tinned, as if to give the impression that they were of gold and silver, but they were not so and only as we have stated. Besides this the sultan had given him on his arrival a hundred thousand silver dinars and two hundred slaves, some of whom he freed and some he took with him.

Account of his gift to Abd al-Aziz of Ardawil

This Abd al-Aziz was a jurist and traditionist who had studied in Damascus. Subsequently he came to the court of the sultan, who received him generously and made rich gifts to him. It happened one day that he expounded before him a number of traditions relating to the merit of al-Abbas and his son (God be pleased with them) and some of the memorable deeds of the caliphs descended from them. The sultan was highly delighted with this because of his attachment to the house of al-Abbas and having kissed this scholar's feet gave orders to fetch a golden tray on which there were two thousand tangahs[21] and poured them over him with his own hand, saying, 'These are for you, and the tray as well.'

Account of his gift to Shams al-Din al-Andukani

The doctor Shams al-Din al-Andukani, who was a philosopher and a gifted poet, wrote a laudatory ode to the sultan in Persian. The ode contained twenty-seven verses, and the sultan gave him a thousand silver dinars for each verse. This is a greater reward than those related of former kings, who used to give a thousand dirhams for each verse, which is only a tenth of the sultan's gift.

Anecdote on the humility of the sultan and his sense of equity

One of the Hindu chiefs brought a claim against him that he had killed the chief's brother without just cause, and cited him to appear before the qadi. Whereupon he went on foot and unarmed to the qadi's tribunal, saluted and made the sign of homage, having previously sent orders to the qadi that on his arrival at the tribunal, he (the qadi) should not stand up for him nor move from his place. He walked up to the tribunal and remained standing before the qadi, who gave judgement against him, decreeing that he should give satisfaction to his opponent for his brother's blood, and he did so.

A similar anecdote

A young boy, one of the sons of the maliks, brought a claim against the sultan that the latter had struck him without just cause, and cited him before the qadi. Judgement was given against the sultan, to the effect that he should give the plaintiff monetary compensation, if he would accept that, or alternatively allow him to exercise his right to retaliate in kind. I was present that day when the sultan returned to his audience hall, and saw him summon the boy, give him a stick and say to him, 'By my head, you shall strike me just as I struck you.' Whereupon the boy took the stick and gave him twenty-one blows, so that I actually saw his high cap fly off his head.

His insistence on the observance of the ritual prayers

The sultan was strict about the observance of the prayers, making congregational attendance at them obligatory, and punishing any dereliction of them most severely. Indeed, he put to death for neglecting them on one day alone nine persons, of whom one was a singer. He gave orders also that the people in general should be required to show a knowledge of the obligations of ablution, prayer, and the binding articles of Islam. They used to be questioned on these matters; if anyone failed to give correct answers he was punished, and they made a practice of studying them with one another in the audience hall and the bazaars, and setting them down in writing.

His distribution of food during the famine

When the severe drought reigned over the lands of India and Sind and prices rose to such a height that the *mann* of wheat reached six dinars, the sultan ordered that the whole population of Dihli should be given six months' supplies from the royal granary, at the rate of one and a half *ratls* (that is to say, Maghribi *ratls*) per day per person, small or great, free or slave.[22] The jurists and qadis went out to compile the registers with the names of the inhabitants of the various quarters; they would then present them to the authorities and each person would be given enough to provide him with food for six months.

This sultan's murders and reprehensible actions

In spite of all that we have related of his humility, his sense of fairness, his compassion for the needy, and his extraordinary liberality, the sultan was far too free in shedding blood. It was but seldom that the entrance to his palace was without a corpse and I used often to see men being executed at his gate and their bodies left to lie there. One day as I arrived my horse shied with me; I saw a white fragment on the ground and said, 'What is this?' One of my companions said, 'It is the torso of a man who was cut into three pieces.' The sultan used to punish small faults and great, without respect of persons, whether men of learning or piety or noble descent. Every day there are brought to the audience hall hundreds of people, chained, pinioned, and fettered, and those who are for execution are executed, those for torture tortured, and those for beating beaten. It is his custom to have all persons who are in his prison brought to the audience hall every day except Friday; on this day they are not hauled before him but it is a day of respite for them, on which they may clear themselves and remain at ease – may God deliver us from misfortune!

His execution of three hundred and fifty men at one time

On one occasion he designated a section of the army to proceed with the Malik Yusuf Bughrah to engage the infidels in part of the hill country bordering on the province of Dihli. Yusuf set out, and most of the troops with him, but a number of them stayed behind. Yusuf wrote to the sultan to inform him of this, whereupon the sultan gave orders for the patrolling of the city and the arrest of all who were discovered of those who had remained. This was done, three hundred and fifty of them were arrested, and he ordered the execution of the whole lot of them, so they were executed.

His torture and execution of the Shaikh Shihab al-Din

The Shaikh Shihab al-Din was one of the major shaikhs noted for probity and virtue, and used to fast uninterruptedly for fourteen days.

The Sultans Qutb al-Din and Tughluq held him in high esteem and used to visit him and to solicit his blessing. When the Sultan Muhammad succeeded, he wished to employ the shaikh in some service of his, for it was his practice to assign offices to jurists, shaikhs and devotees, on the argument that the first generation of the caliphs (God be pleased with them) were not in the habit of appointing to office any but men of religious learning and probity. The Shaikh Shihab al-Din, however, declined to accept office, and when the sultan raised the point with him in his public audience, he openly refused to yield and give his consent.[23] The sultan then commanded the venerable shaikh and jurist Diya al-Din of Simnan to pluck out the hair of his beard. But Diya al-Din refused to do so, and bluntly rejected his command, whereupon the sultan gave orders to pluck out the beards of both of them, and plucked out they were. Shihab al-Din he banished to Dawlat Abad, where he remained for seven years. He then sent for him, received him with great honour and respect and appointed him to high office; indeed, no one in the sultan's palace was higher than he.

When the sultan removed from Dihli to take up residence on the river Gang, where he built the palace known as Sarg Duwar (which means 'the likeness of Paradise'), and ordered the people to build there as well, the Shaikh Shihab al-Din asked his permission to remain in the capital.[24] He was allowed to do so and moved out to some uncultivated land at a distance of six miles from Dihli, where he excavated for himself an immense cave in the interior of which he fitted up chambers, storerooms, an oven and a bath. He stayed there for two and a half years, corresponding to the period of the shaikh's absence.

When the sultan returned to his capital, the shaikh went out to welcome him and meet him some seven miles from the city. The sultan showed him high honour and embraced him on their meeting. Shihab al-Din returned to his cave; then, some days later, when the sultan sent for him, he refused to come at his command. Thereupon the sultan sent an envoy, who spoke to him in a tactful way and warned him of the consequences of the sultan's anger, but he replied, 'Never shall I serve an oppressor.' When the envoy reported this to the sultan on his return, he received the order to fetch the shaikh, which he did. The sultan said to him, 'Is it you who says that I am an oppressor?' The shaikh replied, 'Indeed, you are an oppressor, and such-and-such are instances of your tyrannical conduct,' mentioning a number of things such as his devastation of the city of Dihli and his expulsion of its population.[25] The sultan then took his own sword, handed it to the Grand Qadi Sadr al-Jahan, and said, 'Establish the fact that I am an oppressor, and cut off my head with this sword.' Shihab al-Din said to him, 'Anyone who is willing to offer evidence of this will be put to death, but you yourself are aware of your tyrannical conduct.' The sultan ordered him to be handed over to the Malik Nukbiyah, the chief of the Duwaidars, who put four irons on his feet and pinioned his hands to his neck.[26] He stayed in that condition for fourteen days, fasting continuously, neither eating nor drinking. Every day of the fourteen he was brought to the audience hall, where the jurists and shaikhs were assembled, and they would say to him, 'Withdraw your statement.' But he would say, 'I shall not withdraw it, and I wish to join the ranks of those who have witnessed to the Faith and suffered martyrdom.' On the fourteenth day, the sultan sent him food, but he refused to eat, saying, 'My allotted sustenance from the things of this earth has come to an end – take the food back to him.' When the sultan was informed of this, he straightway ordered that the shaikh should be fed with five *istars* of human excrement – that is, two and a half *ratls* of the Maghribi standard. Those who are charged with carrying out such punishments, who are a body of Indian infidels, took this stuff, stretched out the shaikh on his back, opened his mouth with forceps, dissolved the ordure in water, and made him drink it. On the following day he was brought to the house of the Qadi Sadr al-Jahan. There the jurists, shaikhs, and leading foreign dignitaries were assembled; they admonished him in homilies, they besought him to withdraw his accusation, but he would have none of it and was beheaded – God Most High have mercy on him.

His killing of the jurist and professor Afif al-Din of Kasan and of two other jurists along with him

During the years of the famine, the sultan had given orders to dig wells outside the capital, and have grain crops sown in those parts. He provided the cultivators with the seed, as well as with all that was necessary for cultivation in the way of money and supplies, and required them to cultivate these crops for the royal grain store. When the jurist Afif al-Din heard of this, he said, 'This crop will not produce what is hoped for.' Some informer told the sultan what he had said, so the sultan gaoled him, and said to him, 'What reason have you to meddle with the government's business?' Some time later he released him, and as Afif al-Din went to his house he was met on the way by two friends of his, also jurists, who said to him, 'Praise be to God for your release,' to which our jurist replied, 'Praise be to God who has delivered us from the evildoers.'[27] They then separated, but they had not reached their houses before this was reported to the sultan, and he commanded all three to be fetched and brought before him. 'Take out this fellow,' he said, referring to Afif al-Din, 'and cut off his head baldrickwise,' that is, the head is cut off along with an arm and part of the chest, 'and behead the other two.' They said to him, 'He deserves punishment, to be sure, for what he said, but in our case for what crime are you killing us?' He replied, 'You heard what he said and did not disavow it, so you as good as agreed with it.' So they were all put to death, God Most High have mercy on them.

His killing of two other jurists, men of Sind, who were in his service

The sultan commanded these two Sindi jurists to accompany an amir whom he had appointed to a certain province, and said to them, 'I have committed the affairs of the province and its population to you two, and this amir will go with you only to carry out your instructions to him.' They said to him, 'We should act only as legal witnesses to his administration, and show him the right line of conduct for him to follow,' whereupon he replied, 'All that you want is to devour my revenues and squander them, and lay the blame for it on this Turk, who has no experience.' They said, 'God forbid, O Master of the World; this was not our intention,' but he replied to them, 'You had no other intention. Take them off to the Shaikh-zadah al-Nihawandi,' that is, the officer in charge of punishment by torture.

When they were taken to him, he said to them, 'The sultan intends to put you to death anyway, so admit what he put it into your mouths to say, and don't expose yourselves to the torture.' But they swore, by God, they had meant nothing more than they had said, so he said to his tormentors, 'Give them a taste of something,' meaning of torture. They were laid flat upon their backs and on the chest of each of them there was placed a red-hot iron plate, which was pulled off after a moment and took with it the flesh of their chests. After that, urine and cinders were brought and put on these wounds, whereupon they confessed that their intention had in fact been no other than as the sultan had said, and they were criminals and deserving of death, that there was nothing due to them as of right, nor any claim to retaliation for their blood whether by near relatives or others. They wrote all this down in their own handwriting, and testified to it before the qàdi, who then set his seal upon the attestation. It was stated in the document that their confession had been made without compulsion or coercion, for if they had said that they had been forced to make a confession they would have been most severely tortured, and they held that a quick beheading was better for them than to die under painful torture. So they were put to death, God Most High have mercy on them.

His devastation of Dihli and exile of its population, and killing of the blind man and the cripple

One of the gravest charges against the sultan is his forcing of the population of Dihli to evacuate the city. The reason for this is that they used to write missives reviling and insulting him, seal them, and inscribe them, 'By the head of the Master of the World, none but he may read this.' Then they would throw them into the audience hall by night, and when the sultan broke the seal he found them full of insults and abuse of him. So he decided to lay Dihli in ruins, and having bought from all the inhabitants their houses and dwellings and paid their price to them, he commanded them to move out of the city and go to Dawlat Abad. They refused, so his herald was sent to proclaim that no person should remain in it after three nights. The majority of the citizens left, but some of them hid in the houses. The sultan ordered a search to be made for any persons who had remained in the city, and his slaves found two men in its streets, one of them a cripple and the other blind. They were brought in, and he ordered that the cripple should be flung from a mangonel and the blind man dragged from Dihli to Dawlat Abad, a distance of forty days' journey. He fell to pieces on the road, and all of him that reached Dawlat Abad was his leg. After this action on the part of the sultan, the whole of the population left the town, abandoning furniture and possessions, and the city was left desolate and disintegrating. A person in whom I have confidence told me that the sultan mounted one night to the roof of his palace and looked out over Dihli, where there was neither fire nor smoke nor lamp, and said, 'Now my mind is tranquil and my feelings are appeased.' Afterwards he wrote to the inhabitants of the provinces commanding them to move to Dihli, in order to repopulate it. The result was that their cities were ruined but Dihli remained unrestored, because of its extent and immensity, for it is one of the greatest cities in the world. It was in this condition that we found it on our entry into it, empty and unpopulated save for a few inhabitants.[28]

10 Ibn Battutah's Stay in Dihli

Now let us return to what concerns ourselves in all this, and relate the circumstances of our arrival in the first place at the sultan's court and our changes of fortune until we left his service, and our subsequent departure from the sultan on a mission to China and our return therefrom to our own land, if God Most High will.

Account of our coming to the sultan's palace on our arrival during his absence

When we entered the capital of Dihli we proceeded directly to the sultan's court. On entering from the third door the vast hall called Hazar Ustun, which means 'thousand pillars', met our eyes. Here the sultan sits in public audience. On entering, the vizier made obeisance until his head nearly touched the ground, and we too made obeisance by inclining the body and touched the ground with our fingers, our obeisance being in the direction of the sultan's throne. All who were with us made obeisance also and when we finished this ceremony the *naqibs* cried in a loud voice, '*Bismillah*,' and we all retired.

Account of our visit to the palace of the sultan's mother and of her virtuous qualities

The sultan's mother is called Makhdumah Jahan ['Mistress of the World']. She is one of the most virtuous of women and munificent in charity, and has founded many hospices and endowed them to supply food to all travellers. She is blind, and the reason for this is that when her son came to the throne she was visited by all the princesses and daughters of the maliks and the amirs wearing their finest apparel. As she was sitting on a golden couch encrusted with jewels and they all made obeisance before her, her sight went suddenly and although she has been treated in all kinds of ways it has done no good. Her son is of all men the most filial in his respect for her, and here is an example. Once when she went on a journey with him the sultan returned some time before her, and on her arrival he went out to meet her, alighted from his horse, and kissed her foot as she was in her litter in the sight of all the people.

To return to our subject. When we withdrew from the sultan's palace the vizier went out, taking us in his company, to the Makhdumah Jahan's residence. When we reached her gate we alighted from our mounts, each of us having brought a gift proportioned to his quality. The chief judge of the mamluks went in with us; both he and the vizier did homage at her gate and we did homage in the same manner. The clerk at her gate made a list of our presents and then a company of eunuchs came out, the chief of whom presented themselves to the vizier and spoke with him privately. At length we were commanded to sit down in an arcade at that place, after which they served us with food, bringing drinking vessels, plates and jugs all in gold. We then ate, and after they had brought the barley-water followed by the betel the chamberlains said, '*Bismillah*,' and we all did homage. We were then invited to go to a certain place there and were invested with silk robes of honour embroidered in gold. Next there was brought out from inside the palace a chest containing unsewn fabrics of silk, linen and cotton, and each one of us was given his share of them. Then they brought a golden platter containing dried fruits, a similar platter with juleps, and a third with betel. It is their custom that the person to whom this is brought out takes the platter in his hand, places it on his shoulder and then does homage with his other hand touching the ground. The vizier took the platter in his hand with the purpose of showing me what I should do, out of kindly condescension on his part and courteous solicitude, may God reward him with good, and I did as he had done. We then withdrew to the mansion which had been prepared for our occupation in the city of Dihli and in the neighbourhood of the Gate of Palam, and the hospitality gift was sent to us.

Account of the hospitality gift

On arrival at the mansion which had been prepared for my occupation I found in it everything that was required in the way of furniture, carpets, mats, vessels, and bed. Their beds in India are light and one of them can be carried by a single man; every person when travelling has to transport his own bed, which his slave boy carries on his head. It consists of four conical legs with four crosspieces of wood on which braids of silk or cotton are woven.[1] When one lies down on it, there is no need for anything to make it pliable, for it is pliable of itself. Along with the bed they brought two mattresses and pillows and a coverlet, all made of silk. Their custom is to use white slips made of linen or cotton as cover for the mattresses and coverlets, so that when they become dirty they wash the slips, while the bedding inside is kept clean. That night they came with two men, one of them the miller and the other the butcher. They told us to take from the one so much flour and from the other so much meat – the exact weights I do not remember now. This which we have described was the hospitality gift of the sultan's mother.

Next day we rode to the sultan's palace and saluted the vizier, who gave me two purses, each containing a thousand silver dinars, saying, 'This is *sarshushti*,' which means 'for washing your head', and in addition gave me a robe of fine goathair. A list was made of all my companions, servants, and slave boys, and they were divided into four categories; those in the first category were each given two hundred dinars, in the second a hundred and fifty, the third a hundred, and the fourth sixty-five. There were about forty of them, and the total sum given to them was four thousand odd dinars. After that the sultan's hospitality gift was fixed. This consisted of a thousand Indian pounds of flour, a thousand pounds of flesh-meat, and I cannot say how many pounds of sugar, ghee, *salif*,[2] and arecanuts, with a thousand betel leaves.

Account of the death of my daughter and their action on that occasion

One and a half months after our arrival a daughter of mine died, aged less than a year. When the report of her death reached the vizier he gave orders that she should be buried in a hospice which he had built outside the Gate of Palam. After we had buried her there he wrote to the sultan about her and the reply reached him in the evening of the next day, although the distance between the sultan's hunting field and the capital was ten days' journey.

It is their custom to go to visit the grave of the dead person in the morning of the third day after burial. They spread carpets and silk fabrics on all sides of the tomb and place on it flowers, of which there is a never-ending supply there in all seasons of the year, such as jasmine, and *gul shabah* which has yellow flowers, *raibul* which is white, and *nisrin*, which is of two kinds, white and yellow.[3] They also set up branches of orange and lemon trees with their fruits, and if there should be no fruit on them they attach some to them with threads, and they heap upon the tomb dried fruits and coconuts. Then the people assemble and copies of the scriptures are brought and they recite the Qur'an. When they have completed the recitation servants bring julep and give it to the people to drink, then rose-water is sprinkled over them profusely and they are given betel and retire.

Some days later the eunuchs from the palace of the Makhdumah Jahan brought a *dulah*, that is a litter in which women are carried, though men also use it for journeys, resembling a couch.[4] The roof of the litter is made of braids of silk or cotton and on top of these there is a curved piece of wood like that on the top of parasols in our country, made of curved Indian bamboo. It is carried by eight men in two lots of four, who rest and carry in turn. These *dulahs* in India are like the donkeys in Egypt, for it is on them that most people go about on business; if a man has slaves of his own they carry him, and if he has no slaves he hires men to carry him. In the town there are always a number of these men standing in the bazaars and at the sultan's gate and at the gates of other persons for hire. The *dulahs* of women are covered with silk curtains, and it was a *dulah* of this kind which the eunuchs brought from the palace of the sultan's mother and in which they carried my slave girl, who was the mother of the daughter that died. I for my part sent with her a Turkish slave girl as a gift. The girl that was the mother of the daughter stayed with them for a night and came back the next day after they had given her a thousand silver dinars, and bracelets of gold set with jewels and an amulet case of gold also set with jewels, and a linen chemise embroidered with gold and a silk robe gilded and a chest full of clothing. When she brought all of this I gave it to my companions and to the merchants to whom I was indebted, in order to protect myself and to guard my honour, because the intelligencers were sending reports to the sultan about everything that concerned me.

Account of the generosity shown to me by the sultan and the vizier during the sultan's absence from the capital

While I was waiting, the sultan gave orders to assign to me such a number of villages as would produce a revenue of 5,000 dinars a year. The vizier and the officers of the administration assigned them to me accordingly, and I went out to visit them.

There had arrived in Dihli at that time some captives taken from the infidels and the vizier sent me ten girls from among them. I gave the man who brought them one of them – he was not at all pleased with that – and my companions took three young ones amongst them; as for the rest I do not know what happened to them. Female captives there are very cheap because they are dirty and do not know civilized ways. Even the educated ones are cheap, so that no one there needs to buy captives. The infidels in the land of India inhabit a territory which is not geographically separated from that of the Muslims, and their lands are contiguous, but though the Muslims have the upper hand over them yet the infidels maintain themselves in inaccessible mountains and rugged places, and they have forests of reeds, and as their reeds are not hollow but of large growth and are interlaced with one another, fire makes no impression on them and they are of great strength. The infidels live in these forests which are for them as good as city walls, and inside them they have their cattle and grain and supplies of water collected by the rains, so that they cannot be overcome except by strong armies of men who go into those forests and cut down those reeds with instruments made for the purpose.

Account of the sultan's arrival and our meeting with him

On the fourth of Shawwal [8th June 1334] the sultan alighted at a castle called Tilbat, seven miles from the capital, and the vizier ordered us to go out to him. We set out, each man with his present of horses, camels, fruits of Khurasan, Egyptian swords, mamluks, and sheep brought from the land of the Turks, and came to the gate of the castle where all the newcomers were assembled. They were then introduced before the sultan in order of precedence and were given robes of linen, embroidered in gold. When my turn came I entered and found the sultan seated on a chair. At first I took him to be one of the chamberlains until I saw him with the chief of the royal intimates, whom I had come to know during the sultan's absence. The chamberlain made obeisance and I did so too. After this the chief of the intimate courtiers said to me, '*Bismillah*, Mawlana Badr al-Din,' for in India they used to call me Badr al-Din, and *mawlana* [Our Master] is a title given to all scholars. I approached the sultan, who took my hand and shook it, and continuing to hold it addressed me most affably, saying in Persian, 'This is a blessing; your arrival is blessed; be at ease, I shall be compassionate to you and give you such favours that your fellow-countrymen will hear of it and come to join you.' Then he asked me where I came from and I said to him, 'From the land of the Maghrib.' He said to me, 'The land of Abd al-Mu'min?' and I said, 'Yes.'[5] Every time he said any encouraging word to me I kissed his hand, until I had kissed it seven times, and after he had given me a robe of honour I withdrew.

Account of the sultan's entry into his capital

On the day following that on which we went out to the sultan each one of us was given a horse from the sultan's stables, with a richly ornamented saddle and bridle, and when the sultan mounted for the entry into his capital we rode in the front part of the procession together with the Grand Qadi Sadr al-Jahan. The elephants were decorated and paraded in front of the sultan, with standards fixed on them and sixteen parasols, some of them gilded and some set with precious stones. Over the sultan's head there was displayed a parasol of the same kind and in front of him was carried the *ghashiyah*, which is a saddle-cloth studded with gems. On some of the elephants there were mounted small military catapults, and when the sultan came near the city parcels of gold and silver coins mixed together were thrown from these machines. The men on foot in front of the sultan and the other persons present scrambled for the money, and they kept on scattering it until the procession reached the palace. There marched before him thousands of foot-soldiers, and wooden pavilions covered with silk fabrics were constructed with singing girls in them, as we have already related.

After his entry into the city the sultan used to summon us to eat in his presence and would enquire how we fared and address us most affably. He said to us one day, 'You have honoured us by your coming and we cannot sufficiently reward you. The elder amongst you is in the place of my father, the man of mature age is my brother, and the young man like my son. There is in my kingdom nothing greater than this city of mine and I give it to you,' whereupon we thanked him and invoked blessings upon him.

One day he sent two of his high officers to us to say, 'The Master of the World says to you, "Whoever amongst you is capable of undertaking the function of vizier or secretary or commander or judge or professor or shaikh, I shall appoint to that office."' Everyone was silent at first, for what they were wanting was to gain riches and return to their countries. Then one of the officers said to me in Arabic, 'What do you say, *ya sayyidi*?' (The people of that country never address an Arab except by the title of sayyid, and it is by this title that the sultan himself addresses him, out of respect for the Arabs.) I replied, 'Vizierships and secretaryships are not my business, but as to qadis and shaikhs, that is my occupation, and the occupation of my fathers before me. And as for military commands, you know that the non-Arabs were converted to Islam only at the point of the sword of the Arabs.' The sultan was pleased when he heard what I said.

He was at the time in the Thousand Columns eating a meal, and he sent for us and we ate in his presence as he was eating. We then withdrew to the outside of the Thousand Columns and my companions sat down, while I retired on account of a boil which prevented me from sitting. When the sultan summoned us a second time my companions presented themselves and made excuses to him on my behalf. I came back after the afternoon prayer and I performed the sunset and night prayers in the audience hall. The chamberlain then came out and summoned us. I went in and found the sultan on the terrace of the palace with his back leaning on the royal couch, the Vizier Khwajah Jahan before him, and the 'great king' Qabulah standing there upright. When I saluted him the 'great king' said to me, 'Do homage, for the Master of the World has appointed you qadi of the royal city of Dihli and has fixed your stipend at 12,000 dinars a year, and assigned to you villages to that amount, and commanded for you 12,000 dinars in cash, which you shall draw from the treasury tomorrow (if God will), and has given you a horse with its saddle and bridle and has ordered you to be invested with a *maharibi* robe of honour,' that is, a robe which has on its breast and on its back the figure of a *mihrab*.[6] So I did homage and when he had taken me by the hand and presented me before the sultan, the sultan said to me, 'Do not think that the office of qadi of Dihli is one of the minor functions; it is the highest of functions in our estimation.' I understood what he said though I could not speak in Persian fluently, but the sultan understood Arabic although he could not speak it fluently, so I said to him, 'O Master, I belong to the school of Malik and these people are Hanafis, and I do not know the language.' He replied, 'I have appointed two substitutes for you; they will be guided by your advice and you will be the one who signs all the documents, for you are in the place of a son to us,' to which I replied, 'Nay, but your slave and your servant.' He said to me in Arabic with humility and friendly kindness, 'No, but you are our lord and master.'

On the following day the sultan sent for us and we took possession of the moneys, horses and robes of honour. Each one of us took the sack containing the money, put it on his shoulder, and we came like this into the sultan's presence and did homage. When the horses were brought we kissed their hoofs after some rags of cloth had been put over them, and then led them ourselves to the gate of the sultan's palace, where we mounted them. All this ceremony is customary with them, and after it we withdrew.

Account of my creditors' demand for payment of my debt to them, of my panegyric addressed to the sultan, of his order for the acquittal of my debt, and the suspension of that for some time

As I have already mentioned, I had borrowed from the merchants a sum of money for my expenses on my journey, for the present which I had furnished to the sultan, and what I spent in staying at Dihli. When they were about to set out for their own lands they pressed me for payment of their loans, so I wrote a long ode in praise of the sultan, beginning as follows:

Commander of the Faithful, lord revered,
To thee we come, through deserts toward thee hasting.
A pilgrim I, thy glory's shrine to visit,
A refuge meet for sanctuary thy dwelling.
Had majesty a rank above the sun,
Fit pattern wert thou for its most excelling.
Thou art the Imam, unique and glorious, ever
Thy words infallibly with deeds investing.
I am in need, thy bounty's overflow
My hope, and by thy greatness eased my questing.
Shall I declare it – or thy blush suffice?
—To say 'thy bounty's plash' were seemlier punning.
Make speed to aid the votary to thy shrine,
And pay his debt – the creditors are dunning.

I then presented it to him in person as he was sitting upon a chair; he placed it upon his knee and held one end of it in his hand, with the other end in my hand. Whenever I finished one line of it I said to the Grand Qadi Kamal al-Din of Ghaznah, 'Explain its meaning to the Master of the World,' and he did so, to the sultan's delight, for they are fond of Arabic poetry. When I came to the verse, 'Make speed to aid the votary to thy shrine,' he said, '*Marhamah*,' which means, 'I have compassion upon you,' whereupon the chamberlains took me by the hand to conduct me to their ranks in the audience hall that I should do homage, according to the custom. But the sultan said, 'Leave him until he finishes it,' so I finished it and did homage. Those present congratulated me on this; then I waited for a few days and wrote a petition and delivered it to Qutb al-Mulk, the governor of Sind. He delivered it to the sultan, who said to him, 'Go to the vizier and tell him that the man's debt is to be acquitted.' Qutb al-Mulk therefore went to him and informed him of this, to which he replied, 'Certainly,' but this dragged on for some days, during which the sultan ordered the vizier to set out for Dawlat Abad, and in the meantime the sultan himself went on a hunting expedition. The vizier set out, and so I received none of this money until much later.

The reason for which the payment of this sum was suspended I shall now relate in detail. When my creditors were ready to travel I said to them, 'When I go to the palace of the sultan, "assail" me for your debt according to the custom of this country,' for I knew that when the sultan learned of that he would pay them. Their custom is this:

when anyone has lent money to a person under the sultan's protection and is unable to obtain payment of it, the creditor awaits the debtor at the door of the palace, and when the debtor is on the point of entering he says to him, '*Daruhai al-sultan* ['O enemy of the sultan'], by the head of the sultan you shall not enter until you have paid me what you owe.'[7] The debtor may not leave his place after this until he pays him or obtains a delay from him.

It happened one day that the sultan went out to visit his father's grave and alighted at a palace there. I said to my creditors, 'This is your moment,' so when I was about to enter they waited for me at the gate of the palace and said to me, '*Daruhai al-sultan*, you shall not enter until you pay us what you owe.' The clerks at the gate sent a written report of this to the sultan, whereupon a chamberlain came out and asked them why they had assailed me. When they replied that I was in debt to them, he returned to the sultan with this information, and on receiving the sultan's orders to ask the merchants the size of the debt he asked them and they said to him, 'Fifty-five thousand dinars.' The chamberlain returned to the sultan and informed him of this, whereupon he ordered him to return to them and to say to them, 'The Master of the World says to you, "The money is in my possession, and I shall give you justice; do not demand it of him".' He then commanded two officers to examine and verify the creditors' documents. They did so, the creditors brought their documents, and they went in to the sultan and informed him that the accounts were in order, whereupon he laughed and said jestingly, 'I know he is a qadi and has seen to his business with them.' He then commanded the treasurer to issue that sum, but the latter greedily demanded a bribe to do so and refused to write the authorization. I sent him two hundred tangahs, but he returned them and would not accept that amount. One of his servants told me from him that he demanded five hundred tangahs, but I refused to pay it. This matter came to the ears of the vizier, between whom and the treasurer there was a feud, and he informed the sultan of it, telling him at the same time many of the doings of the treasurer. The sultan, displeased with the latter, ordered him to be detained in the city saying, 'Why has so-and-so given him this money? Suspend this order until it is known whether the treasurer pays out anything when I have given it or refuses to pay when I give it.' So it was for this reason that the payment of my debt was suspended.

Account of the sultan's leaving for the hunt, of my going out with him, and of what I did on that occasion

When the sultan went out to hunt I went out along with him without any delay, as I had already made ready all that was required. I had bought a tent, which is indispensable for all men of high rank, and hired all of the servants that I needed. Indeed, I showed such vigour and energy that I left the city on the same day as the sultan while the rest of the court remained for two or three days after him.

One day when the sultan was in his tent he enquired who was outside. The sayyid Nasir al-Din, one of his familiars, said, 'So-and-so, the Moroccan, who is very upset.' 'Why so?' asked the sultan, and he replied, 'Because of his debt, since his creditors are pressing for payment.' The Malik Dawlat-Shah, whom the sultan used to address as 'Uncle', was present at this conversation and added, 'O Master of the World, every day this man talks to us in Arabic, and I do not know what he is saying. Do you know, Sayyid Nasir al-Din?' Nasir al-Din answered, 'He talks about the debt which he has contracted.' The sultan said, 'When we return to the capital, go yourself, O *Umar* (that is, O Uncle), to the treasury and give him this money.'

Account of the camels and sweetmeats which I presented to the sultan

In the course of the hunt the sultan had asked me whether al-Malik al-Nasir rode camels. I replied, 'Yes, he rides *mahari* camels[8] at the pilgrimage season, and they make the journey to Mecca from Cairo in ten days, but these camels are not like the camels in this country.' I told him that I had with me one of the *mahari* camels and when I returned to the capital I sent for one of the Arabs of Egypt, who made for me a model in wax of the saddle used for riding on *mahari* camels. I showed this to a carpenter, who made the saddle very skilfully, and I covered it with blanket cloth and furnished it with stirrups. I placed on the camel a fine striped cloak and made for it a bridle of silk. I had with me a man from al-Yaman who was very skilful in making sweet-meats, and he prepared some which resembled dates and other objects. I sent the camel and the sweets to the sultan. The sultan was delighted with this gift and said to my man, 'Mount the camel.' So he mounted it and walked it about in front of him, and the sultan ordered him to be given two hundred silver dinars and a robe of honour. When the man came back and told me about it I was full of joy, and I sent him two more camels after his return to the capital. I had two camel-saddles made for them. The front and the back of each I had covered with silver-gilt plates, and for both camels I provided anklets of silver. I prepared also eleven platters and filled them with sweetmeats, and covered each platter with a silk napkin.

When the sultan came back from the hunt and took his seat, on the day after his arrival, in his place of public audience, I put in an early appearance and presented the camels to him, and on his orders they were exercised in front of him. Then the sultan looked at the platters and said, 'Che dari dar an tabaqha halwa ast,' which means, 'What have you got in those plates? Surely it is sweetmeats,' and I said to him, 'Yes.' He then said to the others who were present, 'I have never eaten nor ever seen such sweetmeats as those which he sent to us when we were in the camp.' After this he ordered that the platters should be taken to his private sitting room, which was done, and when he rose to go to his sitting room, he summoned me and ordered food to be brought and I ate.

He then asked me about a particular kind of the sweetmeats which I had sent him previously. I said to him, 'O Master of the World, those sweetmeats were of many kinds and I do not know which kind you are asking about.' He said, 'Bring those plates,' and when they brought them and laid them before him and removed their covers, he said, 'It was about this one that I asked,' and took the dish in which it was. I said to him, 'This kind is called al-muqarrasah,' then he took another kind and said, 'What is the name of this?' and I said to him, 'These are the "judge's sweet-mouthfuls".' Now there was present a merchant whom the sultan used to address as 'My father'. This man was jealous of me, and wishing to humiliate me said, 'These are not the "judge's sweet-mouthfuls" but those are,' and he took a piece of the kind which is called 'horse-skin'. There was opposite him one of the intimate courtiers, who used often to jest with this merchant in the sultan's presence, and he said to him, 'O khoja, you lie and it is the qadi who speaks the truth.'[9] The sultan said to him, 'How so?' He replied, 'O Master of the World, he is the qadi and these are his sweet mouthfuls, for he brought them,' and the sultan laughed and said, 'You are right.'

At the end of the meal the sweetmeats were eaten; after that the barley-water was drunk and we took betel and withdrew. A few moments later the treasurer came to me and said, 'Send your friends to receive the money,' so I sent them, and on returning to my house after the sunset prayer found the money there in three sacks, with which I finally settled with my creditors.

The sultan's departure and command to me to remain in the capital

On the 9th of First Jumada[10] the sultan went out with the design of proceeding to al-Ma'bar and engaging the rebel leader in that province. I was all prepared to accompany the expedition, but at that moment a command was issued that I should remain behind. The sultan ordered that I should be given 6,000 dinars and also commanded me to take charge of the mausoleum of Sultan Qutb al-Din.[11] The sultan used to hold this tomb in great respect because he had been one of Qutb al-Din's servitors. I have seen him on coming to his grave take Qutb al-Din's sandal, kiss it and place it on his head, for it is their custom to put the sandals of the dead man on a cushion beside his grave. Whenever he came to the grave he would do homage to it, as he used to do homage in Qutb al-Din's lifetime, and he held Qutb al-Din's wife in great respect and used to address her as his sister.

When the sultan went out he sent for us to bid us farewell. I came forward after to say farewell, and I was pleased to be staying behind. He said, 'What requests have you?' so I took out a piece of paper on which I had written several petitions, but he said to me, 'Speak with your own tongue.' I said to him, 'The Master of the World has commanded me to act as a qadi but I have not yet sat for that purpose; and I do not desire to have nothing but the honour of the qadiship,' whereupon he commanded me to sit as a judge and that two substitutes should sit with me. Then he said to me, 'Well?' and I said, 'The mausoleum of Sultan Qutb al-Din, what shall I do about it, for I have already given appointments in connection with it to four hundred and sixty persons, and the income from its endowments does not cover their wages and their food?' He said to the vizier, 'Give him a hundred thousand maunds of the corn produce (that is to say wheat and rice) to be expended during this year until the crops of the endowment for the tomb come in.'

He then said to me, 'And what more?' so I replied, 'I have exchanged the villages which you gave me for other revenues; but the officials of the treasury have demanded from me either to pay what I have received from them or to present the order of the Master of the World to be dispensed from that.' He said, 'How much did you receive from them?' I replied, 'Five thousand dinars.' He said, 'They are a gift to you.' I then said to him, 'And my house which you have ordered for me as my residence is in need of repairs.' He said to the vizier, 'Have it repaired,' and went on to say to me, 'Have you anything more to say?' and I said to him, 'No.' He then said to me, 'There is another recommendation, and that is that you incur no debts and so avoid being pressed for payment, for you will not find anyone to bring me news of them. Regulate your expenses according to what I have given you, for as God has said in the Qur'an, *Keep not thy hand bound to thy neck, neither open it to fullest extent*, and again, *Eat and drink, and be not prodigal*, and again, *And those who, when they spend, neither incline to excess nor fall short through niggardliness, but between these there is an upright mean.*' I desired to kiss his foot, but he prevented me and held back my head with his hand, so I kissed that and retired.

I returned to the capital and busied myself with repairing my house; on this I spent four thousand dinars, of which I received from the treasury six hundred and paid the rest myself. I also built a mosque opposite my house, and occupied myself with the dispositions for the mausoleum of the Sultan Qutb al-Din. The sultan had ordered that a dome should be built over it to the height of 100 cubits, exceeding by 20 cubits the height of the dome built over the tomb of Qazan, the king of al-Iraq. He had given orders also that thirty villages were to be purchased to constitute an endowment for it, and he placed them in my hands on the understanding that I should enjoy the tenth part of their revenue according to custom.

Account of the ceremonial which I established for the mausoleum

It is the custom for the people of India to observe in regard to their dead a ceremonial similar to that observed in their lifetime. Elephants fully caparisoned are brought and picketed at the gate of the tomb chamber. I organized everything in this tomb-chamber in accordance with that custom and enrolled of reciters of the Qu'ran a hundred and fifty, of theological students eighty, of assistant teachers eight, one professor, of the sufis eighty, and the imam, the muezzins, reciters who possessed fine voices, rhapsodists, and clerks to note the name of absentees, and announcers of names. I dispensed every day thirty-five maunds of flour and thirty-five of meat, together with the usual subsidiaries of sugar, candy, ghee and betel, in feeding not only the salaried employees but also visitors and travellers. The famine at that time was severe, but the population was relieved by this food, and the news of it spread far and wide. The Malik Sabih, having gone to join the sultan at Dawlat Abad, was asked by him for news of the doings of the people in Dihli and answered, 'If there were in Dihli two such men as so-and-so there would be no complaints of famine.' The sultan was pleased at this and sent me a robe of honour from his own wardrobe.

Account of the sultan's intention to punish me and of my escape from this by the mercy of God

The cause of this was that I went one day to visit Shaikh Shihab al-Din son of Shaikh al-Jam in the cave which he had dug for himself outside Dihli. My object was to see that cave, but when the sultan seized him and asked his sons about those who used to visit him, they mentioned my name amongst those of others. Thereupon the sultan gave orders that four of his slaves should remain constantly beside me in the audience hall, and customarily when he takes this action with anyone it rarely happens that that person escapes. The day on which they began to guard me was a Friday and God Most High inspired me to recite His words *Sufficient for us is God and excellent the Protector*. I recited them that day 33,000 times and passed the night in the audience hall. I fasted five days on end, reciting the Qur'an from cover to cover each day, and tasting nothing but water. After five days I broke my fast and then continued to fast for another four days on end, and I was released after the execution of the shaikh, praise be to God Most High.

Account of my withdrawal from the sultan's service and leaving of the world

Sometime later I withdrew from the sultan's service and attached myself to the shaikh and imam, the learned, devout, ascetic, humble-minded, pious Kamal al-Din Abdallah al-Ghari, the unique and unequalled personality of his age. He was one of the saints and had performed many miracles, some of which that I saw with my own eyes I have already related on speaking of him previously. I devoted myself to the service of this shaikh and gave my possessions to the poor brethren and the needy. The shaikh used to fast for ten days on end, and sometimes for twenty days, but when I wished to fast continuously he would check me and bid me not to overstrain myself in devotional exercise, saying to me, 'He who breaks down from exhaustion has neither covered ground nor spared a mount.' There seemed to me to be a certain sluggishness in me because of something which remained in my possession, so I rid myself of everything that I had, little or much, and I gave the clothes off my back to a mendicant and put on his clothes. I remained with this shaikh as a disciple for five months, the sultan being at that time absent in the land of Sind.

Account of the sultan's sending for me and my refusal to return to his service and my zeal in devotional exercises

When the sultan was informed of my leaving the world he summoned me, being at that time in Siwasitan. I entered his presence dressed as a mendicant, and he spoke to me with the greatest kindness and solicitude, desiring me to return to his service. But I refused and asked him for permission to travel to the Hijaz, which he granted. I withdrew from him and lodged in a hospice. This was in the last days of Second Jumada of the year forty-two.[12] I remained there engaged in devotional exercises during the month of Rajab and ten days of Sha'ban and at length was able to fast for five days in succession, after which I tasted a little rice without any seasoning. I used to recite the Qur'an every day and to keep vigils by night as God willed. Whenever I ate food it was disagreeable to me and when I discarded it I found relief. I remained in this state for forty days and then the sultan sent for me again.

Account of his command to me to proceed
to China on embassy

When I had completed forty days the sultan sent me saddled horses, slave girls and boys, robes and a sum of money, so I put on the robes and went to him. I had a quilted tunic of blue cotton which I wore during my retreat, and as I put it off and dressed in the sultan's robes I upbraided myself. Ever after, when I looked at that tunic, I felt a light within me, and it remained in my possession until the infidels despoiled me of it on the sea. When I presented myself before the sultan, he showed me greater favour than before, and said to me, 'I have expressly sent for you to go as my ambassador to the king of China, for I know your love of travel and sightseeing.' He then provided me with everything I required, and appointed certain other persons to accompany me, as I shall relate presently.

11 From Dihli to Kinbayah

Account of the reason for the sending of the gift to China, of those who were sent with me and of the gift itself

The king of China had sent to the sultan a hundred mamluks and slave girls, five hundred pieces of velvet cloth, five maunds of musk, five robes adorned with jewels, five embroidered quivers, and five swords, with a request that the sultan would permit him to rebuild the idol-temple which is near the mountains called Qarajil [Himalaya].[1] It is in a place known as Samhal, to which the Chinese go on pilgrimage; the Muslim army in India had captured it, laid it in ruins and sacked it. The sultan, on receiving this gift, wrote to the king saying that the request could not be granted by Islamic law, as permission to build a temple in the territories of the Muslims was granted only to those who paid a poll-tax; to which he added, 'If thou wilt pay the tax we shall empower thee to build it. And peace be on those who follow the True Guidance.' He requited his present with an even richer one – a hundred thoroughbred horses saddled and bridled, a hundred male slaves, a hundred Hindu singing- and dancing-girls, fifteen hundred pieces of cloth, unequalled in beauty, a large tent, six pavilions, four candelabra in gold and six in silver enamelled, four golden basins with ewers to match and six silver basins, ten embroidered robes of honour from the sultan's own wardrobe and ten caps also worn by him, one of them encrusted with pearls, ten embroidered quivers one of them encrusted with pearls, ten swords one of them with a scabbard encrusted with pearls, gloves embroidered with pearls, and fifteen eunuchs.

As my fellow-voyagers with this present the sultan appointed the Amir Zahir al-Din of Zanjan, one of the most eminent men of learning, and the eunuch Kafur, the cup-bearer, into whose keeping the present was entrusted. He sent with us the Amir Muhammad of Harat with a thousand horsemen to escort us to the port of embarkation, and we were accompanied by the ambassadors of the king of China, fifteen in number, along with their servants, about a hundred men. We set out therefore in a great company with an imposing body of troops. The sultan gave instructions that we were to be supplied with provisions while we were travelling through his dominions. Our journey began on the 17th of Safar 43 [22 July 1342]. That was the day selected because they choose either the 2nd, 7th, 12th, 17th, 22nd, or 27th of the month as the day for setting out on a journey.

We came to Kuwil [Koel], a pretty town with orchards, most of their trees being mangoes.[2] Here we heard that certain Hindu infidels had invested and surrounded the town of al-Jalali. Now this town lies at a distance of seven miles from Kuwil, so we made in that direction. Meanwhile the infidels were engaged in battle with its inhabitants and the latter were on the verge of destruction. The infidels knew nothing of our approach until we charged down upon them, though they numbered about a thousand cavalry and three thousand foot, and we killed them to the last man and took possession of their horses and their weapons. Of our party twenty-three horsemen and fifty-five foot-soldiers suffered martyrdom, amongst them the eunuch Kafur, the cup-bearer, into whose hands the present had been entrusted. We informed the sultan by letter of his death and halted to await his reply. During that time the infidels used to swoop down from an inaccessible hill which is in those parts and raid the environs of al-Jalali, and our party used to ride out every day with the commander of that district to assist him in driving them off.

Account of my trial by captivity, and of my deliverance from it and from hardships thereafter at the hand of one of the saints of God

On one of these occasions I rode out with several friends and we went into a garden to take our siesta, for this was in the hot season. Then we heard some shouting, so we mounted our horses and overtook some infidels who had attacked one of the villages of al-Jalali. When we pursued them they broke up into small parties; our troop in following them did the same, and I was isolated with five others. At this point we were attacked by a body of cavalry and foot-soldiers from a thicket thereabouts, and we fled from them because of their numbers. About ten of them pursued me, but afterwards all but three of them gave up the chase. There was no track at all before me and the ground there was very stony. My horse's forefeet got caught between the stones, so I dismounted, freed its foot and mounted again. It is customary for a man in India to carry two swords, one called the stirrup-sword, attached to the saddle, and the other in his quiver. My stirrup-sword fell out of its scabbard, and as its ornaments were of gold I dismounted, picked it up, slung it on me and mounted, my pursuers chasing me all the while. After this I came to a deep nullah, so I dismounted and climbed down to the bottom of it, and that was the last I saw of them.

I came out of this into a valley amidst a patch of tanglewood, through which there was a track, so I walked along it, not knowing where it led to. At this juncture about forty of the infidels, carrying bows in their hands, came out upon me and surrounded me. I was afraid that they would all shoot at me at once if I fled from them, and I was wearing no armour so I threw myself to the ground and surrendered, as they do not kill those who do that. They seized me and stripped me of everything that I was carrying except a *jubbah*,[3] shirt and trousers, then they took me into that patch of jungle, and finally brought me to the part of it where they were staying near a tank of water situated amongst those trees. They gave me bread made of *mash*, that is peas, and I ate some of it and drank some water. In their company there were two Muslims who spoke to me in Persian, and asked me all about myself. I told them part of my story, but concealed the fact that I had come from the sultan. Then they said to me: 'You are sure to be put to death either by these men or by others, but this man here (pointing to one of them) is their leader.' So I spoke to him, using the two Muslims as interpreters, and tried to conciliate him. He gave me in charge of three of the band, one of them an old man, with whom was his son, and the third an evil black fellow. These three spoke to me and I understood from them that they had received orders to kill me. In the evening of the same day they carried me off to a cave, but God sent an ague upon the black, so he put his feet upon me, and the old man and his son went to sleep. In the morning they talked among themselves and made signs to me to accompany them down to the tank. I realized that they were going to kill me, so I spoke to the old man and tried to gain his favour, and he took pity on me. I cut off the sleeves of my shirt and gave them to him so that the other members of the band should not blame him on my account if I escaped.

About noon we heard voices near the tank and they thought that it was their comrades, so they made signs to me to go down with them, but when we went down we found some other people. The newcomers advised my guards to accompany them but they refused, and the three of them sat down in front of me, keeping me facing them, and laid on the ground a hempen rope which they had with them. I was watching them all the time and saying to myself: 'It is with this rope that they will bind me when they kill me.' I remained thus for a time, then three of their party, the party that had captured me, came up and spoke to them and I understood that they said to them: 'Why have you not killed him?' The old man pointed to the black, as though he were excusing himself on the ground of his illness. One of these three was a pleasant-looking youth, and he said to me: 'Do you wish me to set you at liberty?' I said, 'Yes' and he answered, 'Go.' So I took the tunic which I was wearing and gave it to him and he gave me a worn double-woven [or indigo-dyed] cloak which he had, and showed me the way. I went off but I was afraid lest they should change their minds and overtake me, so I went into a reed thicket and hid there till sunset.

Then I made my way out and followed the track which the youth had shown me. This led to a pool from which I drank. I went on till near midnight and came to a hill under which I slept. In the morning I continued along the track, and sometime before noon reached a high rocky hill on which there were sweet lote-trees and zizyphus bushes. I started to pull and eat the lote berries so eagerly that the thorns left scars on my arms that remain there to this day. Coming down from that hill I entered a plain sown with cotton and containing castor-oil trees. Here there was a *ba'in*, which in their language means a very broad well with a stone casing and steps by which you go down to reach the water.[4] Some of them have stone pavilions, arcades, and seats in the centre and on the sides, and the kings and nobles of the country vie with one another in constructing them along the highroads where there is no water. We shall have occasion later on to describe some of these that we have seen. When I reached the *ba'in* I drank some water from it and I found on it some mustard shoots which had been dropped by their owner when he washed them. Some of these I ate and saved up the rest, then I lay down under a castor-oil tree. While I was there about forty mail-clad horsemen came to the *ba'in* to get water and some of them entered the sown fields, then they went away, and God sealed their eyes that they did not see me. After them came about fifty others carrying arms and they too went down into the *ba'in*. One of them came up to a tree opposite the one I was under, yet he did not discover me. At this point I made my way into the field of cotton and stayed there the rest of the day, while they stayed at the *ba'in* washing their clothes and whiling away the time. At night time their voices died away, so I knew that they had either passed on or fallen asleep. Thereupon I emerged and followed the trail of the horses, for the nights were moonlit, continuing till I came to another *ba'in* with a dome overlooking it. I went down to it, drank some water, ate some of the mustard shoots which I had, and went into the dome. I found it full of grass collected by birds, so I went to sleep in it. Now and again I felt the movement of an animal amongst the grass; I suppose it was a snake, but I was too worn out to pay any attention.

The next morning I went along a broad track, which led to a ruined village. Then I took another track, but with the same result as before. Several days passed in this manner. One day I came to some tangled trees with a tank of water between them. The space under the trees was like a room, and at the sides of the tank were plants like dittany and others. I intended to stop there until God should send someone to bring me to inhabited country, but I recovered a little strength, so I arose and walked along a track on which I found the traces of cattle. I found a bull carrying a packsaddle and a sickle, but after all this track led to the villages of the infidels. Then I followed up another track and this brought me to a ruined village. There I saw two naked blacks, and in fear of them I remained under some trees there. At nightfall I entered the village and found a house in one of whose rooms there was something like a large jar of the sort they make to store grain in. At the bottom of it there was a hole large enough to admit a man, so I crept into it and found inside it bedding of chopped straw, and amongst this a stone on which I laid my head and went to sleep. On the top of the jar there was a bird which kept fluttering its wings most of the night – I suppose it was frightened, so we made a pair of frightened creatures. This went on for seven days from the day on which I was taken prisoner, which was a Saturday. On the seventh day I came to a village of the infidels which was inhabited and possessed a tank of water and plots of vegetables. I asked them for some food but they refused to give me any. However, in the neighbourhood of a well I found some radish leaves and ate them. I went into the village, and found a troop of infidels with sentries posted. The sentries challenged me but I did not answer them and sat down on the ground. One of them came over with a drawn sword and raised it to strike me, but I paid no attention to him, so utterly weary did I feel. Then he searched me but found nothing on me, so he took the shirt whose sleeves I had given to the old man who had had charge of me.

On the eighth day I was consumed with thirst and I had no water at all. I came to a ruined village but found no tank in it. They have a custom in those villages of making tanks in which the rainwater collects, and this supplies them with drinking water all the year round. Then I went along a track and this brought me to an uncased well over which was a rope of vegetable fibre, but there was no vessel on it to draw water with. I took a piece of cloth which I had on my head and tied it to the rope and sucked the water that soaked into it, but that did not slake my thirst. I tied on my shoe next and drew up water in it, but that did not satisfy me either, so I drew water with it a second time, but the rope broke and the shoe fell back into the well. I then tied on the other shoe and drank until my thirst was assuaged. After that I cut the shoe and tied its uppers on my foot with the rope of the well and bits of cloth which I found there. While I was trying this on and wondering what to do, a person appeared before me. I looked at him, and lo! it was a black-skinned man, carrying a jug and a staff in his hand, and a wallet on his shoulder. He gave me the Muslim greeting, 'Peace be upon you,' and I replied, 'Upon you be peace and the mercy and blessings of God.' Then he asked me in Persian *Chikas*, 'Who are you?' and I answered, 'A man astray,' and he said, 'So am I.' Thereupon he tied a jug to a rope which he had with him and drew up some water. I wished to drink but he, saying, 'Have patience,' opened his wallet and brought out a handful of black chickpeas fried with a little rice. After I had eaten some of this and drunk, he made his ablutions and prayed two prostrations and I did the same. Thereupon he asked my name. I answered, 'Muhammad,' and asked him his, to which he replied, 'al-Qalb al-Farih ["Joyous

Heart"].' I took this as a good omen and rejoiced at it. After this he said to me, 'In the name of God accompany me.' I said, 'Yes,' and walked on with him for a little, then I found my limbs giving way, and as I was unable to stand up I sat down. He said, 'What is the matter with you?' I answered, 'I was able to walk before meeting you, but now that I have met you, I cannot.' Whereupon he said, 'Glory be to God! Mount on my shoulder.' I said to him, 'You are weak, and have not strength enough for that,' but he replied, 'God will give me strength. You must do so.' So I got up on his shoulders and he said to me, 'Say many times, "God is sufficient for us and excellent the Protector".' I repeated this over and over again, but I could not keep my eyes open, and regained consciousness only on feeling myself falling to the ground. Then I woke up, but found no trace of the man and lo! I was at an inhabited village. I entered it and found it was of Hindu peasants with a Muslim governor. They informed him about me and he came to meet me. I asked him the name of this village and he replied, 'Taj Burah.'[5] The distance from there to Kuwil, where our party was, is two *farsakhs*. The governor provided a horse to take me to his house and gave me hot food, and I washed. Then he said to me, 'I have here a garment and a turban which were left in my charge by a certain Arab from Egypt, one of the soldiers belonging to the camp at Kuwil.' I said to him, 'Bring them; I shall wear them until I reach camp.' When he brought them I found that they were two of my own garments which I had given to that very Arab when we came to Kuwil. I was extremely astonished at this, then I thought of the man who had carried me on his shoulders and I remembered what the saint Abu Abdallah al-Murshidi had told me, as I have related in the first volume, when he said to me, 'You will enter the land of India and meet there my brother Dilshad, who will deliver you from a misfortune which will befall you there.'[6] I remembered too how he had said, when I asked him his name, 'Joyous Heart' which, translated into Persian, is Dilshad. So I knew that it was he whom the saint had foretold that I should meet, and that he too was one of the saints, but I enjoyed no more of his company than the short space which I have related.

The same night I wrote to my friends at Kuwil to inform them of my safety, and they came, bringing me a horse and clothes, and rejoiced at my escape. I found that the sultan's reply had reached them and that he had sent a eunuch named Sumbul in place of the martyred Kafur, with orders to pursue our journey. I found too that they had written to the sultan about what had happened to me, and that they regarded this journey as ill-omened on account of what had happened in the course of it to me and to Kafur, and were wanting to go back. But when I saw that the sultan insisted upon the journey, I urged them on with great determination. They answered, 'Do you not see what has befallen us at the very outset of this mission? The sultan will excuse you, so let us return to him or stay here until his reply reaches us.' But I said, 'We cannot stay, and wherever we are his reply will reach us.'

We left Kuwil therefore, and journeyed next to Galyur, a large town with an impregnable fortress isolated on the summit of a lofty hill.[7] Over its gate is the figure of an elephant with its mahout carved in stone. The governor of this town was a man of upright character, and he treated me very honourably when I stayed with him on a previous occasion. One day I came before him as he was about to have an infidel cut in two. I said to him, 'By God I beseech you, do not do this, for I have never seen anyone put to death in my presence.' He ordered the man to be put in prison so my intervention was the means of his escape.

From Galyur we went on to Barwan, a small town belonging to the Muslims, but situated in the land of the infidels.[8] There are many tigers there, and one of the inhabitants told me that a certain tiger used to enter the town by night, although the gates were shut, and used to seize people. It killed quite a number of the townsfolk in this way, and they used to wonder how it made its way in. One of the inhabitants of the town told me that it came into his house by night and carried off a boy who was lying on his bed. Another told me that he was with a party at a wedding celebration and one of them went out to relieve nature, when the tiger seized him; his companions went out in search of him and found him lying in the bazaar. The tiger had drunk his blood but not eaten his flesh and they say that this is the way it does with men. Here is an amazing thing: a certain man told me that it was not a tiger who did this but a human being, one of the magicians known as *jugis*,[9] appearing in the shape of a tiger. When I heard this I refused to believe it, but a number of people told me the same thing; so let us give at this point some of the stories about these magicians.

From Dihli to Kinbayah

Account of the magicians called *jugis*

The men of this sect do some marvellous things. One of them will spend months without eating or drinking, and many of them have holes dug for them under the earth which are then built in on top of them, leaving only a space for air to enter. They stay in these for months, and I heard tell of one of them who remained thus for a year. In the town of Manjarur [Mangalore] I saw a man of the Muslims, one of those who learn the arts of these people, for whom a platform had been put up, on top of which he stayed without eating or drinking for a space of not less than twenty-five days. I left him at that point and I do not know how long he remained after I had gone. The people say that they make up pills, one of which they take for a given number of days or months, and during that time they require no food or drink. They can also tell what is happening at a distance. The sultan holds them in esteem and admits them to his company. Some eat nothing but vegetables, and others, the majority, eat no meat; it is obvious that they have so disciplined themselves in ascetic practices that they have no need of any of the goods or vanities of this world. There are amongst them some who merely look at a man and he falls dead under their glance. The common people say that if the breast of a man killed in this way is cut open, it is found to contain no heart, and they assert that his heart has been eaten. This is commonest in the case of women, and a woman who acts thus is called *kaftar*.[10]

Anecdote

When the great famine was caused in the land of India by the drought, during the sultan's absence in the province of Tiling,[11] he despatched an order that the inhabitants of Dihli should be given an allowance of food at the rate of a pound and a half per person per day. The vizier assembled them and distributed the indigent inhabitants amongst the amirs and qadis so that these latter should be responsible for supplying them with food. My share of them was five hundred souls; I built for them galleries in two houses and lodged them there, and I used to give them provisions for five days every five days. One day they brought me a woman, one of their number, saying that she was a *kaftar* and had eaten the heart of a boy who

209

was beside her, and they also brought the dead body of the boy. I ordered them to take her to the sultan's lieutenant, who commanded that she should be put to the test. They filled four jars with water, tied them to her hands and feet and threw her into the river Jun. As she did not sink she was known to be a *kaftar*; had she not floated she would not have been one. He ordered her then to be burned with fire. The people of the town came and collected her ashes, men and women alike, for they believe that anyone who fumigates himself with them is safe against a *kaftar*'s enchantments during that year.

Anecdote

The sultan sent for me once when I was with him at Dihli, and on entering I found him in a private apartment with some of his intimates and two of these *jugis*. They were wearing long cloaks and had their heads covered, because they remove all their hair with ashes as people generally remove the hair of the armpits. After the sultan had ordered me to sit down and I had done so, he said to them, 'This distinguished man comes from a far country, so show him something that he has not seen,' to which they replied, 'Yes.' One of them squatted on the ground, then rose from the ground into the air above our heads, still sitting. I was so astonished and frightened that I fell to the floor in a faint. The sultan gave orders to administer to me a potion that he had there and I revived and sat up. Meantime this man remained in his sitting posture. His companion then took a sandal from a sack he had with him, and beat it on the ground like one infuriated. The sandal rose in the air until it came above the neck of the sitting man and then began hitting him on the neck while he descended little by little until he sat down alongside us. The sultan said to me, 'The man sitting is the pupil of the owner of the sandal.' Then he said, 'If I did not fear for your reason I would have ordered them to do still stranger things than this you have seen.' I took my leave but was affected with palpitation and fell ill, until he ordered me to be given a draught which removed it all.

To return to our subject. We travelled from the town of Barwan to the post-station of Amwari and on to the post-station of Kajarra.[12] Here there is a large tank, about a mile in length, on the sides of which there are temples containing idols which have been mutilated by the

Muslims. In the centre of the tank there are three pavilions of red stone, three storeys high, and on each of the four corners another pavilion. There live there a company of *jugis* who have matted their hair and let it grow until it has come to be as long as themselves. They are generally of a yellow colour because of their mortifications, and many Muslims become their disciples in order to learn their secrets. They say that if a man suffering from some bodily disease such as leprosy or elephantiasis resorts to them for a long time, he will be cured by the grace of God.

The first time that I saw the men of this company was in the *mahallah* of Sultan Tarmashirin, king of Turkestan. There were about fifty of them for whom a cave had been dug under the earth, and they used to stay in it, never coming out except to satisfy a need. They had a sort of horn which they used to sound at the beginning and end of the day and after the first third of the night. Everything about them is marvellous. It was one of them who made pills for the sultan of the land of Ma'bar, to take as an aphrodisiac. Amongst their ingredients were iron filings, and he was so pleased with their effect that he took more of them than was necessary and died. He was succeeded by his brother's son, who showed high consideration for that *jugi* and raised him in dignity.

We went next to Dawlat Abad, the enormous and important city which rivals Dihli, the capital, in standing and in the spaciousness of its planning. Its citadel is unrivalled and unequalled for its strength and is called Duwaygir.[13] This fortress is a rock situated in a plain; the rock has been excavated and a castle built on its summit. It is reached by a ladder made of leather, which is taken up at night. There is a prison there, in whose dungeons are imprisoned those convicted of serious crime, and in these dungeons there are huge rats, bigger than cats – in fact, cats run away from them and cannot defend themselves, for these rats are too strong for them, so they can be captured only by means of ingenious devices which are employed to deal with them. I saw them there and marvelled at them.

Anecdote

The Malik Khattab al-Afghani told me that he had once been imprisoned in a dungeon in this fortress, which went by the name of 'the pit of the rats'. He said: 'They used to collect together by night to devour me and I fought against them, which I could only do with great difficulty. I then saw in a dream a man who said to me, "Recite the surah of al-Ikhlas a hundred thousand times and God will deliver you".[14] So I recited it and when I had completed this number I was released. The reason for my release was that the Malik Mall was imprisoned in a dungeon adjacent to mine; he fell sick and the rats ate his fingers and his eyes and he died. When this was reported to the sultan he said, "Fetch out Khattab in case the same thing happens to him".'

The inhabitants of Dawlat Abad belong to the tribe of the Marhatah, whose women God has endowed with special beauty, particularly in their noses and eyebrows.[15] They have in intercourse a deliciousness and a knowledge of erotic movements beyond that of other women. The infidels of this city are merchants dealing principally in jewels, and their wealth is enormous. At Dawlat Abad there are grapes and pomegranates, both of which produce fruit twice in the year. It is one of the largest and most important of the provinces in respect of taxes and land revenue, on account of its dense population and the extent of its territory. I have been told that a certain Hindu contracted for the farm of the taxes of the town and its province together (and the latter is, as we have said, a three months' journey) for seventeen crores, the crore being a hundred laks and the lak a hundred thousand dinars. But he was unable to fulfil his obligation; a part of it remained outstanding and his property was seized and he was flayed.

Description of the bazaar of the singers

In the city of Dawlat Abad there is an exceedingly fine and spacious bazaar for singers and singing-girls, called Tarab Abad, containing numerous shops, each of which has a door leading to the house of its proprietor. Each house has another door as well. The shop is beautified with carpets, and in the centre of it there is a sort of large cradle on which the singing-girl sits or reclines. She is adorned with all kinds of ornaments and her attendant girls swing her cradle.

We continued on our way to Nadharbar,[16] a small town inhabited by the Marhatahs, who possess a great skill in the arts, and are physicians and astrologers. The nobles of the Marhatahs are Brahmans and also Katris [Kshatriyas]. Their food consists of rice, vegetables, and oil of sesame, and they do not hold with giving pain to or slaughtering animals. They wash themselves before eating, like our major ablution, and do not marry among their relatives, unless those who are cousins six times removed. Neither do they drink wine, for this in their eyes is the greatest of vices. The Muslims in India take the same view, and any Muslim who drinks is punished with eighty stripes, and shut up for three months in a matamore which is opened only when he is given food.

12 South India

From the aforesaid Nadharbar we travelled on to the town of Kinbayah [Cambay] which is situated on an arm of the sea resembling a river;[1] it is navigable for ships and its waters ebb and flow. I myself saw the ships there lying on the mud at ebb-tide and floating on the water at high tide. This city is one of the finest there is in regard to the excellence of its construction and the architecture of its mosques. The reason is that the majority of its inhabitants are foreign merchants, who are always building there fine mansions and magnificent mosques and vie with one another in doing so.

The governor of Kinbayah at the time of our arrival was Muqbil of Tiling, who was held in high consideration by the sultan. He gave a banquet for us one day in his mansion. By an amusing chance the qadi of the city, who was blind in the right eye, on taking his seat had opposite him a sharif from Baghdad with a marked resemblance to him in his features and his blindness, except for the fact that he was blind in the left eye. The sharif kept looking at the qadi and laughing, and when the qadi rebuked him he replied, 'Do not reprove me, for I am more handsome than you.' 'How's that?' asked the qadi. 'Because you are blind in the right eye and I am blind in the left,' he replied, whereupon the governor and all those present laughed and the qadi was put to shame, but he was unable to make a rejoinder because sharifs are treated in India with the greatest veneration.

We journeyed from this city to Qandahar, a large town belonging to the infidels and situated on a bay of the sea.[2] The sultan of Qandahar is an infidel called Jalansi, who is under Muslim suzerainty and sends a gift to the king of India every year. When we reached Qandahar he came out to welcome us and showed us the greatest honour, himself leaving his palace and installing us in it. The principal Muslims at his court came to visit us, such as the children of the Khwajah Buhrah.[3] One of these is the shipowner Ibrahim, who possesses six vessels of his own. From this city we continued our journey by sea.

Account of our embarkation

We embarked on a ship belonging to the Ibrahim mentioned above, of the type called *jagir*. On this ship we put seventy of the horses of the sultan's present, and the rest we put with the horses of our companions on a ship belonging to this Ibrahim's brother, called a *manurt*. Jalansi gave us a vessel on which we put the horses of Zahir al-Din and Sumbul and their party, and he furnished it for us with water, provisions and forage. He sent his son with us on a ship called an *ukairi*, which resembles a grab, but is rather broader; it has sixty oars and is covered with a roof during battle in order to protect the rowers from arrows and stones. I myself went on board the *jagir*, which had a complement of fifty rowers and fifty Abyssinian men-at-arms. These latter are the guarantors of safety on this sea; let there be but one of them on a ship and it will be avoided by the Indian pirates and idolaters.

Two days later we called at the island of Bairam, which is uninhabited and at a distance of four miles from the mainland.[4] We disembarked on this island and took a supply of water from a tank there. The reason for its devastation is that the Muslims captured it by force from the infidels and it has not been inhabited since. We continued our journey thence and on the following day arrived at the city of Quqah, a large town with important bazaars. We anchored four miles from shore on account of the low tide. I went down into a skiff with some of my associates at the time of low tide, with the object of going into the town, but the skiff stuck in the mud when we were about a mile distant from it. When we sank into the mud I was leaning upon two of my companions, and the men of the place gave me to fear the turn of the tide before I should reach it, since I was not a good swimmer. But finally I did get to it and made the circuit of its bazaars and saw there a mosque attributed to al-Khidr and Ilyas (on them both be peace), in which I made the sunset prayer. I found in the mosque a number of poor brethren of the Haidari order along with a shaikh of theirs. I then returned to the ship.

On setting sail from this town we arrived after three days at the island of Sandabur [Goa], in which there are thirty-six villages. It is surrounded by a gulf, the waters of which are sweet and agreeable at low tide but salt and bitter at high tide. On this occasion we did not stop at this island when we passed by it, but anchored at a smaller one near the mainland, in which there was a temple, an orchard, and a water-tank, and on which we found one of the *jugis*.[5]

The story of this *jugi*

When we landed on this smaller island we found there a *jugi* leaning against the wall of a *budkhanah*, that is an idol-temple; he was between two of its idols and showed the traces of continuous practice of religious austerities. When we spoke to him he did not say a word, and we looked to see if there was any food with him but did not see any. While we were still looking he uttered a great shout, and as he shouted a coconut fell from a coco-palm in front of him. He handed it to us and we in astonishment gave him some dinars and dirhams, which he would not accept, and when we brought him provisions he refused them also. There was a cloak of camel hair lying on the ground in front of him; I took it in hand to examine it and he gave it to me. I had in my hand a chaplet of Zaila; he examined it in my hand so I gave it to him. He rubbed it between his fingers, smelt it, kissed it, and pointed first to the sky and then in the direction of Mecca.[6] My companions did not understand his signs, but I for my part understood him to indicate that he was a Muslim who was concealing his Muslim belief from the people of that island and living on those coconuts. When we were about to leave him I kissed his hand; my companions disapproved of that, but he perceived their disapproval and taking my hand kissed it and smiled and signed to us to go. So we left, I being the last of my party to go out, when he tugged at my cloak; I turned my head towards him and he gave me ten dinars. When we came out of the place my companions said to me, 'Why did he pull you?' and I told them that he had given me those dinars. I gave three of them to Zahir al-Din and three to Sumbul, saying to them, 'The man is a Muslim; do you not see how he pointed to the sky to indicate that he knew God, and then to Mecca to indicate his knowledge of the Apostle (peace be upon him)? And his taking of the chaplet confirms the fact.' They went back when I said this to them but they could not find him.

We set out again immediately and on the next day reached the town of Hinawr, which is on a large inlet into which large ships enter.[7] The town itself is half a mile from the sea. During the *bushkal*, which is the rainy season, this bay is so stormy and boisterous that for four months it is impossible for anyone to sail on it except for fishing.

On the day of our arrival at this place one of the Hindu *jugis* came to me secretly and gave me six dinars saying to me, 'The Brahman has sent this to you,' meaning the *jugi* to whom I had given the chaplet. When he gave me the dinars I took them from him and offered him one of them, but he declined it and withdrew. I told my companions what had happened and said to them, 'If you wish your share of them you may have it.' They both refused but were full of astonishment at the ways of this person and said to me, 'The six dinars which you gave us we left with six others between the two idols in the place where we found him.' I was greatly astonished at our adventure with this person and kept with special care those dinars that he had given me.

The people of the city of Hinawr are Shafi'ites in doctrine, upright, religious, engaged in warfare on the sea, and mighty. The women of this town and of all these coastal districts wear no sewn garments but only unsewn lengths of cloth, one end of which they gird round their waists, and drape the rest over their head and chest. They are beautiful and virtuous, and each wears a gold ring in her nose. One peculiarity amongst them is that they all know the Qur'an by heart. I saw in the town thirteen schools for girls and twenty-three for boys, a thing which I have never seen elsewhere. Its inhabitants live by maritime commerce, and have no cultivated land.

Account of the sultan of Hinawr

He is the Sultan Jamal al-Din Muhammad ibn Hasan, one of the best and most powerful sultans. He is under the suzerainty of an infidel sultan named Haryab.[8] The Sultan Jamal al-Din is assiduous in attending the congregational prayers. It is his custom to come to the mosque before daybreak and to read the Qur'an until the rising of the dawn, when he prays at the earliest moment. He also fasts regularly during the 'white days' [when the moon is at the full]. During my stay with him he used to invite me to break my fast in his company; I and the jurist Ali and the jurist Isma'il would present ourselves, and four small stools would be placed on the ground, on one of which the sultan would sit and each of us on another.

Account of the order observed in his banquet

The order of this was as follows. A brass table is brought in and there is set on it a brass platter. A beautiful slave girl wrapped in a silk robe then comes and sets in front of him the pots of food; she carries a large brown ladle and with it she ladles out a single spoonful of rice and puts it into the platter, then sprinkles over it ghee and puts along with this bunches of salted peppers and green ginger, salted lemons, and mangoes. One eats a mouthful of rice and follows it up with some of these preserves, and when the first ladleful which she placed in the platter is finished she takes out another ladleful of rice and puts a cooked fowl into the bowl, and the rice is eaten with this also. When the second ladleful is finished she ladles out again and puts out another kind of fowl, which one eats with it. When the different kinds of fowls are finished they bring various sorts of fish, with which they eat rice also, and when the different fish dishes are emptied they bring vegetables cooked with ghee and preparations of milk, and they eat rice with these too. When all these are done with they bring curdled milk, with which they end up their service of food. When this is served it is a signal that there is nothing else to be eaten after it. Finally they drink warm water on top of this, for cold water would be harmful to them in the season of the rains.

The clothes worn by their sultan are cloaks of silk and fine linen; he ties a waist-cloth round his middle and puts on two cloaks, one on top of the other. He plaits his hair and winds on a small turban. On this occasion we stayed with him for three days; he supplied us with provisions, and we left him to continue our journey.

Three days later we reached the land of Mulaibar [Malabar], which is the pepper country. It extends for two months' journey along the coast from Sandabur to Kawlam [Quilon]. The road over the whole distance runs beneath the shade of trees, and at every half mile there is a wooden shed with benches on which travellers of every kind, whether Muslims or infidels, may sit. At each shed there is a well for drinking and an infidel who is in charge of it. If the traveller is an infidel he gives him water in vessels; if he is a Muslim he pours the water into his hands. It is the custom of the infidels in the Mulaibar lands that no Muslim may enter their houses or eat from their vessels; if he does so they break the vessels or give them to the Muslims. If a Muslim goes into a place there in which there is no house belonging to Muslims, they cook food for him, putting it on banana leaves, and put the condiments over it, and birds eat what is left. At all the halting-places on this road there are houses belonging to Muslims, at which Muslim travellers alight, and where they buy all that they need, and food is cooked for them. Were it not for these Muslims, no Muslim would travel by this road.

On this road, which, as we have said, extends for a two months' march, there is not a span of ground or more but is cultivated. Every man has his own separate orchard, with his house in the middle and a wooden palisade all round it. The road runs through the orchards, and when it comes to a palisade there are wooden steps to go up by and another flight of steps down into the next orchard. So it goes on for two months. No one travels on an animal in that country, and only the sultan possesses horses. The principal vehicle of the inhabitants is a *dulah* carried on the shoulders of slaves or hired porters; those who do not travel in a *dulah* go on foot, be they who they may. If a man has baggage or merchandise or anything of the kind, it is transported by hired carriers on their backs, and you may see a single merchant with a hundred such or less or more carrying his goods. Each porter has in his hand a stout staff, with an iron ferrule, and at the upper end an iron crook. When he is tired out, and finds no bench on which to rest, he sticks his staff in the ground and hangs his load from the crook, and after resting resumes his load without assistance and goes on with it. I have never seen a safer road than this, for they put to death anyone who steals a single nut, and if any fruit falls no one picks it up but the owner. I was told that some Hindus travelled by this road, and one of them picked up a nut. When the governor was informed of this, he ordered a stake to be fixed in the ground; its upper end was sharpened and inserted into a wooden spar so that it protruded from it. The man was stretched on the spar, belly downwards, and transfixed on the stake until it came out of his back, and he was left like that as an example to the beholders. There are many such stakes on this road, so that people may see them and be warned. We sometimes met infidels during the night on this road, and when they saw us they stood aside to let us pass. Muslims are shown the highest consideration on it except that, as we have said, they do not eat with them nor allow them into their houses.

Description of pepper

The pepper trees resemble grapevines; they are planted alongside coco-palms and climb up them in the same way that vines climb, except that they have no shoots, that is to say tendrils, like those of vines. The leaves of the tree resemble those of stocks [or, according to a variant reading, horses' ears], and some of them resemble the leaves of briar. It produces its fruit in small clusters. In the autumn they gather the grains and spread them on mats in the sun, just as is done with grapes in order to obtain raisins; they keep on turning them until they are thoroughly dried and become black, and then sell them to the merchants. Most people in our country suppose that they roast them with fire and that it is because of that they become crinkled, but it is not so since this results only from the action of the sun upon them. I have seen pepper grains in the city of Qaliqut[9] being poured out for measuring by the bushel, like millet in our country.

The first town in the land of Mulaibar that we entered was the town of Abu Sarur [Barcelore], a small place on a large inlet and abounding in coco-palms. Two days' journey from there brought us to Fakanur [Bacanor], a large town on an inlet;[10] here there is a large quantity of fine-flavoured sugarcanes, which are unexcelled in the rest of that country. Three days after leaving Fakanur we reached Manjarur [Mangalore], a large town on the largest inlet in the land of Mulaibar. This is the town at which most of the merchants from Fars and al-Yaman disembark, and pepper and ginger are exceedingly abundant there. The sultan of Manjarur is one of the principal rulers in that land, and his name is Rama Daw.[11] There is a colony of about four thousand Muslims there, living in a suburb alongside the town. Warfare frequently breaks out between them and the townspeople, but the sultan makes peace between them on account of his need of the merchants.

After staying with them for three days, we set sail for the town of Hili, which we reached two days later.[12] It is large and well built, situated on a big bay which is navigable for large vessels. This is the farthest town reached by ships from China; they enter only this port, the port of Kawlam, and Qaliqut. The town of Hili is venerated both by Muslims and infidels on account of its cathedral mosque, for it is of great blessedness, and resplendent with radiant light. Seafarers make many votive offerings to it, and it has a rich treasury. I met in this mosque a pious jurist from Maqdashaw, called Sa'id, of fine figure and character. He used to fast continually, and I was told that he had studied at Mecca for fourteen years and for the same length of time at al-Madinah, and that he had travelled in India and China.

We then continued our journey from Hili to the town of Jurfattan.[13] Its sultan is called Kuwail, and is one of the most powerful sultans of Mulaibar. He possesses a large fleet of vessels which sail to Oman, Fars, and al-Yaman, and his territories include Dahfattan. We went on from Jurfattan to the town of Dahfattan which is a large town on an inlet with many orchards, in which there are coco-palms, pepper trees, areca palms and betel plants, as well as great quantities of colocasia which they cook along with meat. As for bananas, never have I seen any place in which they are more numerous or cheaper. At Dahfattan there is an immense *ba'in*, five hundred paces in length and three hundred in breadth, cased with red stones squared. Alongside it is a cathedral mosque of the Muslims, which has a flight of steps by which one goes down to the tank, and the people make their ablutions and bathe in it. I heard that the builder of both the mosque and the *ba'in* was a certain ancestor of Kuwail and that he was a Muslim whose conversion was due to a strange event, which we shall relate here.

Account of the marvellous tree which is alongside the mosque

I saw that the mosque was by a tender green tree with leaves like fig leaves, but smooth, surrounded by a wall. Beside it was a mihrab in which I made a prayer of two bowings. This tree is known amongst them as *dirakht al-shahadah*.[14] I was told there that in the autumn of each year a single leaf falls from this tree after it has turned first yellow and then red, and that written on it by the pen of the divine power there are the words, *There is no god but Allah, Muhammad is the apostle of Allah.* At the time of its falling trustworthy persons from among both the Muslims and the infidels sit underneath the tree, and when the leaf falls the Muslims take half of it and the other half is placed in the treasury of the infidel sultan, and they use it for the healing of the sick. This tree was the cause of the conversion to Islam of Kuwail's ancestor who constructed the mosque and the tank. He was able to read the Arabic script and when he read and understood the meaning of what was written on the leaf he embraced Islam and lived as a good Muslim. His story has been handed down amongst them by many witnesses. It was related to me that one of his sons reverted to idolatory after his father's death and governed with violence. He ordered that the tree should be pulled out by the roots, which was done so that no trace was left of it, and afterwards it sprouted up again and became as fine as it had ever been, and the infidel perished swiftly.

From there we continued our journey to town of Qaliqut [Calicut], which is one of the chief ports in Mulaibar. It is visited by men from China, Jawah, Ceylon, the Maldives, al-Yaman and Fars, and in it gather merchants from all quarters. Its harbour is one of the largest in the world. We entered it in great pomp, the like of which I have never seen in those lands, but it was a joy to be followed by distress. We stopped in the port of Qaliqut, in which there were at the time thirteen Chinese vessels, and disembarked. Every one of us was lodged in a house, and we stayed there three months as the guests of the infidel sultan, awaiting the season of the voyage to China. On the sea of China travelling is done in Chinese ships only, so we shall describe their arrangements.

Description of the Chinese vessels

The Chinese vessels are of three kinds: large ships called *junks*, middle sized ones called *zaws*, and small ones called *kakams*.[15] The large ships have anything from twelve down to three sails, which are made of bamboo rods plaited like mats. They are never lowered, but they turn them according to the direction of the wind; at anchor they are left floating in the wind. A ship carries a complement of a thousand men, six hundred of whom are sailors and four hundred men-at-arms, including archers, men with shields and arbalists, that is men who throw naphtha. Each large vessel is accompanied by three smaller ones, the 'half', the 'third', and the 'quarter'. These vessels are built only in the town of Zaitun in China [Quanzhou], or in Sin-Kalan, which is Sin al-Sin [Canton].

Their method of building the ships is to construct two walls of timber, the space between which they fill up with immensely large baulks of wood fastened both in length and breadth by huge nails each of which is three cubits in length. When the two walls are firmly joined together by these baulks they build on top of them the lower deck of the vessel, and launch them into the sea, where they complete the construction of the ship. Since these baulks and side walls remain in contact with the water, they go down to them in order to wash themselves and to relieve nature. At the sides of these baulks are their oars, which are as large as masts, ten or fifteen men joining together to work each of them, and they row standing on their feet. In the vessel they build four decks, and it has cabins, suites and salons for merchants; a set of rooms has several rooms and a latrine; it can be locked by its occupant, and he can take along with him slave girls and wives. Often a man will live in his suite unknown to any of the others on board until they meet on reaching some town. The sailors have their children living on board ship, and they cultivate green stuffs, vegetables and ginger in wooden tanks. The owner's factor on board ship is like a great amir. When he goes on shore he is preceded by archers and Abyssinians with javelins, swords, drums, bugles and trumpets. On reaching the house where he is to stay they stand their lances on both sides of the door, and continue thus during his stay. Some of the Chinese own large numbers of ships on which their factors are sent to foreign countries. There is no people in the world wealthier than the Chinese.

Account of our preparations for the voyage to China, and how it all ended

When the time came for the voyage to China, the Sultan of Qaliqut, who is called al-Samari, equipped for us one of the thirteen junks.[16] The factor on the junk was called Sulaiman of Safad, in Syria. I had made his acquaintance previously and I said to him, 'I want a set to myself because of the slave girls, for it is my habit never to travel without them.' He replied, 'The merchants from China have hired the sets for the outward and return journey. My son-in-law has one which I can give you, but it has no lavatory; perhaps you may be able to exchange it for another.' So I ordered my companions to take on board all my effects, and the male and female slaves embarked on the junk. This was on a Thursday, and I stayed on shore in order to attend the Friday prayers and join them afterwards. The Malik Sumbul and Zahir al-Din also went on board with the present. Early on the Friday morning a slave boy I had named Hilal came to me and said that the set we had taken on the junk was small and unsuitable. When I spoke of this to the captain he said, 'It cannot be helped, but if you like to transfer to the *kakam* there are sets of rooms on it at your choice.' I agreed to this and gave orders accordingly to my companions, who transferred the slave girls and effects to the *kakam* and were settled in it before the hour of the Friday prayer.

Now it is usual for this sea to become stormy every day in the late afternoon, and no one can embark then. The junks had already set sail, and none of them was left but the one which contained the present, another junk whose owners had decided to pass the winter up the coast at Fandaraina, and the *kakam* referred to.[17] We spent the Friday night on the seashore, we unable to embark on the *kakam*, and those on board unable to disembark and join us. I had nothing left but a carpet to spread out. On the Saturday morning the junk and *kakam* were both at a distance from the port, and the junk whose owners were making for Fandarayna was driven ashore and broken in pieces. Some of those who were on board died and some escaped. In it there was a slave girl who belonged to one of the merchants, and a favourite of his. He offered to give ten dinars in gold to anyone who would rescue her (for she had clung to a spar in the stern of the junk). A sailor from Hurmuz undertook to do it, and brought her ashore but would not take the dinars, saying, 'I did this only for the sake of God.'

That night the sea struck the junk which carried the sultan's present, and all on board died. In the morning we went to the scene of the disaster; I saw Zahir al-Din with his head smashed and his brains scattered, and the Malik Sumbul had a nail driven through one of his temples and coming out at the other, and having prayed over them we buried them. I saw the infidel, the sultan of Qaliqut, wearing a large white cloth round his waist, folded over from his navel down to his knee, and with it a small turban on his head, bare-footed, with the parasol carried by a slave over his head and a fire lit in front of him on the beach; his police officers were beating the people to prevent them from plundering what the sea cast up. In all the lands of Mulaibar, except in this one land alone, it is the custom that whenever a ship is wrecked all that is taken from it belongs to the treasury. At Qaliqut, however, it is retained by its owners, and for that reason Qaliqut has become a flourishing and much frequented city. When those on the *kakam* saw what had happened to the junk they spread their sails and went off, with all my goods and slave boys and slave girls on board, leaving me alone on the beach with but one slave whom I had enfranchised. When he saw what had befallen me he deserted me, and I had nothing left with me at all except the ten dinars that the *jugi* had given me and the carpet I had used to spread out.

As I was told that the *kakam* would have to put in at the port of Kawlam,[18] I decided to travel thither, it being a ten days' journey either by land or by the river, if anyone prefers that route. I set out therefore by the river, and hired one of the Muslims to carry the carpet for me. He used to drink wine with the infidels when we went ashore and annoy me with his brawling, which made things all the worse for me. On the fifth day of our journey we came to Kunji-Kari, which is on top of a hill there; it is inhabited by Jews, who have one of their own number as their governor, and pay a poll tax to the sultan of Kawlam.[19]

Account of the cinnamon and brazil trees

All the trees along this river are cinnamon and brazil trees. They use them for firewood in these parts and we used to light fires with them to cook our food on this journey.

On the tenth day we reached the city of Kawlam [Quilon], one of the finest towns in the Mulaibar lands. This city is the nearest of the Mulaibar towns to China and it is to it that most of the merchants from China come. Muslims are honoured and respected there. The sultan of Kawlam is an infidel called Tirawari;[20] he respects the Muslims and he judges severely thieves and profligates.

Anecdote

I was told that the sultan of Kawlam rode out into the environs of the town one day. His road lay between the orchards, and he had with him his son-in-law, his daughter's husband, one of the sons of the *maliks*. This man picked up a mango which had fallen from one of the orchards. The sultan was watching him and gave orders that he should be cut in two on the spot. He was divided into two halves and each half was put on a cross on the right and on the left of the road and the mango also was cut in two, one half of it being placed above each half of him, and he was left there as an example to the beholders.

I stayed at Kawlam for some time in the hospice of the Shaikh Fakhr al-Din, but heard no news of the *kakam*. During my stay there the ambassadors from the king of China who had been with us arrived there also. They had embarked on one of the junks which was wrecked like the others. The Chinese merchants provided them with clothes and they returned to China, where I met them again later.

I intended at first to return from Kawlam to the sultan in Dihli to tell him what had happened to the present, but afterwards I was afraid that he would find fault with what I had done and ask me why I had not stayed with the present. I determined therefore to return to Sultan Jamal al-Din of Hinawr and stay with him until I should obtain news of the *kakam*. On reaching Hinawr, I went ashore to visit the sultan and saluted him; he assigned me a lodging, but without a servant, and asked me to recite the prayers with him. I spent most of my time in his mosque and used to read the Qur'an through every day, and later twice a day, beginning the first recital after the dawn prayer and ending it in the early afternoon, then after making fresh ablutions I would begin the second recital and end it about sunset. I continued to do this for the space of three months, during which I went into retreat for forty days.

Account of our going out on an expedition and conquest of Sandabur

Sultan Jamal al-Din had fitted out fifty-two vessels for an expedition to attack Sandabur [Goa]. A quarrel had broken out there between the sultan and his son, and the latter had written to Jamal al-Din inviting him to seize the town and promising to accept Islam and marry his sister. When the ships were made ready it occurred to me to set out with them to the Holy War, so I opened the Qur'an to take an augury, and found at the top of the page: '*In them is the name of God frequently mentioned, and verily God will aid those who aid Him.*' I took this as a good omen, and when the sultan came for the afternoon prayer I said to him, 'I wish to join the expedition.' 'In that case,' he replied, 'you will be their commander.' I related to him the incident of my augury from the Qur'an, which so delighted him that he resolved to join the expedition himself, though previously he had not intended to do so. He embarked on one of the vessels, I being with him, on a Saturday, and we reached Sandabur on the Monday evening. When we entered its bay, we found its inhabitants prepared for the battle, with mangonels already set up. So we spent that night near the place, and on the next morning, when the drums, trumpets and bugles were sounded, the vessels moved in to the attack, and the defenders bombarded them with the mangonels. I saw a stone hit one of the men who was standing close to the sultan. The men on the ships jumped into the water, shields and swords in hand. I too jumped into the water with the rest of the men. We had with us two tartans, open at the stern, carrying horses; they are so constructed that the horseman mounts his horse inside the vessel, puts on his armour and comes out. They did this and God permitted its conquest and sent down victory to the Muslims. We entered the city at the point of the sword and the greater part of the infidels took refuge in their sultan's palace, but when we set fire to it they came out and we seized them. The sultan thereafter gave them quarter and restored their wives and children to them. They were about ten thousand in number and he assigned to them as residence a suburb of the town and himself occupied the palace, giving the houses in its neighbourhood to his courtiers. He gave me a slave girl called Lamki – I called her Mubarakah, and when her husband wished to ransom her I refused.

I stayed with the sultan at Sandabur from the day of its capture, which was the 13th of Jumada I, until the middle of Sha'ban;[21] I then asked him for permission to travel and he made me promise to return to him. So I sailed to Qaliqut. Two slaves who had been with me on the *kakam* arrived there and told me that the slave girl who had been pregnant, and on whose account I was much upset, had died, and that the ruler of Jawah[22] had taken the rest of my slave girls, that my goods had been seized by various hands, and that my companions were scattered to China, Jawah and Bengal. On hearing this I returned to Sandabur, and I stayed there until the 2nd of Rabi II.[23]

The infidel sultan of Sandabur, from whom we had captured the town, now advanced to recapture it. All the infidels fled to join him, and the sultan's troops, who were dispersed in the outlying villages, abandoned us. We were besieged by the infidels and reduced to great straits. When the situation became serious, I left the town during the siege and returned to Qaliqut, where I decided to travel to Dhibat al-Mahal, of which I had heard.[24]

13 The Maldives

Ten days after embarking at Qaliqut we reached the islands of Dhibat al-Mahal [the Maldives]. These islands are one of the wonders of the world and number about two thousand in all. Each hundred or less of them form a circular cluster resembling a ring, this ring having one entrance like a gateway, and only through this entrance can ships reach the islands. When a vessel arrives at any one of them it must needs take one of the inhabitants to pilot it to the other islands. They are so close-set that on leaving one island the tops of the palms on another are visible. If a ship loses its course it is unable to enter and is carried by the wind to al-Ma'bar or to Ceylon.

The inhabitants of the Maldives are all of them Muslims, pious and upright. The islands are divided into twelve districts, each under a governor. The inhabitants live on a fish which they call *qulb al-mas*;[1] it has red flesh and no grease, and smells like mutton. On catching it, they cut the fish in four, cook it lightly, then smoke it in palm-leaf baskets. When it is quite dry, they eat it. Some of these fish are exported to India, China and al-Yaman.

Description of their trees

Most of the trees on these islands are coco-palms, and they provide food for the inhabitants along with fish. We have already spoken of the coco-palm. These trees are quite extraordinary: each palm bears twelve bunches a year, one coming out every month; some are small, some large, some dry and some green, it is always so. They make milk, oil and honey from it, as we have related in the first volume. From its honey they make sweetmeats which they eat along with the dried coconut. All these products of the coco-palm and the fish which they live on have an amazing and unparalleled effect in sexual inter-course, and the people of these islands perform wonders in this respect. I had there myself four wives, and concubines as well, and I used to visit all of them every day and pass the night with the wife whose turn it was, and this I continued to do the whole year and a half that I was there.

Among their trees also are the *jamun*, the citron, orange and colocasia.[2] From the roots of this last they grind a flour, with which they make vermicelli, and they cook this in the milk of the coconut. This is one of the most delicious dishes; I was very fond of it, and used to eat it often.

Account of the people of these islands, and of some of their customs, and a description of their dwellings

The people of these islands are upright and pious, sound in belief, and sincere in purpose; they keep to lawful foods, and their prayers are answered. When one of them sees a man he says to him, 'God is my Lord and Muhammad my Prophet, and I am an ignorant and miserable creature.' Their bodies are weak, they are unused to fighting and warfare, and their armour is a prayer. Once when I ordered a thief's hand to be cut off, a number of those who were in the room fainted. In each island of theirs there are beautiful mosques, and most of their buildings are made of wood. They are very cleanly and avoid filth; most of them bathe twice a day to cleanse themselves, because of the extreme heat there and their profuse perspiration. They make plentiful use of perfumed oils, such as oil of sandalwood, and they smear them-selves with *ghaliyah* brought from Maqdashaw.[3] It is their custom when they have prayed the dawn prayer that every woman comes to her husband or her son, bringing the antimony jar, rose water and *ghaliyah*; she then paints his eyes with the antimony so that his skin shines and the traces of fatigue are removed from his face. Their garments are simply aprons; they tie one round their waists in place of trousers, and on their backs they place cloths. Some wear a turban, others a small kerchief instead. When any of them meets the qadi or preacher, he removes his cloth from his shoulders, uncovering his back, and accompanies him thus to his house. All of them, high or low, are bare-footed; their lanes are kept swept and clean and are shaded by trees, so that to walk in them is like walking in an orchard. In spite of that, every person entering a house must wash his feet with water from the jar kept at the entrance to the guest room, and wipe them with a rough towel of fibre matting which he finds there, after which he enters the room. The same practice is followed on entering a mosque.

It is a custom of theirs when a vessel arrives at their island that small boats go out to meet it, loaded with people from the island carrying betel and green coconuts. Each man of them gives these to anyone whom he chooses on board the vessel, and that person becomes his guest and carries his goods to his host's house as though he were one of his relatives. Any of the visitors who wishes to marry may do so, but when it is time for him to leave he divorces the woman, because their women never leave the country. If a visitor does not marry, the woman in the house where he lodges cooks for him, serves him and gives him provisions when he sets out on his journey. In return for that she is content to receive from him the smallest pittance of charity. The people buy pottery, when it is brought to them, with chickens, so that a cooking pot is sold amongst them for five or six chickens.

From these islands there are exported by ship the fish we have mentioned, coconuts, cloths and cotton turbans, as well as brass utensils, of which they have a great many, cowrie shells and *qanbar*.[4] This is the hairy integument of the coconut, which they tan in pits on the shore, and afterwards beat out with bars; the women then spin it and it is made into cords for sewing the planks of ships together. These cords are exported to India, China, and al-Yaman, and are better than hemp. The Indian and Yemenite ships are sewn together with them, for that sea is full of reefs, and if a ship is nailed with iron nails it breaks up on striking the rocks, whereas if it is sewn together with cords, it is given a certain resilience and does not fall to pieces.

The inhabitants of these islands use cowrie shells as money. This is an animal which they gather in the sea and put into pits there where its flesh disappears, leaving a white shell. They buy and sell with these at the rate of four hundred thousand for a gold dinar, but they often fall in value to a million for a dinar. They sell them in exchange for rice to the people of Bengal, who also use them as money, as well as to the Yemenites, who use them instead of sand as ballast in their ships. These cowries are used also by the negroes in their lands; I saw them being sold at Malli and Gawgaw at the rate of 1,150 for a dinar.[5]

Account of their women

Their womenfolk do not cover their heads, not even at one side. Most of them wear only one apron from the navel to the ground, the rest of their bodies being uncovered. It is thus that they walk abroad in the bazaars and elsewhere. When I was qadi there, I tried to put an end to this practice and ordered them to wear clothes, but I met with no success. No woman was admitted to my presence in a lawsuit unless her body was covered, but apart from that I was unable to effect anything. Some of them wear shirts in addition to the waistcloth, their shirts having short and wide sleeves. I had some slave girls who wore garments like those worn at Dihlị and who covered their heads, but it was more of a disfigurement than an ornament in their case, since they were not accustomed to it. The women's ornaments consist of bracelets, of which each woman wears so many on her forearm as to cover the arm from wrist to elbow. They are made of silver, and no one wears bracelets of gold except the sultan's wives and relatives. They wear anklets also, and necklaces of gold on their chests.

It is easy to get married in these islands on account of the smallness of the dowries and the pleasure of their women's society. When ships arrive the crews marry wives and when they want to sail they divorce them; it is really a sort of temporary marriage, and the women never leave their country. I have never found in the world any women more agreeable to consort with than they are. Among these people the woman never entrusts the service of her husband to anyone but herself; it is she who brings him his food and removes it from his presence, who washes his hand and brings him the water for his ablutions, and who covers his feet when he sleeps. It is one of their customs that the woman does not eat with her husband, nor does the man even know what she eats. I married several women there, and some of them ate with me after some effort on my part, but some of them never did so, nor was I able to see them eating and no ruse of mine for this purpose succeeded.

Account of the reason for the conversion to Islam of the inhabitants of these islands and of the evil spirits of the jinn which used to do injury to them every month

A number of trustworthy persons among the population told me that these islanders were infidels and that every month there would appear to them an evil spirit of the jinn, coming from the direction of the sea and resembling a ship filled with lights. On seeing him it was their custom to take a virgin girl and, after dressing her in finery, to conduct her to the *budkhanah*, that is the idol-temple, which was built on the seashore and had a window looking out on the sea. There they would leave her for a night and when they came back in the morning they would find her violated and dead. So they went on drawing lots every month amongst themselves, and the one on whom the lot fell gave up his daughter. Then there came amongst them a man from the Maghrib called Abu'l-Barakat al-Barbari, who could recite by heart the Holy Qur'an, and he lodged in the house of an old woman of their people in the island of Mahal.[6] One day when he visited her he found that she had called together all her kinswomen and they were weeping as though they were at a funeral ceremony. He asked them what was the matter with them but they did not explain it to him. Then an interpreter came and told him that the lot had fallen on the old woman, and she had but one daughter whom the evil spirit would kill. Abu'l-Barakat said to her, 'I shall go in place of your daughter tonight,' for he was beardless, having no hair at all on his face. So they took him that night and brought him into the *budkhanah*, he having previously made his ablutions, and he stayed there reciting the Qur'an. Then the evil spirit appeared to him from the window but he continued his recitation and when the spirit came so near as to hear the recital he plunged into the sea. In the morning the Maghribi was still occupied in his recitation when the old woman came with her kinsfolk and the people of the island to bring out the girl, as they had been accustomed to do, and burn her body. They found the Maghribi reciting, took him to their king who was called Shanurazah, and told the latter his story. The king was astonished at it and when the Maghribi expounded Islam to him and interested him in it he replied, 'Stay with us until the next month; then if you repeat this action and escape the evil spirit I shall become a Muslim.' So he stayed with them and God opened the breast of the king to Islam and he was converted before the end of the month, and his children and his court also.[7]

When the next month opened the Maghribi was taken to the *budkhanah*, but the demon did not come; he continued to recite the Qur'an till dawn, and when the sultan came along with the people and found him occupied in recitation they broke up the idols and destroyed the *budkhanah*. The population of the island embraced Islam and sent word to all the other islands, whose populations were converted also. The Maghribi settled down among them, greatly venerated, and they adopted his rite, namely the rite of the imam Malik, may God be pleased with him, and to this day they continue to hold the Maghribis in high respect because of him. He built a mosque which is known by his name and I read the following words on a screen in the cathedral mosque, carved in wood: 'The Sultan Ahmad Shanurazah accepted Islam at the hand of Abu'l-Barakat al-Barbari al-Maghribi.' This sultan assigned the third of the tax receipts of the islands as alms for travellers, since it was through them that his conversion to Islam had happened, and for that reason his name is remembered to the present day.[8]

On account of that demon many of these islands were uninhabited before the introduction of Islam. When we came to them I was still ignorant of this event. One night when I was engaged in some business or other I heard the people shouting *tahlils* and *takbirs*[9] and saw the boys carrying copies of the Qur'an on their heads and the women beating on basins and copper utensils. Greatly astonished at all this I asked what was afoot and they said, 'Just look out to sea,' so I looked and there was something like a great ship which seemed as though it were full of lamps and torches. They said, 'That is the demon, whose habit it is to appear once a month, but when we do what you have seen he goes away without doing any harm to us.'

Account of the sultanah of these islands

It is a strange thing about these islands that their ruler is a woman, Khadijah, daughter of the Sultan Jalal al-Din Omar, son of the Sultan Salah al-Din Salih of Bengal. The sovereignty belonged to her grandfather, then to her father, and after his death to her brother Shihab al-Din. It is told of this Sultan Shihab al-Din that he used to frequent the wives of his nobles and chief courtiers at night, on account of which they deposed him, exiled him to the region of Haladutani, and sent someone there who killed him.[10] None of the royal house was now left but his sisters Khadijah the eldest, and Maryam and Fatimah, so they raised Khadijah to the throne. She was married to their preacher, but orders are executed in her name only. They write the orders on palm leaves with a curved iron instrument resembling a knife; they write nothing on paper but copies of the Qur'an and works of theology.

Account of my arrival at these islands and of the course of my fortune there

When I arrived at these islands I disembarked at the one called Kannalus,[11] a fine island containing many mosques, and I put up at the house of one of the pious persons there. On this island I met a man called Muhammad, belonging to Dhofar, who showed me hospitality and warned me that if I entered the main island of Mahal the vizier, who is the sultanah's deputy, would detain me there, because they had no qadi. Now my design was to sail from there to Ma'bar, Sarandib,[12] and Bengal, and thence on to China. But I wished first to see this island of Mahal, so I enjoined the captain of the ship to say, if he were asked about me there, 'I do not know him.' On reaching Mahal he was asked about me and duly answered, 'I do not know him.' Afterwards they brought out betel and rose-water to us, this being their mark of honour, and lodged us in a house, where they sent us food, consisting of a large platter of rice surrounded by plates containing salted meat, chickens, ghee, and fish. On the following morning the vizier sent to me a robe and a hospitality gift including rice, ghee, salted meat, coconuts and the honey made from them, and along with this they brought 100,000 cowries for my expenses.

At first they did not know that I was qadi of Dihli. But when ten days had passed a ship arrived from Ceylon bringing some poor brethren, Arabs and Persians, who recognized me and told the vizier's attendants who I was. This made him still more delighted to have me. Not long afterwards the vizier invited me to accompany him. As we passed by an orchard belonging to the treasury he said to me, 'This orchard is yours, and I shall build a house in it for you to live in.' I thanked him and prayed for his happiness. Then on the next day he sent me a slave girl, and his servant who brought her said to me, 'The vizier says to you that if this girl is agreeable to you she is yours, but if not he will send you a Marhatah girl.' Now the Marhatah girls were much to my liking, so I said to him, 'I should prefer the Marhatah,' and he sent her to me. Her name was Qulistan, which means 'Flower of the Garden', and she knew the Persian language, so she pleased me, for the people of those islands have a language of their own which I did not understand. Then on the following day the vizier sent me a Ma'bari slave girl.

In addition to all this, he wished to marry me to his daughter. But I for my part refused that, in fear of the ill-luck attached to her, for she had already had two husbands who had died before consummating the marriage. Meanwhile I was seriously attacked by fever, for every person who comes to this island inevitably contracts fever. I firmly determined therefore to leave it and hired a vessel to take me to Bengal. When the vizier heard of this, he did everything possible to prevent my leaving. So reasoning with myself that I was in their power and that if I did not stay of my own free will I should be kept by main force, I decided that it was better to stay of my own choice.

Account of my marriage and my appointment as qadi

On the second of Shawwal[13] I made an agreement with the naval commander to marry his daughter, so I sent to the vizier requesting that the ceremony might be held in his presence at the palace. He gave his consent, and sent the customary betel and sandalwood. The guests arrived but the bride's father delayed. He was sent for but still did not come, and on being summoned a second time excused himself on the ground of his daughter's illness. The vizier then said to me privily, 'His daughter has refused and she is her own mistress. The people have assembled, so what do you say to marrying the sultanah's mother-in-law?' I said, 'Very well,' so the qadi and notaries were summoned, and the profession of faith recited. The vizier paid her dowry, and she was conducted to me a few days later. She was one of the best of women, and was so affectionate that when I married her she used to anoint me with perfume and cense my garments, laughing all the while and without showing any displeasure.

After this marriage the vizier forced me to take the office of qadi.

When I was appointed, I strove my utmost to establish the prescriptions of the Sacred Law. Lawsuits there are not like those in our land. The first bad custom I changed was the practice of divorced wives staying in the houses of their former husbands, for they all do so till they marry another husband. I put a stop to that. About twenty-five men who had acted thus were brought before me; I had them beaten and paraded in the bazaars, and the women put away from them. Afterwards I gave strict injunctions that the prayers were to be observed, and ordered men to go swiftly to the streets and bazaars after the Friday service; anyone whom they found not having prayed I had beaten and paraded. I tried also to determine how women dressed, but I could not manage this.

After my appointment as qadi I also married another wife, a descendant of Sultan Ahmad Shanurazah. Afterwards I married a wife who had formerly been married to the Sultan Shihab al-Din, and I built three houses in the garden which the vizier had given me. My fourth wife, another lady of good family, used to live in her own house, and she was my favourite among them. After I had become thus allied by marriage to many important persons the islanders stood in awe of me, because of their weakness, and they exerted themselves to turn the vizier against me by slanders, until our relations became strained.

Account of my separation from them and the reason for it

It happened one day that a slave of the late Sultan Jalal al-Din was complained of to the vizier by his wife, who informed him that he was at the house of one of the late sultan's concubines and committing adultery with her. The vizier sent witnesses who entered the concubine's house, found the slave sleeping with her in one bed, and arrested them both. On the following morning, when I learned of the event I gave orders that both of them should be beaten because of their intimacy, and then set the woman at liberty and imprisoned the slave. On my return to my house the vizier sent some of his principal attendants to ask me to set him at liberty. I said to them, 'Are you going to intercede for a negro slave who has violated his master's honour, when you yourselves but yesterday deposed the Sultan Shihab al-Din and put him to death because he had entered the house of one of his slaves?' Thereupon I sent for the slave and had him beaten with bamboo rods, which give heavier blows than whips, and paraded round the island with a rope round his neck. When they went to the vizier and told him of this he was much agitated and fell into a violent rage, assembled the ministers and army commanders and sent for me. I came to him, and said to those present, 'Be my witnesses that I resign the office of qadi because of my inability to carry out its duties.' The vizier addressed me, whereupon I mounted to the dais, sat down in a place facing him, and answered him in the most uncompromising manner. At this point he went into his palace saying, 'I sent for this fellow to vent my wrath on him and he vented his wrath on me.' The respect in which I was held amongst them was due solely to the sultan of India, for they were aware of the regard in which he held me, and even though they are far distant from him yet the fear of him is in their hearts.

Shortly after this the vizier sent a representative to see me. This man had an arrogant tongue, and said to me, 'Our master knows that you are aiming only at leaving us; give back your wives' dowries and pay your debts and go, if you will.' On hearing this I went to my house and acquitted all the debts I had contracted. Then when the vizier heard that I had acquitted my debts and was indeed bent upon going, he repented of what he had said and withheld his permission for my departure. So I swore with the most solemn oaths that I had no alternative but to leave. The chief men came to me and begged me not to go. I said to them, 'If I had not sworn I should not go.' They said, 'Go to one of the islands so as to keep your oath and then return,' so I said, 'Very well,' in order to satisfy them, although I had no intention of returning. When the night fixed for my departure came I went to take leave of the vizier, and he embraced me and wept so copiously that his tears dropped on my feet.

Having divorced my wives I set sail. We came to a little island in the archipelago in which there was but one house, occupied by a weaver. He had a wife and family, a few coco-palms and a small boat, with which he used to fish and to cross over to any of the islands he wished to visit. His island contained also banana bushes, but we saw no land birds on it except two crows, which came out to us on our arrival and circled above our vessel. And I swear I envied that man, and wished that the island had been mine, that I might have made it my retreat until the inevitable hour should befall me.

I then came to the island of Muluk where the ship belonging to the captain Ibrahim was lying.[14] This was the ship in which I had decided to travel to Ma'bar. Ibrahim and his companions met me and showed me great hospitality. The vizier had written to me that I was to receive in this island twelve million cowries, along with twenty bowls of coconut honey and a stated quantity of betel, areca nuts, and fish every day. I stayed seventy days at Muluk and married two wives there.

14 Ceylon and Coromandel

Before leaving the Maldives, I made a compact with two of the high military officers there that I should go to the land of Ma'bar and fetch troops to bring the islands under the authority of its sultan. (The sultan of Ma'bar and I were related by marriage, for he had married the sister of one of my wives in Dihli.) I arranged with these officers that the signal between us should be the hoisting of white flags on the ships; when they saw these they were to rise in revolt on the shore. I therefore sailed for Ma'bar with the object of realizing this plan.

We travelled for nine days, emerging on the ninth day at the island of Ceylon. We saw the mountain of Sarandib there, rising into the heavens like a column of smoke.[1] When we came to the island, the sailors said, 'This port is in the territory of the infidel Sultan Ayri Shakarwati who is an evildoing tyrant and keeps pirate vessels.'[2] We were afraid to put into this harbour, but as a gale arose thereafter and we dreaded drowning, I said to the captain, 'Put me ashore and I shall get you a safe conduct from this sultan.' He did as I asked and put me ashore, whereupon the infidels came to us and said, 'What are you?' I told them that I was the brother-in-law and friend of the sultan of Ma'bar, that I had come to visit him, and that the contents of the ship were a present for him. They went to their sultan and informed him of this. Thereupon he summoned me, and I visited him in the town of Battalah [Puttalam], which is his capital. It is a small and pretty town, surrounded by a wooden wall with wooden towers. The whole of its coasts are covered with branches of cinnamon trees brought down by torrents and heaped up like mounds on the shore. They are taken without payment by the people of Ma'bar and Mulaibar, but in return for this they give presents of woven cloth and similar articles to the sultan. It is a day and a night's journey from

243

this island to the land of Ma'bar. It has also much brazil wood and Indian aloes.

When I entered the presence of the infidel sultan, he rose to meet me, seated me beside him, and spoke most kindly to me. He said, 'Your companions may land in safety and will be my guests until they sail, for the sultan of Ma'bar and I are friends.' He then gave orders for my lodging and I stayed with him three days, enjoying great consideration which increased every day. He understood Persian and was delighted with the tales I told him of kings and countries. One day, when I came into his presence, he had before him a large quantity of pearls which had been brought from the pearl dives in his country, and his entourage were separating out the valuable ones from the others. He said to me, 'Have you seen pearl dives in the countries that you have come from?' I replied, 'Yes! I have seen them in the island of Qais and the island of Kish.'[3] He said, 'I have heard of them,' then taking some pearls from those in front of him he said, 'Are there in that island pearls like these?' I replied, 'I have seen only smaller ones,' which so pleased him that he said, 'They are yours,' and added, 'Do not be shy, but ask me for anything that you want.' I replied, 'Since reaching this island I have but one desire, to visit the blessed Foot, the Foot of Adam.' (They call him Baba, and Eve they call Mama.) 'That is simple,' he answered. 'We shall send an escort with you to take you to it.' 'That is what I want,' said I, then I added, 'And this ship that I came in can set out in safety for Ma'bar, and when I return from the Foot you will send me in your own vessels.' 'Certainly,' he replied. When I related this to the captain, however, he said to me, 'I shall not set sail until you return, even if I wait a year on your account,' so I told the sultan this and he said, 'He will remain as my guest until you come back.'

The sultan then gave me a palanquin, which was carried by his slaves on their shoulders, and sent with me four *jugis*, whose custom it is to make an annual pilgrimage to the Foot, three Brahmans, ten other persons from his entourage, and fifteen porters. Our way lay through rugged and well-watered country. In this part there are many elephants, but they do no harm to pilgrims and strangers, through the blessed virtue of the Shaikh Abu Abdallah b. Khafif (God's mercy on him) who was the first to open up this road for the pilgrimage to the Foot. These infidels used formerly to prevent Muslims from making this pilgrimage and would maltreat them, and neither eat nor trade with them, but since the adventure that happened to the Shaikh Abu Abdallah, as we have related, when the elephants killed his companions and he alone of them escaped, the infidels honour the Muslims, allow them to enter their houses, eat with them, and have no suspicions regarding their dealings with their wives and children. To this day they continue to pay the greatest veneration to this shaikh, and call him 'the Great Shaikh'.[4]

After this we came to the town of Kunakar, which is the capital of the principal sultan in this land.[5] It is built in a narrow valley between two hills, near a great channel called the Channel of Rubies, because rubies are found in it. Outside this town is the mosque of Shaikh Othman of Shiraz; the sultan and inhabitants of the town visit his tomb and venerate him. He was the guide to the Foot, and when his hand and foot were cut off, his sons and slaves took his place as guides. The reason for his mutilation was that he killed a cow. The Hindu infidels have a law that anyone who kills a cow is slaughtered in the same fashion or else put in its skin and burned. As Shaikh Othman was so highly revered by them, they cut off his hand and foot instead, and assigned to him the revenues of one of the bazaars.

Description of the sultan of Kunakar

He is called the Kunar, and possesses a white elephant, the only white elephant I have seen in the world. He rides on it at festivals and puts great rubies on its forehead. It happened that his officers of state revolted against him, blinded him, and made his son ruler, but he is still there, though blind.

Description of the rubies

The marvellous rubies called *bahraman* [carbuncles] are found only in this town. Some are taken from the channel, and these are regarded by them as the most valuable, and some are obtained by digging. In the island of Ceylon rubies are found in all parts. The land is private property, and a man buys a parcel of it and digs for rubies. He finds white stones, deeply cracked, and it is inside these that the rubies are formed. He gives them to the lapidaries who scrape them down until they split away from the ruby stones. Some of them are red, some yellow, and some blue.[6] Their custom is that all rubies of the value of a hundred *fanams* belong to the sultan, who pays their price and takes them; those of less value belong to the finders. A hundred *fanams* equal in value six gold dinars.

All the women in the island of Ceylon have necklaces of rubies of different colours and wear them also on their arms and legs in place of bracelets and anklets. The sultan's slave girls make a network of rubies and wear it on their heads. I have seen on the forehead of the white elephant seven ruby stones each larger than a hen's egg, and I saw in the possession of the Sultan Ayri Shakarwati a ruby bowl as large as a man's hand, containing oil of aloes-wood. When I showed my astonishment he said, 'We have things larger than that.' We next set out from Kunakar and halted at a channel called Khor Buznah, the word *buznah* meaning 'monkeys'.

Account of the monkeys

There are in these mountains vast numbers of monkeys. They are black and have long tails, and their males are bearded like men.[7] Shaikh Othman and his son and others as well told me that these monkeys have a chief, whom they obey as if he were a sultan. He fastens on his head a fillet of leaves and leans upon a staff. On his right and his left are four monkeys carrying staves in their hands. When the chief monkey sits down the four monkeys stand behind him, and his female and young come and sit in front of him every day. The other monkeys come and sit at a distance from him, and then one of the four monkeys addresses them and all the monkeys withdraw. After this each one brings a banana or an orange or some such fruit, and the monkey chief with his young and the four monkeys eat. One of the *jugis* told me that he had seen the four monkeys in the presence of their chief beating a monkey with sticks and after the beating pulling out its hair. Some trustworthy persons told me as a fact that when one of these monkeys seizes a girl who is unable to defend herself he has intercourse with her. I was told by one of the inhabitants of this island that there was in his house a monkey of this kind; one of his daughters went into a chamber and the animal followed her in, and though she screamed at it, it got the better of her, and he added, 'When we came into the room after her it was between her legs and so we killed it.'

Account of the flying leeches

In this place we saw the flying leech, which they call *zulu*.[8] It is found in trees and in the vegetation near water. When a man approaches, it jumps out at him, and wheresoever it alights on his body the blood flows. The inhabitants keep a lemon in readiness for it; they squeeze this over it and it falls off them; then they scrape the place on which it alighted with a wooden knife which they have for the purpose. It is related that as a certain traveller was passing by this place the leeches fastened on him. He took no notice and did not squeeze lemons on them, and he lost so much blood that he died.

Description of the mountain of Sarandib

This is one of the highest mountains in the world.[9] We saw it from the sea when we were nine days' journey away, and when we climbed it we saw the clouds below us, shutting out our view of its base. On it there are many evergreen trees and flowers of various colours, including a red rose as big as the palm of a hand. They maintain that on these roses there is writing, in which can be read the name of Allah and the name of His Apostle (peace be upon him). There are two tracks on the mountain leading to the Foot, one called the Baba track and the other the Mama track, meaning Adam and Eve (peace be upon them). The Mama track is easy and is the route by which the pilgrims return, but anyone who goes by that way is not considered by them to have made the pilgrimage at all. The Baba track is difficult and stiff climbing. Former generations cut a sort of stairway on the mountain, and fixed iron stanchions on it, to which they attached chains for climbers to hold on by.[10] There are ten such chains, and the tenth is the 'Chain of the Profession of Faith', so called because when one reaches it and looks down to the foot of the hill, he is seized by apprehensions and recites the profession of faith for fear of falling. When you climb past this chain you find a badly kept track. From the tenth chain to the cave of al-Khidr is seven miles; this cave lies in a spacious place, where there is a spring which is also called by his name; it is full of fish, but no one catches them. Close to this there are two tanks cut in the rock on either side of the path. At the cave of al-Khidr the pilgrims leave their belongings and ascend thence for two miles to the summit of the mountain where the Foot is.

Description of the Foot

The blessed Footprint, the Foot of our father Adam (God bless him and give him peace) is on a lofty black rock in a wide plateau. The blessed Foot sank into the rock far enough to leave its impression hollowed out. It is eleven spans long. In the rock where the Foot is there are nine holes cut out, in which the infidel pilgrims place offerings of gold, rubies and pearls. You can see the faqirs, after they reach the cave of al-Khidr, racing one another from there to take what there is in these holes. We, for our part, found nothing in them but a few small stones and a little gold, which we gave to the guide. It is customary for the pilgrims to stay at the cave of al-Khidr for three days, visiting the Foot every morning and evening, and we followed this practice.

When the three days were over we descended by the Mama track and returned to Battalah. I found the captain Ibrahim awaiting me and we set sail for the land of Ma'bar.

During the voyage a gale sprang up and our ship nearly took in water. We had no knowledgeable pilot on board. We came to some rocks on which the ship narrowly escaped being wrecked, and then into some shallows where the ship ran aground. We were face to face with death, and people jettisoned all that they had, and bade farewell to one another. We cut down the mast and threw it overboard, and the sailors made a wooden raft. We were then about two *farsakhs* from the shore. I was going to climb down to the raft, when my companions (for I had two slave girls and two of my companions with me) said to me, 'Are you going to go down and leave us?' So I put their safety before my own and said, 'You two go down and take with you the girl that I love.' The other girl said, 'I am a good swimmer and I shall hold on to one of the raft ropes and swim with them.' So both my companions (the one being Muhammad b. Farhan al-Tuzari, and the other an Egyptian) and the one girl went on the raft, the other girl swimming. The sailors tied ropes to the raft, and swam with their aid. I sent along with them all the things that I valued and the gems and ambergris, and they reached the shore in safety because the wind was in their favour. I myself stayed on the ship. The captain made his way ashore on the rudder. The sailors set to work to make four rafts, but night fell before they were completed, and the ship took in water. I climbed on the poop and stayed there until morning, when a party of infidels came out to us in a boat and we went ashore with them to the coast of Ma'bar. We told them that we were friends of their sultan, under whose protection they live, and they wrote informing him of this. He was then two days' journey away, on an expedition against the infidels, and I too wrote to him telling him what had happened to me. Those infidels took us into a great jungle. We stayed there three days at the end of which an amir arrived from the sultan and escorted us to his camp.

Account of the sultan of the country of al-Ma'bar[11]

He is Ghiyath al-Din of Damaghan. The land of Ma'bar had been under the rule of the Sultan Muhammad, the king of Dihli. Then his governor in Ma'bar, my father-in-law the Sharif Jalal al-Din, revolted. After reigning there for five years he was killed and one of his amirs ruled after him for a year. He then made an expedition against the infidels but, after defeating them with enormous slaughter, it chanced that he took his helmet from his head to drink, was hit by a stray arrow, and died on the spot. They appointed as ruler his son-in-law; but after forty days, disliking his conduct, they killed him, and the Sultan Ghiyath al-Din succeeded him as ruler. He married the daughter of the Sultan Sharif Jalal al-Din, and it was her sister that I had married in Dihli.

Account of my coming to the Sultan Ghiyath al-Din

When we reached the neighbourhood of his camp, he sent one of his chamberlains to welcome us. He himself was lodging in a fort made of wood. Now, it is a custom throughout India that no person enters the sultan's presence without boots on. I had no boots with me so one of the infidels gave me a pair. There were a number of Muslims there and I was astonished to find an infidel show greater courtesy than they did.

Afterwards I met the sultan and proposed to him the business of the Maldives and that he should send troops there. He decided to do this and designated the ships for the purpose. He entrusted me with drawing up a contract of marriage between him and the sultanah's sister and ordered that three ships should be loaded with alms for the poor people of the islands. He said to me, 'You will come back after five days.' But his admiral said to him, 'It is impossible to travel to the islands except after three months from now.' The sultan said to me, 'If that is so, then let us bring this expedition to an end.'

I therefore remained with him during his march. The country through which we were passing was one continuous jungle of trees and reeds. Any infidel whom they found in the jungle they took prisoner. They made wooden stakes sharpened at both ends and put them on the prisoners' shoulders to carry. Their wives and children were with them and they brought them to the camp. In the morning the infidels taken prisoner the day before were divided into four groups which were taken to each of the four gates of the camp. The stakes they had carried the day before were fixed in them and driven through them. Their women were killed and tied by the hair to the stakes. The little children were killed in their laps and left there. This was an abomination which I have not known of any other king and it is why God hastened the sultan's death. Also, I was in his presence one day when an infidel man had been brought to him. He said something I did not understand and immediately some of his myrmidons drew their knives. I got up at once and he said to me, 'Where are you going?' I said, 'I am going to pray the afternoon prayer.' He understood and laughed. He ordered his hands and feet to be cut off. When I returned I found him wallowing in his blood.

In the end, the infidels were disastrously routed. Their leader was eighty years old, and Nasir al-Din, the son of the sultan's brother, seized him and took him to his uncle, who treated him with apparent respect until he had extracted from him his wealth, his elephants and his horses. He was promising to set him at liberty, but when he had extorted everything he possessed, he killed and flayed him, stuffed his skin with straw, and hung it on the wall of Mutrah, where I saw it hanging.

The sultan's own death occurred not long after this; I have already related how it took place. A *jugi* made pills for him, to give him strength in copulation. It was said that the mixture included iron filings and that he ate more of them than was necessary and fell ill. Some weeks later, he died.

Sultan Ghiyath al-Din was succeeded by Nasir al-Din, his brother's son. He ordered that the ships which his uncle had designated for the expedition to the islands should be assembled for me but then a fever, fatal in that country, attacked me. I thought it meant death for me, but God inspired me to resort to the tamarind, which is abundant there. I took about a pound of it in water and drank it; it purged me for three days and God cured me of my illness. By now I was disgusted with Mutrah and sought permission to leave it. The sultan said to me, 'How should you leave when not a single month is left before the time for sailing to the islands? Stay till you are given everything that has been ordered for you.' But I refused and he wrote on my behalf and found eight ships going to al-Yaman, in one of which I travelled. Eventually we reached Kawlam. I still had some of my illness left in me and I stayed there for three months and then embarked on a ship to go to Sultan Jamal al-Din of Hinawr, but infidels attacked us between Hinawr and Fakanur.

Account of how the infidels plundered us

When we reached the little island between Hinawr and Fakanur the infidels came out against us in twelve warships, fought fiercely against us and overcame us.[12] They took everything I had preserved for emergencies; they took the pearls and rubies that the king of Ceylon had given me, they took my clothes and the supplies given me by pious people and saints. They left me no covering except my trousers. They took everything everybody had and set us down on the shore.

I returned to Qaliqut and went into one of the mosques. One of the jurists sent me a robe, the qadi a turban and one of the merchants another robe. I learnt there that a wife I had left pregnant in the Maldives had given birth to a male child, so I thought of going to the islands but remembered the enmity between me and some of the islanders. I therefore opened the Qur'an [for an augury] and found:

'The angels will descend to them saying, "Do not be afraid and do not grieve."' Thereupon I asked God's blessing and set out. After ten days I reached the islands. My son was brought to me, but it appeared to me that it would be best for him to stay with them, so I returned him to them and stayed for five more days, after which I thought it best to hasten my journey and asked permission to leave. The vizier summoned me and I went in to him. He seated me beside him and asked me about my circumstances. I ate with him and washed my hands in the bowl with him, something he never does with anyone. Betel was brought, and then I left. He sent me robes and quantities of cowries and behaved as well as possible.

15 Bengal, Assam and South-East Asia

I left and we were at sea for forty-three days and then reached the country of Bengal. It is a spacious country, producing rice in abundance. Nowhere in the world have I seen cheaper produce than there, but it is gloomy and the people of Khurasan say, '*duzakhast pur ni'mah*', meaning 'it is a hell full of blessings'.

The first city we entered in Bengal was Sudkawan, a very big city on the shore of the Great Sea.[1] The rivers Gang, to which the Indians go to pilgrimage, and Jun unite there and flow into the sea. From here I travelled to the mountains of Kamaru, a journey of one month.[2] They are extensive mountains which join China and also Tibet, where are the musk gazelles. The people of these mountains look like Turks. They are strong workers and a slave of that race is twice as good as a slave of another. They are also famous for resorting to magic and for their involvement in it. My object in going to these mountains was to meet a saint living there, Shaikh Jalal al-Din of Tabriz.[3]

Account of the Shaikh Jalal al-Din

This shaikh is among the greatest saints and most remarkable men, responsible for famous miracles and wonderful achievements. He was an aged man. He told me he had even set eyes on – God's mercy on him – the Caliph al-Musta'sim in Baghdad and was there when he was killed. Later on his companions told me that he had fasted for about forty years, breaking the fast only at intervals of ten days. He had a cow and used to break his fast with its milk. He also used to stand up all night. In appearance he was thin, tall and had little hair on his cheeks. He converted the people of those mountains to Islam, and that is why he stayed among them.

A miracle of his

When I was on my way to visit this shaikh four of his companions met me two days' journey from the place where he lived. They told me that the shaikh had said to the faqirs who were with him, 'The traveller from the Maghrib has come to you. Go and receive him.' They had set out accordingly by his order. He had no knowledge whatever of me; this had been divinely revealed to him. I went with them to the shaikh and came to his hospice outside the cave. When I entered his presence he rose, embraced me, and asked about my country and my travels, about which I informed him. He said to me, 'You are the traveller of the Arabs.' One of his companions who was present said, 'And of the non-Arabs, my master.' He said, 'And of the non-Arabs. Treat him with respect.' They took me to the hospice and gave me hospitality for three days.

When I had said farewell to Shaikh Jalal al-Din I travelled to the city of Habanq, one of the biggest and most beautiful cities.[4] It is divided by a river which flows from the mountains of Kamaru, called the Blue River, by which one goes to Bengal. After travelling on this river for fifteen days, we reached the city of Sunarkawan.[5] When we arrived there we found a junk intending to go to the country of al-Jawah which is forty days' sail away, on which we embarked.

After fifteen days we arrived at the country of the Barahnakar, who have mouths like those of dogs.[6] They are sottish and do not adhere to the religion of the Indians or to any other. They live on the sea-shore in houses of reeds roofed with dried grass, and have many bananas, areca palms and betel bushes. Their men are like us except that their mouths are like those of dogs. Their women are not like that, however, and are of outstanding beauty. The men are naked with no covering except that some of them put their male organs and testicles in a painted holder made of reeds and attached to their bellies. The women cover themselves with tree leaves. There is a community of Muslims among them, people from Bengal and al-Jawah who live in a separate quarter. They told us that the Barahnakar copulate like beasts and do not hide what they are doing. A man has thirty wives, more or less, and they do not commit adultery. If one does commit adultery the penalty for the man is that he is fixed to a cross till he dies, unless his friend or slave is fixed to the cross in his stead, when he is freed. The penalty for the woman is that the sultan orders all his household attendants to copulate with her, one after the other till she dies, in his presence. Then they throw her into the sea.

Account of their sultan

Their sultan came to us riding on an elephant on which was a kind of pack saddle made of skins. He was dressed in a goatskin robe, the hair on which was turned outwards. On his head were three coloured silk fillets and in his hand was a javelin of reed. Some twenty of his relatives accompanied him on elephants. He sent us a gift of pepper, ginger, cinnamon, fish and Bengali cloths. They do not wear these but deck the elephants with them on feast days. For every ship that docks in his country he takes a slave girl, a male slave, elephant cloths, and gold ornaments which his wife puts in her girdle and on her toes. If anyone does not give them this tribute they use magic against him. The sea becomes rough for him and he perishes, or almost so.

Anecdote

It happened that one night while we were in their port a slave of the master of the ship, who had repeatedly visited these people, left the ship one night for an assignation with the wife of one of their chief men, in a place like a cave on the shore. The husband knew of this and came to the cave with a party of his friends, found them there and they were taken to the sultan. He ordered that the slave's testicles should be cut off and he should be crucified. By his orders people copulated with the woman till she died. Then the sultan came to the shore and excused himself for what had happened, saying, 'We have to enforce our laws.' He then gave the master of the ship a slave in place of the one he had crucified.

We left these people and after twenty-five days we reached the island of al-Jawah [Sumatra], from which Jawi incense takes its name. We saw it at a distance of half a day's sail. It is green and very well-wooded. We landed at the port, where the vice-admiral wrote to the sultan informing him of my arrival. The notables then came out and brought a horse from the sultan's stables and other horses. I and my companions mounted and we entered the sultan's capital, the city of Sumutrah, a fine, big city with wooden walls and towers.[7]

Account of the sultan of al-Jawah

He is Sultan al-Malik al-Zahir,[8] one of the noblest and most generous of kings, a Shafi'i in rite and a lover of jurists, who come to his audiences for the recitation of the Qur'an and for discussions. He often fights against and raids the infidels. He is unassuming and walks to the Friday prayer on foot. The people of his country are eager to fight infidels and readily go on campaign with him. They dominate the neighbouring infidels who pay the poll tax in return for peace.

I stayed in Sumutrah with the sultan for fifteen days. After that I sought permission to travel, for it was the season of the voyage to China which is not organized at any other time. The sultan prepared a junk for us, stocked it with provisions, and was most generous and kind. May God reward him! He sent one of his companions with us to be host to us on the junk. We sailed along his country for twenty-one nights. Then we reached Mul Jawah, which is a country of infidels.[9] It extends for two months' travel. It has aromatics, and good aloes of Qaqulah and Qamarah, both places being in the country. In the country of Sultan al-Zahir, that is in al-Jawah, there are only incense, camphor, some cloves and some Indian aloes.

We arrived at the port of Qaqulah, a fine city with a wall of cut stone wide enough to take three elephants. The first thing I noticed outside the city was elephants with loads of Indian aloes wood which they burn in their houses; it is the price of firewood among us, or even cheaper. That, however, is when they sell it to each other. When they sell to [foreign] merchants a load costs a robe of cotton, cotton being more expensive than silk among them. Elephants are very common; they ride on them and use them as beasts of burden. Everyone who has a shop ties up his elephant beside it, and rides it to go home and to carry goods.

Account of the sultan of Mul Jawah

He is an infidel. I saw him outside his palace before a pavilion sitting on the ground with no mat. He summoned me, so I came to him and said, 'Greetings to whoever follows the true guidance.' They understood only the word *salam*. The sultan welcomed me and ordered a cloth to be spread for me to sit on. I said to the interpreter, 'How shall I sit on a cloth when the sultan is sitting on the ground?' He said, 'This is his custom. He sits on the ground as a mark of humility. You are a guest and you have come from a great sultan. You must be treated with honour.' I sat down and he asked me about the sultan of India. His questions were terse. He said to me, 'You will stay as our guest for three days and then depart.'

Account of a wonderful thing I saw in his assembly

In this sultan's assembly I saw a man with a knife like a billhook. He laid it on his neck and spoke at length although I did not understand. Then he took the knife in both hands and cut his own throat. His head fell to the ground because the knife was so sharp and his grip of it so strong. I was astounded at what he had done. The sultan said, 'Does anyone do this among you?' I said, 'I have never seen this anywhere.' He laughed and said, 'These are our slaves and they kill themselves for love of us.' He ordered the body to be carried away and burnt. The sultan's deputies, the state officials, the troops and the common people went out to the cremation. He granted ample pensions to his children, wife and brothers, and they were highly honoured because of what he had done. Someone who had been present at that assembly told me that what the man had said had been an affirmation of his love for the sultan, and a declaration that he was killing himself for love of him, as his father had killed himself for love of the sultan's father, and as his grandfather had done for love of the sultan's grandfather.

We set sail from Qaqulah and after thirty-four days reached the Sluggish or Tranquil Sea, which has a reddish colour; they claim that this is because of the earth of the land which bounds it. It has no wind and no waves and no movement in spite of its extent. For this reason every Chinese junk is accompanied by three boats, as we have said.

They are rowed and tow it. Besides, there are in every junk about twenty very big oars like masts. Some thirty men assemble by each oar and stand in two ranks facing each other. Two very big ropes like cables are attached to each oar. One party pulls the rope and then lets it go; then the other party pulls it. They sing with fine voices as they do this, and usually they sing *La'la, la'la.*

We sailed on this sea for thirty-seven days, then reached the country of Tawalisi.[10] The people of this country worship idols. They are of handsome appearance and resemble the Turks, most of them having reddish colouring. They are brave and intrepid and their women ride horses, understand archery, and fight just like the men. We anchored in one of their ports in the city of Kailukari, one of their finest and largest cities. The king had appointed his daughter to govern that city, and her name is Urduja.

Account of this princess

On the second day after our arrival at the port of Kailukari the princess summoned the captain, officers and merchants to a banquet she had prepared for them according to her custom. The captain wanted me to attend with them, but I refused, for they are infidels and it is not lawful to eat their food. When the guests attended upon her she said, 'Is there any one of you who has stayed behind and has not come?' The captain said to her, 'Only one man has stayed behind. He is the qadi and he does not eat your food.' She said, 'Summon him.' Her bodyguards and the captain's companions came and said, 'Obey the princess,' so I went to her. She was receiving in full state. Around her were women past child-bearing who were her viziers. They sat below the throne on sandalwood chairs. The men were before her. Her seat was covered in silk and had silk curtains; it was of sandalwood inlaid with many gold plaques. In the assembly hall were benches of carved wood on which were many gold vessels, both large and small, such as amphoras, jugs and goblets. The captain told me they were filled with a drink that induces cheerfulness, sweetens the breath, helps digestion, and enhances sexual intercourse.[11]

When I greeted the princess she said to me in Turkish, 'How are you? Are you well?' She seated me near her. She wrote Arabic well and said to one of her attendants, 'Bring an inkwell and paper.' They were brought and she wrote, 'In the name of God the merciful, the compassionate.' She said, 'What is this?' I said, 'That is God's name.' She said, 'Good.' Then she asked me from which country I came. I said, 'From India.' She said, 'The pepper country?' I said, 'Yes.' She asked me about that country and events there and I answered her. She said, 'I must invade it and take possession of it. Its wealth and its soldiers please me.' I said to her, 'Do so.' She ordered that I should be given robes, two elephant loads of rice, two buffalo cows, ten sheep, four pounds of julep, and four *martabans*, which are big vessels,[12] filled with ginger, pepper, citrus fruit and mangoes, all salted with what is used in preparing for sea voyages.

The ship owner told me that this princess had in her army women, serving women and slaves, who fought like men, and that she goes out among her troops of men and women, invades the territory of her enemies, is present at the fighting, and engages the champions. He told me there was a fierce battle between her and one of her enemies in which many of her soldiers were killed and her army was on the point of fleeing; but she forced her way forwards and broke through the armies till she reached the king against whom she was fighting, pierced him with a lance thrust and killed him. At this point his troops fled, and she brought his head on a spear, which his family recovered from her for much treasure. When she returned to her father he made her ruler of that city. He told me also that the kings' sons used to ask for her in marriage, and she used to say, 'I shall marry only a man who fights against me and defeats me.' They avoided doing this, being afraid of the disgrace if she were to defeat them.

16 China

We left the country of Tawalisi, and after seventeen days of sailing very rapidly and comfortably with a favourable wind we reached the country of China. The Chinese clime is extensive and is rich in resources, fruits, cereals, gold and silver; no other clime in the world compares with it in this respect. A river known as Ab-i Hayat, meaning 'the water of life', divides it. It rises in the mountains near the city of Khan Baliq and flows through China for a distance of six months' travel to finish at Sin al-Sin.[1] It is encompassed by villages, cultivated fields, orchards and bazaars, like the Nile in Egypt, but here there is more settlement.

Account of Chinese pottery

Chinese pottery is made only in the city of Zaitun[2] and in Sin Kalan. It is made from an earth from mountains there which burns like charcoal. They add to it a stone which is found there and burn it for three days. Then they pour water on it and it becomes powdery again. Then they ferment it. The best is that which has fermented for a whole month, but no more. What has fermented for ten days is inferior. The price is that of earthenware in our country, or less. It is exported to India and other parts of the world till it reaches our country in the Maghrib, and it is the most superb kind of pottery.

Account of the Chinese fowls

The hens and cocks of China are very fat, fatter indeed than our geese. We bought a hen which we wanted to cook but it would not fit into one pot, so we used two. The cock in China is the size of an ostrich. Sometimes its feathers fall out and a mass of red flesh is left. The first time I saw the Chinese cock was in the city of Kawlam. I thought it was an ostrich and was astonished, but its owner said to me, 'In China there are bigger ones than this.' When I arrived in China I saw the proof of what he had told me.

Account of some particulars of the Chinese

The Chinese are infidels. They worship idols and burn their dead as the Indians do. The king is a Tatar of the lineage of Tankiz Khan.[3] In every city of China is a quarter where the Muslims live separately and have mosques for their Friday prayers and other assemblies. They are highly regarded and treated with respect. The Chinese infidels eat the meat of pigs and dogs and sell it in the bazaars. They live comfortably and in affluence but take little care about their food and clothing. You will see an important merchant, whose wealth is beyond reckoning, wearing a tunic of coarse cotton. All the Chinese pay attention only to gold and silver vessels. Every one of them has a walking stick on which to lean when walking and they call it the third leg.

Silk is extremely plentiful, for the worms attach themselves to fruit, eat it and need little care. This is why it is plentiful and the poor and the destitute dress in it. If it were not for the merchants trading in it, it would have no value. Among them a single robe of cotton is sold for the price of many of silk.

Account of the paper dirham with which they buy and sell

The people of China do not do business for dinars and dirhams. In their country all the gold and silver they acquire they melt down into ingots. They buy and sell with pieces of paper the size of the palm of the hand, which are stamped with the sultan's stamp. Twenty-five such pieces are the same as dinar among us. If these pieces of paper become tattered from handling, they take them to a house which is like our mint and receive new ones instead. If anyone goes to the bazaar with a silver dirham or a dinar intending to buy something with it, it is not accepted and he is disregarded.

Account of the crafts in which the Chinese have special skill

The Chinese are of all peoples the most skilful in crafts and attain the greatest perfection in them. This is well known and people have described it and spoken at length about it. No one, whether Greek or any other, rivals them in mastery of painting. They have prodigious facility in it. One of the remarkable things I saw in this connection is that if I visited one of their cities, and then came back to it, I always saw portraits of me and my companions painted on the walls and on paper in the bazaars. I went to the sultan's city, passed through the painters' bazaar, and went to the sultan's palace with my companions. We were dressed as Iraqis. When I returned from the palace in the evening I passed through the said bazaar and I saw my and my companions' portraits painted on paper and hung on the walls. We each one of us looked at the portrait of his companion; the resemblance was correct in all respects. I was told the sultan had ordered them to do this, and that they had come to the palace while we were there and had begun observing and painting us without our being aware of it. It is their custom to paint everyone who comes among them. They go so far in this that if a foreigner does something that obliges him to flee from them, they circulate his portrait throughout the country and a search is made for him. When someone resembling the portrait is found, he is arrested.

Account of their way of preventing depravity among the merchants

When a Muslim merchant arrives in a Chinese town he chooses whether to stay with one of the Muslim merchants designated among those domiciled there, or in the *funduq*.[4] If he prefers to stay with the merchant his money is impounded, the merchant with whom he is to reside takes charge of it, and spends from it on his behalf honestly. When he wishes to leave, his money is examined and if any of it is missing the merchant with whom he has stayed and to whom it was entrusted makes it good. If he wishes to stay in the *funduq* his money is entrusted to the master of the *funduq*, who is put in charge of it; he buys for the merchant what he wants on his account. If he wants to take a concubine, he buys a slave girl for him. He puts him in a room inside the *funduq* and he meets the expenses of them both. Slave girls are cheap in price, but all the Chinese sell their sons and daughters, and it is not thought shameful among them. They do not all the same compel them to travel with their purchasers, nor do they prevent them if they wish to do so. So if the foreign merchant wants to marry, he gets married, but there is no way he can spend his money on debauchery. They say, 'We do not want it said in the Muslim countries that they lose their money in our country, and that it is the land of debauchery and fleeting pleasure.'

Account of the protection they afford to travellers on their roads

China is the safest and best country for the traveller. A man may travel for nine months alone with great wealth and have nothing to fear. What is responsible for this is that in every post station in their country is a *funduq*, which has a director living there with a company of horse and foot. After sunset or nightfall the director comes to the *funduq* with his secretary and writes down the names of all the travellers who will pass the night there, seals it and locks the door of the *funduq*. In the morning he and his secretary come and call everybody by name and write down a record. He sends someone with the travellers to conduct them to the next post station, and he brings back a certificate from the director of that *funduq* confirming that they have all arrived. If he does not do this he is answerable for them. This is the procedure in every post station in their country from Sin al-Sin to Khan Baliq. In them is everything the traveller needs by way of provisions, especially hens and geese. Sheep are rare among them.

Let us return to our journey. When we had crossed the sea the first city to which we came was Zaitun. It is a huge and important city in which are manufactured the fabrics of velvet, damask and satin which are known by its name. Its harbour is among the biggest in the world, or rather is the biggest; I have seen about a hundred big junks there and innumerable little ones. The Muslims live in a separate city. On the day I arrived I saw there the amir who had been sent to India as ambassador with the present, had been in our company and had been in the junk which sank. He greeted me and installed me in handsome lodgings. I received visits from the qadi of the Muslims and from the important merchants. As these merchants live in an infidel country they are delighted when a Muslim arrives among them. They say, 'He has come from the land of Islam', and give him the legal alms due on their property so that he becomes as rich as one of them.[5]

We sailed from Zaitun on the river for twenty-seven days till we reached the city of Sin Kalan, which is the city of Sin al-Sin. Among the largest bazaars there is that of the potters, whose wares are exported to other provinces of China and to India and al-Yaman. In the middle of the city is a huge temple with rooms in which blind people and chronic invalids live. They are all maintained and clothed from the endowments of the temple. There is also a hospital for the sick, a kitchen for cooking food, and there are physicians and attendants in the temple. I was told that old men no longer strong enough to earn their living are maintained and clothed in this temple. It is the same with orphans and widowed people without means. The temple was built by one of their kings, who made this city and the villages and orchards depending on it into an endowment for its benefit. The portrait of that king is in the aforesaid temple and people worship it.

In one part of this city is the town of the Muslims who have there the congregational mosque, the hospice and the bazaar. They have a qadi and a shaikh and in every town in China there is a Shaikh al-Islam to whom all the affairs of the Muslims are referred. There is also a qadi who gives judgements among them. I lodged with Awhad al-Din of Sinjar, a distinguished, important and very wealthy man, and stayed with him for fourteen days. Gifts to me from the qadi and the other Muslims came continuously, and every day there was a fresh banquet to which people came in splendid skiffs with singers. There is no city, either of infidels or of Muslims, beyond this city. Between it and the rampart of Yajuj and Majuj is sixty days' travel, as I have been told.[6] Wandering infidels live there who eat the sons of Adam if they overcome them, which is why people do not pass through their country or travel to it. I did not meet in that country anyone who had seen the rampart, or had seen anyone who had seen it.

A marvellous anecdote

When I was in Sin Kalan I heard that there was there a venerable shaikh over two hundred years old who neither ate nor drank nor excreted nor had intercourse with women, though his powers were intact, and that he lived in a cave outside the city, giving himself to devotion. I went to the cave and saw him at the entrance. He was thin, very ruddy, showed the traces of his devotional practices, and had no beard. I greeted him; he took my hand, sniffed it, and said to the interpreter, 'This man is from one end of the world and we are from the other.' Then he said to me, 'You have seen a miracle. Do you remember the day you arrived at an island where there was a temple and a man sitting among the idols who gave you ten gold dinars?' I said, 'Yes.' He said, 'I am that man.' At this I kissed his hand. He thought for a while and then entered the cave and did not come out to us again, as though he regretted what he had said. We burst into the cave after him but did not find him. We did, however, find one of his companions who had a bundle of paper notes and said to us, 'This is your guest money. Take your departure.' We said to him, 'We are waiting for the great man.' He replied, 'If you were to wait for ten years you would not see him. It is his practice that he does not see again anyone to whom one of his secrets has been made known. Do not suppose he has gone away from you. On the contrary, he is present with you.'

I was amazed at this and went away. When I told the qadi and the Shaikh al-Islam and Awhad al-Din of Sinjar about what had happened, they said, 'This is how he behaves with strangers who come to see him. No one knows what religion he follows. Moreover, the one you supposed to be one of his companions was the shaikh himself.' They also told me that he had been away from this country for about fifty years and had come back a year ago. Sultans, amirs and important people used to come and visit him and he gave them presents according to their rank; faqirs came to him every day and he gave something suitable to each one, though there was nothing to be seen in the cave in which he lived. They said too that he told of things in past years and spoke of the Prophet, God bless and give him peace, and used to say, 'If I had been with him I would have helped him.' He used to speak with the greatest respect of the two Caliphs Omar b. al-Khattab and Ali b. Abi Talib and praise them both, and used to curse Yazid b. Mu'awiyah and abuse Mu'awiyah.[7] They told me many things about him.

Awhad al-Din of Sinjar said, 'Once, when I visited him in the cave, he took my hand and I imagined I was in a vast palace and that he was sitting on a throne with a crown on his head. On either side of him were beautiful maidservants, and fruits were dropping into rivers which were there. I imagined I took an apple to eat and lo! I was in the cave, in front of him, and he was laughing at me. After this severe illness afflicted me and stayed with me for months. I did not go to him again.'

The people of that country believe he is a Muslim, but nobody has seen him pray. As for fasting, he fasts perpetually. The qadi said to me, 'One day I spoke to him about prayer and he said to me, "Do you know what I do? My prayer is certainly not the same as your prayer."' Everything one is told about this man is strange.

On the second day after meeting him I set out to return to Zaitun. Some days after arriving there an order came from the qan, who is the sultan, for me to go to his capital in security and honour, either by river or by land as I wished. I chose to travel by river. A handsome boat, one of those used by the amirs, was prepared for me. The amir sent his companions with me, and he and the qadi and the Muslim merchants sent us ample provisions. We travelled as official guests, having our morning meal in one village and our evening meal in another. After travelling for ten days we reached the city of Qanjanfu, which is a big and handsome city in an extensive plain.[8] Orchards surround it as if it were the Ghutah of Damascus.

Anecdote

One day when I was in the house of the Shaikh al-Islam, a big ship arrived belonging to one of the jurists most highly regarded by them. I agreed to receive him, and they introduced him as 'Mawlana Qiwam al-Din of Ceuta.'[9] I was surprised at his name, but when we conversed after our formal greetings it occurred to me that I knew him. I looked at him for a long time, and he said, 'I see you looking at me as though you knew me.' I said, 'Which country are you from?' He replied, 'From Ceuta.' I said, 'I am from Tangier.' He greeted me again, weeping, and I wept too. I said, 'Have you been to India?' He said, 'Yes, I have been to the capital, Dihli.' When he said that to me I remembered him and said, 'Are you al-Bushri!' He said, 'Yes.' He had come to Dihli with his maternal uncle. He was then young and beardless but one of the ablest students, for he had memorized the *Muwatta*.[10] I had told the sultan of India about him and he had given him three thousand dinars and asked him to remain with him. But al-Bushri refused and left for China, where he prospered and acquired considerable wealth. He told me he had about fifty male and as many female slaves. He gave me two of each and many presents. Later on I met his brother in the country of the Blacks. How far apart they were!

I stayed in Qanjanfu for fifteen days and then left. China, for all its magnificence, did not please me. I was deeply depressed by the prevalence of infidelity, and whenever I left my lodging I saw many offensive things which distressed me so much that I tended to stay at home as much as possible. When I saw Muslims it was as though I had met my family and my relatives.

We sailed from Qanjanfu on the river until after seventeen days we reached the city of al-Khansa.[11] It is the biggest city I have seen on the face of the earth. It takes three days to cross it, the traveller journeying on and stopping for the night in the city. It is laid out in the Chinese style of building, everyone having his own orchard and house. The number of Muslims here is great. We stayed with them for fifteen days; every day and night we attended a fresh banquet, at which they always paid much attention to the food they offered. Every day they rode out with us on pleasurable excursions in the quarters of the city. One day they rode with me into the fourth city, which is where the government house is and the house of the great Amir Qurtay.

Account of the great amir Qurtay

He is the supreme commander in China. He gave us hospitality in his house and held a reception at which the principal men of the city were present. He brought Muslim cooks to kill the animals and cook the meat, and for all his high rank this amir brought us the food and carved the meat with his own hand. We stayed as his guests for three days. He then sent his son with us on to the canal, on which we sailed in a ship like a fire-ship. The amir's son sailed in another with musicians and singers who sang in Chinese, Arabic and Persian. The amir's son much admired the Persian songs, and they sang a song which he made them repeat time and again so that I learnt it by heart. It has a wonderful tune. Here it is:

> *Ta dil bamihnat dadim*
> *Dar bahr-i fikr uftadim*
> *Chun dar namaz istadim*
> *Qawi bimihrab andarim*[12]

A large number of ships assembled on that canal, with coloured sails, silk awnings and intricate paintwork. They attacked one another, throwing oranges and lemons. In the evening we returned to the amir's house and spent the night there; the musicians came and sang all kinds of attractive songs.

Anecdote of the conjuror

That night a conjuror who was one of the qan's slaves was present. The amir said to him, 'Show us some of your tricks.' He took a wooden ball in which were holes through which were long cords. He threw it up and it rose till it disappeared from sight, for we were in the courtyard in the middle of the citadel, this being the last season of intense heat. When only a little of the cord was left in his hand he ordered an apprentice of his to cling to it and climb up till he disappeared. The conjuror called to him three times, but he did not answer. Then he took a knife in his hand as if he were infuriated and climbed up the cord till he too disappeared. Next he threw down to the ground the youth's hand, then his foot, then his other hand, then his other foot, then his trunk, then his head. Finally he came down, panting and his robe bloodstained. He kissed the ground in front of the amir and spoke to him in Chinese. The amir told him to do something and he took the youth's limbs, attached them to each other, kicked him with his foot, and he stood up intact. I was so amazed at this that I suffered palpitation of the heart, just as I did in Dihli when I had seen a similar sight. They poured out a draught for me, however, which relieved me. The qadi Afkhar al-Din was at my side and said, 'By God, there was no climbing up or down or cutting off of limbs. It is all conjuring.'

Next day we visited the quarter of the artisans. Among the wonderful things made there are dishes fashioned from reeds, pieces of which are fitted together very skilfully and given a shining red tincture. Ten of these dishes are fitted together, each one in the hollow of another, and so perfect that they look as if they were one dish. They make a lid which covers them all. They also make platters which have remarkable properties; they can fall from a great height without breaking, and hot food can be put in them without their colours changing or being spoiled. These are exported to India, Khurasan and elsewhere.

At length we left this city, which is the last province of China, and entered the country of Khita.[13] This is the finest country in the world in respect of cultivation, for there is no place in its whole extent which is not planted. Orchards, villages and cultivated fields are ranged on both sides of the river from the city of Khansa to the city of Khan Baliq, which is sixty-four days' travel. In it there are no Muslims except for casual passers-by who do not have a home there, for it is not suited to fixed residence for them. Every night we stopped at a village and received hospitality, until we reached the city of Khan Baliq, also called Khaniqu. It is the qan's capital, and the qan is their supreme sultan, whose dominion is China and Khita. We anchored, as is their custom, at a distance of ten miles from the city. A written report on us was sent to the naval commanders, who allowed us to enter the port. Khan Baliq is one of the largest cities in the world. It is not laid out as in China with orchards inside it, but as in other countries, with them outside. The sultan's city is in the middle like a citadel, as we shall explain.

Account of the sultan of China and Khita called the qan

Qan is the designation of whoever governs the kingdom and rules its different regions. His name is Pashay.[14] The infidels have no kingdom bigger than his on the face of the earth. His palace is in the middle of the city designated for his residence and is built mostly of carved wood. It is admirably planned and has seven gates.

When we arrived at the capital, Khan Baliq, we found the qan was away. He had gone to encounter the son of his paternal uncle, who had rebelled against him in the district of Qaraqurum and Bish Baligh in Khita;[15] from the capital to these places is three months' journey. During this expedition, the qan was killed and his forces were routed.[16] The news of these events arrived some days after we had reached the capital. The city was decorated, drums were beaten, trumpets and bugles were played, and amusements and entertainments were organized for the space of a month. Then the bodies of the dead qan and about a hundred of his uncle's sons, his relatives and his favourites were brought to the capital. They dug for the qan a big *na'us*, which is an underground chamber, spread with the finest carpets. The qan and his weapons were then placed in it, with the gold and silver vessels from his palace. Four slave girls and six of his favourite mamluks with jars of drink were placed with them. The entrance to the chamber was built up, and earth was piled over it all until it formed a big hill. Then they brought four horses and made them run at the grave till they collapsed. They erected a wooden structure over the grave and fixed the horses to it, after driving a wooden stake through each horse from the anus to the mouth. The aforesaid relatives of the qan were placed in *na'uses* with their weapons and their household vessels. Over the graves of the great men among them, of whom there were ten, they impaled three horses for each grave. Over the rest they impaled one horse for each.[17]

When the qan was killed as we have related, his uncle's son took possession of the kingdom and chose as his capital the city of Qaraqurum. Then the amirs who had not been present when the qan was killed rebelled against him; they cut communications and there was great disorder.

17 From China to Morocco, then Spain

Account of my return to China and then to India

When the rebellion broke out and disorders flared up the principal Muslims advised me to return to China before disorder became prevalent. We therefore returned to Zaitun. When I arrived there I found the junks about to sail for India. Among them was a junk belonging to al-Malik al-Zahir, the lord of al-Jawah, the crew of which were Muslims. His agent recognized me and was delighted that I had come. We set sail and encountered favourable winds for ten days, but when we were near the country of Tawalisi, the wind changed, the sky became dark, and there was heavy rain. For ten days we did not see the sun. Then we entered an unknown sea, the crew of the junk were frightened, and they wanted to return to China, but it was not possible. We spent forty-two days without knowing in which sea we were.

Account of the Rukhkh[1]

At first light on the forty-third day a mountain became visible in the sea about twenty miles away. The wind was carrying us directly towards it. The sailors were amazed and said, 'We are not near land and there is no knowledge of a mountain in the sea. If the wind drives us on to it we shall perish.' Everyone resorted to self-abasement, to devotion, and to renewed repentance, supplicating God in prayer. We sought Him through His prophet, on whom be the Blessing and Peace of God. The merchants swore to give plentiful alms, which I recorded in my own writing. The wind became somewhat calmer, but at sunrise we saw that the mountain had risen into the air and that there

273

was light between it and the sea. We were amazed at this and I saw the sailors weeping and saying goodbye to each other. I said, 'What is the matter?' They said, 'What we took for a mountain is the *rukhkh*. If it sees us we shall perish.' We were then less then ten miles from it. Then God Most High gave us the blessing of a favourable wind which took us directly away from it. We did not see it or know its true shape.

Two months after that day we reached al-Jawah and landed at Sumutrah. I stayed in this island for two months and then embarked in one of the junks. The sultan gave me a great deal of aloes, camphor, cloves and sandalwood, and dismissed me. I left him and after forty days I reached Kawlam. From here I took ship and after twenty-eight nights I reached Zafar. Travelling thence by sea to Hurmuz, then by land through Persia and al-Iraq, I came eventually to the city of Damascus of Syria, from which I had been absent fully twenty years. I had left there a pregnant wife, and while I was in India I learnt that she had given birth to a male child. I had then sent forty Indian gold dinars for his mother to his grandfather, who was from Miknasah [Meknes] in the Maghrib. When I came to Damascus this time I had no other concern than to ask after my son, so I went into the mosque and luckily found the imam of the Malikis. I greeted him but he did not recognize me, so I let him know who I was and asked him about my son. He said, 'He died twelve years ago,' and told me that a jurist from Tangier lived in the Zahiriyah *madrasah*. I went there to ask him about my father and my family, and found him to be a venerable shaikh. When I informed him of my origin and family, he told me my father had died fifteen years ago, and that my mother was still living.

I stayed in Damascus of Syria for the rest of the year, then proceeded to Aleppo. In the first days of the month of Rabi II in the year forty-nine,[2] news reached us here that plague had broken out in Ghazzah and that the number of dead there exceeded a thousand a day. I went next to Hims and found that the plague had already struck there; about three hundred persons died on the day of my arrival. I returned to Damascus and arrived on a Thursday; the people had been fasting for three days. On Friday they went to the Mosque of the Footprints, as we have related in the first book, and God alleviated their plague. The number of deaths among them had risen to two thousand four hundred a day. Then we went on to Ghazzah and found most of it deserted because of the numbers that had died during the plague. The qadi told me that only a quarter of the eighty notaries there were left, and that the number of deaths had risen to eleven hundred a day. We then went by land to Cairo and were told that during the plague the number of deaths there had risen to twenty-one thousand a day. I found that all the shaikhs I had known were dead – may God Most High have mercy upon them.

In Cairo we learnt that Our Master the Commander of the Faithful, the Protector of True Religion, who places his trust in the Lord of the Worlds, Abu Inan, may God Most High assist him, had under God brought together the scattered pieces of the Marinid dominion and by his blessing had healed the countries of the Maghrib after their being near to death, had poured forth benefits on high and low, and had en-wrapped all the people in a profusion of favours. Thereupon I sought to make my way to his exalted capital. The memory of my homeland moved me, together with affection for my people and friends, and love for my country which for me is better than all others,

> A land where charms were hung upon me
> Whose earth my skin first touched[3]

I sailed in stages to Tunis, and from there continued by sea with the Catalans. We reached the island of Sardaniyah [Sardinia], a Christian island in which there is a wonderful harbour with huge beams of wood around it and an entrance like a gate, which is opened only with their permission.[4] In the island are fortresses, one of which we entered and in which there were many bazaars. I vowed to God Most High that if He delivered us from this island I would fast for two months, because we had learnt that its people had resolved to follow us and take us prisoner when we left. But we departed from the island in safety, and after ten days reached the coast of the Maghrib. I travelled inland to the city of Taza, where I learnt that my mother had died of the plague, God Most High have mercy upon her.[5]

I left Taza and on the last Friday of Sha'ban the blessed in the year seven hundred and fifty I reached the capital city of Fez, where I stood before our exalted master, the most generous imam, the Commander of the Faithful, who puts his trust in the Lord of the Worlds, Abu Inan, God establish his grandeur and crush his enemies. His majesty caused me to forget the majesty of the sultan of Iraq, his beauty to forget that of the king of India, his gracious manners those of the king of al-Yaman, his courage that of the king of the Turks, his clemency that of the king of the Greeks, his devotion that of the king of Turkestan, his theological learning that of the king of al-Jawah.

I laid down my travelling staff in his noble country after verifying, with superabundant impartiality, that it is the best of countries. Its fruits are plentiful, water and provisions are easy to get, and few regions of the world have all these together. The poet spoke well who said:

> The West is the best of lands as I can prove
> The full moon is near to it and the sun runs thither.

When it had been granted to me to see the noble residence of our master Abu Inan, and I had been overwhelmed by the favours of his universal benevolence, I sought to visit my mother's grave. I reached my native town of Tangier, visited it, and went on to the city of Sabtah [Ceuta], where I stayed for some time. I was ill for three months; then God cured me and I resolved to take part in the holy war and the frontier fighting. I sailed from Ceuta in a *shatti*[6] and reached al-Andalus, God Most High guard her, just after the death of the Christian tyrant Adfunus.[7] He had besieged the Mountain of Victory for ten months, supposing he would get possession of all of al-Andalus that still belonged to the Muslims. But God took him unprepared and he died of the plague, which he feared more than anyone else.

The first town I saw in the Andalusian country was the Mountain of Victory. I made the circuit of the mountain and saw the wonderful works constructed by our master Abu'l-Hasan,[8] God be pleased with him, the military equipment he had installed, and what our master, God strengthen him, had added further. I would have liked to be one of those serving there till the end of my life.

Our master Abu'l-Hasan, the favour of God be with him, conquered it and recovered it from the hands of the Christians after they had ruled it for twenty years and more. He sent his son, the illustrious Amir Abu Malik, to besiege it, and helped him with a great deal of money and numerous soldiers. It was taken after a siege of six months, in the year seven hundred and thirty-three.[9] At that time it was not as it is now. Our master Abu'l-Hasan, God's mercy on him, built the huge Calahorra Tower at the top of the fortress; till then there had only been a small turret which was destroyed by stones from the mangonels. He built the tower in its place. He also built there an arsenal, which had been lacking before then, and a big wall surrounding the

Red Mound, going from the arsenal to the tileyard. Later on our master the Commander of the Faithful Abu Inan, God strengthen him, renewed the fortifications and their embellishments and added to the wall at the end of the Mount of Victory, which is the most effective of the walls and the most generally useful. He sent ample munitions, foodstuffs, and general supplies, acting to God Most High with pious intent and sincere devotion. His concern for the affairs of the Mount was such that he, God strengthen him, ordered the construction of a model of the said Mount. In it were simulated the walls, the turrets, the fortress, the gates, the arsenal, the mosques, the magazines for munitions of war, the granaries, the shape of the Mount and the Red Mound adjoining it. This was made in the auspicious audience hall. It is a wonderful model, which the craftsmen made perfectly. Anyone who has seen the Mount and has seen this model will recognize its worth.

I left the Mount of Victory for the city of Rundah [Ronda], which is one of the strongest and best sited Muslim fortresses. I stayed there for five days and then went to the city of Marbalah [Marbella]. The road between these two cities is difficult and very rough, but Marbella is a pretty little town with abundant supplies of food. I found there a cavalry troop going to Malaqah [Malaga], and I wished to travel in their company; however, God Most High in His grace preserved me, for the troop left before me and were taken prisoner on the road, as we shall relate. I left in their wake, and when I had gone beyond the limits of Marbella and entered those of Suhail I passed a dead horse in a ditch.[10] Then I passed a basket of fish abandoned on the ground. This alarmed me. The guardian's watchtower was in front of me, and I said to myself, 'If the enemy had appeared here the warden of the tower would have given warning.' I then went on to a house and found in front of it a horse that had been killed. While I was there I heard cries from behind me. I had gone ahead of my companions, but I returned to them and found the commander of the Suhail fort with them. He informed me that four enemy war galleys had appeared there, some of those manning them had landed, the warden had not been in the tower, and horsemen coming from Marbella, twelve in number, had passed by them. The Christians had killed one of them, one had fled, and ten had been taken prisoner. A fisherman had been killed with them; it was he whose basket I had found lying on the ground.

The commander advised me to stay in his station so that he could conduct me to Malaga. I therefore spent the night with him in the fort, the aforesaid war galleys being moored nearby. Next day the commander accompanied me on horseback and we reached the city of Malaga, one of the capitals of al-Andalus and one of its finest cities, combining as it does the amenities of land and sea. It has ample resources and fruits, and I saw grapes sold in the bazaars at eight pounds for a small dirham; its Murcian ruby-red pomegranates have no equal in the world, and its figs and almonds are exported from Malaga and its neighbourhood to the East and the West.

Ibn Juzayy remarks: 'This is what the preacher Abu Muhammad Abd al-Wahhab b. Ali of Malaga was referring to when he wrote, in a witty play on words:

Malaqah, how many figs (*tinaha*) you produce. Because of you
   ships load (*ya'tinaha*) them.
My doctor forbade (*naha*) you to me when I was ill, but he does
   not have the equal (*naha*) of my life.'

At Malaga is made the wonderful gilded pottery that is exported to the remotest countries. The Great Mosque is very big in extent, and is famous for its sanctity. Its courtyard is of unparalleled beauty, with very tall bitter orange trees. When I came to Malaga I found its qadi sitting in this mosque. With him were jurists and prominent citizens, who were collecting money for the ransom of the captives who have been mentioned. I said to him, 'Praise be to God Who protected me and did not make me one of them.' I told him what had happened to me, and he was astonished at my story and offered me hospitality, God be merciful to him. I then travelled to the city of Ballash [Velez], twenty-four miles away, and from there to al-Hammah [Alhama], a little town with a beautifully situated and wonderfully constructed mosque. There is a hot spring about a mile from the town on the river bank, in which there is a bath-house for men and another for women.[11] From there I went to the city of Gharnatah [Granada], the capital of al-Andalus and the bride of its cities. Its dependent lands are unequalled in any country of the world. They extend for forty miles and are divided by the famous Shannil [Jenil] river and many others, and the city is surrounded on all sides by orchards, gardens, meadows, palaces and vineyards. One of the wonderful places there is the Fountain of Tears, which is a mountain with meadows and orchards, quite without equal.

Ibn Juzayy remarks: 'If I were not afraid of being charged with excessive local patriotism I would try to describe Granada, since I have the opportunity. However, such is its fame that there is no sense in speaking at length about it.'

The king of Granada at the time I arrived was Sultan Abu 'l-Hajjaj Yusuf.[12] I did not meet him because of an illness he had, but his nobly born, pious and excellent mother sent me some gold dinars, of which I made good use. In Granada I met a number of its eminent men, among them the rarity of the age and masterpiece of the times, Abu 'l-Barakat al-Balfiqi.[13] He had come from Almariyah [Almeria] recently, and I encountered him in the garden of the jurist Abu 'l-Qasim. We stayed there for two days and a night.

Ibn Juzayy remarks: 'I was with them in that garden. Shaikh Abu Abdallah delighted us with the story of his travels. I took down from him the names of famous people he had met, and we profited greatly from him. A group of the notable people of Granada were with us, among them the gifted poet, the remarkable Abu Ja'far al-Judhami. The story of this young man is astonishing. He grew up in the country-side, did not study or frequent the learned, yet he came to write excellent poetry of a quality rare among masters of eloquence and eminent men of letters, for example:

> You who have made my heart your home, its door is the eye that
> glances at it.
> My insomnia opened the door after you left. Send your spectre
> who will lock it.

I also met in Granada a group of foreign faqirs who have settled there because it is like their own country; among them are al-Hajj Abu Abdallah of Samarqand, al-Hajj Ahmad of Tabriz, al-Hajj Ibrahim of Quniyah [Konya], al-Hajj Husain of Khurasan, and the two Hajjis Ali and Rashid, the Indians, and others. Then I returned to the Mount of Victory and embarked in the galley in which I had previously made the crossing, and which belonged to the people of Asila. I went with them to Asila, where I stayed some months, then to the city of Sala. From Sala I travelled to the city of Marrakush.[14]

It is one of the most beautiful cities, spacious and extending over a very wide area, and has ample resources. It has magnificent mosques, like the principal mosque, which is known as the Kutubiyin Mosque [Mosque of the Booksellers]. This has a wonderful awe-inspiring minaret, which I climbed and from which the whole town can be seen. However, ruin has overtaken the city and I can compare it only with Baghdad, except that the bazaars of Baghdad are better.

18 The Country of the Blacks

I left Marrakush in the company of the exalted cortège, that of our master, God strengthen him, and we reached the city of Sala [Sallee], then the city of Miknasah [Meknes], the wonderful, the green, the brilliant, with orchards and gardens and with plantations of olives surrounding it on all sides. Then we arrived at the capital, Fa's [Fez], God Most High guard it. There I said farewell to our master, God strengthen him, and set out on a journey to the country of the Blacks. I first reached the city of Sijilmasah, a very beautiful city.[1] It has abundant dates of good quality. Here I stayed with the jurist Abu Muhammad al-Bushri, whose brother I had met at Qanjanfu in China. How far apart they are! He treated me with the greatest generosity. In Sijilmasah I bought camels and four months' fodder for them.

On the first day of God's month of Muharram in the year fifty-three[2] I set out in a caravan with a number of merchants from Sijilmasah and other places. After twenty-five days we reached Taghaza. It is a village with no attractions. A strange thing about it is that its houses and mosque are built of blocks of salt and roofed with camel skins.[3] There are no trees, only sand in which is a salt mine. They dig the ground and thick slabs are found in it, lying on each other as if they had been cut and stacked under the ground. A camel carries two slabs. The only people living there are the slaves of the Massufah, who dig for the salt.[4] The Blacks come from their country to Taghaza and take away the salt. A load of it is sold at Iwalatan [Walata][5] for eight to ten *mithqals*, and in the city of Malli for twenty to thirty, sometimes forty. The Blacks trade with salt as others trade with gold and silver; they cut it in pieces and buy and sell with these. For all its squalor, *qintars* of *qintars* of gold dust are traded in Taghaza.

We spent ten days there, under strain, for the water is brackish and it is the most fly-ridden place anywhere. Here water is taken in for the journey into the desert that lies beyond, which is ten days' travel in extent with no water, or only rarely. We, however, found a pool between two hills of rock which was sweet; we quenched our thirst and washed our clothes. Truffles are plentiful in that desert, and so are lice, so much so that people wear round their necks string necklaces containing mercury, which kills them.

In those days we used to go ahead of the caravan, and when we found a suitable place we pastured the animals there. We went on doing this till a man called Ibn Ziri was lost in the desert, after which I did not go ahead or fall behind the caravan. There had been a quarrel between Ibn Ziri and the son of his paternal uncle and they had exchanged insults, so Ibn Ziri had fallen behind the caravan and lost his way. When the caravan halted there was no news of him. I advised his cousin to hire one of the Massufah to follow his tracks and perhaps find him, but he refused. We met a caravan on the way, and they told us that some men had become separated from them; they had found one of them dead under one of the bushes that grow in the sand. He had his clothes on him and a whip in his hand. There was water about a mile away.

We then came to Tasarahla, where there is underground water.[6] Caravans stop there for three days to rest, and to repair and fill their waterskins and sew on to them coarse bags to protect them from the wind. The *takshif* is sent forward from here.

Account of the *takshif*

Takshif is the name given to any man of the Massufah whom the people of the caravan hire to go ahead of them to Iwalatan with letters from them to their friends there, asking them to let houses to them and come four days' journey to meet them with water. Anyone who has no friend in Iwalatan writes to a merchant there known for his benevolent character, who then enters into the same relationship with him. Sometimes the *takshif* perishes in this desert and the people of Iwalatan known nothing of the caravan, and its people or most of them perish too. There are many demons in that desert. If the *takshif* is alone they play tricks on him and delude him till he loses his way and perishes. There is no road to be seen in the desert and no track, only sand blown about by the wind. You see mountains of sand in one place, then you see they have moved to another. A strange thing I saw is that our guide was blind in one eye and diseased in the other, but he knew the route better than anybody else. The *takshif* we hired for this journey cost a hundred *mithqals* of gold, and was one of the Massufah. On the night of the seventh day we saw the lights of those who had come to meet us, and we were extremely pleased.

This desert is luminous, radiant, one's chest is dilated, one is in good spirits, and it is safe from robbers. There are many wild cattle.[7] A troop of them will approach so near that the people can hunt them with dogs and wooden arrows. However, eating their meat produces thirst and so many people avoid it. It is remarkable that if these cattle are killed water is found in their stomachs. I have seen the Massufah squeezing the stomach and drinking the water in it. There are also many snakes in this desert.

Anecdote

There was in the caravan a merchant of Tilimsan [Tlemcen] who had a habit of taking hold of these snakes and playing about with them. I had told him not to do this, but he did not stop. One day he put his hand into a lizard's hole to pull it out and found a snake there instead. He grasped it in his hand and was going to mount his horse but it bit the index finger of his right hand, giving him severe pain. It was cauterized, but in the evening the pain grew worse, so he cut the throat of a camel and put his hand in its stomach and left it there for the night. The flesh of his finger dropped off and he cut off his finger at the base. The Massufah told me that the snake had drunk water before biting him; if not the bite would have killed him.[8]

When the people coming to meet us with water had reached us, our mounts were given drink. We then entered an extremely hot desert, not like the one we had experienced. We used to set off after the afternoon prayer, travel all night and halt in the morning. Men from the Massufah and other tribes used to bring us loads of water for sale. We reached the city of Iwalatan at the beginning of the month of Rabi I, after a journey of two full months from Sijilmasah.[9] It is the first district of the country of the Blacks. The sultan's deputy there was Farba Husain, *farba* meaning 'deputy'.

When we arrived the merchants deposited their goods in an open space and the Blacks took responsibility for them. The merchants then went to the Farba, who was sitting on a rug under a shelter; his officials were in front of him with spears and bows in their hands, and the Massufah notables were behind him. The merchants stood in front of him and he spoke to them through an interpreter as a sign of his contempt for them, although they were close to him.[10] At this I was sorry I had come to their country, because of their bad manners and contempt for white people.

The inspector of Iwalatan invited those who had come in the caravan to a reception, and I refused to be present. But my companions urged me very strongly to accept, so I went with the rest. At the reception coarsely ground *anli* was served mixed with a little honey and curdled milk.[11] This was put in a half gourd which they had made like a large bowl. Those present drank and then left. I said to them, 'Is it for this that the Blacks invited us?' They said, 'Yes. For them it is the greatest hospitality.' I then became convinced that no good was to be hoped for from these people, and considered joining the pilgrims travelling from Iwalatan; but I decided to go and see the capital of their king. I stayed in Iwalatan about fifty days.

Account of the Massufah inhabitants of Iwalatan

Conditions among these people are remarkable, and their way of life is strange. The men have no jealousy. No one takes his name from his father, but from his maternal uncle. Sons do not inherit, only sisters' sons! This is something I have seen nowhere in the world except among the infidel Indians of al-Mulaibar. Nevertheless, these people are Muslims. They are strict in observing the prayers, studying the religious law, and memorizing the Qur'an. Their women have no shame before men and do not veil themselves, yet they are punctilious about their prayers. Anyone who wants to take a wife among them does so, but they do not travel with their husbands, and even if one of them wished to, her family would prevent her. Women there have friends and companions among men outside the prohibited degrees for marriage, and in the same way men have women friends in the same category. A man goes into his house, finds his wife with her man friend, and does not disapprove.

Anecdote

One day I called upon the qadi at Iwalatan and found him with a young and exceptionally beautiful woman. When I saw her I hesitated and was going to go back, but she laughed at me and showed no embarrassment. The qadi said to me, 'Why are you turning back? She is my friend.' I was astonished at them, for he was a jurist and a Hajj.

Comparable anecdote

One day I called on one of the Massufah in whose company we had arrived, and found him sitting on a rug. In the middle of the room was a canopied couch and upon it was a woman with a man sitting and talking together. I said to him, 'Who is this woman?' He said, 'She is my wife.' I said, 'What about the man who is with her?' He said, 'He is her friend.' I said, 'Are you happy about this, you who have lived in our country and know the content of the religious law?' He said, 'The companionship of women and men among us is a good thing and an agreeable practice, which causes no suspicion; they are not like the women of your country.' I was astonished at his silliness. I left him and did not visit him again. Afterwards he invited me a number of times but I did not accept.

When I decided to travel to Malli, which is twenty-four days' journey from Iwalatan for one who hurries, I hired a Massufah guide.[12] There is no need to travel in a caravan for the road is safe. I set out with three of my companions. The road has many trees of great age and size; a caravan can shelter under a single one of them.[13] Some of them have no branches or leaves, but the trunk gives enough shade to shelter men. Some of these trees have rotted inside and rainwater has collected there, as if it were a well, and people drink this water. In some of the trees are bees and honey, which people collect. I passed by one of these trees and found a man inside weaving; he had set up his loom and was working at it. I was amazed at him.

Ibn Juzayy remarks: 'In al-Andalus there are two chestnut trees and in the hollow trunk of each of them is a weaver making cloth; one of them is on the slope of Wadi Ash [Guadix], the other in Bush-sharah [Alpujarras] in Granada.'

After travelling for ten days from Iwalatan we reached the village of Zaghari, near which is the great river, the Nile.[14] From here the Nile descends to Tunbuktu [Timbuktu] and then to Gawgaw [Gao], of both of which we shall speak later. Then it flows down to the country of the Nubians, who are Christians, then to Dunqulah [Dongola], the biggest of their towns. Then it flows down to the Cataracts, which is in the frontier district of the Blacks and the first district of Aswan in Upper Egypt.

At a town on the Nile called Karsakhu I saw near the bank a crocodile the size of a small boat.[15] One day I went down to the Nile to satisfy a need and one of the Blacks came and stood in the space between me and the river; I was amazed at his appalling manners and lack of decency. I mentioned it to someone, who said, 'He did that only to protect you from the crocodile by putting himself between you and it.' We left Karsakhu and arrived in the city of Malli, the capital of the kings of the Blacks, alighted at the cemetery, and proceeded to the quarter of the white people. I met the qadi of Malli, Abd al-Rahman, who came to me; he is a Black, a Hajj, an excellent man with noble qualities, and he sent me a cow as a welcoming gift. I also met the dragoman Dugha, one of the most distinguished and important of the Blacks; he sent me a bull. They provided for me completely, God recompense their kindnesses.

Ten days after our arrival we ate *asidah* made from something like taro called *qafi*, which is the food they prefer to all others.[16] All six of us were taken ill and one of us died. I myself attended the dawn prayer and fainted while it was in progress. I asked one of the Egyptians for a purgative and he brought me something made from the roots of plants, mixed it with aniseed and sugar and stirred it in water. I drank it and vomited what I had eaten together with much bile. God spared me from death but I was ill for two months.

Account of the sultan of Malli

He is the Mansa Sulaiman; *mansa* means sultan and Sulaiman is his personal name.[17] He is a miserly king and a big gift is not to be expected from him. It happened that I spent all this time in Malli without seeing him because of my illness. Then he arranged a mourning meal for our master Abu'l-Hasan. When this was over I advanced and greeted Mansa Sulaiman. The qadi told him about me, and he replied in their language. They said to me, 'The sultan says to you, "Give thanks to God".' I said, 'Praise and thanks be to God in all circumstances.'

Account of their meagre hospitality and exaggerated opinion of it

When I had left, a gift of welcome was sent to me. The man who brought it said, 'Stand up! The sultan's things and his gift have come for you.' I stood up, supposing them to be robes of honour and money, but there were three rounds of bread, a piece of beef fried in oil, and a calabash with curdled milk. When I saw it I laughed and was greatly surprised at their feeble intelligence and exaggerated opinion of something contemptible.

Account of what I said to the sultan afterwards and of his kindness to me

After I had received this gift I spent two months during which nothing reached me from the sultan. The month of Ramadan began and in the meantime I had been going repeatedly to the audience hall, greeting him, and sitting with the qadi and the preacher. I talked to Dugha the dragoman, who said, 'Speak in his presence. I shall explain on your behalf what is necessary.' I stood before him and said, 'I have travelled through the countries of the world and I have met their kings. I have been in your country for four months, but you have not treated me as a guest, and you have not given me anything. What am I to say about you before other sultans?' He said, 'I have not seen you and I know nothing about you.' The qadi stood up and answered him, saying, 'He greeted you and you sent food to him.' Thereupon he ordered that a house should be provided for my lodging, and my current expenses met. On the night of the twenty-seventh of Ramadan he gave me thirty-three and a third mithqals. When I left he gave me a hundred mithqals of gold.

Account of his audience in his cupola

He has a raised cupola the door of which is in his house and where he sits most of the time. On the side of this audience hall are three arches of wood covered with silver plates, below which are three more, covered with plates of gold, or silver gilt. They have curtains of blanket cloth. On a day when there is an audience in the cupola, the curtains are raised and it is known that there is a session. When he takes his seat a silk tassel is put through the grille of one of the arches, to which is tied a striped Egyptian handkerchief. When people see the handkerchief drums are beaten and trumpets sounded. Then some three hundred slaves come out from the door of the palace, some with bows in their hands and some with short spears and leather shields. Dugha the dragoman stands at the door of the audience hall, dressed in splendid clothes; on his head is a turban with borders, arranged with exceptional artistry; he is girded with a sword with a gold scabbard; on his feet are boots and spurs. No one except him wears boots that day. In his hand he has two short spears, one of gold and the other silver, tipped with iron. The soldiers, the governors, the pages and the Massufah and the rest sit outside the audience hall in a wide thoroughfare with trees. Each amir has in front of him his men with spears, bows, drums, trumpets made from elephants' tusks, and musical instruments made from reeds and gourds, which are struck with sticks and make a pleasant sound.

Account of the humility of the Blacks before their king, how they pour dust on themselves, and other things about them

The Blacks are the most respectful of people to their king and abase themselves before him. If he summons one of them at his session in the cupola we have mentioned, the man summoned removes his robe and puts on a shabby one, takes off his turban, puts on a dirty skullcap and goes in with his robe and his trousers lifted half way to his knees. He comes forward humbly and abjectly, and strikes the ground hard with his elbows. He stands as if he were prostrating himself in prayer, and listens to what the sultan says. If one of them speaks to the sultan and he answers him, he takes his robe off his back, and throws dust on his head and back like someone making his ablutions with water. I was astonished that they did not blind themselves.

Account of what he did about the prayer on the Feast days

I was in Malli for the Feasts of Sacrifice and of Breaking the Fast. On the two feasts the sultan sits on his dais after the afternoon prayer. The armour bearers come with splendid weapons, quivers of gold and silver, swords and scabbards ornamented in gold, spears of gold and silver, and maces of crystal. Four amirs stand by his head driving off the flies; in their hands they have a silver ornament like a stirrup. Dugha the dragoman comes in with his four wives and his concubines, who are about a hundred, in fine clothes; on their heads are gold and silver bands with gold and silver apples attached to them. A chair is placed for Dugha, where he sits playing an instrument made from reeds with tiny calabashes underneath. He sings poems praising the sultan and recounting his campaigns and his exploits, and his wives and concubines sing with him.

Account of the comical way poetry is recited to the sultan

On the feast day when Dugha has finished his playing, the poets come in. Each of them is inside a costume made of feathers on which is a wooden head with a red beak like the head of the *shaqshaq*.[18] They stand before the sultan in this laughable get-up and recite their poems. I have been told that their poetry is a sort of admonition, and that they say to the sultan, 'This dais, formerly such and such a king sat on it and performed noble actions, and so and so did such and such; do you do noble acts which will be recounted after you.'

Then the chief poet climbs the steps of the dais and puts his head in the sultan's lap; after this he climbs to the top of the dais and puts his head on the sultan's right shoulder, then on his left shoulder, talking all the time in their language. Finally he comes down. I have been told that this custom has continued among them since ancient times before Islam, and that they have persisted in it.

Account of what I found good and what I found bad in the conduct of the Blacks

Among their good practices are their avoidance of injustice, for there is no people more averse to it, and their sultan does not allow anyone to practise it in any measure; the universal security in their country, for neither the traveller nor the resident there has to fear thieves or bandits; and their punctiliousness in praying and compelling their children to do so. They dress in clean white clothes on Fridays; if one of them has only a threadbare shirt he washes it and cleans it and wears it for Friday prayers. They also pay great attention to memorizing the Holy Qur'an. If their children appear to be backward in learning it they put shackles on them and do not remove them till they learn it. I called on the qadi on the feast day and found his children in shackles. I said to him, 'Are you not going to free them?' He said, 'Not till they learn the Qur'an by heart.' One day I passed by a handsome youth, who was very well dressed, with a heavy shackle on his foot. I said to the person with me, 'What has he done? Has he killed someone?' The youth understood what I said and laughed. I was told, 'He has been shackled to make him memorize the Qur'an.'

Among their bad practices are that the women servants, slave girls and young daughters appear naked before people, exposing their genitals. Women who come before the sultan are naked and unveiled, and so are his daughters. On the night of the twenty-seventh of Ramadan I saw about a hundred naked slave girls come out of his palace with food; with them were two daughters of the sultan with full breasts and they too had no veil. Also they put dust and ashes on their heads as a matter of good manners. Other bad practices are the clowning we have described when poets recite their works, and the fact that many of them eat carrion, dogs and donkeys.

Account of my departure from Malli

I arrived there on the fourteenth of Jumada the First in the year fifty-three and left on the twenty-second of Muharram in the year fifty-four.[19] I was accompanied by a merchant named Abu Bakr b. Ya'qub. I rode a camel, for horses are very dear, one costing a hundred mithqals. We came to a big channel which runs from the Nile and can be crossed only in boats. That place abounds in mosquitoes and no one passes it except by night. We reached the channel in the first third of the night, which was moonlit.

Account of the horses there are in the Nile

When we reached the channel I saw on the bank sixteen beasts with huge bodies. I wondered at them and supposed they were elephants, which are numerous there. Then I saw they had gone into the river. I said to Abu Bakr b. Ya'qub, 'What are these beasts?' He said, 'They are hippopotamuses which have come out to graze on land.' They are bigger than horses, they have manes and tails, their heads are like horses' heads, and their feet are like elephants' feet. I saw them another time when I was sailing on the Nile from Tunbuktu to Gawgaw. They swim in the river and lift their heads and blow. The boatmen were afraid of them and drew near to land to avoid being drowned by them. They have an ingenious trick for hunting them, using spears pierced with holes through which they put strong cords. They strike the hippopotamus with them and, if the blow strikes the foot or the neck, it pierces right through and they pull on the rope till it comes to the bank when they kill the hippopotamus and eat the flesh. There are many of the bones lying on the bank.

We stopped by the channel in a big village whose governor was a black Hajj, an excellent man named Farba Magha. He was one of those who had accompanied the Sultan Mansa Musa when he went on pilgrimage.

Anecdote

Farba Magha told me that when Mansa Musa reached this channel there was with him a white qadi known as al-Dukkali. Subsequently this qadi acted dishonestly, and the sultan banished him to the country of the infidels who eat the sons of Adam. He spent four years there, then the sultan brought him back to his own country. The infidels had not eaten him because he was white, for they say that eating a white man is harmful because he is unripe. They claim that a Black is ripe.

Anecdote

A group of these Blacks who eat the sons of Adam came to the Sultan Mansa Sulaiman with their amir. It is their custom to put in their ears big pendants, the opening of each pendant being half a span across.

They wrap themselves in silk, and in their country is a gold mine. The sultan treated them with honour and gave them in hospitality a slave woman, whom they killed and ate. They smeared their faces and hands with her blood and came to the sultan to thank him. I was told that this is their custom whenever they come on an embassy to him. It was reported of them that they used to say that the best parts of the flesh of human females were the palm of the hand[20] and the breast.

We travelled from this village by the channel and reached the town of Quri Mansa.[21] Here the camel I was riding died. The driver told me this and I went out to look at it, but I found that the Blacks had already eaten it in accordance with their practice of eating carrion. I sent two young men whom I had hired for my service to buy a camel for me at Zaghari, which is two days' journey away. Then we travelled to the city of Tunbuktu [Timbuktu] which is four miles from the Nile. Most of the inhabitants are Massufah, the people of the *litham*.[22] Their governor is named Farba Musa. I was present one day when he promoted one of the Massufah to be amir of a group. He gave him a robe, turban and trousers, all coloured, and seated him on a leather shield. The chiefs of the tribe then lifted it up above their heads. In this town is the grave of the illustrious poet Abu Ishaq al-Sahili of Granada, known in his own country as al-Tuwaijin [the little cooking pan].[23]

At Tunbuktu I embarked on the Nile in a little boat hollowed out from a single piece of wood. Every night we stopped at a village where we used to buy the food and butter we needed, paying with salt, aromatics and glass trinkets. We reached a town whose name I have forgotten; the amir was an excellent man, a Hajj, named Farba Sulaiman, famous for his courage and strength. I saw none of the Blacks taller or with a bigger body than he. He took me by the hand and brought me into his audience hall, where there were many weapons, leather shields, bows, and spears. I found he had the *Kitab al-mudhish* of Ibn al-Jawzi[24] and I began to read it.

A five-span-high slave boy came in, and the amir called him and said to me, 'This is your welcoming gift. Guard him so that he does not escape.' I accepted him and wanted to leave, but he said, 'Stay till food is brought.' A slave girl of his, a Damascene Arab, came to us and spoke to me in Arabic. While this was going on we heard crying inside his house, so he sent the girl to find out what was happening. She came back and told him that one of his daughters had died. He said, 'I do not like lamentations. Come, let us go to the river,' meaning the

Nile, where he had houses on its banks. A horse was brought and he said to me, 'Mount.' I said, 'I shall not ride when you walk,' so we walked together and came to his houses by the Nile, where food was brought. We ate and I said farewell to him, and left. I saw no one among the Blacks more generous and more admirable than he. The boy he gave me is still with me to this day.

I travelled to the city of Gawgaw [Gao] on the Nile. It is one of the finest and biggest cities of the Blacks, and amply supplied with provisions. It has plentiful rice, curds, chickens, fish and has the 'tabby' cucumber, which is incomparable. Its inhabitants transact business, buying and selling, with cowries, as do the people of Malli. I stayed there about a month.

I travelled from there overland in the direction of Takadda with a big caravan.[25] We came first to the country of the Bardamah, who are a Berber tribe. Their women are the most perfectly beautiful of women and have the most elegant figures; they are pure white and very fat. I have never seen any who are as fat as they. They feed on cows' milk and pounded millet, which they drink mixed with water, uncooked, night and morning. Anyone who wants to marry among them settles with them as near to their country as possible and does not go with them further than Gawgaw and Iwalatan.

In this country I fell ill from the extreme heat and excess of bile. We hastened our march, however, to reach the city of Takadda, and I lodged there near the shaikh of the Maghribis. The houses of Takadda are built of red stone. Its water runs through copper mines, spoiling its colour and taste. There are many scorpions here, which kill young children who have not reached puberty, but only rarely kill adults. The inhabitants of Takadda have no occupation except trade. Every year they travel to Egypt and import some of the fine fabrics and other such things there are in that country. These people live in ease and luxury, vying with one another in the number of their male and female slaves as do the people of Malli and Iwalatan. They sell educated females only rarely and at a high price.

Anecdote

When I came to Takadda I wanted to buy an educated slave woman, but could not find one. Later the qadi sent me one belonging to one of his friends. I bought her for twenty-five mithqals. Then her former owner regretted it and wanted to revoke the sale. I said, 'If you show me another like her I will revoke the deal.' He pointed out to me a slave woman belonging to a certain Maghribi. I bought her from him, and she was better than the first slave so I revoked the deal with the first owner. Later on the Maghribi also regretted the sale of the slave and wanted to revoke it. He begged me to do so but I refused, and he nearly went mad or died of vexation. Afterwards I cancelled the deal.

Account of the august command I received

When I returned to Takadda a young slave arrived with an order from our master the Commander of the Faithful, commanding me to come to his exalted capital. I kissed it and obeyed instantly. I bought two riding camels for thirty-seven and a third mithqals, and left Takadda on Thursday the eleventh of Sha'ban in the year fifty-four[26] with a big caravan in which there were some six hundred female slaves. We first came to the country of Air, a land rich in pasture. People buy sheep from the Berbers there and cut their meat into strips, which they dry. From there we entered a plain where there was no cultivation and no water for three days' journey. Then for fifteen days we travelled over a plain without cultivation but with water. We reached the place where the road to Ghat, which leads to Egypt, divides from the road to Tawat.[27]

We travelled from there for ten days and reached the country of the Hakkar [Ahaggar], a Berber clan who wear the *litham* and who are scoundrels. One of their chiefs met us and stopped the caravan till they were forced to give him cloth and other such things. We travelled for a month in Hakkar country. It has little vegetation and is stony, and the road is rough. Then we arrived at Buda, which is one of the biggest villages of Tawat.[28] The soil is sand and salt flats, but dates are plentiful, though they are not good. There is no other cultivation, no butter, and no olive oil; these are imported from the Maghrib. The people eat dates and locusts; the latter are plentiful, and they store them as they do dates. They go out to collect them before sunrise, as they do not fly then because of the cold.

We stayed in Buda for some days, then left by caravan and reached Sijilmasah. I left it on the second of Dhu 'l-Hijjah.[29] It was a time of intense cold, and a great deal of snow had settled on the road. Indeed, I have seen difficult roads and much snow in Bukhara, Samarqand, Khurasan, and the country of the Turks, but I never saw one more difficult than the Umm Junaibah road.[30]

I arrived at the capital city of Fez, the residence of our master the Commander of the Faithful, God strengthen him. I kissed his noble hand and I had the happiness of seeing his blessed countenance. I have taken shelter in his benevolence after long travelling. May God Most High reward him for his profuse favours and abundant bene- factions to me, prolong his days, and cause the Muslims to rejoice by the long duration of his life.

Here ends the book of travels entitled *A Gift to Those Who Contemplate the Wonders of Cities and the Marvels of Travelling.* Its composition was completed on the third day of Dhu 'l-Hijjah of the year seven hundred and fifty-six.[31] Praise be to God and peace to those of his servants whom he has chosen.

Ibn Juzayy remarks: 'This completes the epitome I made of the composition of the Shaikh Abu Abdallah Muhammad Ibn Battutah, God ennoble him. It is obvious to anyone of intelligence that this shaikh is the traveller of the age. If anyone were to call him "the traveller of this [Muslim] community" he would not exaggerate. He travelled to the countries of the world, and then chose the capital city of Fez in which to settle and make his home, certain that our master, God strengthen him, is the greatest of kings, who has the most merit, bestows the most favours, has the most concern for those who visit him, and who bestows the fullest protection on those intent on seeking knowledge.

'It is fitting that someone like me should praise God Most High for the good fortune he accorded me when I set out to make my home in this capital, the very city which this shaikh chose after travelling for twenty-five years. It is an inestimable blessing for which sufficient thanks are not possible. May God Most High extend His help to us in the service of our master, the Commander of the Faithful, and may He cause the shadow of his protection and his mercy to remain over us. May He also recompense him, on behalf of us who are strangers devoted to him, with the best recompense of the beneficent.

God grant His blessing and His peace to our lord, our master, our prophet Muhammad, the seal of the prophets, the imam of His messengers. Praise be to God the lord of the worlds.

*The copying of this was completed in Safar
of the year seven hundred
and fifty-seven.*[32]
*God reward
him who
copied it.*

Notes

Ibn Battutah is referred to as IB throughout the notes.

Introduction by Ibn Juzayy

1. Sultan of the Marinid dynasty of Morocco, reigned 1348–58. It was he who caused IB to set down his *Travels*.
2. Noted Andalusian scholar, lived 1321–56 or 58. IB's amanuensis and editor.

1 North-West Africa and Egypt

1. In Tangier, Thursday 13 June 1325. Islamic months begin with the sighting of the new moon, which can vary from place to place.
2. Africa (Arabic Ifriqiya) is the name of the old Roman province, comprising modern Tunisia and eastern Algeria.
3. IB probably means that he took an augury from the Qur'an.
4. Milyanah is fifty-five miles south-west of Algiers.
5. An Islamic judge.
6. i.e. towards Mecca and al-Madinah.
7. The *madrasah* or college is devoted to the teaching of the religious sciences of Islam. It usually contains a mosque, lecture rooms and accommodation for teachers and students. *Madrasahs* often also provided lodging for travelling scholars.
8. A large open-air area for prayer, used particularly at the two major Islamic feasts (those of Fast-breaking and of Sacrifice).
9. The allocution is a formal sermon preached at the Friday and the festival prayers.

10. Wordplay – here between Safaqus and *safa* – is a common, indeed almost obligatory, feature of traditional Arabic poetry.
11. About 17 November 1325.
12. Literally 'I set up my tent over her', a traditional bedouin phrase.
13. Literally 'student', in Marinid Morocco the word signified a salaried jurist and doctor of religion.
14. This passage and other similar ones in the earlier part of the *Travels* are in elegant rhyming prose.
15. Sudaq is in the Crimea; Zaitun (Quanzhou) is on the Strait of Formosa.
16. The ancient Pharos.
17. North-west Africa.
18. Al-Malik al-Nasir, Mamluk sultan of Egypt and Syria, succeeded in 1293 and reigned with two short breaks until his death in 1341.
19. Known to European travellers as Pompey's Pillar.
20. The saint Burhan al-Din the Lame has so far defied identification. The brothers to whom he refers in India, Sind and China are brothers by spiritual affiliation rather than blood.
21. Al-Shadhili (d. 1258) is one of the great figures of medieval mysticism. He was of Moroccan origin. The tomb-mosques of his disciple Abu 'l-Abbas al-Mursi (i.e. of Murcia in Spain, d. 1287) and of al-Mursi's disciple Yaqut al-Habashi ('the Abyssinian', d. 1337) stand beside each other in Alexandria and are still greatly venerated.
22. Al-Hasan b. Ali was the Prophet Muhammad's grandson. On IB's visit to Humaithira, see below, p. 23.
23. Jedda, port for the holy cities of the Hijaz.
24. This and other passages in italics are direct quotations from the Qur'an.
25. Allusions to various Qur'anic passages which relate the deliverance of Abraham from a fire, the instruction of David in the art of metalworking, and the subjugation of demons and jinn to Solomon.
26. The initial letters of chapter xix of the Qur'an. Supernatural powers have been ascribed to them and to similar introductory letters in other chapters.
27. i.e. the bridge that takes believers across hell.
28. Al-Murshidi (d. 1337) was the author of many saintly miracles. His tomb-mosque still exists near Mutubis, north of Fawwa. Both these towns are on the Rosetta branch of the Nile.
29. i.e. towards Mecca, where the Ka'bah forms the *qiblah* or 'direction' in which all Muslims face in their prayers.
30. The *buri* is the grey mullet.
31. i.e. those who have devoted themselves to poverty and dependence on God. Faqirs are mendicants, living monastically or wandering from place to place.
32. In fact it was razed by the Mamluk Sultan Aibek to prevent its recapture by the Franks, or Crusaders.

33. Usually Qalandariyah. The Qalandars were a group of antinomian mendicants founded in the thirteenth century by Jamal al-Din al-Sawi (i.e. from Saveh in Iran). IB tells his story below.
34. The Way is the *tariqah*, i.e. a set of spiritual observances.
35. i.e. the heretical shaikh.
36. The story of Jamal al-Din's miraculous beard appears in a book on mystic masters by Hamid Qalandar, a contemporary of IB's in Delhi. Could the traveller have been the source for this tale?
37. 'The Conquering One' is the name given by the Fatimid dynasty to their capital, founded in 969 north of the old metropolis. It is the origin of the name Cairo.
38. The Mosque of Amr b. al-As was founded by the Arab conqueror of Egypt in 641.
39. Al-Shafi'i (d. 820) was the eponymous imam of one of the four orthodox rites in Sunni Islam.
40. Al-Mansur Qala'un (reigned 1279–90) was the father of al-Malik al-Nasir. His great mausoleum still exists in Bain al-Qasrain ('between the two castles'), the street named after a pair of Fatimid palaces which had formerly flanked it. Although the attached Maristan, or hospital, is now in ruins, an eye clinic still operates on the site.
41. The night following 14 Sha'ban (the eighth month of the Muslim year) has always been regarded as particularly holy.
42. Al-Husain b. Ali was the Prophet Muhammad's grandson, brother of al-Hasan. Al-Husayn was martyred in Iraq in 681, and his shrine in Cairo is perhaps the most sacred Islamic monument in Egypt.
43. So called in contradistinction to the Sudanese Nile, i.e. the Niger.
44. The Egyptian Arabic term for pharaonic temples.
45. IB at first speaks of the pyramids as if they were a single building; it seems unlikely that he visited them in person. All medieval Arabic descriptions, however, call them conical, since the word for 'pyramidal' did not then exist.
46. Reigned at Baghdad 813–33.
47. The Mamluk sultanate of Egypt and Syria is named after the slaves (mamluks), at this time predominantly of Kipchak Turkic origin, who were imported for military service. Those with ability and luck would rise to the rank of amir (commander); on the death of the reigning sultan the amirs would, in theory, acknowledge one of their own number as his successor. At times however during the sultanate's 250-year history, power descended in a particular house. The dynasty founded by Qala'un, and which ruled (with a few breaks) until 1390, is the most notable case.
48. Mamluk amirs often bore titles such as *saqi*, cup-bearer, and *dawadar*, keeper of the inkstand.
49. 'Ill-starred limper', because al-Nasir was lame in the right foot.

50. Upper Egypt.
51. The relics were removed in 1888 from Dair al-Tin, now in the southern suburbs of Cairo, to the Mosque of al-Husain.
52. Munyat Ibn Khasib is the modern Minya. Gibb calls IB's story of Khasib – who, far from being a bath-stoker, was in fact a Persian aristocrat – 'an odd deformation of history into legend'. The verse quoted by IB below relies on wordplay and allegory: *khasib* means 'fertile' and, by extension, 'generous'; the Nile is always referred to by Egyptians as the Sea; and water is a common poetical metaphor for generosity.
53. The tall pulpit from which sermons are preached on Fridays and festivals.
54. *Waqf* is the charitable endowment of land or other immovable property.
55. The titles sayyid and sharif indicate his descent from the Prophet Muhammad; the surname al-Hasani specifies descent through the Prophet's grandson al-Hasan.
56. The tomb of al-Shadhili at Humaithira, recently rebuilt, is now a popular place of visitation despite its isolated location.
57. One of the most important ports in medieval east–west trade, Aidhab was destroyed by the Mamluk sultan in 1426. Its site has been located twelve miles north of Halaib on the Red Sea coast, in an area disputed between Egypt and Sudan.
58. The Bujah, or Bejas, are a people who at this time were only partly islamized. Their *mahri* dromedaries were originally bred in Mahrah, in south-eastern Yemen. There is still a clan called al-Hadrabi, who claim descent from the old ruling family.

2 Syria

1. Sha'ban 726 corresponds with 3–31 July 1326.
2. Qatya was on the coast east of the present Suez Canal. *Zakat* is the canonical alms tax. The standard weight of a gold dinar was 4.23 grammes.
3. The Mongol rulers of Iraq were seen, perhaps with good reason, as an ever-present threat to the Mamluk state.
4. Al-Sham, Syria, denoted a wider area than the modern state, taking in present-day Jordan, Palestine and Lebanon.
5. The Arabic name of Hebron comes from the epithet of Abraham, Khalil Allah, 'the Friend of God'.
6. As stated above, the direction of Mecca; also, as here, a niche indicating this direction usually known as a *mihrab*.
7. The reference to the palm trunk alludes to the Qur'anic version of the birth of Jesus, in which 'the pains of travail caused her [Mary] to grasp the trunk of the palm tree'.

8. Al-Bait al-Muqaddas, Bait al-Maqdis and al-Quds are all variants of the Arabic name of Jerusalem.

9. This reference is to the miraculous night journey of the Prophet, when he was transported to Jerusalem and thence to heaven.

10. The point of the lie is that since Islamic doctrine states that Jesus was not crucified, another figure being substituted for him, He had no grave.

11. The hinterland of Tyre has been, from early times, a centre of Shi'ite Islam, whose adherents were scathingly referred to by orthodox Sunnis such as IB as Rafidis, 'Deserters', i.e. Schismatics. The Sunni order for ritual ablution is face then hands then feet.

12. Acre.

13. The Biqa al-Aziz is the Bekaa Valley. The Maghribi ruler Abu Ya'qub Yusuf (reigned 1163–84) died in Portugal and was buried in southern Morocco, and the identity of IB's character is uncertain.

14. Nur al-Din (d. 1174) was sultan of Aleppo from 1146 and of Damascus from 1154.

15. See below, pp. 33–4, for the story of Ibrahim b. Ad'ham.

16. Hisn al-Akrad, Castle of the Kurds, was known to the Crusaders as Crac des Chevaliers. Hims is generally transliterated as Homs, which is nearer to the colloquial pronunciation.

17. The Arabic name of the Orontes is derived from its Greek name, Axios, but rationalized by the explanation that, in contrast to the other rivers in Syria, it 'rebelliously' flows from south to north. Hamah is still famous for its waterwheels, at least one of which dates back almost to the time of IB.

18. IB's term 'revilers' apparently refers to an extremist schismatic sect; 'the Ten' are the Ten Companions of the Prophet to whom he promised Paradise. The Turk of the story was an orthodox Sunni.

19. IB's greatest travel-writing predecessor, Ibn Jubair of Valencia (1144–1217), wrote an elegant and justly famous account of his journey to Mecca. IB (or perhaps his editor Ibn Juzayy) often quotes from Ibn Jubair in the earlier part of the *Travels*; he does not always acknowledge his source.

20. 'The Iron Grey'.

21. A complex of shops and markets.

22. The pulpit described by IB is still in place.

23. The castles listed by IB are situated in the mountains between Hamah and the coast. The Fidawis, generally known as Assassins, were the active members of the Isma'ili sect. Other texts corroborate IB's statement that they were used as hit-men by the Mamluk regime. In the popular imagination, the Assassins carried out their operations under the influence of hashish, from which they derived their name, al-Hashishiyin. It is noteworthy, however, that IB does not ascribe the use of the drug to them.

24. Jabalah is on the Syrian coast south of al-Ladhiqiyah (Latakiya).

25. Ibrahim b. Ad'ham (d. about 780), renounced his rank and adopted the ascetic life. One of the earliest and most celebrated saints of Islam, his biography has gained many legendary accretions.

26. The Nusairiyah are now usually known now as Alawis, from the importance given to the Prophet's son-in-law Ali in their beliefs. By saying that they do not 'purify themselves', IB means that they do not practise circumcision. Some of his statements about them are exaggerated, although as late as the 1970s the Alawis were apparently still reluctant to build mosques.

27. The name seems to have been applied particularly to the northern part of the Lebanon range.

28. This and *mulabban*, 'in the form of bricks or tiles', are usually alternative names for a paste made from apricot pulp.

29. Damascus. The date of IB's arrival was 7 August 1326.

30. Founded by Ahmad b. Ali al-Sharabishi, whose surname means 'the cap-maker'. The building has disappeared.

31. i.e. the maidens and youths who attend the blessed in Paradise.

32. Umayyad Caliph, reigned 705–15.

33. i.e. mosaics, many panels of which still survive.

34. The single remaining footprint is now ascribed to the Prophet Muhammad.

35. i.e. the Black Death.

36. The *Sahih* of al-Bukhari (d. 870) is one of the two main compilations of Traditions (i.e. sayings) of the Prophet Muhammad. To hear such a text read aloud and explained, as IB did, was the only acceptable method of studying it. A *hafiz*, such as the scholar mentioned below, is one who has memorized the Qur'an by heart.

3 The Pilgrimage to Mecca

1. Bosra lies in the south of present-day Syria, al-Karak in Jordan.

2. According to many accounts, the *samum* could be fatal (see below, pp. 99 and 147–8). Al-Ukhaidir, 'the little green place', is presumably an ironical name.

3. This pre-Islamic site is now called Mada'in Salih; IB's 'dwellings of Thamud' are rock-cut tombs. In the Qur'an, the Prophet Salih urged the tribe of Thamud to worship the One God, and miraculously brought out a she-camel from the rock. The Thamudites slaughtered it and in punishment were struck dead in their houses, as 'a warning example'.

4. The name Taibah, connected with the Arabic root meaning 'sweet, pleasant', is often applied to al-Madinah.

5. The Garden is the metaphorical name applied to the space, as delineated by IB, inside the Prophet's mosque. The fragment of the palm trunk mentioned below has now disappeared. The story goes that the Prophet originally

preached his sermons leaning against this trunk, and that when he began to use a pulpit 'the palm-trunk whimpered for him as a she-camel whimpers for her calf'.

6. Abu Bakr (632–4) and Umar/Omar (634–44) were the first two *khalifahs* (caliphs, i.e. 'successors') of the Prophet.

7. The repetition of this formula, which is taken to mean 'At Thy service, O God!', is one of the essential rites of the Pilgrimage; so too is the wearing of garments which are not tailored, i.e. pieces of unsewn cloth.

8. i.e. the exchange of profit and worldly advantages for the labours and reward of the Pilgrimage.

9. Taken from the roots of the shrub *Salvadora persica*.

10. In English, 'fustian'. This Shaikh Abu Abdallah was the Maliki imam of Mecca.

11. 17 November 1326.

12. Mongol ruler of Persia and Iraq (reigned 1316–35). His territory is sometimes called 'the Two Iraqs', i.e. Arab Iraq (Mesopotamia) and Persian Iraq (ancient Media).

13. Zubaidah was the wife of the Abbasid caliph Harun al-Rashid (d. 809).

14. The poet Jamil was the creator of a type of romantic poetry called 'Udhrite', after the name of his tribe. Much of his verse is addressed to his inamorata Buthainah.

15. The Battle of al-Qadisiyah in 637 was the decisive victory by the Arabs over the Sasanid kings of Persia, the Magians (i.e. Zoroastrians) of the text.

16. Ali b. Abi Talib, the Prophet's cousin and son-in-law, was elected caliph in 656 and murdered in 660. His alleged tomb at al-Najaf and that of his son al-Husain at Karbala (both in southern Iraq) have long been revered by the Shi'ites.

17. The ceramics of the Iranian city of Qashan, and particularly its cobalt glazed tiles, were among the most celebrated in the Islamic world. IB compares the tiles to the Maghribi-Andalusian *zalij*, tile-mosaic, the name of which derives ultimately from Perso-Arabic *lazward*, or lapis lazuli.

18. i.e. Persia and Anatolia. The Rum are the Byzantine Greeks.

19. This official, found in many districts and cities, was in charge of keeping the register of sharifs, or descendants of the Prophet.

4 Southern Persia and Iraq

1. IB's 'jungle of reeds' is the marshland of southern Iraq, described in Wilfred Thesiger's *The Marsh Arabs*.

2. Founded in about 703 as a garrison town, midway (which is the meaning of its name) between al-Kufah and al-Basrah.

3. Shaikh Ahmad (d. 1183) was founder of the Rifa'i (or Ahmadi, as IB calls it) brotherhood of sufis. Their thaumaturgic practices, described below, are still perpetuated by the Kasnazani brotherhood.

4. Literally 'remembering, making mention', this became the technical term for the chants in which sufis praise God.

5. The school of al-Basrah once set the standard for correct Arabic usage. The 'leader' of the grammarians was Sibawaih (d. 796), a Persian by origin.

6. IB, by substituting the name of the Caliph Abu Bakr for that of Ali, is advertising his rigid Sunni loyalty. Shaking minarets are not as rare as one might think: there was one in the Spanish town of Purchena, and a pair still exists outside Isfahan.

7. The Persian Sea, i.e. the Arabian Gulf.

8. Abbadan is now better known for its oil refineries. The hermitage named after al-Khidr and Ilyas, mentioned below, is one of many thus ascribed which IB visited. Most of them were situated on or near the sea, and/or on hilltops. Al-Khidr (also written 'al-Khadir') is an immortal wandering saint, often credited with protective powers; he is frequently associated with or identified as Ilyas, i.e. Elijah (Greek Elias).

9. IB uses the word *nafs*, with the sense here of his worldly, appetitive spirit.

10. Shushtar, in the Khuzistan Province of Iran. IB's al-Azraq, 'the Blue River', is the Karun. He compares it below to 'the river of Balakhshan', i.e. the Badakhshan district of Afghanistan, an affluent of the Oxus known today as the Kokcha. The Atabek referred to here was ruler of the local Greater Lur or Hazaraspid dynasty.

11. Idhaj, south-east of Shushtar, is situated on a tributary of the Karun.

12. If IB was here in 1327, as it would seem from the text, Atabek Ahmad (reigned 1298–1333) would still have been on the throne. However, the traveller passed this way again on his way back from China twenty years later, when Atabek Afrasiyab was ruling. It seems likely, therefore, that he or his editor has combined reminiscences from the two visits, sacrificing chronology to literary neatness. (A similar solution has been suggested for problems of chronology arising from IB's Syrian visit.)

13. Faqihs are professional religious teachers or jurists. The term *mawlana*, 'our master', used later (p. 67), is the origin of the Persian and Indian term mulla. Khatibs, below, are preachers.

14. IB's view contrasts with that of the Persians themselves, who have long accused the Isfahanis of meanness. An old Persian proverb runs, 'As mean as the merchants of Isfahan, who put their cheese in a bottle, and rub their bread on the outside to give it a flavour.'

15. Ali b. Sahl, a famous ascetic, d. 919 or 920. His tomb still exists in the northern part of Isfahan.

16. Literally, '[garment] of a thousand wedges'. This is the patched robe of the sufis, an outward sign of worldly renunciation.

17. 7 May 1327. By this investiture, IB became affiliated to the Suhrawardi order of sufis, founded by Shihab al-Din al-Suhrawardi (d. 1234). In the full text and in common with all sufi spiritual 'pedigrees', IB continues the chain of investitures back to the Prophet's cousin and son-in-law, Ali b. Abi Talib. The Suhrawardis were a widespread brotherhood, and IB's affiliation to them provided valuable connections for his future journeys.

18. Ruknabad earned enduring literary fame through the poems of IB's younger contemporary, the Shirazi poet Hafiz (d. 1389). One of the best-known, translated by Sir William Jones (1746–94), includes the stanza:

> Boy, let yon liquid ruby flow,
> And bid the pensive heart be glad,
> Whate'er the frowning zealots say:
> Tell them, their Eden cannot show
> A stream so clear as Rocnabad,
> A bower so sweet as Mosellay.

19. Majd al-Din was born in 1272 or 1273 and died in 1355. The 'evident "graces"' referred to by IB are saintly miracles.

20. Khudabandah (reigned 1304–16), the Mongol ruler of Persia and Iraq, was also known as Öljaitu.

21. Many Mongol and Turkic rulers maintained the nomadic habit of migrating to the mountain pastures for the summer. The name Qarabagh, in the mountains north of the Aras river, is preserved in that of the present-day region of Nagorno-Karabagh.

22. AH 748 began on 13 April 1347.

23. Abu Abdallah b. Khafif (d. 982) was the founder of orthodox sufism in Shiraz. Although it seems likely that he travelled to the Indies, the story below of his visit to the mountain of Sarandib, i.e. Adam's Peak, is not found in any of the saint's biographies. A similar tale appears in Rumi's *Mathnawi* (see above, p. 107), but with an anonymous hero.

24. The tomb of the poet Sa'di (d. 1292) is still one of the most popular attractions of Shiraz.

25. Kazarun is fifty-five miles west of Shiraz. Al-Kazaruni (963–1035) was a pupil of Abu Abdallah b. Khafif, and founded a missionary order whose members were active as far away as India and China.

26. One of the most celebrated Arab poets (d. 846).

27. The Mustansiriyah college, built in 1234, still stands. The four schools referred to are the four orthodox rites of Islamic law: Maliki, Shafi'i, Hanafi and Hanbali.

28. Mention has already been made of both these monarchs, the last in the line of Chingiz (Genghis) Khan to rule Iraq and Persia. Khudabandah's given name was Öljaitu-buqa (Good Augury in Mongol), but this was later

changed to Timur and then Kharbandah, following a Mongol custom of altering a child's name to protect him against the evil eye. Muhammad was the name he took on conversion to Islam.

29. Khatun is a Turco-Mongol title meaning 'lady'.
30. The mobile camp of the Mongol khans.
31. The amir jandar was chief of the bodyguard.
32. An empty litter with a pyramidal top covered with embroidered brocade and decorated with gold, silver and gems. It was sent annually to accompany the pilgrim caravan to Mecca and back.
33. The 'Standing' on Jabal Arafat, to hear the delivery of sermons, is an essential rite of the Pilgrimage. The date on this occasion was Monday 26 October 1327.

5 Southern Arabia, East Africa and the Arabian Gulf

1. A wooden vessel, the planks of which are sewn together with coir. It is the origin of the English term 'jolly-boat'. Abu Numayy, father of IB's sharif Mansur, held office 1254–1301.
2. Ra's Dawa'ir is situated in the region of the modern Port Sudan. Sawakin (or Suakin), said below to be 'six miles off the coast', is in fact within an almost land-locked bay.
3. In the province of Asir, under Saudi administration since 1934.
4. Al-Sarjah was correctly Sharjah, on the Yemeni coast near al-Luhayyah. It has now disappeared. Sa'da, however, is still a thriving town inland.
5. At this time, Zabid was the winter capital of Yemen, and al-Ahwab its port.
6. The Tradition continues, 'for there are women there who resemble the dark-eyed maidens of Paradise'. The *subut al-nakhl* described below are, literally, Palm Saturdays. Apparently, a genteel version of this date festival still takes place.
7. Ahmad b. Musa b. Ali Ujail (1212–91) was one of the celebrated jurists of his time. The miraculous story told by IB is not found in any of the other sources. It hinges on the fact that the Zaidiyah – the rite to which most of the inhabitants of northern Yemen adhere – had been influenced by Mu'tazilite teachings, which admit a certain freedom of will in human actions. The grave visited by IB still exists although Ghassanah has long been called, after its most famous resident, Bait al-Faqih (the House of the Jurist).
8. Now usually spelled Jiblah, in the mountains seventy-five miles east-south-east of Zabid.
9. IB's comment about the people of Ta'izz no longer applies; but the Yemeni historian al-Khazraji, writing on the Ta'izzis of the period of the traveller's visit, agrees that they were 'dreadfully contrary and abusive'.

10. Al-Mujahid reigned 1321–63, with some intervals of dethronement. The missions of his ancestor, known as *Rasul*, had in fact been to Egypt and Syria.
11. Not the ruler of Iraq already mentioned but his namesake, the Marinid Sultan of Morocco. The king of the Lurs is the Atabek described above, pp. 64–7.
12. In the name of God.
13. This is one of the few passages in the *Travels* of which the veracity is in doubt, and not only because the account of San'a is borrowed from the works of earlier geographers. Even if he had failed to mention the scenery on his journey (a round trip of three weeks through spectacular mountains), IB would surely have recalled that the people of San'a adhered to 'evil' Zaidi doctrines; and, moreover, that the Zaidi imamate was at the time the subject of a violent dispute between several claimants. The passage may well be an interpolation by Ibn Juzayy.
14. The reservoirs are the famous pre-Islamic Aden Tanks, restored by the British in the nineteenth century.
15. The ports listed are described later in the Indian section of the *Travels*. The one exception is Tanah, situated twenty miles north-east of Bombay.
16. Zaila is on the Somali coast near the present-day border with Djibouti. 'Barbarah', preserved in the toponym Berbera, was the term used by Arab geographers for the Hamitic peoples and especially the Somalis. Maqdashaw, i.e. Mogadishu, was founded in the tenth century as a trading colony by Arabs from the Gulf.
17. Somalia is still the world's biggest producer of camels.
18. *Sawahil*, plural of *sahil*, is the origin of 'Swahili'. IB's Kulwa is Kilwa Kisiwani in Tanzania, 340 miles south of Mambasa, i.e. Mombasa. 'Zinj' is the usual word for negroes.
19. The Indian *jamun* (*Eugenia jambolata*).
20. The enclave of Zafar (Dhofar), on the southern Arabian coast, is now in the Sultanate of Oman. The ruins of the city visited by IB, from which the province takes its name, are now known as al-Balid; they lie to the east of the modern Salalah.
21. This belief is based on legends which state that the pre-Islamic Himyarite kings of Yemen conquered the Maghrib, and that their troops settled there.
22. Abu Muhammad b. Abu Bakr b. Isa may well be Shaikh Muhammad b. Abu Bakr b. Sa'd b. Ali al-Damrini (d. 1315), whose tombstone from Zafar is now in the Victoria and Albert Museum in London.
23. The isolated settlement of Hasik, eighty miles east of Salalah, produces what is generally agreed to be the best frankincense. Trade in this product and in dried shark were still the main occupations of its inhabitants a few decades ago. IB clearly did not personally observe the harvesting of frankincense, which exudes from the trunk of the tree, not from its leaves.

24. Despite its relative proximity to Hasik, this seems to be Hallaniyah, the main island of the Kuria Muria or Hallaniyat group. The name Lum'an is otherwise unknown.
25. Although another of the Kuria Murias, al-Hasikiyah, has also been known as the Island of Birds, this is probably the small island off the western coast of the Gulf of Masirah called al-Humar, or Humar Nafun. It is a seasonal roost for large numbers of Socotra Cormorant. Below, IB reproves the merchant for eating the birds because their throats have not been cut before death, a stipulation of Islamic dietary regulations.
26. The feast day was 14 September 1331. Gibb would wish to put this date back two years, as it is clear that IB's chronology is by now confused. The whole thorny issue of dating has been discussed at length by Gibb, in an appendix to the second volume of the Hakluyt edition of the *Travels*, and by Ivan Hrbek, 'The Chronology of Ibn Battuta's Travels', *Archiv Orientalni* 30, 1962, pp. 409–86.
27. Masirah, forty miles long and ten miles across, lies off the southern coast of Oman.
28. The distance from Sur, near the extreme eastern tip of the Arabian Peninsula, to Qalhat is thirteen miles in a direct line. Qalhat, one of the chief ports of IB's time, is now an extensive ruin field.
29. The lote-tree or jujube, *Zizyphus spina-Christi*.
30. Bibi Maryam, the wife of Ayaz, a former ruler of Qalhat and Hurmuz, continued to rule for some years after his death in 1311 or 1312. Both were originally Turkish slaves of the ruler of Hurmuz. Bibi Maryam's tomb-chamber is the most conspicuous feature of the ruins at Qalhat, and an object of veneration by local people. The site of the mosque mentioned above has recently been identified.
31. The term is used in its original sense, that of the settled area around Jabal Akhdar in the interior of the modern Sultanate of Oman. Nazwa, often spelled Nizwa, is 130 miles from Qalhat in a direct line.
32. Old Hurmuz was situated on the mainland; Mughistan was the name of the province. New Hurmuz was founded on the island of Jarawn, or Jarun, shortly after 1300.
33. Probably the tribesmen of southern Iraq now called Qashqa'is, who are of Turkic origin.
34. IB is confused here. Qais is an island, now called Kish, off the Gulf coast of Iran. Siraf was on the mainland, over a hundred miles to the north-west. The latter was a place with scant water supplies, and had never recovered from a devastating earthquake in 977; IB's description therefore applies more closely to the island.
35. Although Gibb accuses IB of exaggeration here, the Arabic text could be understood as meaning 'in the water', rather than 'under water'. It seems very likely, however, that IB did not personally observe pearl diving.

6 Asia Minor, the Steppe and Constantinople

1. On the Red Sea coast of Egypt, and a place of importance as it is the nearest of the Red Sea ports to the Nile.
2. The Land of the Rum, the Byzantine Greeks, is Anatolia. At this period the Genoese dominated maritime trade in the Mediterranean. 'Martalamin' may be IB's rendering of 'Bartolomeo'.
3. Al-Alaya, now Alanya, took its name from the Seljuk sultan Ala al-Din. His citadel, mentioned below, dates from after the Seljuk capture of the city in 1220.
4. The Turks have always been predominantly Hanafi in rite. i.e. following the Sunni legal school of Abu Hanifah. As an orthodox Sunni, IB disapproved of the four sects named. 'Innovator' carries the implication of 'heretic'.
5. Now spelled Antalya. The Christian inhabitants of al-Mina, the Harbour, were those from the western countries outside the Byzantine Empire.
6. *Akhi* is a Turkish word meaning 'generous'. The Akhi organizations, which combined features of guild and religious brotherhood, were flourishing at the time of IB's visit but declined as the Ottoman Empire became established. The traveller's comment about them killing 'the agents of police' seems strange; but at this time the police were often little more than bandits who extorted money from traders. In colloquial speech *shurti*, policeman, came to be used for a thief or pickpocket.
7. Akridur is Eğridir, also spelled Eğirdir. Akşehir and Beyşehir in fact both lie at some distance from Eğridir Lake. The college in which IB lodged still exists, as does the mosque with its wooden platform.
8. The present town of Gölhisar ('Lakecastle') lies at some distance from the lake. Nothing of the town seen by IB exists above ground, and the lake has been partially drained; the causeway, however, still exists.
9. 'Ladhiq' comes from the ancient name, Laodicea-on-Lykos. The modern name, Denizli, '[town] of flowing waters', is a euphemistic version of its old alternative title.
10. The canonical poll tax on Christians and Jews living under the protection of a Muslim ruler.
11. Konya, the ancient Iconium. Jalal al-Din Rumi, also called Mevlana (Arabic *mawlana*, our master), was one of the most famous Persian mystical poets and inspirer of the Mevlevis, the so-called 'whirling dervishes'. Also regarded as a 'pole', the highest rank of sufi master, he died in Konya in 1273. The story of the sweet-seller below is a variant of the traditional account of Mevlana's meeting with his spiritual director Shamsi Tabriz.
12. The modern Erzerum.
13. A small town north-east of Ödemiş, in the Küçük Menderes (Little Maeander) valley.

14. The mountain is Bozdağ, still a popular summer retreat.
15. Sultan Muhammad (d. 1344) was the founder of the house of Aydın, one of the many independent sultanates which were eventually swallowed up by the Ottomans.
16. *Kharqah* is the Persian name for the tent now often called yurt.
17. The ability to recite *hadiths* (Traditions, i.e. sayings of the Prophet) extempore was regarded as one of the chief accomplishments of a religious scholar. Sultan Muhammad seems to have had a particular interest in *hadiths*: the pulpit and window shutters of his mosque in Birgi are profusely carved with them.
18. Elsewhere in the *Travels*, IB shows no antipathy to Jews. His indignation here was at the breach of protocol caused by the physician's sitting 'above the readers of the Qur'an'.
19. The mithqal is a measure for precious metals, equal in weight to that of the dinar. Silver dirhams varied slightly in weight; the average was around 2.97 grammes.
20. Aya Suluq is the modern Selçuk, the ancient Ephesus. The church here mentioned seems to be the Church of Mary; the congregational mosque described below, formerly the Church of St John, was reputedly destroyed by Timur (Tamerlane) in 1402.
21. Yazmir is the present-day İzmir, or Smyrna. The amir Omar Bak succeeded his father as Sultan of Birgi. IB must have heard of his death, which occurred in 1348, during his return journey from the East. His account is slightly incorrect: the Christians had in fact captured İzmir and its citadel in 1344, and Omar was killed trying to regain it.
22. In modern Turkish, Manisa.
23. Perhaps an Islamized version of the old Siberian practice of placing corpses in trees to desiccate.
24. Bergama, the ancient Pergamon. IB has mistakenly substituted the name of Plato for that of the physician Galen (129–c. 200), whose supposed house may be the second-century brick building known as the Kızıl Avlu, or Red Hall.
25. The modern Balikesir.
26. The curative hot springs of Bursa, captured from the Byzantines by Urkhan (see next note), are still famous.
27. Urkhan (or Orkhan, reigned 1326–59) was second sultan of the Ottoman dynasty, so named after his father Othman.
28. Now İznik, the ancient Nicaea.
29. Makaja is now spelled Mekece; Yanija (below) is known as Tarakli. The Sakarya river sounded to IB as if its name were derived from *Saqar*, one of the Qur'anic names of Hell.
30. Modern Geyve.

31. Kainuk is now Göynük, Muturni (below) Mudurnu.
32. Qastamuniyah, now Kastamonu, is situated around a hundred miles north-north-east of Ankara, on IB's route to the Black Sea coast.
33. Modern Bolu.
34. Now Gerede and Safranbolu, the latter so called from the cultivation of saffron in the district.
35. Since al-Mustansir died in 1242, the shaikh could not have been more than 120 years old.
36. Sanub is the Black Sea port of Sinop. The gateway mentioned below (in fact at the west of the town) still exists, as do the associated city walls.
37. Ghazi Chalabi, in modern Turkish Gazi Çelebi, was the son of the Seljuk Sultan Mas'ud II (d. 1302). His tomb, now much neglected, is in a side chamber in a *madrasah* beside the Friday Mosque of Sinop. His exploits against the 'Greeks' seem in fact to have been directed against the Genoese: Genoese sources tell of how one 'Zarabi', in 1324, treacherously attacked their fleet while its leaders were being entertained by him ashore.
38. i.e. the Crimea. The city, from which the name of the peninsula derives, is described below, p. 121.
39. Kerch, at the eastern end of the Crimea. IB's meeting, below, with the monk probably took place in the extant church of St John the Baptist. The monk's surprising comment about what is clearly an icon looks, Gibb says, 'like a natural confusion with Elias, the Greek genitive of which is Elía'. It would, however, be difficult to accommodate IB's description of the figure with the usual iconography of Elias, i.e. the Prophet Elijah. Perhaps the icon represented St George, and the monk was aware of the traditional identification of al-Khidr-Elias (see above, p. 304 n. 8) with that saint. It is also noteworthy that, some three centuries later, Pietro della Valle reported that Shah Abbas of Persia was convinced that Ali and St George were 'one and the same person'.
40. The Turkic Qifjaqs, or Kipchaks, gave their name to the steppes of what is now southern Russia and Ukraine.
41. Muhammad Özbeg (reigned 1312–41) was khan of the Mongol apanage that came to be known as the Golden Horde.
42. The Genoese trading centre of Kafa, or Keffe, is the modern Feodosia. IB's French translators suggested that 'al-Damdir' conceals the name Demetrio. Below, IB uses the word 'clappers' to signify the wooden gongs used by the Greek churches; he may also have heard the bells of Latin churches.
43. Here IB refers to the Crimean capital of the time, now known as Stary Krim. The Christian monk referred to below may have lived in the nearby Armenian monastery of St Gyorgi, or in that of Surb-Khatch. The latter was built a few years after IB's visit, but probably on an earlier foundation.
44. New Saray, Özbeg's recently founded metropolis, was situated on the Volga 225 miles upstream from Astrakhan. See also p. 136.

45. Koumiss, the well-known drink of the Tatar and Turkic peoples.
46. Azaq is now Azov, near the north-eastern shore of the sea of that name. Al-Machar has been identified with Burgomadzhary, on the Kuma river in southern Russia.
47. The Jarkas are the Circassians, inhabitants of the lands at the eastern end of the Black Sea.
48. Now Pyatigorsk – a literal translation of the Turkish name – in the sub-Caucasian region of southern Russia. It is still a famous spa town.
49. 6 May 1334, or in Gibb's revised chronology 27 May 1332.
50. Turkic *ordu*, residence of a (nomadic) prince, and the origin of both 'horde' and 'Urdu', i.e. the language of the army camp.
51. Surdaq/Sudaq is a port in the Crimea. On Khwarizm, see pp. 137–40 and p. 313 n. 70.
52. The allusion is to a story, with its origins in the Qur'an, concerning a wife of Solomon. She was deceived by a demon into giving him Solomon's magic ring, by means of which he occupied Solomon's throne for forty days.
53. 'Takfur' was the usual Arab name for the Byzantine emperor, said to be derived from Armenian *tagavor*. The princess's name is Turkic and was presumably given to her on her marriage, an alliance confirmed by contemporary sources.
54. Bulghar, originally the capital of the Volga Bulgars, lay near the left bank of the Volga some seventy miles south of Kazan. IB's account of the journey – a 1,600-mile round trip, impossible in the time stated – is drawn from literary sources and may well be an interpolation by his editor. Geographical texts have also supplied the subsequent information on the Land of Darkness, a semi-legendary region beyond the trans-Ural steppe.
55. 5 June 1334. Since this was in fact a Sunday, the date in Gibb's revised chronology – Friday 26 June 1332 – would fit better.
56. Itil is the usual Arabic name for the Volga. Al-Hajj Tarkhan is Astarkhan, i.e. Astrakhan.
57. 14 June 1334, or 5 July 1332 by Gibb's dating.
58. A town on the Sea of Azov. IB's statement about the Rus, i.e. the Russians, no doubt reflects information given him by the Turks.
59. Baba Saltuq has been identified as being situated either near the lower Dnieper or in the Dobruja area of Romania. 'Mahtuli' is otherwise unknown; the Byzantine frontier city at this time was Diampolis, later Jamboli, in Bulgaria. Since IB was travelling in a large party, he was probably unable to get accurate information on the route. Kifali Niqulah, below, must be the 'head' (Greek *kephalé* – perhaps in the sense of 'governor') Nicholas.
60. The word heard by IB is *sarakenoi*, 'Saracens'.
61. As stated in n. 53 above, 'Takfur' is the Arabic title for the Byzantine emperor. The reigning emperor was Andronicus III of the Palaeologue dynasty, grandson

of his predecessor Andronicus II. On the name 'Jirjis', see below, n. 65. A ruinous wing of the Palaeologues' palace of Blachernae, described below, still survives. It is known as Takfur-saray.

62. The Arabic name for the Church of the Holy Sepulchre.

63. IB's river is the Golden Horn; he seems to have heard and misremembered the Greek word *potamos*, 'river'. The quarter of al-Ghalatah, i.e. Galata, is still known by this name.

64. See p. 301 n. 10.

65. Andronicus II was deposed by his grandson in 1328 and entered the monastic life. His monastic name, however, was not Jirjis (i.e. George) but Antonius. More of a problem is that the ex-Emperor died in February 1332: no revision of IB's chronology yet proposed allows him to have entered Constantinople before this date. We can only assume that IB misunderstood, or was misled by his guide, about the monk's identity.

66. IB's *al-barbarah* is the Byzantine gold *hyperperon*. He is correct in implying that at this time the coinage had become debased.

67. IB's departure, by Gibb's chronology, would have been on about 24 October 1332.

68. The Ossetes, whose name is preserved in the modern Caucasian republics of North and South Ossetia. The Mughals are the Mongols, usually termed Tatars by IB.

69. IB has confused *tash*, 'stone' with *bash*, 'head'.

70. Properly the name of the region, it was often applied to its chief city, at this time Urgench in the Amu Darya delta south of the Aral Sea.

7 Turkestan and Afghanistan

1. This is the Ural river; Sarachuq, or Saraychik, lies about forty miles from its outflow into the Caspian Sea.

2. The Jaihun is the Amu Darya, or Oxus.

3. Al-Tuzari, a Tunisian, has been mentioned before in passing. He was IB's companion during some fifteen years of travels; even in the full text, however, we learn little of him beyond his name and the fact that he died in Goa. Al-Kat, below, is Kath, on the right bank of the Amu Darya about thirty-five miles north-east of Khiva.

4. Persian *alu*, 'plum'.

5. Chingiz Khan sacked Bukhara in 1220, but the city soon recovered. The Mongol rulers of Persia had however attacked it again, in 1273 and 1316.

6. IB had studied the *Sahih*, the great compilation of Traditions of the Prophet, in Damascus.

7. Tarmashirin (reigned 1326–34 or 35) was ruler of the Chagaday khanate of

Central Asia, and a descendant of Chingiz Khan. Nakhshab, now Karshi, is about 100 miles south-east of Bukhara.

8. A ceremony on the seventh day after the birth of a child, when it is given a name.

9. Gibb dates IB's stay from mid-March to early May 1333.

10. Wadi 'l-Qassarin in fact flows by Nakhshab. The river of Samarqand is the Zarafshan.

11. On the upper Amu Darya river, the modern border between Tajikistan and Afghanistan.

12. South of the Amu Darya, near Mazar-i Sharif.

13. IB is referring to the huge Mosque of Hassan in Rabat. The building was started at the end of the twelfth century but never completed. The story below is otherwise unknown.

14. i.e. those male relatives with whom marriage is forbidden (father, brother, son and other ascendants and descendants).

15. Qunduz, as it is spelled now, is east of Balkh. Baghlan was the name of the region to the south of Qunduz.

16. The old name was later replaced by 'Panjshir', *shir* meaning lion. The *balakhsh* rubies mentioned below are the balas rubies of European accounts, a type of spinel.

17. The name of a tribe in the Panjhir valley and the region to the south of it.

18. Mahmud (reigned 999–1030) was the most celebrated ruler of the Turkic dynasty of Ghaznah.

19. Kandahar lies 200 miles south-west of Ghaznah, and is nearly 4,000 feet lower in altitude.

20. The term seems to have been applied at this time only to the tribes of what is now south-eastern Afghanistan. Kuh Sulaiman is still known as the Sulaiman range, and lies to the east of Quetta.

21. IB's route to the Indus river is very unclear from the text. Gibb believes he may have travelled south from Ghaznah through the desert, arriving at the Indus some 300 miles from its mouth. Other commentators have suggested a route through the Khyber Pass. So far, the puzzle remains unsolved. Note that IB does not distinguish between the Indus proper and the five-river complex of the Panjab. The date of IB's arrival, by Gibb's reckoning, was 12 September 1333.

8 Sind and North-Western India

1. Of Sultan Muhammad b. Tughluq (reigned 1324–51), second ruler of the Tughluqid dynasty which ruled the Delhi Sultanate, we shall hear much more later. His father, Tughluq (reigned 1320–4), was probably in origin a Qarawnah, a term applied to Turkic tribes living in the region of Afghanistan

towards India. Tughluq had been a loyal officer of the previous dynasty, the Khaljis, who were extinguished in a coup by the Indian convert Khusraw Khan; he defeated the usurper and founded a line which was to rule for the best part of a century. Arab writers always distinguished between Sind, i.e. the land of the Indus conquered by the Arabs in 712, and Hind, the rest of India, into which Muslim incursions began in the eleventh century.

2. The city in the Deccan which Sultan Muhammad made his capital for some years. (See below, pp. 211–13.)
3. Janani is no longer known. The Samirah mentioned below are in fact a Rajput tribe, the Sumras.
4. A town 120 miles north of Karachi.
5. i.e. the gecko.
6. A ruined port, later known as Larrybunder, twenty-eight miles south-east of Karachi.
7. The title malik, 'king', was in Indian usage applied to high officers of the sultanate. Gibb usually leaves it in the original.
8. Bakar is Bhakkar, a fortified island in the Indus 110 miles north of Sehwan.
9. Uch is now reduced to a group of three small villages.
10. The name of this river is not otherwise known; it probably refers to the Ravi.
11. 'Dihli' is the original Perso-Arabic spelling, and correctly reflects the name as pronounced by its Indo-Muslim population. 'Delhi' was a nineteenth-century slip which took root and spread.
12. Abohar, in the Firozpur district of the Panjab, now on the Indian side of the border. IB has placed it in error before his next major halt at Ajodhan.
13. Ajodhan, now in Pakistan, lies on the Sutlej river and was renamed Pakpattan, 'Holy Ferry', in Mughal times. The shrine of Farid al-Din ('Baba Farid') is still an important place of visitation. The Farid al-Din whom IB met was a descendant of the original saint, who died in 1271.
14. Amjhera, twelve miles west of Dhar in Madhya Pradesh.
15. IB's French translators suggested that 'Kusay' stands for Krishna.
16. Sarasati is now Sirsa; Hansi bears the same name. The ruins of Mas'ud Abad are near Najafgarh, to the east of New Delhi.

9 The City of Dihli and Sultan Muhammad ibn Tughluq

1. The city was founded by a Rajput chief in the eleventh century and captured by Qutb al-Din Aibak, who became the first sultan of Delhi. The date of the capture was in fact 588/1192. Siri, two or three miles to the north-east, was founded by the Khalji Sultan Ala al-Din. Tughluqabad lies some four miles east of the earliest city, and Jahan Panah ('Refuge of the World') between the latter and Siri.

2. Called Quwwat al-Islam ('the Strength of Islam'). It was built in the original Rajput city, as IB states, on the site of a Hindu temple. The term for the latter, *budkhanah*, is Persian; the element *bud* derives from 'Buddha', although the word was used indiscriminately for any temple containing idols. The iron pillar, still standing, was taken from a fourth-century temple. Perhaps IB's explanation of its name should be amended to 'of seven temperaments', in reference to its remarkable resistance to rust.

3. The famous Qutb Minar, currently over 240 feet in height. The top has been rebuilt on several occasions and the 'apples' mentioned by IB – presumably spherical ornaments – have disappeared. The minaret was in fact begun by Aibak, the conqueror of Delhi, not by the later Mu'izz al-Din. Similarly, the unfinished larger minaret, also extant, was started by Ala al-Din (reigned 1295–1315) and not by his son, Qutb al-Din.

4. Lalmish (reigned 1210–36) is more correctly called Iltutmish. The Shamsi Tank, to the west of Mehrauli village, is still in use although reduced in size. The 'private tank' mentioned below, al-Hawd al-Khass, now dry, has given its name to the modern suburb of Hauz Khas some two miles north of the first city of Delhi.

5. Mahmud al-Kubba is unknown, but has been identified with the saint Chiragh-i Dihli (d. 1356). Al-Nili died in 1361. Both Chiragh-i Dihli and al-Nili were disciples of Nizam al-Din Awliya (1238–1324), the greatest of the Delhi saints and a promoter of the Chishti order of sufism.

6. Al-Ghari (on whom see also p. 198) has not yet been identified. Troglodytism was practised by several Muslim ascetics in medieval Delhi.

7. Now the ruined site of Gaur in Bangladesh, Laknawti was capital of the Muslim governors of Bengal.

8. Afghanpur was a village to the south-east of Tughluqabad. The word *kushk* is Persian, and the origin of the English 'kiosk'.

9. Tughluq's magnificent tomb still stands.

10. The *kunyah* was a type of throne-title. Sultan Muhammad's coins do not in fact bear 'Abu 'l-Mujahid', which means literally 'Father of the Holy Warrior', but 'al-Mujahid fi Sabil Allah', 'the Holy Warrior in the Cause of God'.

11. The remains of the palace still exist in Muhammad's city of Jahanpanah.

12. In this context, the term *naqib* applies to a marshal or usher.

13. 'Thousand' is not to be taken literally; rather, it implies 'very many'. Some of the stone column bases have been excavated.

14. Firuz succeeded Sultan Muhammad and reigned (1357–88) as Firuz Shah.

15. Literally 'commanders', but the term is also applied to holders of civilian posts.

16. *Qamari* is cognate with 'Khmer', i.e. Cambodian. *Qaquli* is harder to pin down (IB later visits a town apparently in Java which he calls 'Qaqulah') but may refer to a place on the coast of present-day Burma, south of the Irawaddy river. Benzoin (also 'benjamin'), a name derived from the Arabic *luban jawi* or 'Javanese incense', is the resin of *Styrax benzoin*.

17. It was such statements that led many of IB's countrymen to claim he was a liar (see above, Foreword, pp. xv–xvii). In fact the scattering of coins in this manner is attested in local histories of the sultanate of Delhi.

18. Samosas, triangular envelopes of pastry with savoury or sweet fillings (from Persian *sanbusah*, 'triangular').

19. i.e. 'honourable'.

20. Al-Ma'bar is the usual Arabic name for the Coromandel region of south-east India, corresponding with modern Tamil Nadu. *Maqasiri* sandalwood is probably that from the island of Macassar. The reference below to the black robe alludes to Sultan Muhammad's attachment to the Abbasid line of caliphs, who at their outset adopted black as their official colour. The Abbasids had been extinguished as a power by the Mongol assault on Baghdad some eighty years before, but the Mamluk regime always maintained a scion of the house in Cairo as a nominal caliph. Sultan Muhammad obtained diplomas from these puppet-caliphs, permitting him to rule in their name.

21. The principal coinage of the Delhi sultanate at this time. Tangahs were minted in both gold and silver, but IB always refers to the latter as 'dinars'.

22. The *mann* (Anglo-Indian 'maund') was a measure of about 31 lb, and the *ratl* of Delhi half that amount. The Maghribi *ratl*, however, was approximately one pound avoirdupois.

23. The more scrupulous religious leaders made a point of refusing to serve or associate with temporal rulers, on the grounds that the practice of administration was tainted by illegalities and abuses.

24. As a result of a severe famine in the Delhi area, the sultan moved in 1338 to a temporary capital near the Ganges some 200 miles south-east of Delhi. The site of Sargadwari (i.e. Sarg-dvara, 'the Gate of Paradise') has been located near Kannauj. The 'people' ordered to build there were presumably the court and the civil and military officers.

25. i.e. to Dawlat Abad in the Deccan. (See below, pp. 211-13.)

26. The Duwaidars, literally 'pen-holders', were military officers in charge of the chancery.

27. A quotation from the Qur'an.

28. The most reliable contemporary sources suggest that IB's account is greatly exaggerated, and that relocation orders applied mainly to the court and other Muslim notables.

10 Ibn Battutah's Stay in Dihli

1. The reference is to the charpoy, from Persian *chihar-pai* meaning 'four-feet'.
2. This may be the substance known in India as *saleb*, the dried and powdered tubers of a variety of orchid used in the making of various sweets and decoctions.

3. *Gul shabah* is 'night-scented rose', and *nisrin* the musk rose. *Raibul* is probably the Arabian jasmine.

4. IB's *dulah* is the Indian *doli*, a small palanquin or litter.

5. Abd al-Mu'min (reigned 1130–63), founder of the Almohad dynasty, was ruler of much of North Africa and of Muslim Spain.

6. The *mihrab* is a niche in a mosque indicating the direction of prayer.

7. *Daruhai al-sultan* was an exclamation uttered by a petitioner for redress by the ruler. Commonly the first word was *dohai*, meaning 'justice'. The phrase was still in use in the nineteenth century.

8. IB noted the use of *mahri*, plural *mahari*, camels by the Bejas (see p. 23).

9. *Khoja* or *khwajah*, is a respectful title, although perhaps in this case it was uttered with a touch of irony.

10. 5 January 1335.

11. Last ruler of the Khalji dynasty, Qutb al-Din Mubarak Shah succeeded (by deposing his brother) in 1316 and was murdered by his favourite, the Indian convert Khusraw Khan, in 1320.

12. 13 June 1341. Even in the unabridged text IB says remarkably little about his experiences since the last date he mentioned.

11 From Dihli to Kinbayah

1. The name Qarajil seems to be from the Turkic *qar-achil*, 'opening in the snow'. It may refer particularly to Kashmir, where there are two places near Srinagar named Sumbal, one of which may correspond with IB's Samhal.

2. Aligarh, originally the name of the citadel of Koel, is now applied to the whole town. Al-Jalali, below, is a small town some ten miles east of Aligarh.

3. A loose robe, open at the front, with wide, short sleeves.

4. IB's *ba'in* is the Hindi *baoli*. His definition is correct.

5. Tajpur, about three miles north of Jalali.

6. See above, pp. 12–13.

7. Galyur is the famous fortress-town of Gwalior.

8. Professor Beckingham identified Barwan with Narwar in the former Gwalior State. It may in fact be the village beside the lake of Barwa Sagar, which is directly on the route to IB's next halt.

9. i.e. yogis.

10. Persian for 'hyena'.

11. The Hindu kingdom of Telingana, situated between the Godavari and Krishna rivers.

12. Amwari must be the modern Nivari; Kajarra is Khajuraho, famous for its temple sculptures.

13. Deogiri.

14. The surah of al-Ikhlas is the shortest chapter of the Qur'an, and an assertion of the unity and uniqueness of God. It has always been credited with talismanic properties.
15. The Marhatah are the Mahrattas.
16. Nandurbar, south of the Tapti river.

12 South India

1. Cambay, on the gulf of the same name, is in Gujarat State. At this time it was the most important port of the region; it later silted up and was overtaken by Surat.
2. Qandahar is Ghandar, now a fishing village near the mouth of the Dhandar river.
3. The Bohras, still numerous in Gujarat and Bombay, are followers of a branch of the Isma'ili sect.
4. Bairam is Perim or Piram Island, near the mouth of the Gulf of Cambay. Ququah, below, is Goga, on the eastern shore of the gulf near Bhavnagar.
5. This smaller island is almost certainly Anjidiv, near Karwar in Karnataka. It is now a naval base.
6. The 'chaplet of Zaila' is an Islamic rosary, probably of black coral, a material that exudes a distinctive scent when rubbed in the hand.
7. Hinawr is Honavar, on the Karnataka coast. IB's *bushkal* represents the Hindi *pashkal*.
8. Haryab, who is not mentioned again, must be Harihara I of the Kingdom of Vijayanagar.
9. Calicut, now spelled Kozhikode, in Kerala State.
10. Barcelore, or Basrur, is east of Coondapur in Karnataka. Bacanor, to the south, is now called Barkur.
11. Rama Daw represents the name Ram Deo.
12. Hili appears in later European accounts as Mount Dely, a conspicuous hill overlooking the sea near Nileshwar in the north of Kerala.
13. This place has been tentatively identified as Cananore (now Kannur), but there are other candidates in the vicinity. Dahfattan, below, is Dharma-pattanam, further down the coast and north of Tellichery (now Thalasseri). IB's 'Kuwail' seems to stand for 'Kolattiri', the title of the local rajas.
14. The Tree of the Creed (Perso-Arabic).
15. *Zaw* has been identified with 'dhow', a word of uncertain origin (but not apparently used in any form in Arabic). *Kakam* may represent a Chinese term, although it has also been suggested that is a corruption of the Italian *cocca*.
16. 'Al-Samari' is an arabization of the vernacular title of the ruler of Calicut, 'Samuri'; this in turn is a condensed form of a Sanskrit phrase meaning 'lord of the sea'. It entered European languages, via Portuguese, as 'Zamorin'.

17. Fandaraina is Pantalayini Kollam, north of Quilandi.
18. Quilon of later European accounts, now spelled Kollam.
19. Kunji-Kari has been identified with the stretch of water known as Kanjirapuzha, east of Chennamangalam, an old Jewish settlement near Cochin (Kochi).
20. Probably a title meaning, roughly, 'sacred lord'.
21. 15 October 1342 to mid-January 1343.
22. The name Jawah, i.e. Java, was applied by the Arabs to Sumatra.
23. 24 August 1343.
24. Dhibat al-Mahal is Male-dvipa, i.e. the Maldives.

13 The Maldives

1. Maldivian *kalu bili mas*, the black bonito. IB is generally accurate in his rendering of Maldivian words. Indeed, his account of the islands is by far the best until that of Pyrard de Laval (1570–1621).
2. IB's colocasia is in fact another plant, *Dioscorea oppositifolia*.
3. *Ghaliyah* is a scent of Yemeni origin, composed of musk and ambergris.
4. English 'coir', from Tamil *kayiru*.
5. Malli and Gawgaw are Mali and Gao in West Africa.
6. Male, the main island of the archipelago and source of its name.
7. According to a nineteenth-century local history, the conversion to Islam took place in 1153.
8. The story of the conversion is current in the Maldives today. The inscription IB saw, or a replacement of it, is also still extant.
9. The formulas 'There is no god but God' and 'God is great'.
10. Haladutani is Hadhdhunmathi or Laamu atoll, about 180 miles south of Male. Banishment to a distant island is still a common punishment for Maldivian offenders.
11. Kinolhas, in North Maalhosmadulu or Raa atoll.
12. Serendip, i.e. Ceylon.
13. 17 February 1344.
14. 'Muluk' probably represents Fua Mulaku, near the southern end of the archipelago.

14 Ceylon and Coromandel

1. The mountain of Sarandib is Adam's Peak, to which Adam is supposed to have descended when expelled from Paradise. IB later visits Adam's footprint on its summit.

2. Arya Chakravarti is a title. The ruler IB visited was probably Martanda Singai Ariyan.
3. In the Arabian Gulf.
4. IB has already recounted the story of Shaikh Abu Abdallah b. Khafif. (See above, pp. 72–3.)
5. The location of this place is uncertain, but the form of the name and that of the ruler mentioned below, 'the Kunar', probably reflect Ajakkonara, the name of a powerful family of South Indian origin.
6. The Arabic term *yaqut* covers ruby, topaz, sapphire and other similar stones.
7. These have been identified as wanderoo monkeys, *Macacus silenus*, which are black with long tails and prominent beards.
8. A Persian word. The leeches are probably *Haemobdella ceylanica*.
9. Its height is 7,357 feet.
10. The chains, sometimes attributed to Alexander the Great, still exist.
11. The short-lived sultanate of Madurai, IB's Mutrah, in Ma'bar (Coromandel) was one of a number of states that broke away from the rule of Delhi. IB's father-in-law's revolt probably occurred in 1333 or 34.
12. The island is Nitran or Pigeon Island, or one of the other small islands nearby off the coast near Mavalli, north of Bhatkal in Karnataka.

15 Bengal, Assam and South-East Asia

1. Although some commentators have identified Sudkawan as Satgaon, north of Calcutta, it seems more likely that it represents Chittagong, now in south-eastern Bangladesh. The river Jun, i.e. the Yamuna, mentioned below is not that which flows past Delhi, but another of the same name.
2. Kamaru is the Kamrup district of Assam. IB's comparison of its people with Turks, i.e. the Mongoloid race, is a description of the Shan and related peoples.
3. IB has confused this person, one of the founders of the Suhrawardi order of sufis in India who had at this time been dead for about a century, with Shah Jalal, Islamic missionary to the Sylhet district. 'It is strange,' wrote Professor Beckingham, 'that IB should have travelled from Madurai to Sylhet to meet someone who had died about a hundred years before, and have spent three days there with someone else whom he still supposed to be the man he wanted to meet.' In defence of the traveller, it should be noted that among the Bengalis 'Shah Jalal' came to be used as the generic name for any powerful saint, and that tombs of 'Shah Jalal' abound in the region. The date of the death of al-Musta'sim, referred to below, was 1258.
4. The name Habanq seems to survive in that of a small hill overlooking the Chingra Khal river, near Sylhet. Gibb believed, however, that IB's Blue River must have been the Meghna.

5. Sonargaon, south-east of modern Dhaka.
6. The people or place IB calls Barahnakar has never been satisfactorily identified. Most commentators, however, agree that the location should be somewhere on the Arakan coast of Burma.
7. Samudra, IB's Sumutrah, was the commercial centre of the island to which it later gave its name. The medieval city was located in the northern Acheh region of Sumatra on the Strait of Malacca; its name survives in that of the village of Samoedra, on the Pasé river.
8. This throne title was borne by several rulers. The one IB met must have been Sultan Ahmad (reigned 1326–c. 1360).
9. Mul Jawah is the usual Arabic name for Java. On Qaqulah and Qamarah, see p. 316 n. 16. It will have become apparent that his geography on this further eastern leg of his travels is shaky, to say the least; he may have misplaced these toponyms from an earlier section of his sea voyage.
10. This place has been identified variously with Cambodia, Cochin China, Champa, Tonking, the Celebes (Sulawesi), Tawal Island in the Moluccas, Brunei and Sulu. The mystery, and that of the turcophone princess below, remains unsolved.
11. Could this drink be tea, or a decoction of ginseng?
12. These large glazed storage pots have long been popular in south-east Asia, and are still to be found in households in, e.g., Borneo.

16 China

1. Much, but not all, of the journey from Khan Baliq ('the Khan's City', i.e. Peking) to Sin al-Sin (or Sin Kalan, i.e. Canton) could have been done by water, using canals. IB's river does not exist.
2. Quanzhou.
3. The ruling emperor was Toghon Temür, an eighth-generation descendant of Chingiz (Tankiz) Khan. He was the last emperor of the Mongol Yuan dynasty, and was expelled by the Ming in 1368.
4. An alternative name for the *khan*, or caravanserai, derived from the Greek *pandokheion*.
5. Muslims who are able to do so should give alms to various groups, including wayfarers.
6. Yajuj and Majuj are Gog and Magog. The rampart was supposedly built by Alexander the Great to protect the civilized world from northern savages. Usually located at Derbend on the western shore of the Caspian, it was sometimes confused with the Great Wall of China.
7. The shaikh's stance towards these various early caliphs is in accordance with Sunni political correctness.

8. Qanjanfu is probably Fuzhou. IB compares its surroundings to the Ghutah, the plain around Damascus famous for its fertility. It should be noted that IB's Chinese trip henceforward becomes confused and blurred, and that it is doubtful whether he penetrated any distance inland.

9. i.e. Sabtah, in northern Morocco. The town is about a day's journey from IB's native Tangier.

10. *The Beaten Track*, a collection of Hadiths of the Prophet compiled by Malik b. Anas, founder of the Maliki rite to which IB adhered.

11. Hangzhou. At the time, it may indeed have been the most populous city on earth.

12. The verses are by the poet Sa'di, whose tomb IB visited in Shiraz:

> When we gave our hearts to sorrow
> We sank in an ocean of care,
> But we were stalwart in standing
> Upright at the *mihrab* in prayer.

13. i.e. Cathay, or northern China.

14. This has been explained as a corruption of the Persian title Padshah.

15. Karakorum and Beshbaliq, in what is now the far west of the Republic of China, were the original centres of Mongol rule.

16. No Yuan emperor was killed in battle. Two, however, were assassinated, and the later years of the dynasty witnessed several rebellions.

17. IB's description of pagan Mongol funerals is plausible, although the custom of burying slaves with their dead masters seems to have fallen out of use well before the end of the thirteenth century.

17 From China to Morocco, then Spain

1. IB's 'roc' may have been a cloud formation accompanying the onset of a storm – perhaps an arch-squall, a well known phenomenon in these waters. At no point does he personally identify it as the giant bird of legend.

2. May/June 1348. The plague is the Black Death.

3. The reference to charms is an allusion to the practice of attaching amulets to new-born babies.

4. The harbour is evidently Cagliari, then an Aragonese possession.

5. Taza is east of Fez. The date of IB's departure from it was 6 November 1349.

6. A small two-masted ship, from Latin *sagitta*, 'arrow'.

7. Alfonso XI of Castile, who died of the plague on 20 March 1350 while besieging Gibraltar, IB's Mountain of Victory.

8. Marinid Sultan of Morocco, reigned 1331–48.

9. 1333. The Calahorra Tower still exists.

10. Suhail is the modern Fuengirola.
11. The name al-Hammah itself means 'hot spring'.
12. Sultan of the Nasrid dynasty, reigned 1333–54.
13. i.e. of Velefique in Almeria province. On this distinguished qadi (lived 1265–1370) and his reaction to IB, see the Foreword, pp. xvi–xvii above.
14. IB travelled to Marrakesh via Asila, south-west of Tangier, and Sala (Salé or Sallee), further down the coast and across the Bou Regreg river from Rabat.

18 The Country of the Blacks

1. The ruins of Sijilmasah lie some 200 miles to the south of Fez, beyond the Atlas.
2. 14 February 1352.
3. Taghaza is in the far north of the modern state of Mali. The ruins of salt structures are still visible.
4. The Massufah are a pastoral Berber people of the western Sahara.
5. Now in the extreme south-east of Mauretania. The phrase *'qintars* of *qintars'*, below, might be rendered 'hundreds of hundredweights'; a *qintar* is a weight of 100 *ratls* (see p. 317 n. 22).
6. The only well on IB's route to Iwalatan is the one now called Bir al-Kusaib, some 150 miles south-south-west of Taghaza.
7. *Addax nasomaculatus.*
8. Apparently a similar treatment, involving the warm stomach of a chicken, is practised in the Setif region of Algeria.
9. The date is 17 April 1352.
10. The use of an interlocutor was normal in Sudanic courts, and did not signify contempt.
11. *Anli* is *Pennisetum typhoideum*, a type of millet.
12. The location of the capital of the medieval empire of Mali at this period has long been the subject of debate. It may have been situated south of the Niger in the modern Republic of Guinea, or north of the Niger and east of Bamako, in present-day Mali.
13. The tree is the baobab.
14. The Niger, or 'Sudanese Nile', was thought to be connected with the Egyptian Nile. The notion persisted into the nineteenth century. Zaghari was probably in the region of Sokolo, in the modern state of Mali.
15. Karsakhu is perhaps Kara Sakho, 'Kara Market', on the Niger south-east of Sokolo.
16. *Asidah* is a dish of porridge- or polenta-like constituency. The *qafi* (in the Fula language *kahe*) is the yam, which needs to be carefully washed and cooked for a long time before being eaten.

17. Mansa Sulaiman reigned for twenty years or more and died in 1360. His late brother was the famous Mansa Musa who, when in Cairo on his way to Mecca, caused a fall in the price of bullion by his generous distribution of gold.
18. The woodpecker, although the bird represented may have been the hornbill.
19. 29 June 1352 and 28 February 1353.
20. There may be something in this: Robert Louis Stevenson wrote of a 'cannibal grandee' of the Marquesas whose favourite morsel was the hand.
21. This place has not been identified.
22. The veil covering the face below the eyes, worn by Tuareg men.
23. Al-Tuwaijin was a poet and jurist who accompanied Mansa Musa on the Pilgrimage and returned with him to Mali. He designed several buildings in the capital and in Timbuktu, where he died in 1346. The reason for his nickname is unknown.
24. *The Book of Amazing Retorts* by Ibn al-Jawzi of Baghdad (d. 1200 or 1201) is a miscellany of Qur'anic, legal and historical apothegms.
25. Takadda seems to be Azelik in the modern state of Niger, an oasis southwest of the Saharan highland region of Air.
26. 12 September 1353.
27. Probably this fork in the road is the one at Azawa, north of Air and in present-day Algeria.
28. Buda, in the Tawat (Tuat) region, is north-west of Adrar on the Trans-Saharan motor road.
29. 29 December 1353.
30. A defile in the Atlas fifty-seven miles south-east of Fez.
31. 13 December 1355.
32. February 1356.